FR

MW00680212

COMPREHENSIVE TRAVEL GUIDE

WASHINGTON, D.C. '94

Shop
Creptal City Mall
Union sta—Daytime
georgstown—Fossy Bottom

by Rena Bulkin

Clydes—
~~Chesfields~~ closed
casual

georgetown—
Dupancirde

PRENTICE HALL TRAVEL

NEW YORK • LONDON • TORONTO • SYDNEY • TOKYO • SINGAPORE

FROMMER BOOKS

Published by Prentice Hall General Reference
15 Columbus Circle
New York, NY 10023

ISBN 0-671-84903-4
ISSN 0899-3246

Design by Robert Bull Design
Maps by Geografix Inc.

Frommer's Editorial Staff
Editorial Director: Marilyn Wood
Senior Editor/Editorial Manager: Alice Fellows
Senior Editors: Sara Hinsey Raveret, Lisa Renaud
Editors: Charlotte Allstrom, Thomas F. Hirsch, Peter Katucki, Theodore
   Stavrou
Assistant Editors: Margaret Bowen, Christopher Hollander, Alice
   Thompson, Ian Wilker
Editorial Assistants: Gretchen Henderson, Douglas Stallings
Managing Editor: Leanne Coupe

Special Sales
Bulk purchases (10+ copies) of Frommer's Travel Guides are available to
corporations at special discounts. The Special Sales Department can produce
custom editions to be used as premiums and/or for sales promotion to suit
individual needs. Existing editions can be produced with custom cover
imprints such as a corporate logo. For more information write to: Special
Sales, Prentice Hall Travel, Paramount Communications Building, 15 Columbus Circle, New York, NY 10023.

Manufactured in the United States of America

CONTENTS

LIST OF MAPS

By Arthur Frommer

Once a sleepy, southern-style town, Washington, D.C., has now become the communications capital of the nation, ousting New York from that position (to the dismay of New Yorkers like me). It's hard to admit that Washington, D.C., is now the publishing site of so many major U.S. newspapers, magazines, and books, that Dupont Circle has world-class salons and galleries, that great theatrical pageants open here before they come to Broadway, or that the city's Georgetown is as vital as Greenwich Village—but there it is. Washington, D.C., is now as cosmopolitan as any U.S. city (a sharp reversal of its previous status), and some visitors come here for recreation, leisure, and learning that have nothing at all to do with the federal government.

For that matter, several of its museums are today among the nation's greatest, and one of them—the new United States Holocaust Memorial Museum—is thoroughly unique and just as important. The magnificent Gothic National Cathedral has become a must-see, the restored Ford Theatre provides a touching moment, and a score of other nongovernment buildings, collections, and memorials—the Phillips Collection (European masters of the 19th and 20th centuries), Dumbarton Oaks (pre-Columbian art), the Corcoran Gallery of Art—would do credit to any city.

Still, it is Washington's status as capital of this country that provides its most essential sights. Although my own list of indispensable attractions won't differ much from anyone else's, it's important always to include such a recital at the outset of any guidebook to Washington, D.C., to prevent any highlight from being overlooked, either by inattention or because there is so much else to see here. My own unsurprising checklist is as follows:

(1) The Capitol, sessions of Congress, and meetings of Congressional committees. The latter can be attended by simply wandering into the appropriate committee rooms—without tickets or advance appointments; these meetings often provide insights into the workings of Congress as important as do the full sessions of the House or Senate (for which you'll need a ticket from your representative).

(2) The Supreme Court, especially on an "arguments-day" (for this information call 202/479-3030), and also courtroom lectures presented every half-hour on other weekdays.

(3) The Library of Congress, for such absorbing exhibits as the first rough drafts of the Declaration of Independence and the Gettysburg Address.

(4) The Washington, Lincoln, and Jefferson Memorials.

(5) The Folger Shakespeare Library, which the casual traveler will value for its important exhibits, if not for its research resources.

(6) The National Archives.

(7) Arlington National Cemetery, with its tomb of the Unknowns, the Kennedy gravesites, and Arlington House.

(8) The several museums of the Smithsonian Institution on the Mall, every one of them free of charge and together comprising the world's greatest array of artifacts and art.

(9) The new United States Holocaust Memorial Museum.

(10) The special tours of "working agencies" such as the Bureau of Engraving and Printing and the FBI.

And when you've completed the in-city sights, there are almost as many interesting trips to make to the outskirts and nearby: to the home of Washington at Mount Vernon some 20 miles away, to the U.S. Naval Academy at Annapolis about 30 miles away, and many more.

Of all the activities in Washington, D.C., the most rewarding to see may be a political gathering of citizens outside the Capitol, a "March on Washington" at the Mall, or a demonstration at Lafayette Square (opposite the White House) or elsewhere. Having participated in such weekend rallies myself for causes in which I believed, I can attest that nothing is more worthy of the capital city than these direct demonstrations of democracy by citizens who have come long distances to convey their views to their representatives. It is a glorious sight, whether or not you believe in the particular cause.

The reasons for coming to Washington, D.C., are fairly obvious, as can be confirmed from my short list above; no one can be at a loss for how to spend their time here—there are never enough hours in the day! But the best options for choosing lodgings and meals, in particular (selected from hundreds of alternatives and options)—have required months and months of research and repeated trips over the years. Rena Bulkin, our author, has been doing this book for nearly two decades, and having hired her initially for that task, I'm proud of her achievement. On these pages, you'll find the kind of skilled judgment and suitable choices made from long experience that are the hallmarks of a Frommer guide. And for added pleasure, I don't think you'll find another text that presents its information as lucidly and delightfully as Rena does.

Our very best wishes for your Washington, D.C., trip.

INVITATION TO THE READERS

In researching this book, I have come across many wonderful establishments, the best of which I have included here. I'm sure that many of you will also come across special hotels, inns, restaurants, guesthouses, shops, and attractions. Please don't keep them to yourself. Share your experiences, especially if you want to comment on places that have been included in this edition that have changed for the worse. You can address your letters to:

Rena Bulkin
Frommer's Washington, D.C. '94
c/o Prentice Hall Travel
15 Columbus Circle
New York, NY 10023

A DISCLAIMER

Readers are advised that prices fluctuate in the course of time and travel information changes under the impact of the varied and volatile factors that affect the travel industry. Neither the author nor the publisher can be held responsible for the experiences of readers while traveling. Readers are invited to write to the publisher with ideas, comments, and suggestions for future editions.

SAFETY ADVISORY

Whenever you're traveling in an unfamiliar city or country, stay alert. Be aware of your immediate surroundings. Wear a moneybelt and keep a close eye on your possessions. Be particularly careful with cameras, purses, and wallets, all favorite targets of thieves and pickpockets.

INTRODUCING WASHINGTON, D.C.

As home to one of the world's major powers, Washington, D.C., offers its own special brand of excitement. Here, visitors can linger in the halls and chambers where great leaders formulated the democratic process; listen to Senate debates; hear the Supreme Court in session; visit the National Archives, where the most cherished U.S. documents—the Declaration of Independence, the Constitution, and the Bill of Rights—are enshrined; find inspiration in magnificent monuments to the greatest American presidents and check out the palatial digs of the current chief executive; learn how the FBI works to thwart crime; and see dollar bills being churned out at the Bureau of Engraving and Printing. In short, visitors can experience firsthand just how the government of the United States works.

Edifices of gleaming marble are the background to Washington sightseeing. And surrounding the city's grand beaux arts buildings are spacious boulevards and tranquil tree-lined streets, grassy malls and parks, and circular plazas with splashing fountains and statuary at the focal points. This is a lushly verdant city. Millions of flowers create a dazzling riot of color in spring and summer, and every April the famous Japanese cherry trees burst into bloom along the Tidal Basin like a pink snowstorm. In almost every respect, the capital is a showplace, one of the most beautiful cities in the country. But that hasn't always been the case. . . .

1. CULTURE, HISTORY & BACKGROUND

Probably not an American alive thinks of Washington as a capital in the wilderness. But back in 1800, when Congress moved from its temporary home in Philadelphia to its new permanent seat of government on the Potomac, that's precisely what it was.

The Continental Congress had decided as early as 1783 that a federal city should be established as a permanent locale for its meetings. But even then, the question of slavery created a gap between the North and the South. The northern states insisted that

☑ # WHAT'S SPECIAL ABOUT WASHINGTON, D.C.

Government Buildings

- ☐ The White House, the Capitol, two of America's most visited shrines.
- ☐ The Supreme Court, Cass Gilbert's marble-columned temple.
- ☐ The National Archives, displaying original parchments of the Constitution, Declaration of Independence, and Bill of Rights.

Monuments

- ☐ Monuments to Presidents Washington, Lincoln, and Jefferson.
- ☐ The Vietnam Veterans Memorial, a poignant tribute.

After Dark

- ☐ The John F. Kennedy Center for the Performing Arts—our national cultural facility.
- ☐ The Arena Stage, repertory theater at its very best.
- ☐ Wolf Trap Farm Park, bucolic setting for a prestigious summer performing-arts festival.

Zoo

- ☐ National Zoo, home to more than 5,000 animals.

Architectural Highlights

- ☐ Library of Congress—the ornate Italian Renaissance-style Thomas Jefferson Building (1897).
- ☐ Smithsonian "Castle" (1849), Victorian red-turreted and towered James Renwick building, the first in the famed museum complex.

- ☐ Union Station (1907), modeled after Rome's Baths of Diocletian and Arch of Constantine.
- ☐ Old Post Office Pavilion (1899), in Romanesque style, crowned by a 315-foot clock tower.
- ☐ Old Stone House (1765), probably the city's oldest surviving pre-Revolutionary building.
- ☐ The Renwick Gallery (1859), a landmark building of the French Second Empire style.

Parks and Gardens

- ☐ West Potomac Park, site of the famous cherry trees.
- ☐ C&O Canal, built in the 1800s when inland water routes were vital to transportation; today a major D.C. recreational area.
- ☐ The National Arboretum, containing the National Bonsai Collection.
- ☐ Rock Creek Park, a 1,754-acre playground in the heart of the city.

For Kids

- ☐ The National Air & Space Museum, where exhibits range from the 1903 Wright Brothers' plane to the *Apollo 11* command module.
- ☐ The Museum of Natural History Discovery Room, for a hands-on learning experience.
- ☐ The FBI building, where exhibits range from the DNA lab to weapons used by notorious 1930s gangsters.

the new capital be in the North, while southerners championed a national seat of government in their precincts.

Wrangling about a location for the capital continued until 1790, when New Yorker Alexander Hamilton and Virginian Thomas

Jefferson resolved the dispute (over dinner in a Manhattan restaurant) with a compromise. In exchange for the South's agreement to pay the national Revolutionary War debts, the capital would be located in the South. Furthermore, it would be named Washington after the first U.S. president and (probably more important) a resident of the Commonwealth of Virginia.

By Act of Congress, George Washington was given full authority to choose a site "not exceeding ten miles square on the River Potomac . . . for the permanent seat of the Government of the United States."

ENTER PIERRE L'ENFANT

Virginia and Maryland, by agreement, ceded land for the new capital. It was to be known as the Federal District and to include Georgetown in Maryland and Alexandria in Virginia. In 1791 Pierre Charles L'Enfant was employed by George Washington to survey the land and plan the city. L'Enfant, a Frenchman, had distinguished himself as an engineer in the Revolutionary Army. He had also remodeled New York's City Hall to serve as the first seat for our federal government.

L'Enfant's masterplan (which you can see in the Library of Congress) proposed "a presidential palace" linked to the "home of Congress" by a vast green mall. Asked how he happened to choose the hill at the west end of Jenkins Heights as the site for the Capitol, he responded, "it stands as a pedestal waiting for a monument."

Assisting L'Enfant in laying out the design was Benjamin Banneker, an African-American surveyor, inventor, and mathematician. He was specifically responsible for drawing up the District boundary that affected the state of Maryland.

L'Enfant, though a genius, was also a temperamental artist. He had no patience for practical politics and refused to cooperate with building commissioners or Washington's appointed surveyor, Andrew Ellicott. And he ignored Washington's repeated requests to produce a preliminary blueprint so that fund-raising could begin. His situation became increasingly difficult, and in 1792 he was fired. For the next few decades, the embittered L'Enfant was often seen "haunting the lobbies of the Capitol . . . pacing the newly marked avenues"— keeping a jaundiced eye on the developing city. Architect Benjamin Latrobe wrote in his diary: "Daily through the city stalks the picture of famine, L'Enfant and his dog."

DATELINE

- **1608** Capt. John Smith sails up Potomac River from Jamestown; for next hundred years Irish-Scotch settlers colonize area.
- **1783** Continental Congress proposes new "Federal Town"; North and South vie for it.
- **1790** A compromise is reached: If South pays off North's Revolutionary War debts, new capital will be situated in its region.
- **1791** French engineer Pierre Charles L'Enfant designs capital city but is fired within year.
- **1792** Cornerstone is laid for Executive Mansion.
- **1793** Construction begins on Capitol.
- **1800** First wing of Capitol completed; Congress moves from Philadelphia; President John Adams moves into Executive Mansion.
- **1801** Library of Congress established.
- **1812** War with England.

(continues)

4 • INTRODUCING WASHINGTON, D.C.

DATELINE

- **1814** British burn Washington.
- **1817** Executive Mansion rebuilt, its charred walls painted white; becomes known as White House.
- **1822** Population reaches 15,000.
- **1829** Smithsonian Institution founded for "increase and diffusion of knowledge."
- **1847** Cornerstone laid for first Smithsonian museum building.
- **1861** Civil War: Washington becomes North's major supply depot.
- **1865** Capitol dome completed; Lee surrenders to Grant April 8; Lincoln assassinated at Ford's Theatre April 14.
- **1871** Alexander "Boss" Shepherd turns Washington into a showplace, using many L'Enfant plans.
- **1889** National Zoo established.
- **1900** Population reaches about 300,000.
- **1901** McMillan Commission plans development of Mall from Capitol to Lincoln Memorial.
- **1907** Union Station opens, largest train station in country.
- **1908** Federal Bureau of Investigation (FBI) created.
(continues)

When L'Enfant died in 1825, the fact that he had designed Washington had been practically forgotten. His superb plans were gathering dust; the city that had begun with such grandiose vision muddled along as a nondescript small town. L'Enfant was buried without fanfare, and it wasn't until 1909 that his grave was moved to Arlington Cemetery to rest on a hill looking out over the city that owes him so much.

LAYING THE FOUNDATION

Back in 1792, a nationwide competition was held for the design of the Capitol Building to be erected on the hill L'Enfant had designated. The winner was a young physician, an amateur architect named William Thornton, who later founded the Patent Office. (Architects in those days had little professional standing.) In the words of Thomas Jefferson, another "amateur" architect, the Capitol plan "captivated the eye and judgment of all." George Washington noted that "grandeur, simplicity, and convenience appear to be . . . well combined in this plan." The cornerstone for the Capitol Building was laid September 18, 1793, beside the banks of what the Native Americans called "The River of Swans," the Potomac.

The competition to design the "presidential palace" was won by an Irishman, James Hoban, who received $500 for his plan. (Other entrants included Thomas Jefferson, who submitted his design anonymously.) Hoban hailed from North Carolina, where he had designed that state's capitol building. Because the White House cornerstone was laid in 1792, it holds the distinction of being the oldest public building in Washington. George Washington, however, never occupied the mansion and is, in fact, the only American president never to have resided there. John Adams, the second president, became the first tenant on November 1, 1800—before the house was fully completed.

A CITY RISES

In the considerable period before the public buildings were finished, it was suggested that Congress meet alternately in Trenton, New Jersey, and Annapolis, Maryland—that is, part of the time in the North, part of the time in the South. This idea of shifting meetings was rejected when Francis Hopkinson suggested, sardonically, that a federal town be built on a platform on wheels and rolled back and forth between two places of residence.

By 1800 one wing of the Capitol Building was ready for the legislators. They moved down from Philadelphia, the last temporary capital, in the fall of that year.

As the first tenants in the White House, President and Mrs. Adams headed from Baltimore cross country, and they got so hopelessly lost that they "wandered for two hours without finding a guide or path." When they finally arrived, however, Abigail Adams pronounced her new home "a beautiful spot, capable of any improvement." Mrs. Adams, a Yankee girl of grit and gumption, finding "not the least fence, yard, or other convenience," hung the laundry out to dry in the East Room.

Pennsylvania Avenue, on paper the principal boulevard between the Capitol and the presidential palace, was then a muddy morass of a pathway covered with alder bushes. Where the path reached Georgetown, "houses had been erected, which bore the name of *The Six Buildings*," a put-down to those who harbored ideas that it was a blossoming megalopolis.

Never mind. The new federal capital was in business. And John Adams wasted no time in delivering his presidential address to the first joint session of Congress. Yet the grumbling continued.

John Cotton, a congressman from Connecticut, complained: "A sidewalk was attempted in one instance by a covering formed of the chips hewed from the Capitol. It extended but a little way and was of little value, for in dry weather the sharp fragments cut our shoes, and in wet weather covered them with white mortar."

Newspapers all over the country quipped about "the palace in the wilderness" and referred to Pennsylvania Avenue as "the great Serbonian bog." Georgetown was called "a city of houses without streets" and Washington "a city of streets without houses."

Speculation escalated land prices in the capital. Congress had agreed to purchase land for public building sites. Land surrounding these sites was to be sold, with half the proceeds from the sale of lots to go to

DATELINE

- **1912** Cherry trees, gift from Japan, planted in Tidal Basin.
- **1914** World War I begins.
- **1922** Lincoln Memorial completed.
- **1941** National Gallery of Art opens; U.S. declares war on Japan.
- **1943** Pantheon-inspired Jefferson Memorial and Pentagon completed.
- **1949** Interior of White House rebuilt.
- **1957** Helicopters first seen on White House lawn.
- **1960** Population reaches almost 800,000.
- **1961** John F. Kennedy becomes first Catholic president.
- **1971** John F. Kennedy Center for Performing Arts opens.
- **1976** Metro, city's first subway system, opens in time for Bicentennial.
- **1982** Vietnam Veterans Memorial erected in Constitution Gardens.
- **1987** Arthur M. Sackler Gallery, a new Smithsonian facility focusing on Asian art, opens on Mall; expanded Museum of African Art, also part of Smithsonian, moves to Mall.
- **1991** Population *(continues)*

DATELINE

exceeds three mil-
lion.

• **1993** U.S. Holo-
caust Memorial Mu-
seum, documenting
the horror and trage-
dy of Nazi era,
opens near Mall.

the landowners, half to the government for the erection of government buildings.

But as land prices rose ferociously high around the Capitol Building, those who would have preferred to live in the area were forced to buy elsewhere. As a result, settlement shifted toward the northwest, and, even today, most fashionable town houses and embassies are found in the Northwest section. The area along Pennsylvania Avenue remained a soggy bog. And when the land speculation syndicate fell apart in 1796, financial support for constructing government buildings went down the drain too.

Jefferson, when he assumed the presidency in 1801, had to secure money from Congress for public buildings. He planted poplar trees along Pennsylvania Avenue, doing what he could to make that "Appian Way of the Republic" something better than a "slough of despond." The Library of Congress was established, too, at this time.

Thomas Moore, Ireland's national lyricist, on a visit in 1804 cracked:

> *And what was Goose Creek once is Tiber now.*
> *This fam'd metropolis, where fancy sees,*
> *Squares in morasses, obelisks in trees;*
> *Which second-sighted seers e'en now adorn,*
> *With shrines unbuilt and heroes yet unborn.*

Building went on slowly, but no sooner had the youthful Congress seen James and Dolley Madison installed in the White House than it became necessary to declare war. England had been impressing American seamen, and disputes over western land worsened the situation. The War of 1812 had begun.

A CITY BURNS

On August 24, 1814, the British fleet sailed into Chesapeake Bay and marched on the capital. Admiral George Cockburn (pronounced Co-burn by the British) was in charge of the attack.

Fortunately, everybody knew that they were coming. Dolley Madison stubbornly stayed on in the White House, determined to save all she could. She hustled important documents off to Lewisburg, 35 miles northwest of Washington, for protection. When friends insisted that she leave for her own safety, at the last minute she cut Gilbert Stuart's portrait of George Washington out of its frame, rolled it up, and hied off to a nearby army camp where she spent the night in a tent, a soldier guarding the entrance. This famous portrait, probably the oldest original possession in the White House, hangs today in the East Room. Dolley Madison knew George Washington well—her younger sister, Lucy, was married to Washington's nephew—and she considered the portrait a remarkable likeness. Dolley saved another painting too—a portrait of herself—which also hangs in the White House.

Luckily for the budding nation, the rains came on that fateful night. A torrential storm halted the flames that might have destroyed the city completely.

Then, the British gone, the Madisons moved back into town. They set up housekeeping at Octagon House, on the corner of 18th Street and New York Avenue, and the gala parties Dolley threw helped relieve the pall over Washington left by the war.

The Madisons remained at Octagon House until 1815, when they moved to the northwest corner of Pennsylvania Avenue and 19th Street, to a place known simply as "The Seven Buildings," early housing for the Department of State. There they stayed until the executive mansion was rebuilt, its charred walls painted white in March 1817. Ever since, the "president's palace" has been called the White House.

A CITY REBUILDS

After the British withdrew, Congress first met in the Blodgett Hotel, then moved into a brick building across from the burned-out Capitol. James Monroe took the presidential oath on the porch of what became known as the "Brick Capitol," which stood where the Supreme Court now stands, beginning the tradition of taking the presidential oath in open air, sometimes a chilly event in January.

Monroe also refurnished the burned-out White House with $15,567.43 in French-designed furniture. Jefferson, Madison, and Monroe all had a taste for things French, and it's still reflected throughout the White House. More recently, First Lady Jacqueline Kennedy, also a Francophile, was responsible for refurnishing and redecorating the White House to reveal its original French character.

Repair work on the Capitol Building was directed by Benjamin Latrobe, an Englishman who had taken over responsibility for its construction in 1803. Slowly he replaced the gutted wood with marble, brick, and metal. It was reoccupied by Congress in 1819.

By 1822, only 22 years after its founding and 8 years after being burned, the capital city boasted a population of nearly 15,000 people.

In 1829 the Smithsonian Institution was created when an Englishman, James Smithson, left half a million dollars "to found at Washington, under the name of the Smithsonian Institution, an establishment for the increase and diffusion of knowledge. . . ." Smithson never visited the United States, but the cornerstone for his great legacy, the now-sprawling Smithsonian, was laid in 1847. The first building in the complex is a red sandstone castle of Norman inspiration. That original building is located on the Mall, and it was reopened to the public after undergoing considerable restoration in 1972. Today it serves as a visitor information center for the Smithsonian complex.

Government building continued to boom. By 1842 the present Treasury Building—blocking the vista from the White House to the Capitol and spoiling L'Enfant's original plan—was completed. Andrew Jackson had tired of waiting for the appointed commission to choose a Treasury site, so he marched out of the White House one day, pointed to a spot, and said that the Treasury cornerstone would be laid there. His will was done . . . plunk in the middle of Pennsylvania Avenue!

MID-19TH-CENTURY WASHINGTON

From all this, you might assume that Washington was well on its way from villagehood to cityhood. Gas lights were lit on the Capitol

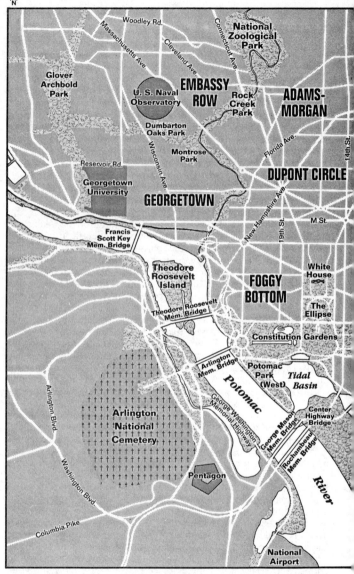

grounds in 1847. But by 1860 no more than Pennsylvania Avenue had been lit. "Pigs roamed the principal thoroughfares, pavements but for a few patches were lacking, and open sewers carried off refuse." Visiting author Anthony Trollope declared Washington "as melancholy and miserable a town as the mind of man could conceive." Soon things would get even worse.

The Civil War turned the capital into an armed camp. It was the principal supply depot of the North and an important medical center. The rotunda of the Capitol Building—its nine-million-pound

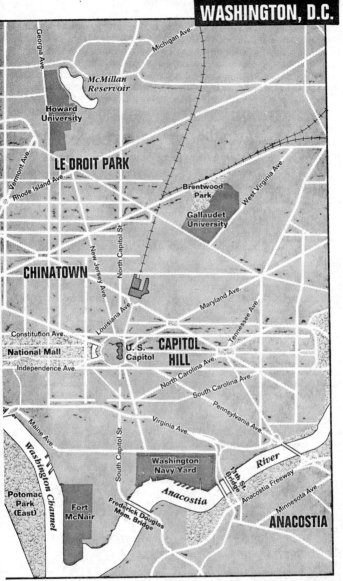

cast-iron dome completed in 1865—was used as a barracks, referred to by the soldiers as "the big tent." Later it became a troop hospital, and here American poet Walt Whitman wandered among the wounded, helping where he could. Altogether, 3,000 troops were billeted in the Capitol, and basement committee rooms were converted into bakeries.

The Civil War ended when Lee surrendered to Grant on April 8, 1865. The greatest parade in the capital's history celebrated this event. To the tune of fife and drums, troops marched down

Pennsylvania Avenue for two full days and nights. Less than a week later, on April 14, President Abraham Lincoln was shot at Ford's Theatre by John Wilkes Booth, and the city went into mourning.

The war's legacy was poverty, unemployment, and disease. Washington's population swelled with uneducated freed slaves, and tenement slums arose within a stone's throw of the Capitol.

SUDDEN EXPANSION

In 1870 several factions attempted to transfer the national capital to another city. St. Louis bid several million dollars for the honor, and Horace Greeley suggested that the capital go west. But the move never got seriously under way, and Congress went ahead and voted $500,000 to build the Departments of State and War and the Navy Building.

Enter "Boss" Shepherd and another era. Governor Alexander R. Shepherd was chosen to head a territorial government established in the District of Columbia from 1871 to 1874. Shepherd was a handsome, strapping man with blustery charm. He'd been a successful plumber, an alderman, a newspaper owner, and president of the City Reform Association. He was a natural to become governor of the territorial government. Once installed in office, though, he ignored budgets and followed a bankruptcy course to beautify his domain. Under his guidance, the L'Enfant plan was finally executed in earnest. Three hundred miles of half-laid streets were improved. Nearly every thickly populated thoroughfare was paved with wood, concrete, or macadam. Some 128 miles of sidewalks were built, and 3,000 gas lamps and a system of sewers were installed. Old Tiber Creek was filled in. Scores of new parks were graded and beautified with fountains. A special park commission planted 6,000 trees.

Soon there were more paved streets in Washington than in any other city in the country. And President Ulysses S. Grant declared in a message to Congress, "Washington is rapidly becoming a city worthy of the nation's capital." Grant temporarily swept a few facts about the grand public works under the rug—like the whopping $20-million bill for the improvements.

Before long Congress reacted, and Shepherd was nearly booed out of town. In 1874 the territorial form of government gave way to a trio of commissioners. Shepherd took his family to Mexico. But when he returned to the United States in 1887, he was acclaimed as the man who had made Washington a showplace. And he certainly had.

The nation's Centennial Celebration of 1876 in Philadelphia and the Chicago Exposition of 1893 brought about a cultural awakening throughout the country. Following that period, the Corcoran Art Gallery was built in Washington, the Metropolitan Museum in New York, and the Museum of Fine Arts in Boston. In 1884 the Washington Monument was completed. And in 1897 the Library of Congress, which took 11 years to build, also was completed. During the following year, 1898, L'Enfant's plan was dusted off again, and adjustments were made to suit the District to the motor age.

But the capital of the United States was 100 years old and home to 300,000 before the plan for development and improvement drawn up by the McMillan Commission was enacted in 1901. At his own

IMPRESSIONS

*I know of no other capital in the world which stands on so wide
and splendid a river. But the people and the mode of life are
enough to take your hair off!*
—HENRY ADAMS

*My God! What have I done to be condemned to
reside in such a city!*
—A FRENCH DIPLOMAT IN THE EARLY DAYS

*The whole aspect of Washington is light, cheerful, and airy; it
reminds me of our fashionable watering places.*
—MRS. FRANCES TROLLOPE

*Washington . . . enormous spaces, hundreds of miles of asphalt,
a charming climate, and the most entertaining society in America.*
—HENRY JAMES

expense, James McMillan, a senator from Michigan, sent an illustrious committee—New York's Central Park landscapist Frederick Law Olmsted, sculptor Augustus Saint-Gaudens, and noted architects Daniel Burnham and Charles McKim—to Europe on a seven-week study tour, to absorb the architecture and landscaping of the world's great capitals. It was a committee worthy of L'Enfant's vision, backed up by the necessary political clout to get the job done.

The principal thrust of the commission's plan was to develop the Mall, at the turn of the century still little more than a pasture traversed by the tracks of the Pennsylvania Rail Road. The company agreed to remove its tracks in return for funding to construct Union Station.

The Mall, in addition to housing the National Gallery of Art and the Smithsonian Institution, was to become the site for the Department of Agriculture and other important structures. When finished, it would extend one mile in length, 300 feet in width, from the Capitol through the Washington Monument, beyond to the Lincoln Memorial. Projected plans also included several public buildings—office buildings for members of the House, Senate, and the Supreme Court (which had met in the Capitol until then).

Aesthetics came into play in 1910, when the National Commission of Fine Arts was created by President Taft. Its duty was to advise on fountains, statues, and monuments in public squares, streets, and parks throughout the District of Columbia. Thanks to Mrs. Taft, the famous cherry trees presented to the United States by the Japanese in 1912 were planted in the Tidal Basin. And thanks to Taft's commission, neoclassic architecture and uniform building height became the order of the day. This is when the commission fixed the 110-foot maximum rooftop height limit for buildings in the downtown district, so that the Capitol dome might be seen from miles around.

WASHINGTON TODAY

Until Franklin D. Roosevelt came along, only President Grant had really changed Washington—and Grant got the credit only because Boss Shepherd had spent too much! During the Great Depression in the 1930s, FDR's Works Progress Administration—WPA, *We Do*

Our Part—put the unemployed to work erecting public buildings and artists to work beautifying them.

More recently (1971), the John F. Kennedy Center for the Performing Arts, on the Potomac's east bank, filled a longtime need for a cultural haven.

In 1974 the opening of the New Hirshhorn Museum and Sculpture Garden on the Mall provided a much-needed major museum of modern art. Another storehouse of art treasures is the magnificent East Building of the National Gallery of Art, which opened in 1978. It was built to handle the overflow of the gallery's burgeoning collection and to accommodate traveling exhibits of major importance.

In time for the Bicentennial, the National Air and Space Museum opened in splendid new quarters. Also in time for the nation's big birthday party, the first leg of the capital's much-needed subway system, Metro, was completed. The 45 acres between the Washington Monument and the Lincoln Memorial were transformed into Constitution Gardens, and in 1982 the park became the site of the Vietnam Veterans Memorial.

In 1987 Washington got a new $75-million Smithsonian complex on the Mall; it houses the Arthur M. Sackler Gallery of Art, the relocated National Museum of African Art, the International Center, and the Enid A. Haupt Garden. In 1989 the renovation of the city's magnificent Union Station (inspired by the Baths of Diocletian) was completed. And 1993 saw the opening of the United States Holocaust Memorial Museum, adjoining the Mall.

The capital has changed for the better, and the people are changing too. Washingtonians are becoming much more sophisticated and much more demanding. Today, D.C. can hold its own as a great town for theater, dining, shopping, concert-going, and other metropolitan pleasures.

So it's no wonder Washington attracts over 19 million tourists each year. History and heritage, art and politics, cuisine and culture combine to make this a vital and beautiful city—a fitting capital for a great nation.

2. FAMOUS WASHINGTONIANS

Benjamin Banneker   (1731–1806) When Pierre L'Enfant left Washington in 1792, Banneker, a black mathematician, astronomer, and surveyor, re-created his maps and city plans from memory.

Art Buchwald   (b. 1925) Pulitzer Prize–winning syndicated columnist and political satirist.

Frederick Douglass   (1818–95) Born in slavery, he escaped and fled north to become a driving force in the abolitionist movement and its most impassioned voice.

Edward (Duke) Ellington   (1899–1974) Native Washingtonian, bandleader, pianist, and songwriter, he composed "Mood Indigo," "Sophisticated Lady," and "Take the 'A' Train."

Helen Hayes   (1900–93) The First Lady of the American Theater is well known for her roles in *Long Day's Journey into Night* and *The Glass Menagerie*.

Pierre Charles L'Enfant (1754–1825) Brilliant French military engineer who, invited by George Washington, laid out plans for the national capital in 1791.

Dolley Madison (1769–1849) President Madison's wife and capital society's first queen, she rescued Gilbert Stuart's famous portrait of George Washington from the British in the War of 1812.

Perle Mesta (1891–1975) Official Washington's "hostess with the mostest," especially during the Truman years. She was the inspiration for the musical *Call Me Madam.*

James Smithson (1765–1829) Although he never set foot in the United States, he should be considered an honorary Washingtonian as he left his fortune to this country for the museum complex that, bearing his name, has become the largest in the world.

John Philip Sousa (1854–1932) America's bandmaster, known as "The March King," composer of "Semper Fidelis," "Stars and Stripes Forever," and "The Washington Post."

Walt Whitman (1819–92) American poet, author of *Leaves of Grass* and "O Captain, My Captain," the latter a tribute to Lincoln, whom he greatly admired.

---

3. RECOMMENDED BOOKS & FILMS

BOOKS

As the capital of the United States, Washington probably is better documented than any other American city. The following list is a good starting point for further reading.

ECONOMIC, POLITICAL & SOCIAL HISTORY

Adler, Bill. *Washington, a Reader.* Meredith, 1967.

Arnebeck, Bob. *Through a Fiery Trial: Building Washington, 1790–1800.* Madison, 1991.

Bishop, Jim. *The Day Lincoln Was Shot.* Harper & Row, 1955.

Cooke, Alistair. *One Man's America.* Knopf, 1952.

Duncan, Don. *Washington: The First One Hundred Years.* Seattle Times, 1989.

Kite, Elizabeth S. *L'Enfant and Washington, 1791–92.* Ayer, 1970.

Loftin, T. L. *Contest for a Capital.* T. L. Loftin, 1989.

Schlesinger, Arthur M., Jr. *The Birth of the Nation.* Houghton Mifflin, 1968.

Terrell, John Upton. *The Key to Washington.* J. B. Lippincott, 1962.

ARCHITECTURE & THE ARTS

Aylesworth, Thomas, and Virginia Aylesworth. *Washington, the Nation's Capital.* Gallery Books, a division of W. H. Smith, 1986.

Carter, Edward C., et al. *Latrobe's View of America, 1795–1820* (Selections from the Watercolors and Sketches). Yale University Press, 1985.

Reed, Robert. *Old Washington, D.C. in Early Photographs.* Dover, 1980.

FICTION & MYSTERY

Drury, Allen. *Advise and Consent*. Doubleday, 1959.
McCarthy, Abigail. *Circles, a Washington Story*. Doubleday, 1977.
Roosevelt, Elliott. *The White House Pantry Murder* and others in
the Eleanor Roosevelt as sleuth series. St. Martin's Press, 1987.
Truman, Margaret. *Murder at the Smithsonian, . . . at the FBI, . . .
at the CIA, . . . in Georgetown;* and six others in the Capital
Crimes Series. Fawcett, 1985–1990.

HUMOR

Adler, Bill. *The Washington Wits*. Macmillan, 1967.
Pitch, Anthony S. *Exclusively Washington Trivia*. Mino, 1989.
Rash, Bryson B. *Footnote Washington*. EPM, 1983.

FOR KIDS

Krementz, Jill. *A Visit to Washington, D.C.* Scholastic, 1987.
Loewen, N. *Washington, D.C.* Rourke, 1989.
Petersen, Anne. *Kidding Around Washington, D.C.: A Young
Person's Guide to the City*. John Muir, 1989.
Weston, Marti, and Florri DeCell. *Washington! Adventures for
Kids*. Vandemeer, 1989.

FILMS

Hundreds of film companies have used the streets and famous
interiors of Washington, D.C., as a setting for films for some 80 years.
Some of the more memorable include *Birth of a Nation* (1915), *Mr.
Smith Goes to Washington* (1939), *Born Yesterday* and *Magnificent
Yankee* (1950), *The FBI Story* (1959), *Advise and Consent* (1962),
Seven Days in May (1964), *The Last Detail* (1974), *All the
President's Men* (1976), *The Seduction of Joe Tynan* (1978), *Heart-
burn* (1985), *No Way Out* (1986), and *Broadcast News* (1987).

CHAPTER 2

PLANNING A TRIP TO WASHINGTON, D.C.

A lot of what you'll want to see and do in the capital can be arranged after you arrive, but some things should be planned in advance, while you're still home.

1. BEFORE YOU GO

Before you leave, contact the **Washington, D.C., Convention and Visitors Association,** 1212 New York Ave. NW, Washington, DC 20005 (tel. 202/789-7000), and ask for free maps and brochures detailing sights in and around the District, restaurant and hotel guides, and events calendars. They'll also be happy to answer specific questions.

SPECIAL PASSES FOR VIP TOURS

Senators and/or congressional representatives can provide their constituents with passes for VIP tours of the Capitol, the White House, the FBI, the Bureau of Engraving and Printing, and the Kennedy Center. This is no secret. Thousands of people know about it and do write, so make your request as far in advance as possible—even six months ahead is not too early—specifying the dates you can visit and the number of tickets you need. Their allotment of tickets for each sight is limited, so there's no guarantee you'll secure tickets, but it's worth a try. At the very least you can get some general information about Washington.

Address requests to representatives to: U.S. House of Representatives, Washington, DC 20515; and to senators to: U.S. Senate,

Washington, DC 20510. Don't forget to include the exact dates of your Washington trip. When you write, also request tourist information and literature.

Note: Before writing, you might try calling a senator or congressperson's local office; in some states you can obtain passes by phone.

THE CAPITOL The 8am weekday VIP tour of the Capitol is 15 minutes longer than the regular tour and includes both the House and Senate chambers (the regular tour visits only one).

THE WHITE HOUSE Between 8 and 8:45am the doors of the White House are open for special VIP tours to those with tickets. Once again, write far, far in advance, because each senator receives only 15 tickets a week to distribute, and each representative only 10. These early tours ensure your entrance in the busy tourist season when thousands line up during the two hours daily that the White House is open to the public. They're also more extensive than later tours, with guides providing explanatory commentary as you go; on later tours, docents are on hand to answer questions but don't give formal talks in each room.

THE FBI The line for this very popular tour can be extremely long. One way to beat the system is to ask a senator or representative to make a reservation for you for a scheduled time.

BUREAU OF ENGRAVING & PRINTING Guided VIP tours are offered weekdays at 8am, except on holidays and the days after holidays. Later, non-VIP tours are self-guided.

THE KENNEDY CENTER The VIP tour offered Monday through Saturday at 9:30am allows you to avoid a long wait with the masses who did not take the trouble to write to a senator or representative.

WHAT THINGS COST IN WASHINGTON   U.S. $

Taxi from National Airport to downtown	10.00–12.00
Bus from National Airport to downtown	8.00 (12.00 round-trip)
Local telephone call	.25
Double at the Jefferson Hotel (expensive)	225.00–265.00
Double at the Hotel Anthony (moderate)	109.00–133.00
Double at the Days Inn Downtown (inexpensive)	87.00–97.00
Double at the Hosteling International (budget)	18.00
Three-course dinner at the Willard Room (very expensive)	50.00

	U.S. $
Three-course dinner at Petitto's (expensive)	35.00
Three-course dinner at Clyde's (moderate)	18.00–22.00
Three-course dinner at Scholl's Cafeteria (budget)	7.00
Bottle of beer (restaurant)	2.75
Coca-Cola (restaurant)	1.50
Cup of coffee (restaurant)	1.25
Roll of ASA 100 Kodacolor film, 36 exposures	4.50
Admission to all Smithsonian museums	Free
Theater ticket at the National	22.50–60.00

2. WHEN TO GO — CLIMATE & EVENTS

THE CLIMATE

Washington weather is a bit unpredictable. Winter can be pretty cold, with lots of snow. Occasionally, the weather is unexpectedly warm. Advantages of winter visits are low hotel prices and no lines at attractions.

Springtime, especially in April when the cherry trees are in bloom, is the most popular season for visitors.

In summer, heat and humidity can be high, and if you aren't accustomed to them, you'll feel limp. Most places are air-conditioned, however. Hotels with swimming pools make a summer vacation much more enjoyable.

Autumn in Washington is an unqualified delight. The weather is comfortable, the tourist throngs have abated, and I recommend it as the best time for a vacation visit.

Average Temperatures [°F] in Washington, D.C.

	Jan	Feb	Mar	Apr	May	June	July	Aug	Sept	Oct	Nov	Dec
High	44	44	53	64	75	83	87	84	78	68	55	45
Low	24	28	35	44	55	64	68	66	60	48	38	30

WASHINGTON
CALENDAR OF EVENTS

The District is the scene of numerous daily special events, fairs, and celebrations. Listed below are the major annual events. When in town, check the *Washington Post,* especially the Friday "Weekend" section, and pick up an events calendar at the Washington Visitor Information Center, 1455 Pennsylvania Ave. (tel. 789-7038). The Smithsonian Information Center, 1000 Jefferson Dr. SW (tel. 357-2700), is another good source. For annual events in Alexandria, see Chapter 10.

JANUARY

☐ **Washington Antique Show,** Omni Shoreham Hotel, 2500 Calvert St. NW, at Connecticut Avenue (tel. 234-0700). About 50 East Coast dealers display their wares. Admission is charged, and profits go to charities. This is an impressive show, with displays of artifacts relating to the annual theme (for example, historical preservation). Catalogs include articles by scholars and museum curators, and there are guest speakers—people like George Plimpton and Henry Kissinger. Early in January.

☐ **Presidential Inauguration,** on the Capitol steps. After the swearing-in, the crowd follows the new president down Pennsylvania Avenue to the White House. The event is heralded by parades, concerts, parties, plays, and other festivities. For details, call 789-7038. January 20 in years following a national election.

☐ **Martin Luther King, Jr.'s Birthday.** Events include speeches by prominent civil-rights leaders and politicians; readings; dance, theater, and choral performances; prayer vigils; a wreath laying at the Lincoln Memorial; and concerts. Many events take place at the Martin Luther King Memorial Library, 901 G St. NW (tel. 727-1186). Call 789-7000 for further details. Third Monday in January.

☐ **Chinese New Year celebration,** in Washington's small Chinatown. A friendship archway, topped by 300 painted dragons and lighted at night, marks Chinatown's entrance at 7th and H Streets NW. The celebration goes on for 10 days, with traditional firecrackers, dragon dancers, and colorful street parades. Some area restaurants offer special menus. For details, call 789-7000 or 724-4093. Late January or early to mid-February.

FEBRUARY

☐ **Black History Month.** Features numerous events, museum exhibits, and cultural programs celebrating contributions of African Americans to American life. For details, call 357-2700 or 789-7000.

☐ **Abraham Lincoln's Birthday,** Lincoln Memorial. Marked by the laying of a wreath and a reading of the Gettysburg Address at noon. Call 426-6895. February 12.

☐ **George Washington's Birthday,** Washington Monument. Similar celebratory events. Call 426-6839 for details. Both presidents' birthdays also bring annual citywide sales. February 22 (celebrated the third Monday in February as Presidents Day).

MARCH

☐ **Spring Antiques Show,** D.C. Armory, 2001 E. Capitol St. Features close to 200 dealers from the United States, Canada, and Europe. Admission is charged. Call 301/738-1966 for details. Usually the first week in March.

☐ **St. Patrick's Day,** on Constitution Avenue NW from 7th to 17th Streets. A big parade that's all you'd expect—floats, bagpipes, marching bands, and the wearin' o' the green. Past grand marshals have included Tip O'Neill, Redskins' "player of the decade" John Riggins, Helen Hayes, and Eunice Shriver. For parade information, call 424-2200 or 789-7000. On the Sunday before March 17 (unless March 17 falls on a Sunday).

✪ *SMITHSONIAN KITE FESTIVAL A delightful event if the weather cooperates—an occasion for a trip in itself. Throngs of kite enthusiasts fly their unique creations and compete for ribbons and prizes.*
   ***Where:** On the Washington Monument grounds. **When:** On a Saturday in mid- or late March. **How:** If you want to compete, just show up with your kite and register between 10am and noon. Call 357-2700 for details.*

✪ *CHERRY BLOSSOM EVENTS Washington's best-known annual event—the blossoming of the famous Japanese cherry trees. Festivities include a major parade with princesses, floats, and VIPs, not to mention fireworks, fashion shows, concerts, a Japanese lantern-lighting ceremony, a ball, and a marathon race.*
   ***Where:** The trees bloom by the Tidal Basin in Potomac Park. Related events take place throughout the town. **When:** Late March or early April (national news programs monitor the budding). **How:** For parade and ball information, call the DC Downtown Jaycees (tel. 728-1135). For other cherry-blossom events, check the Washington Post or call 789-7000.*

APRIL

Cherry blossom events continue (see above).

☐ **Easter Sunrise Services,** Memorial Amphitheater at Arlington Cemetery. There are free shuttle buses to the site from the visitor center parking lot. Call 475-0856 or 789-7000 for details. Date varies.

✪ *WHITE HOUSE EASTER EGG ROLL The biggie for kids 8 and under. In past years, entertainment has included clog dancers, clowns, storytellers, Easter bunnies, Ukrainian egg-decorating exhibitions, puppet and magic shows, military drill teams, an egg-rolling contest, and a hunt for 1,000 or so hidden wooden eggs, many of them signed by celebrities (like Michael Jackson) or the Clintons.*
   ***Where:** On the White House lawn and on the Ellipse;*

enter at the southeast gate on East Executive Avenue.
When: *Easter Monday between 10am and 2pm; arrive early.* **How:** *Just show up. Call 456-2200 for details.*

☐ **Filmfest DC,** at theaters throughout the city. Premieres dozens of international and American films. Check the *Washington Post* for film schedules and locations, or call 727-2396. April and May.
☐ **Thomas Jefferson's Birthday,** Jefferson Memorial. Celebrated with a wreath-laying and military ceremony. Call 426-6822 for time and details. April 13.
☐ **The Imagination Celebration,** Kennedy Center for the Performing Arts. At this two-week festival of performing arts for young people, events are free for moderately priced. Call 467-4600 for details. Mid-April.
☐ **White House Gardens.** These beautifully landscaped creations are open to the public for special free tours between 2 and 5pm. Call 456-2200 for details. Two days only, in mid-April.
☐ **Georgetown Garden Tour.** View the remarkable private gardens of one of the city's loveliest neighborhoods. Admission is charged, but high tea is included. Call 333-4953 for details. Mid- or late April (or early May).
☐ **Georgetown House Tour.** The interiors of beautiful old Georgetown homes can be seen. Admission is charged, and includes a tea at St. John's Georgetown Parish Church. Call 338-1796 for details. Late April.
☐ **Justice Douglas Reunion Hike,** C&O Canal. If you love hiking, don't miss this event. Douglas, bless him, once walked the entire 184½-mile towpath in protest against a plan to build a scenic parkway along the canal. The annual hike covers about 12 miles, on a different section each year. A buffet banquet wraps up the day's activities, and there's a bus back to town. For details and tickets (there's a charge for the bus and buffet), contact the C&O Canal Association, P.O. Box 366, Glen Echo, MD 20812 (tel. 703/356-1809 or 301/739-4200). Usually the last Saturday in April.

MAY

☐ **Washington National Cathedral Annual Flower Mart,** on the cathedral grounds. Includes displays of flowering plants and herbs, decorating demonstrations, ethnic food booths, children's rides and activities (including an old-fashioned carousel), costumed characters, puppet shows, and other entertainments. Call 537-6200 for details. First Friday and Saturday in May.
☐ **Asian Pacific American Heritage Festival,** Freedom Plaza, on Pennsylvania Avenue between 13th and 14th Streets NW. Honors the contributions of Asian Americans to this country and presents their varied cultural heritages. All of Washington's Asian communities participate. There are cultural displays, crafts booths, ethnic foods, dragon dances, and martial arts exhibitions. For information, call 703/354-5036. Weekend day early in May.
☐ **Memorial Day.** At 11am, a wreath-laying ceremony takes place at the Tomb of the Unknowns in Arlington National Cemetery, followed by military band music, a service, and an address by a high-ranking government official (some years, the president); call

475-0856 for details. There's also a ceremony at 1pm at the Vietnam Memorial—wreath laying, speakers, and the playing of taps; call 634-1568 for details. In the evening the National Symphony Orchestra performs a free concert at 8pm on the West Lawn of the Capitol; call 619-7222 for details. Last Monday in May.

JUNE

☐ **Spirit of America Pageant,** Capital Centre, Landover, Md. Programs tracing the history of America in music and skits. The concerts are given by the Third U.S. Infantry and the U.S. Army Band. Call 475-0685 for details. Mid-June.

✪ *SMITHSONIAN FESTIVAL OF AMERICAN FOLKLIFE* *A major event with traditional American music, crafts, foods, games, concerts, and exhibits. Past performances have ranged from Appalachian fiddling to Native American dancing, and demonstrations from quilting to coal mining. All events are free.*

Where: Most events take place on the Mall. When: Late June and early July. How: Call 357-2700, or check the listings in the Washington Post, for details.

JULY

✪ *INDEPENDENCE DAY* *There's no better place to be on the Fourth of July than Washington, D.C. The festivities include a massive National Independence Day Parade down Constitution Avenue, complete with lavish floats, princesses, marching groups, and military bands. Other events include baseball games, a jazz festival, dances, arts and crafts exhibits, celebrity entertainers, concerts, and food booths. A Revolutionary War encampment is set up on Constitution Avenue in front of the National Archives, where a program includes military demonstrations, period music, and a reading of the Declaration of Independence. In the evening the National Symphony Orchestra plays on the west steps of the Capitol with guest artists (for example, Leontyne Price). And big-name entertainment also precedes the fabulous fireworks display over the Washington Monument.*

Where: Most events take place on the Washington Monument grounds. When: July 4, all day. How: Just show up. Check the Washington Post or call 789-7000 for details.

☐ **Men's Tennis Classic,** Rock Creek Park at 16th and Kennedy Streets NW. Top-seeded players compete. Call 703/276-3030 for details, 432-SEATS for tickets. Mid- or late July.

AUGUST

☐ **Tchaikovsky's *1812* Overture,** Sylvan Theatre on the Washington Monument grounds. The U.S. Army Band gives a free performance of this famous work, complete with roaring cannons. For details, call 703/696-3718. Sometime during the month.

SEPTEMBER

☐ **National Frisbee Festival,** on the Mall near the Air and Space Museum. See world-class Frisbee champions and their disc-catching dogs at this noncompetitive event. For details, call 301/645-5043. First weekend in September (some years, in late August).

☐ **International Children's Festival,** Wolf Trap Farm Park in Vienna, Va. At this three-day arts celebration, the entertainment—all of it outdoors—includes clowns, musicians, mimes, puppet shows, and creative workshops from 10am to 4pm each day. Admission is charged. For details, call 703/642-0862. Early September.

☐ **Washington National Cathedral's Open House.** Celebrates the laying of the foundation stone in 1907. Events include exhibits of stone carving and other crafts utilized in building the cathedral, carillon and organ demonstrations, and performances by dancers, choirs, strolling musicians, jugglers, and puppeteers. This is the only time visitors are allowed to ascend to the top of the tower to see the carillon; it's a tremendous climb, but you'll be rewarded with a spectacular view. For details, call 537-6200. A Saturday in late September.

☐ **Rock Creek Park Day.** A birthday party for Washington's largest park (1990 was its centennial). The celebration includes music, folk dancing, balloons, pony rides, international crafts and food booths, children's activities, and environmental exhibits. Call 426-6832 for details.

OCTOBER

☐ **Taste of D.C. Festival,** Pennsylvania Avenue between 9th and 14th Streets. Dozens of Washington's restaurants offer international food-tasting opportunities, along with live entertainment, dancing, storytellers, and games. Admission is free; purchase tickets for tastings. Call 724-4091 for details. Columbus Day weekend (second Monday in October).

☐ **White House Fall Garden Tours.** For two days visitors have an opportunity to see the famed Rose Garden and South Lawn. Admission is free. A military band provides music. For details, call 456-2200. Mid-October.

☐ **Washington International Horse Show,** Capital Centre, Landover, Md. This is one of the nation's most important equestrian events. Admission is charged. Call 301/840-0281 for details. Late October.

☐ **Halloween.** Never officially organized, but with costumed revels on the increase every year. Giant block parties take place in the Dupont Circle area and Georgetown. Check the *Washington Post* for special parties and activities. October 31.

NOVEMBER

☐ **Marine Corps Marathon.** A 26-mile race beginning at the Iwo Jima Memorial in Arlington and passing some of Washington's major monuments. World-class runners compete. Call 703/690-3431 for details. First Sunday in November.

☐ **Veterans Day.** The nation's war dead are honored with a wreath-laying ceremony at 11am at the Tomb of the Unknowns in Arlington National Cemetery. The President of the United States or a very high ranking government personage officiates. Military music is provided by the U.S. Army Band. Call 475-0843 for information. At the Vietnam Memorial (tel. 619-7222), observances include speakers, a wreath laying, a color guard, and the playing of taps at 1pm. November 11.

DECEMBER

☐ **Christmas Open House,** at the National Cathedral. An evening for families that includes a visit from St. Nicholas, dancers, choral groups, crafts, caroling, bell ringing, and much more. Call 537-6200 for more information, or to inquire about other Christmas concerts, pageants, services, and children's activities. First week of December.

☐ **Christmas Pageant of Peace / National Tree Lighting,** at the northern end of the Ellipse. On a selected Thursday in early December between 5 and 6pm, the President lights the national Christmas tree to the accompaniment of orchestral and choral music. The lighting inaugurates the two-week Pageant of Peace, a tremendous holiday celebration with seasonal music, caroling, a Nativity scene, 50 state trees, and a burning Yule log. Call 619-7222 for details. Early December.

☐ **White House Candlelight Tours.** On three evenings from 6 to 8pm, visitors can see the President's Christmas holiday decorations by candlelight. String music enhances the tours. Call 456-2200 for dates and details. Late December.

3. WHAT TO PACK

The most important aspect of a traveler's wardrobe is comfort. It can get very unpleasant trekking around even the most fascinating attractions when your shoes hurt or your clothing is too warm. In summer especially, the ideal ensemble is sneakers, shorts, and a T-shirt. You might, however, wish to carry a light jacket or shawl in hot weather, since interior spaces are almost always frigidly air-conditioned.

In winter, pack a coat, hat, and boots, but don't get carried away—this isn't Wisconsin. And since not every museum or attraction has a checkroom, light outerwear—like an easy-to-carry down jacket—is preferable. A fold-up umbrella is always a good idea, and if you don't use it, so much the better. People definitely dress up for dinner and evening entertainments (theater, concerts), so be sure to bring along one or two elegant outfits for nighttime wear. Jackets and ties for men are essential if you're going to an upscale restaurant, the theater, or a nightclub.

You don't need to pack a travel iron. Almost all hotels these days provide irons at the front desk, albeit with those tiny boards that make ironing even more hateful than usual. Find out if your hotel offers hairdryers before you pack one.

4. TIPS FOR THE DISABLED, SENIORS, SINGLES, STUDENTS & FAMILIES

FOR THE DISABLED

Some nationwide resources include the following: For accessibility information, call the **Travel Information Service,** Moss Rehabilitation Hospital (tel. 202/456-9900).

Recommended tour packagers include **Evergreen Travel Service/Wings on Wheels Tours,** 4114 198th Ave. SW, Suite 13, Lynwood, WA 98036 (tel. 206/776-1184, or toll free 800/435-2288), offers tours designed for the blind, the visually impaired, the hearing impaired, the elderly, and the physically or mentally disabled.

And a publisher called **Twin Peaks Press,** P.O. Box 129, Vancouver, WA 98666 (tel. 206/694-2462, or toll free 800/637-2256 for orders only), specializes in books for the disabled. Write for their *Disability Bookshop Catalog,* enclosing $2.

Finally, a Washington phone number to keep on hand is 202/966-8081, the **Information, Protection and Advocacy Center for Handicapped Individuals.** This organization responds quickly to the needs of the handicapped visitor, whether it's locating emergency attendant care or replacing a missing part of a wheelchair. It also publishes a series of pamphlets called "Access Washington: A Guide to Metropolitan Washington for the Physically Disabled," which cover everything from hotels to restaurants to sightseeing attractions. There's a nominal fee for mailing, but it's well worth it. The center can help make your stay in Washington a worry-free, enjoyable experience.

SIGHTSEEING ATTRACTIONS Washington, D.C., is one of the most accessible cities in the world for the disabled. The **White House** has a special entrance on Pennsylvania Avenue for visitors arriving in wheelchairs, and White House guides usually allow visually handicapped visitors to touch some of the items being described on tours. For details, call 456-2200.

All **Smithsonian museum buildings** (and the National Gallery) are accessible to wheelchair visitors, as are all museum floors. To receive a copy of the Smithsonian's publication "A Guide for Disabled Visitors," call 357-2700 or 357-1729 (TTY) or write to the Visitor Information Associates Reception Center, Smithsonian Institution Building, Smithsonian Institution, Washington, DC 20560. The Smithsonian publishes large-print, braille, and cassette materials for several of its museums, and its monthly calendar of events is also available on audiocassette tape. On advance request, you may be able to arrange for a sign-language interpreter on museum tours. For details, and more specific information on programs of special interest to disabled visitors, call 357-1697 or 357-1696 (TTY).

The **Lincoln and Jefferson Memorials** and the **Washington Monument** are also equipped to accommodate disabled visitors. The last-named keeps a wheelchair on the premises and allows disabled visitors to go to the head of the waiting line.

Call ahead to other sightseeing attractions for accessibility information and special services.

SHOPPING   For shoppers, places well equipped with wheelchair ramps and other facilities for the disabled include the Shops at National Place, the Pavilion at the Old Post Office, and Georgetown Park Mall.

THEATER   The **John F. Kennedy Center for the Performing Arts** rents headphones to hearing-impaired patrons that allow them to adjust volume as needed. All theaters in the complex are wheelchair accessible. Also inquire (in advance) about cassettes for the visually impaired, offering audio descriptions at select performances. For details, call 416-8340; for other questions regarding patrons with disabilities, call 416-8727.

The **National Theatre** features special performances of its shows for visually and hearing-impaired theatergoers. To obtain earphones for narration, simply ask an usher prior to the performance. The National also offers a limited number of half-price tickets to handicapped patrons on Tuesday, Wednesday, and Thursday evenings and Sunday matinees. For details, call 628-6161.

GETTING AROUND TOWN   Each **Metro** station is equipped with an elevator (complete with brailled number plates) to train platforms. Conductors make station and on-board announcements of train destinations and stops. The TTD number for Metro information is 638-3780.

Regular **Tourmobile** trams are accessible to physically impaired visitors. The company also operates special vans for immobile travelers, complete with wheelchair lifts. For the vans, reservations must be made at least 24 hours in advance. For information, call 554-7020.

TRAVELING BY BUS, TRAIN & PLANE   A companion can accompany a disabled person at no charge aboard a **Greyhound** bus. This is available only to disabled people who have a letter from their doctor certifying that they are handicapped and cannot negotiate the bus steps alone. Call toll free 800/752-4841 at least 48 hours in advance to discuss special needs.

Amtrak offers a handicapped person's fare of at least 25% off regular coach fare. Amtrak also provides wheelchair-accessible sleeping accommodations. Although pets are not allowed, guide dogs are permissible and travel free of charge. Contact your reservation agent to discuss any special needs at least 72 hours in advance of traveling.

Note: Not all stations offer redcap service.

When making your flight reservations, ask the airline or travel agent where your wheelchair will be stowed on the plane and if seeing or hearing guide dogs can accompany you.

FOR SENIORS

Bring some form of photo ID as many city attractions, theaters, transportation facilities, hotels, and restaurants grant special senior discounts.

If you haven't already done so, think about joining the **American Association of Retired Persons (AARP),** 601 E St. NW, Washington, DC 20049 (tel. 202/434-2277). Membership ($8 per year) entitles you to discounts at hotels, motels, car-rental agencies, and Gray Line tours. You must be 50 or older to join.

The **AARP Travel Experience from American Express,** 400 Pinnacle Way, Suite 450, Norcross GA 30071 (tel. toll free 800/927-0111 for land tours, 800/745-4567 for cruises), arranges a wide array of discounted group tours for members. Nonmembers can travel with AARP members at the same discounted prices.

Another good source of reduced-price information is *The Discount Guide for Travelers Over 55* by Caroline and Walter Weinz (E.P. Dutton).

Elderhostel, a national organization that offers low-priced educational programs for people over 60, runs frequent week-long residential programs in Washington. Some of these focus on government and American history, others on art, literature, and other diverse subjects. Cost averages about $355 per person, including meals, room, and classes. For information, call 410/830-3437 or contact Elderhostel headquarters at 75 Federal St., Boston, MA 02110 (tel. 617/426-7788).

Amtrak (tel. toll free 800/USA-RAIL) offers a 15% discount off the lowest available coach fare (with certain travel restrictions) to people 62 or over.

Greyhound also offers discounted fares for senior citizens. Call your local Greyhound office for details.

FOR SINGLE TRAVELERS

The main problem for single travelers is meeting other people. There is, of course, the bar scene (see Chapter 9). Another good way to meet people is to go on a hike, river-rafting trip, or other such excursion, many of which are listed in the *Washington Post* Friday "Weekend" section. You'll find other people-meeting activities listed there as well.

Another tip: Choose a bed-and-breakfast facility; it's easy to meet people over coffee and muffins in the communal dining room.

FOR STUDENTS

The key to securing discounts is a valid student ID. Be sure to carry one, and keep your eyes open for special student prices at attractions, theaters, transportation facilities, and other places.

FOR FAMILIES

Careful planning makes all the difference between a successful, enjoyable vacation and one that ends with exhausted, irritable parents and cranky kids. Here are a few helpful hints:

Get the kids involved Let them, if they're old enough, write to the tourist offices for information and color brochures. Give them a map on which they can outline the route; let them help decide the itinerary.

Packing Although your home may be toddler-proof, accommodations are not. Bring portable gates for stairways and other off-limits areas, and also some blank plugs to cover electrical outlets.

En route Carry a few simple games to relieve boredom while traveling. A few snacks will also help and will save money. Check Amtrak for special family discounts; the airlines, too, have reduced airfares for those under 17; both let under-2s travel free.

Accommodations   Children under a certain age usually stay free in their parents' room. Look for establishments that have pools and other recreational facilities. Reserve equipment such as cribs and playpens in advance.

Resources   For ideas on what to do with the kids this year: *Traveling with Children in the U.S.A.* by Leila Hadley (Morrow), *Travel with Children* by Maureen Wheeler (Lonely Planet), and *How to Take Trips with Your Kids* by Joan and Sanford Portnoy (Harvard Common Press).

5. GETTING THERE

BY AIR

Washington is served by three major airports—**Washington National Airport,** just across the Potomac in Virginia and a 15-minute drive from downtown; **Dulles International Airport,** about 45 minutes from downtown, also in Virginia; and **Baltimore-Washington International Airport,** between Baltimore and Washington, about 45 minutes from downtown. Most visitors come in via National, which is served by American, America West, Continental, Delta, Northwest, TWA, United, and USAir.

BEST-FOR-THE-BUDGET FARES   When evaluating airline fares, take into consideration bus and/or taxi fares to and from departure and arrival airports. Taxi and bus fares listed below will help you make these computations.

As we go to press, there's a major airline price restructuring going on throughout the country. With everything up in the air (so to speak), quoting specific fares here would be meaningless. Always remember, however, that it pays to book flights as far in advance as possible, since advance-purchase fares are often substantially lower. When you call, also inquire about money-saving packages that include essentials like hotel accommodations, car rentals, and tours with your airfare.

SHUTTLES TO & FROM NEW YORK   The **Delta Shuttle,** which flies out of LaGuardia's Marine Terminal in New York and Washington National Airport, has flights departing New York every hour on the half hour Monday through Friday from 6:30am to 8:30pm, with an extra departure at 9pm. Saturday flights are offered every hour on the half hour between 8:30am and 8:30pm. Sunday flights are the same, with an extra departure at 9pm. The first weekday flight leaves Washington National at 6:30am, with flights every hour on the half hour after that until 9:30pm. Saturday and Sunday flights leave every hour on the half hour from 8:30am to 8:30pm. At press time, the price was $142 each way Monday through Friday and on Sunday after 2:30pm, and $72 all day Saturday and through 1:30pm on Sunday. Since it's possible for prices and/or flight

**FROMMER'S SMART TRAVELER:
AIRFARES**

VALUE-CONSCIOUS TRAVELERS SHOULD TAKE
ADVANTAGE OF THE FOLLOWING:

1. Shop all the airlines that fly to Washington, D.C.
2. Always ask for the lowest fare, not just a discount fare.
3. Keep calling the airline to check fares. Availability of inexpensive seats changes daily, and as the departure date
   draws nearer, more seats are sold at lower prices.
4. Ask about discounts for seniors (usually 10%), children, and
   students.
5. Book in advance to obtain lower advance-purchase fares.

schedules to change, double-check the above by calling Delta (tel. toll
free 800/221-1212). Do inquire about special fares for seniors,
children, and youth (up to age 24), as well as 7- and 14-day
advance-purchase fares.

The same prices are offered by the **USAir Shuttle,** which
departs from its own terminal at LaGuardia. Flights to Washington
National Airport leave New York Monday through Saturday every
hour on the hour from 7am to 9pm, and on Sunday on the hour from
9am to 9pm. Washington–New York flights leave at the same hours.
You can call USAir toll free at 800/428-4322.

BY TRAIN

Historic **Union Station,** at Massachusetts Avenue and North
Capitol Street, is the Amtrak terminal in Washington. In the late
1980s, this turn-of-the-century beaux arts structure was magnificently restored at a cost of more than $180 million, with a three-level
marketplace of shops and restaurants. It's conveniently located and
connects with Metro service. There are also plenty of taxis here at all
times. For rail reservations, contact Amtrak (tel. toll free 800/USA-
RAIL). There's more on Union Station in Chapters 6, 7, and 8.

Like the airlines, Amtrak also offers discounted fares. A limited
number of seats are set aside for these special fares, so the sooner you
reserve them, the greater your likelihood of success. Many people
reserve these seats months in advance, so the minute you know the
dates of your trip, make your reservations. Coach fares are usually
refundable, so, in most cases, you don't lose anything by reserving far
in advance. There are some restrictions as to the dates you may travel,
mostly around very busy holiday times. At this writing, regular
round-trip coach fares and discount fares are as follows between
Washington's Union Station and five selected cities:

	Regular Fare	**Discount**
N.Y.–D.C.	$136	$92
Chicago–D.C.	$242	$128
Atlanta–D.C.	$238	$126
L.A.–D.C.	$494	$259
Boston–D.C.	$202	$132

I also suggest that you inquire about money-saving packages that include hotel accommodations, car rentals, tours, etc., with your train fare. Call toll free 800/321-8684 for details. Note: Metro liner fares are substantially reduced on weekends.

BY BUS

Greyhound buses connect just about the entire United States with Washington, D.C. They pull in at a terminal at 1st and L Streets NE (tel. toll free 800/231-2222). The closest Metro station is Union Station, four blocks away. The bus terminal area is not what you'd call a showplace neighborhood, so if you arrive at night, a taxi is advisable.

Fare structure on these buses is a little complex, not always based on distance traveled. The good news is that when you call Greyhound to make a reservation, the company will always offer you the lowest fare options. Call in advance, and know when you plan to travel, since some discount fares require advance purchase.

BY CAR

Major highways approach Washington, D.C., from all parts of the country. The District is 240 miles from New York City, 40 miles from Baltimore, and 600 miles from Chicago and Atlanta.

CHAPTER 3

FOR FOREIGN VISITORS

1. **PREPARING FOR YOUR TRIP**
2. **GETTING TO & AROUND THE U.S.**
- **FAST FACTS: THE FOREIGN TRAVELER**
- **THE AMERICAN SYSTEM OF MEASUREMENTS**

Although American fads and fashions have spread across Europe and other parts of the world so that America may seem like familiar territory before your arrival, there are still many peculiarities and uniquely American situations that any foreign visitor will encounter. This chapter is meant to clue you in on what they are. International visitors should also read the introductory chapters carefully.

---

1. PREPARING FOR YOUR TRIP

The **International Visitors Information Service (IVIS),** 1623 Belmont St. NW, between Florida Avenue and Kalorama Road (tel. 202/939-5566), is a nonprofit, community volunteer organization that provides special services to D.C.'s many visitors from abroad. Here you can obtain foreign-language publications and brochures. IVIS has a language bank of volunteers on call who speak dozens of languages. They'll provide assistance (by phone) with accommodations, sightseeing, dining, and other traditional tourist needs.

IVIS is open weekdays from 9am to 5pm, but phones are answered seven days a week from about 6am to 10pm.

ENTRY REQUIREMENTS

DOCUMENT REGULATIONS Canadian citizens may enter the United States without visas; they need only proof of residence.

British, Dutch, French, German, Italian, Japanese, Swedish, and Swiss citizens traveling on valid national (or EC) passports do not need a visa for holiday or business travel in the United States of 90 days or less if they hold round-trip or return tickets and if they enter the country on an airline or cruise line that participates in the no-visa travel program.

Note: Citizens of these visa-exempt countries who first enter the United States may then visit Mexico, Canada, Bermuda, and/or the Caribbean islands and then reenter the United States, by any mode of transportation, without a visa. Further information is available from any U.S. embassy or consulate.

Citizens of other countries require both of the following:

- a valid **passport,** with an expiration date at least six months later than the scheduled end of the visit to the United States; and
- a **tourist visa,** available without charge from the nearest U.S. consulate; the traveler must submit a completed application form (either in person or by mail) with a passport photograph attached.

Usually you will be given your visa at once, or within 24 hours at most; try to avoid the summer rush from June to August. If applying by mail, enclose a large stamped, self-addressed envelope, and expect an average wait of two weeks. Visa application forms are available at airline offices or from leading travel agents as well as from U.S. consulates. The U.S. tourist visa (visa B-2) is theoretically valid for a year, and for any number of entries, but the U.S. consulate that issues you the tourist visa will determine the length of stay for a multiple- or single-entry visa. However, there is some latitude here, and if you are of good appearance and can give the address of a relative, friend, or business connection living in the United States (useful, too, for car rental, passage through Customs, etc.), you have an excellent chance of getting a longer permit if you want one.

MEDICAL REQUIREMENTS   No inoculations are needed to enter the United States unless you are coming from areas known to be suffering from epidemics, especially of cholera or yellow fever.

If you require treatment with medications containing controlled drugs, carry a valid, signed prescription from your physician to allay any suspicions that you are smuggling drugs. Ditto for syringes.

TRAVEL INSURANCE (BAGGAGE, HEALTH & ACCIDENT)

All travel insurance is voluntary in the United States. Given the very high cost of medical care, however, I cannot too strongly advise every traveler to arrange for appropriate coverage before setting out. There are specialized insurance companies that will, for a relatively low premium, cover:

- loss or theft of your baggage;
- trip-cancellation costs;
- guarantee of bail in case you are arrested;
- sickness or injury costs (medical, surgical, and hospital); and
- costs of an accident, repatriation, or death.

Such packages (for example, "Europe Assistance" in Europe) are sold by automobile clubs at attractive rates, as well as by banks and travel agencies.

2. GETTING TO & AROUND THE U.S.

Travelers from overseas can take advantage of the **APEX (Advance Purchase Excursion) fares** offered by all the major U.S. and European air carriers. Aside from these, attractive values are offered by **Icelandair** on flights from Luxembourg to New York, Fort

Lauderdale, or Orlando; and by **Virgin Atlantic** from London to New York/Newark or Miami.

Some large airlines (for example, Delta, TWA, American, Northwest, and United) offer travelers on their transatlantic or transpacific flights special discount tickets under the name **Visit USA,** allowing travel between any U.S. destinations at minimum rates. They are not on sale in the United States, and must therefore be purchased before you leave your foreign point of departure. This system is the best way of seeing the States at low cost. You should obtain information well in advance from your travel agent or the office of the airline concerned, since the conditions attached to these discount tickets can be changed without advance notice.

For information on transportation to Washington, D.C., from elsewhere in the United States, see "Getting There," in Chapter **2**.

FAST FACTS FOR THE FOREIGN TRAVELER

Accommodations See Chapter 5.

Automobile Organizations Auto clubs will supply maps, recommended routes, guidebooks, accident and bail-bond insurance, and, most important of all, emergency road service. The leader, with over 1,000 offices and 34 million members, is the **American Automobile Association (AAA),** with national headquarters at 1000 AAA Dr., Heathrow, FL 32745 (407/444-7000). Check a telephone directory for the local office. Membership for both U.S. citizens and foreign visitors ranges from $21 to $67, depending on the particular local office where you join. AAA also has a 24-hour emergency toll-free number: 800/336-4357. The AAA can provide you with an International Driving Permit validating your foreign driving license. Members of some foreign auto clubs that have reciprocal arrangements with AAA enjoy AAA's services at no charge.

Auto Rentals To rent a car you need a major credit card or you'll have to leave a sizable cash deposit ($100 or more for each day). Minimum driver age is usually 21, and you'll need a valid driver's license. Rates vary from company to company, from location to location (airport vs. downtown, Florida vs. New York City). In addition, companies offer unlimited-mileage options or per-mile charges as well as special discounts on weekends. So it pays to shop around. Use the major companies' toll-free numbers to do this. Other variable costs include drop-off charges if you're picking up the car in one city and leaving it in another and the cost of daily collision damage and personal accident insurance. Always return your car with a full tank—the rental companies charge excessive prices for gasoline.

Business Hours Public and private **offices** are usually open from 9am to 5pm Monday through Friday. **Banking hours** are generally 9am to 3pm Monday through Friday, but in some cases until 6pm on Thursday or Friday, and sometimes also on Saturday morning. **Post offices** are open from 8am to 5:30 or 6pm Monday through Friday and 8am to noon on Saturday; some locations offer extended hours. **Store hours** are 9:30 or 10am to 5:30 or 6pm

Monday through Saturday, though often until 9pm on one or more evenings a week; shopping centers, drugstores, and supermarkets are open from 9am to 9pm six days a week (and even in some cases 24 hours). **Museum hours** vary widely: The norm for big cities is 10am to 5pm six days a week (closing day is usually Monday); all Smithsonian museums are open daily.

Climate See "When to Go—Climate and Events," Chapter 2.

Currency and Exchange The U.S. monetary system has a decimal base: one **dollar** ($1) = 100 **cents** (100¢).

The commonest **bills** (all green) are the $1 ("a buck"), $5, $10, and $20 denominations. There are also $2 (seldom encountered), $50, and $100 bills (the last two are not welcome when paying for small purchases).

There are six basic denominations of **coins:** 1¢ (one cent, or "penny"); 5¢ (five cents, or "nickel"); 10¢ (ten cents, or "dime"); 25¢ (twenty-five cents, or "quarter"); 50¢ (fifty cents, or "half dollar"), and $1 (both the old "silver dollar" and the rarer new Susan B. Anthony coin).

If they're denominated in *dollars,* traveler's checks are accepted without demur at hotels, motels, restaurants, and large stores.

However, the method of payment most widely used is the **credit or charge card:** VISA (BarclayCard in Britain), MasterCard (EuroCard in Europe, Access in Britain, Diamond in Japan, etc.), American Express, Diners Club, and Carte Blanche, in descending order of acceptance. You can save yourself trouble by using "plastic money," rather than cash or traveler's checks, in 95% of all hotels, motels, restaurants, and retail stores. A credit or charge card can serve as a deposit when renting a car, as proof of identity (often carrying more weight than a passport), or as a "cash card," enabling you to draw money from banks that accept them.

Note: The "foreign-exchange bureaus" so common in Europe are rare even at airports in the United States, and nonexistent outside major cities. Try to avoid changing foreign money, or traveler's checks denominated in other than U.S. dollars, at a small-town bank, or even a branch bank in a big city. In fact, leave any currency other than U.S. dollars at home—it may prove more nuisance to you than it's worth.

Customs and Immigration Every adult visitor may bring in, free of duty: one liter of wine or hard liquor; 200 cigarettes or 100 cigars (but *no* cigars from Cuba) or three pounds (1.35kg) of smoking tobacco; and $400 worth of gifts. These exemptions are offered to travelers who spend at least 72 hours in the United States and who have not claimed them within the preceding six months. It is forbidden to bring into the country foodstuffs like cheese, fruit, cooked meats, and canned goods and plants (vegetables, seeds, tropical plants, etc.). Foreign tourists may bring in or take out up to $10,000 in U.S. or foreign currency with no formalities; larger sums must be declared to Customs on entering and leaving.

The visitor arriving by air, no matter what the port of entry— New York, Boston, Miami, Honolulu, Los Angeles, or the rest— should cultivate patience and resignation before setting foot on U.S. soil. The U.S. Customs and Immigration Services are among the slowest and most suspicious on earth. Make a generous allowance for delay in planning connections between international and domestic flights—an average of two to three hours at least.

In contrast, for the traveler arriving by car or by rail from Canada, the border-crossing formalities have been streamlined to the vanishing point. And for the traveler by air from Canada, Bermuda, and some points in the Caribbean, you can go through Customs and Immigration at the point of *departure,* which is much quicker and less painful.

Drinking Laws As with marriage and divorce, every state, and sometimes every county and community, has its own laws governing the sale of liquor. The only federal regulation (based on a judgment of the U.S. Supreme Court on June 23, 1987) restricts the consumption of liquor in public places anywhere in the country to persons aged 21 or over (states not respecting this rule may be penalized by a withdrawal of federal highway funds). In D.C., establishments can serve alcoholic beverages from 8am to 2am Monday through Thursday, until 2:30am on Friday and Saturday, and from 10am to 2am on Sunday. Liquor stores are closed on Sunday.

Electricity U.S. wall outlets give power at 110–115 volts, 60 cycles, compared to 220 volts, 50 cycles, in most of Europe. Besides a 110-volt transformer, small appliances of non-American manufacture, such as hairdryers or shavers, will require a plug adapter with two flat, parallel pins.

Embassies and Consulates All embassies are located in Washington, D.C., as it's the nation's capital, and many consulates are located here as well. Among the embassies here are those for **Australia,** 1601 Massachusetts Ave. NW (tel. 202/797-3000); **Canada,** 501 Pennsylvania Ave. NW (tel. 202/682-1740); **France,** 4101 Reservoir Rd. NW (tel. 202/944-6000); **Germany,** 4645 Reservoir Rd. NW (tel. 202/298-4000); **Netherlands,** 4200 Linnean Ave. NW (tel. 202/244-5300); and the **United Kingdom,** 3100 Massachusetts Ave. NW (tel. 202/462-1340). You can obtain the telephone numbers of other embassies and consulates by calling "Information" in Washington, D.C. (dial 411 within D.C.'s 202 area code; elsewhere, dial 202/555-1212). Or consult the phone book in your hotel room.

Emergencies In all major cities you can call the police, an ambulance, or the fire brigade through the single emergency telephone number **911.** Another useful way of reporting an emergency is to call the telephone-company operator by dialing **0** (zero, *not* the letter "O"). Outside major cities, call the county sheriff or the fire brigade at the number you'll find in the local telephone book.

If you encounter such travelers' problems as sickness, accident, or lost or stolen baggage, it will pay you to call the **Travelers Aid Society,** 512 C St. NE (tel. 546-3120), an organization that specializes in helping distressed travelers, whether American or foreign. See "Networks and Resources," in Chapter 4, for further details.

Gasoline [Petrol] One U.S. gallon equals 3.75 liters, while 1.2 U.S. gallons equals one Imperial gallon. You'll notice several grades (and price levels) of gasoline at most gas stations. And you'll also notice that their names change from company to company. The unleaded grades with the highest octane are the most expensive (most rental cars take the least expensive "regular" unleaded) and leaded gas is the least expensive (if available), but only older cars can take this anymore, so check if you're not sure.

Holidays On the following national legal holidays, banks, government offices, post offices, and many stores, restaurants, and museums are closed: January 1 (New Year's Day), the third Monday in January (Martin Luther King, Jr., Day), the third Monday in February (Presidents Day, Washington's Birthday), the last Monday in May (Memorial Day), July 4 (Independence Day), the first Monday in September (Labor Day), the second Monday in October (Columbus Day), November 11 (Veterans Day/Armistice Day), the fourth Thursday in November (Thanksgiving Day), and December 25 (Christmas Day).

Finally, the Tuesday following the first Monday in November is Election Day, a legal holiday in presidential-election years.

Legal Aid   The foreign tourist will probably never become involved with the American legal system. If you are cited for a minor infraction (for example, of the highway code, such as speeding), *never* try to pay the fine directly to a police officer; you may wind up arrested on the much more serious charge of attempted bribery. Pay fines by mail or directly to the clerk of a court. If accused of a more serious offense, it is wise to say and do nothing before consulting a lawyer. Under U.S. law, an arrested person is allowed one telephone call to a party of his or her choice. Call your embassy or consulate.

Mail   If you want your mail to follow you on your vacation, you need only fill out a change-of-address card at any post office. The post office will also hold your mail for up to one month. If you aren't sure of your address, your mail can be sent to you, in your name, **c/o General Delivery** at the main post office of the city or region where you expect to be. The addressee must pick it up in person, and produce proof of identity (driver's license, credit card, passport, etc.).

Generally found at major road or street intersections, mailboxes are blue with a red-and-white stripe, and carry the inscription U.S. MAIL. If your mail is addressed to a U.S. destination, don't forget to add the five-figure postal code or ZIP Code, after the two-letter abbreviation of the state to which the mail is addressed (CA for California, NY for New York, DC for the District of Columbia, and so on).

In Washington, the **main post office** is located opposite Union Station at Massachusetts Avenue and North Capitol Street (tel. 523-2628). It's open Monday through Friday from 7am to midnight, and on Saturday and Sunday until 8pm.

Newspapers/Magazines   National newspapers include *The New York Times, USA Today,* and *The Wall Street Journal.* There are also innumerable national newsweeklies including *Newsweek, Time,* and *U.S. News & World Report.* For information on local Washington, D.C., periodicals, see "Newspapers/Magazines" in "Fast Facts: Washington, D.C.," in Chapter 4.

Foreign newspapers and magazines are available at Periodicals, 3109 M St. NW.

Radio and Television   Audiovisual media, with three coast-to-coast networks—ABC, CBS, and NBC—joined in recent years by the Public Broadcasting System (PBS) and the cable network CNN, play a major part in American life. In big cities like Washington, D.C., televiewers have a choice of about a dozen channels, most of them transmitting 24 hours a day, without counting the pay-TV channels showing recent movies or sports events. All options are indicated on your hotel TV set. You'll also find a wide choice of local radio stations, each broadcasting particular kinds of talk shows and/or music, punctuated by news broadcasts and frequent commercials.

Safety   Whenever you're traveling in an unfamiliar city, stay alert. Be aware of your immediate surroundings. Wear a moneybelt—or better yet, check valuables in a safety-deposit box at your hotel. Keep a close eye on your possessions and be sure to keep them in sight when you're seated in a restaurant, theater, or other public place. Don't leave valuables in your car—even in the trunk. Every city has its criminals. It's your responsibility to be aware and be alert even in the most heavily touristed areas.

Taxes In the United States there is no VAT (value-added tax) at the national level. Every state, and each city in it, can levy its own local tax on purchases, including hotel and restaurant checks, airline tickets, etc. It is automatically added to the price of certain services such as public transportation, cab fares, phone calls, and gasoline. It varies from 4% to 10%, depending on the state and city, so when you are making major purchases such as photographic equipment, clothing, or high-fidelity components, it can be a significant part of the cost.

Each locality can levy its own separate tax on hotel occupancy. Since this tax is in addition to any general sales tax, taken together these two taxes can add a considerable amount to the cost of your accommodations.

In the District, in addition to your hotel rate, you pay 11% sales tax and $1.50 per room per night in occupancy tax. In Virginia, sales tax is 4.5%, while occupancy tax varies throughout the state. In Maryland, sales tax is 5%; occupancy tax, 9.5%.

Telephone, Telegraph, Telex Almost everywhere, **pay phones** are an integral part of the American landscape. You'll find them at street corners; in bars, restaurants, public buildings, stores, service stations; along highways; etc. Telephones are provided by private corporations, which perhaps explains the high standard of service. In the District, local calls cost 20¢.

For **long-distance** or **international calls,** stock up on a supply of quarters; the pay phone will instruct you when, and in what quantity, you should put them into the slot. For direct overseas calls, first dial 011, followed by the country code and then by the city code and the number of the person you wish to call. For Canada and long-distance calls in the U.S., dial 1 followed by the area code and number.

Before calling from a hotel room, always ask the hotel phone operator if there are telephone surcharges. These are best avoided by using a public phone, calling collect, or using a telephone charge card.

For **reversed-charge or collect calls,** and for **person-to-person calls,** dial 0 (zero, *not* the letter "O") followed by the area code and number you want; an operator will then come on the line, and you should specify that you are calling collect, or person-to-person, or both. If your operator-assisted call is international, ask for the overseas operator.

For local **directory assistance** ("information"), dial 411; for **long-distance information,** dial 1, then the appropriate area code and 555-1212.

Like the telephone system, **telegraph** and **telex** services are provided by private corporations, such as ITT, MCI, and above all, Western Union, the most important. You can bring your telegram in to the nearest Western Union office (there are hundreds across the country), or dictate it over the phone (tel. toll free 800/325-6000). You can also telegraph money, or have it telegraphed to you, very quickly over the Western Union system.

Telephone Directory   See "Yellow Pages," below.

Time   The continental United States is divided into four **time zones** (six, if Alaska and Hawaii are included). From east to west, these are: eastern standard time (EST), central standard time (CST), mountain standard time (MST), Pacific standard time (PST), Alaska standard time (AST), and Hawaii standard time (HST). Always change time zones in your mind if you're traveling (or even telephoning) long distances in the States. For example, noon in Washington (EST) is 11am in Chicago (CST), 10am in Denver (MST), 9am in Los Angeles (PST), 8am in Anchorage (AST), and 7am in Honolulu (HST).

Also, **daylight saving time** is in effect from the first Sunday in April through the last Saturday in October (actually, the change is made at 2am on Sunday) except in Arizona, Hawaii, part of Indiana, and Puerto Rico. Daylight saving time moves the clock one hour ahead of standard time.

Tipping   Service charges are not normally collected as part of the bill, so tipping has become part of the American way of life, on the principle that you must pay for any service received. (In fact, most service personnel receive only minimal salaries, since it is expected that they will receive tips.) Here are some rules of thumb:

In **hotels,** tip bellhops at least 50¢ per piece of luggage, $2 to $3 if you have a lot of baggage; chambermaids, $1 a day; parking attendants, $1 per vehicle. Tip the doorman only if he performs a special service (like hailing a cab).

In **restaurants, theaters, and nightclubs,** tip checkroom attendants $1 per garment; waiters, waitresses, and other service staff, 15% to 20% of the check; bartenders, 10% to 15% of the drink charges (tip as you pay for each drink at the bar). Tip the doorman only if he performs a special service (like hailing a cab).

For **other service personnel,** tip cab drivers 15% of the fare (including any additional charges); hairdressers and barbers, 15% to 20% (which is shared with the shampooer and other staff); parking lot attendants, 50¢ per vehicle; redcaps (porters in airports and railroad stations), at least 50¢ per piece of luggage, $2 to $3 if you have a lot of baggage; train sleeping-car porter, $2 to $3 per night.

Note: Tipping is not expected for the staff in cafeterias and fast-food restaurants; for ushers in cinemas, movies, and theaters; and for gas station attendants.

Toilets   Foreign visitors often complain that public toilets are hard to find in most U.S. cities. True, there are none on the streets, but the visitor can usually find one in a bar, restaurant, hotel, museum, department store, or service station. Note, however, a growing practice in restaurants and bars of displaying a notice like TOILETS ARE FOR THE USE OF PATRONS ONLY. You can ignore this sign, or better yet, avoid arguments by purchasing a cup of coffee or a soft drink, which will qualify you as a patron. The cleanliness of toilets at railroad stations and bus depots may be open to question. Some public places are equipped with pay toilets, which require you to insert one or two 10¢ coins (dimes) into a slot on the door before it will open.

White and Yellow Pages   There are two kinds of telephone directories. The general directory is the so-called **White Pages,** in which private and business subscribers are listed in alphabetical order. The inside front cover lists emergency numbers for police, fire, and ambulance as well as other vital numbers (like the

Coast Guard, poison-control center, crime-victims hotline, etc.). The first few pages include community service numbers and a guide to long-distance and international calling, complete with country codes and area codes.

The second directory, the **Yellow Pages,** lists local services, businesses, and industries by type of activity, with an index at the back. The listings cover not only such obvious items as automobile repairs by make of car, or drugstores (pharmacies), often by geographical location, but also restaurants by type of cuisine and geographical location, bookstores by special subject and/or language, places of worship by religious denomination, and other information that the tourist might otherwise not readily find. The Yellow Pages also include city plans or detailed area maps, often showing postal ZIP Codes and public transportation routes.

THE AMERICAN SYSTEM OF MEASUREMENTS
LENGTH

1 inch (in.)	=	2.54cm				
1 foot (ft.)	=	12 in.	=	30.48cm	=	.305m
1 yard (yd.)	=	3 ft.	=	.915m		
1 mile	=	5,280 ft.	=	1.609km		

To convert miles to kilometers, multiply the number of miles by 1.61. Also use to convert speeds from miles per hour (m.p.h.) to kilometers per hour (kmph).

To convert kilometers to miles, multiply the number of kilometers by .62. Also use to convert kmph to m.p.h.

CAPACITY

1 fluid ounce (fl. oz.)	=	.03 liter				
1 pint	=	16 fl. oz.	=	.47 liters		
1 quart	=	2 pints	=	.94 liters		
1 gallon (gal.)	=	4 quarts	=	3.79 liters	=	
		.83 Imperial gal.				

To convert U.S. gallons to liters, multiply the number of gallons by 3.79.

To convert liters to U.S. gallons, multiply the number of liters by .26.

To convert U.S. gallons to Imperial gallons, multiply the number of U.S. gallons by .83.

To convert Imperial gallons to U.S. gallons, multiply the number of Imperial gallons by 1.2.

WEIGHT

1 ounce (oz.)	=	28.35g				
1 pound (lb.)	=	16 oz.	=	453.6g	=	.45kg
1 ton	=	2,000 lb.	=	907kg	=	.91 metric tons

To convert pounds to kilograms, multiply the number of pounds by .45.
To convert kilograms to pounds, multiply the number of kilos by 2.2.

AREA

    1 acre   =   .41ha
    1 square mile   =   640 acres   =   259ha   =   2.6km²

To convert acres to hectares, multiply the number of acres by .41.
To convert hectares to acres, multiply the number of hectares by 2.47.
To convert square miles to square kilometers, multiply the number of square miles by 2.6.
To convert square kilometers to square miles, multiply the number of square kilometers by .39.

TEMPERATURE

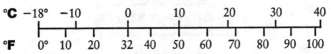

To convert degrees Fahrenheit to degrees Celsius, subtract 32 from °F, multiply by 5, then divide by 9 (example, 85°F − 32 × 5/9 = 29.4°C).
To convert degrees Celsius to degrees Fahrenheit, multiply °C by 9, divide by 5, and add 32 (example, 20°C × 9/5 + 32 = 68°F).

CHAPTER 4

GETTING TO KNOW WASHINGTON, D.C.

1. ORIENTATION
2. GETTING AROUND
 • FAST FACTS:
   WASHINGTON, D.C.
3. NETWORKS &
   RESOURCES

Washington is one of America's most delightful cities—a fitting showplace for the nation's capital. It's a city designed for strolling, offering both natural beauty and stunning architecture. Learning your way around is quick and easy.

1. ORIENTATION

ARRIVING

BY PLANE Washington National Airport is right on the Blue and Yellow **Metro** Lines from which you can reach just about any point in town. Courtesy van service is provided between the airport terminal and the Metro station.

The Washington Flyer (tel. 703/685-1400 or 703/271-7765) operates buses between the very centrally located Airport Terminal Building at 1517 K St. NW and both Dulles and National airports. Fares to/from Dulles are $16 one way, $26 round-trip; to/from National, $8 one way, $12 round-trip. Children 6 and under ride free. There are departures in each direction about every 30 minutes. From the K Street Terminal Building you can pick up a free loop shuttle that goes to eight Washington hotels—the Sheraton Washington, Omni Shoreham, Washington Hilton, Mayflower, Washington Renaissance, Grand Hyatt, J. W. Marriott, and Harrington. The Harrington alone requires advance reservation, since it's not on the loop unless someone requests it.

The Airport Connection II (tel. 301/261-1091 or 301/441-2345) runs buses between the Airport Terminal Building at 1517 K St. NW and Baltimore-Washington International Airport, with departures about every one to two hours in each direction; call for exact times. The fare is $14 one way, $25 round-trip, free for children 6 and under.

Taxi fares come to about $8 between National Airport and the White House, $42 to $45 between the White House and Dulles or BWI. (From National, take a D.C. rather than a Virginia cab—it's cheaper.)

Note: There have been price-gouging incidents in which tourists arriving from the airports have been overcharged by taxi drivers. If you think you're being ripped off, make sure to write down the company name and number of the cab (they're on the door), get an accurate receipt for the fare, and, if possible, the license plate number of the cab and the driver's name. Call 331-1671 to report any problems.

BY TRAIN   If you're traveling by train, Amtrak will deposit you in historic **Union Station,** at Massachusetts Avenue and North Capitol Street. It's conveniently located and connects with Metro service. There are also plenty of taxis available at all times.

BY BUS   Greyhound buses pull in at a terminal on 1st and L Streets NW (tel. toll free 800/231-2222); the closest Metro stop is Union Station. This is not a particularly safe neighborhood, so if you arrive at night, consider taking a taxi to your hotel.

BY CAR   If you're driving from New York or other points north, you'll probably take I-95 south to U.S. 50 west, which becomes New York Avenue in D.C. This avenue will be on your map, so you can easily figure directions to your hotel.

   If you start elsewhere, your best bet, if you're a member, is to call AAA for exact directions. Otherwise, the Convention & Visitors Association (tel. 202/789-7038) can help you find the way; have a map in front of you when you call.

TOURIST INFORMATION

On arrival in D.C., be sure to visit the **Washington Visitor Information Center** in the Willard Collection of Shops (next to, but not in, the Willard Inter-Continental Hotel) between 14th and 15th Streets on Pennsylvania Avenue NW (tel. 789-7038). A block from the White House, the center provides information on every aspect of Washington and stocks a vast supply of free maps, brochures, and literature of interest to visitors. The center's friendly and knowledgeable staff can answer all your Washington-related questions. This service is open Monday through Saturday from 9am to 5pm.

CITY LAYOUT

Pierre Charles L'Enfant designed Washington's great sweeping avenues crossed by numbered and lettered streets. At key intersections he placed spacious circles. Although the circles are enhanced with monuments, statuary, and fountains, L'Enfant planned them with a dual motive—they were also designed to serve as strategic command posts to ward off invaders or marauding mobs. After what had happened in Paris during the French Revolution—and remember,

---

IMPRESSIONS

If Washington should ever grow to be a great city, the outlook from the Capitol will be unsurpassed in the world. Now at sunset I seemed to look westward far into the heart of the continent from this commanding position.
—RALPH WALDO EMERSON

Like a city in dreams, the great white capital stretches along the placid river from Georgetown on the west to Anacostia on the east.
—ALLEN DRURY

that was current history at the time—his design views were most practical.

MAIN ARTERIES & STREETS   The primary artery of Washington is **Pennsylvania Avenue,** scene of parades, inaugurations, and other splashy events. Pennsylvania runs northwest in a direct line between the Capitol and the White House, continuing on a northwest angle to Georgetown from the White House.

Constitution Avenue, paralleled to the south most of the way by **Independence Avenue,** runs east-west flanking the Capitol and the Mall.

Washington's longest avenue, **Massachusetts Avenue,** runs north of and parallel to Pennsylvania. Along the way you'll find Union Station and Dupont Circle, central to the area known as Embassy Row. Farther out are the Naval Observatory (the vice-president's residence is on the premises), Washington National Cathedral, American University, and, finally, Maryland.

Connecticut Avenue, running more directly north, starts at Lafayette Square directly facing the White House. It's the city's Fifth Avenue, the boulevard with elegant eateries, posh boutiques, and expensive hotels.

Wisconsin Avenue, from the point where it crosses M Street, is downtown Georgetown. Antiques shops, trendy boutiques, discos, restaurants, and pubs all vie for attention. Yet somehow Georgetown manages to keep its almost European charm.

FINDING AN ADDRESS   Once you understand the city's layout, it's very easy to find your way around. You'll find it helpful, when reading this, to have a map handy.

The city is divided into four basic quadrants—**northwest, northeast, southwest,** and **southeast.** If you look at your map, you'll see that some addresses—for instance, the corner of G and 7th Streets—appear in four different places. There's one in each quadrant. Hence you must observe the quadrant designation (NW, NE, SW, or SE) when looking for an address.

The **Capitol** dome is the center of the District of Columbia—the dividing point for the four quadrants: Each of the four corners of the District of Columbia is exactly the same distance from the dome. The White House and most government buildings and important monuments are west of the Capitol (in the northwest and southwest quadrants); so are important hotels and tourist facilities.

Numbered streets run north-south, beginning on either side of the Capitol with East 1st Street and West 1st Street. **Lettered streets** run east-west.

Avenues, named for U.S. states, run at angles across the grid pattern and often intersect at traffic circles. For example, New Hampshire, Connecticut, and Massachusetts Avenues intersect at Dupont Circle.

With this in mind, finding an address is a cinch. On **lettered streets,** the address tells you exactly where to go. For instance, 1776 K Street NW is between 17th and 18th Streets (the first two digits of 1776 tell you that) in the northwest quadrant (NW). *Note:* I Street is often written Eye Street to prevent confusion with 1st Street.

To find an address on **numbered streets** you'll probably have to use your fingers. For instance, 623 8th Street SE is between F and G Streets (the sixth and seventh letters of the alphabet; the first digit of

623 tells you that) in the southeast quadrant (SE). One thing to remember though—there's no J Street (skipping the letter J was meant as a slap in the face to unpopular Chief Justice John Jay). So when counting, remember that K becomes the 10th letter, L the 11th, and so on.

As you go farther out—beyond Washington's original layout—the letter alphabetical system ends and a new one begins—two-syllable names in alphabetical order: Adams, Bryant, Channing, and so forth. When the two-syllable alphabet is used up, the system begins anew with three-syllable names—Albemarle, Brandywine, Chesapeake, and so on.

NEIGHBORHOODS IN BRIEF

The Mall   This lovely tree-lined stretch of open space between Constitution and Independence Avenues, extending for 2½ miles from the Capitol to the Lincoln Memorial, is the hub of tourist attractions. It includes most of the Smithsonian Institution museums, and many other visitor attractions are close by. The 300-foot-wide Mall is used by natives as well as tourists—joggers, food vendors, kite-flyers, and picnickers among them.

Downtown   Roughly the area between 7th and 22nd Streets NW going east to west, and P Street and Pennsylvania Avenue going north to south, downtown is a mix of Federal Triangle's government office buildings, K Street and Connecticut Avenue restaurants and shopping, F Street department stores, and much more. Too large an area to have a consistent character, it contains lovely Lafayette Park, Washington's tiny porno district, its slightly larger Chinatown, the Convention Center, and a half dozen or so sightseeing attractions.

Capitol Hill   Everyone's heard of "the Hill," the area crowned by the Capitol. When people speak of Capitol Hill, they refer to a large section of town, extending from the western side of the Capitol to RFK Memorial Stadium going east, bounded by H Street NE and the Southwest Freeway north and south. It contains not only the chief symbol of the nation's capital, but the Supreme Court building, the Library of Congress, the Folger Shakespeare Library, Union Station, and the Botanic Gardens. Much of it is a quiet residential neighborhood of tree-lined streets and Victorian homes. Many restaurants are in the vicinity.

Foggy Bottom   The area west of the White House to the edge of Georgetown, Foggy Bottom was Washington's early industrial center. Its name comes from the foul fumes emitted in those days by a coal depot and gasworks, but its original name, Funkstown (for owner Jacob Funk), is perhaps even worse. There's nothing foul about the area today. The Kennedy Center and George Washington University are located here. Constitution and Pennsylvania Avenues are Foggy Bottom's southern and northern boundaries, respectively.

Dupont Circle   Generally, when Washingtonians speak of Dupont Circle they don't mean just the park, they mean the area around it. The park itself, named for Rear Adm. Samuel Francis Dupont of the U.S. Navy, is centered around D.C.'s most famous fountain, at the intersection of Connecticut and Massachusetts Avenues, and is a popular rendezvous spot. Dupont Circle is one of the liveliest sections in town, rivaled only by Georgetown and Adams-Morgan for nightspots, movie theaters, and restaurants.

Georgetown This historic community dates back to coloni-al times. It was a thriving tobacco port long before the District of Columbia was formed, and one of its attractions, the Old Stone House, dates to pre-Revolutionary days. Georgetown action centers on M Street and Wisconsin Avenue NW, where you'll find numerous boutiques (see Chapter 8 for details), chic restaurants, and popular pubs. But do get off the main drags and see the quiet tree-lined streets of restored colonial row houses, stroll through the beautiful gardens of Dumbarton Oaks, and check out the C&O Canal. One of the reasons so much activity flourishes in Georgetown is that it contains the campus of Georgetown University.

Adams-Morgan This increasingly trendy multiethnic neighborhood is popular for its restaurants serving Jamaican, Ethiopian, Spanish, and other international cuisines. Try to plan at least one meal up here; it's a good opportunity to see an authentic untouristy area of Washington. Adams-Morgan centers around Columbia Road and 18th Street NW.

2. GETTING AROUND

Washington is one of the easiest towns in the country to get around in. Only New York rivals its comprehensive transportation system, but Washington's clean, efficient subways put the Big Apple's underground nightmare to shame. There's also a complex bus system with routes covering all major D.C. arteries, and it's easy to hail a taxi anywhere at any time. Finally, Washington—especially the areas of interest to tourists—is pretty compact, and often the best way to get from here to there is on foot.

BY METRO

The Metrorail stations are immaculate, cool, and attractive, with terra-cotta floors and high, vaulted ceilings; the sleek subway cars are air-conditioned, carpeted, furnished with upholstered seats, and fitted with picture windows; the tracks are rubber-cushioned so the ride is quiet; the service is frequent enough so you usually get a seat; and the system is so simply designed that a 10-year-old can under-stand it.

Metrorail's 74 stations and 89 miles of track (83 stations and 103 miles of track are the eventual goal) include locations at or near almost every sightseeing attraction and extend to suburban Maryland and northern Virginia. If you're in Washington even for a few days you'll probably have occasion to use the system, but if not, I suggest you create one—perhaps dinner at a Dupont Circle restaurant. The Metro is a sightseeing attraction in its own right.

There are five lines in operation at this writing—**Red, Blue, Orange, Yellow,** and **Green**—with extensions in the works for the future. The lines connect at several points, making transfers easy. All but Yellow and Green Line trains stop at Metro Center; all but Red Line trains stop at L'Enfant Plaza.

Metro stations are indicated by discreet brown columns bearing the station's name and topped by the letter M. Below the M is a colored stripe or stripes indicating the line or lines it serves. When entering a Metro station for the first time, go to the kiosk and ask the station manager for a free "Metro System Pocket Guide." It contains a map of the system, explains how it works, lists parking lots at Metrorail stations, and indicates the closest Metro stops to points of interest. The station manager can also answer questions about routing or purchase of farecards.

To enter or exit a Metro station you need a computerized **farecard,** available at vending machines near the entrance. The minimum fare to enter the system is $1, which pays for rides to and from any point within seven miles of boarding during non-rush hours; during rush hours (Monday through Friday from 5:30 to 9:30am and 3 to 7pm) $1 only takes you for three miles. The maximum value allowed per card is $100. The machines take nickels, dimes, quarters, $1 bills, and $5 bills (some new machines also accept $10 and $20 bills), and they can return change (in coins only). If you plan to take several Metrorail trips during your stay, put more value on the farecard to avoid having to purchase a new card each time you ride. Otherwise you might waste time standing in long lines. There's a 5% fare discount on everything you purchase over $10, 10% on all farecards over $20. Up to two children under 5 ride free with a paying passenger.

When you insert your card in the entrance gate, the time and location are recorded on its magnetic tape and your card is returned. Don't forget to snatch it up, and keep it handy—you have to reinsert it in the exit gate at your destination, where the fare will automatically be deducted. The card will be returned if there's any value left on it. If you arrive at a destination and your farecard doesn't have enough value, add what's necessary at the Exitfare machines near the exit gate.

If you're planning to continue your travel via Metrobus, pick up a **transfer** at the station where you enter the system (*not* your destination station) from the transfer machine on the mezzanine. It's good for full fare within D.C., and gives you a discount on bus fares in Maryland and Virginia. There are no bus-to-subway transfers.

Metrorail operates Monday through Friday from 5:30am to midnight and on Saturday and Sunday from 8am to midnight. A weekend schedule is in effect on most holidays. Call 637-7000 for information on Metro routes.

BY BUS

While any 10-year-old could understand the Metrorail system, the Metrobus system would probably perplex Einstein. The 13,000 stops on the 1,500-square-mile route (it operates on all major D.C. arteries and in the Virginia and Maryland suburbs) are indicated by red, white, and blue signs. However, the signs just tell you what buses pull into a given stop (if that), not where they go. For **routing informa-tion,** call 637-7000; a transit information agent can tell you the most efficient route from where you are to where you want to go (using bus and/or subway) almost instantly. Calls are taken daily between 6am and 11:30pm, but the line is often busy, so don't wait until the last minute to call.

If you travel the same route frequently and would like a free map and time schedule, ask the bus driver or call 637-7000. Information about free parking in Metrobus fringe lots is also available from this number.

Base fare in the District is $1, and transfers are free. There are additional charges for travel into the Maryland and Virginia suburbs. Bus drivers are not equipped to make change, so be sure to *carry exact change or tokens.* The latter are available at 398 ticket outlets (call 637-7000 for locations and hours of operation). If you'll be in Washington for a while, and plan to use the buses a lot, consider a two-week pass such as the **$21 D.C. Base Flash Pass,** good for unlimited Metrobus rides within the District and $4 worth of Metrorail rides. These are also available at ticket outlets. Other passes include zones in Virginia or Maryland.

Most buses operate daily just about around the clock. Service is very frequent on weekdays, especially during rush hours. On weekends, and late at night, your wait will be longer, but never more than 15 minutes.

There's a full bus information center (the Metro Sales Facility) at Metro Center Station (12th and F Streets), where tokens, special bus tickets, and all else is available.

Up to two children under 5 ride free with a paying passenger on the Metrobus, and there are reduced fares for senior citizens (tel. 962-1179) and the handicapped (tel. 962-1245).

Should you leave something on a bus, on a train, or in a station, call Lost and Found (tel. 962-1195).

BY CAR

Within the District a car is a luxury, as public transportation is so comprehensive. Having a car can even be an inconvenience, especially during spring and summer, when traffic jams are frequent, parking spaces almost nonexistent, and parking lots ruinously expensive. But there's a great deal to see in the D.C. vicinity, and for most attractions in Virginia and Maryland you will want a car.

All the major car-rental companies are represented here. Some handy phone numbers: **Budget** (tel. toll free 800/527-0700), **Hertz** (tel. toll free 800/654-3131), **Thrifty** (tel. toll free 800/367-2277), **Avis** (tel. toll free 800/331-1212), and **Alamo** (tel. toll free 800/327-9633).

BY TAXI

Surprise! You can take taxis in Washington without busting your budget—at least in some cases. District cabs work on a zone system. If you take a trip from one point to another in the same zone, you pay just $3 ($2.60 within a subzone of Zone 1), regardless of the distance traveled. So it would cost you $3 to travel a few blocks from the U.S. Botanic Garden to the Museum of American History, the same $3 from the Botanic Garden all the way to Dupont Circle. They're both in Zone 1. Also in Zone 1 are most other tourist attractions: the Capitol, the White House, most of the Smithsonian, the Washington Monument, the FBI, the National Archives, the Supreme Court, the Library of Congress, the Bureau of Engraving and Printing, the Old Post Office, and Ford's Theatre. If your trip takes you into a second zone, the price is $4.20, $5.20 for a third zone, $6.20 for a fourth, and so on. You're unlikely to travel more than three zones unless you're staying in some remote section of town.

So far fares are pretty low. Here's how they can add up: There's a

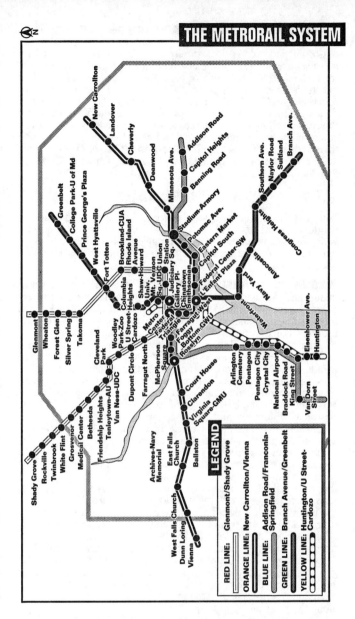

LEGEND

RED LINE: Glenmont/Shady Grove

ORANGE LINE: New Carrollton/Vienna

BLUE LINE: Addison Road/Franconia-Springfield

GREEN LINE: Branch Avenue/Greenbelt

YELLOW LINE: Huntington/U Street-Cardozo

$1.25 charge for each additional passenger after the first, so a $3 Zone 1 fare becomes $6.75 for a family of four (though one child under 6 can ride free). There's also a rush-hour surcharge of $1 per trip between 4 and 6:30pm weekdays. And there are surcharges as well for large pieces of luggage and for arranging a pickup by telephone ($1.50).

Note: A fare hike is under discussion at press time.

The zone system is not used when your destination is an

out-of-district address (like an airport); the fare is then based on mileage covered—$2 for the first half mile or part thereof and 70¢ for each additional half mile or part. You can call 331-1671 to find out the rate between any point in D.C. and an address in Virginia or Maryland. Call 767-8380 for inquiries about fares within the District.

It's generally easy to hail a taxi. There are about 7,500 cabs, and drivers are allowed to pick up as many passengers as they can comfortably fit. Expect to share. You can also call a taxi, though there's that $1.50 charge. Try **Diamond Cab Company** (tel. 387-6200), **Yellow Cab** (tel. 544-1212), or **Capitol Cab** (tel. 546-2400).

BY TOURMOBILE

You can save on shoe leather and see most Washington landmarks in comfort aboard Tourmobiles (tel. 554-7950)—open-air blue-and-white sightseeing trams that run on routes along the Mall and as far out as Arlington National Cemetery and even (with coach service) Mount Vernon.

WASHINGTON/ARLINGTON TOUR   You may take the Washington and Arlington Cemetery tour or tour Arlington Cemetery only. The former visits 15 different sights on or near the Mall and three sights at Arlington Cemetery: the gravesites of the Kennedy brothers, the Tomb of the Unknowns, and Arlington House.

Here's how the Tourmobile system works. You may board vehicles at 15 different locations: the White House, the Washington Monument/U.S. Holocaust Memorial Museum, the Arts and Industries Building/Hirshhorn Museum, the National Air and Space Museum, Union Station, the Capitol, the National Gallery of Art, the Museum of Natural History, the Museum of American History, the Bureau of Engraving and Printing, the Jefferson Memorial, West Potomac Park, the Kennedy Center, the Lincoln Memorial/Vietnam Veterans Memorial, and Arlington National Cemetery.

You pay the driver when you first board the bus. Along the route, you may get off at any stop to visit monuments or buildings. When you finish exploring each area, you step aboard the next Tourmobile that comes along without extra charge. The buses travel in a loop, serving each stop every 20 to 30 minutes. One **fare** allows you to use the buses for a full day. The charge for the Washington/Arlington tour is $8.50 for adults, $4 for children under 12. For Arlington only, adults pay $2.75; children, $1.25. Buses follow "figure-8" circuits from the Capitol to Arlington and back. Children under 3 ride free. Between June 15 and Labor Day you can also buy a ticket after 4pm good for the rest of the afternoon and the following day ($10.50 for adults, $5 for children); the rest of the year the same offer pertains after 2pm. Well-trained narrators give commentaries about sights along the route and answer questions.

Tourmobiles operate daily year-round on the following schedules. From June 15 through Labor Day, they ply the Mall between 9am and 6:30pm. After Labor Day, hours are 9:30am to 4:30pm. From Arlington, between October and March, they start at 8am and end at 5pm. April through September, the hours are 8am to 7pm.

OTHER TOURS   Tourmobiles also run round-trip to **Mount Vernon** from April to October. Coaches depart from the Arlington National Cemetery Visitors Center and the White House at 10am,

LEGEND:

Zone Fares	Single Passenger and Shared Riding Rate Per Passenger
Subzone	$2.60
1 Zone	3.00
2 Zones	4.20
3 Zones	5.20
4 Zones	6.20
5 Zones	7.20
6 Zones	8.20
7 Zones	9.20
8 Zones	10.20

Group Rates:
$1.25 extra for each additional passenger after first passenger in group

P.M.:
Rush-hour (4:00-6:30 P.M.)
Surcharge—$1.00 per trip

Radio Dispatch:
Surcharge—$1.50

NOTE: Fares are doubled during periods of snow emergency as Declared by the District of Columbia Taxicab Commission.

▬▬▬ MAJOR ZONE BOUNDARIES
▬ ▬ ▬ SUBZONE BOUNDARIES

noon, and 2pm, and from the Washington Monument at 10:15am, 12:15pm, and 2:15pm. The price is $16.50 for adults, $8 for children, including admission to Mount Vernon. A combination tour of Washington, Arlington Cemetery, and Mount Vernon is $25.50 for adults, $12.50 for children—much cheaper than the Gray Line equivalent. Another offering (June 15 through Labor Day) is the **Frederick Douglass National Historic Site Tour,** including a guided tour of Douglass's home, Cedar Hill. Departures are from Arlington National Cemetery at 10am. Adults pay $5; children,

$2.50. A two-day **Combination Frederick Douglass Tour and Washington-Arlington National Cemetery Tour** is also available at $16 for adults, $8 for children. For both the Mount Vernon and Frederick Douglass tours you must reserve at least an hour in advance.

BY OLD TOWN TROLLEY

A service similar to Tourmobile's is Old Town Trolley Tours of Washington (tel. 301/985-3020), in operation since 1986. For a fixed price, you can get on and off these green-and-orange vehicles as many times as you like within one loop at 16 locations (listed below) in the District and Arlington. Most stops are at or near major sightseeing attractions, including Georgetown. The trolleys operate seven days a week: Memorial Day to Labor Day hours are 9am to 5pm; the rest of the year, 9am to 4pm. The cost is $15 for adults, $7 for ages 5 to 12, free for children under 5. The full tour, which is narrated, takes two hours, and trolleys come by every 15 to 30 minutes. Stops are made at Union Station, the Hyatt Regency Hotel (near the National Gallery), the Pavilion at the Old Post Office, the Grand Hyatt (near Ford's Theatre), the J. W. Marriott (near the Renwick and Corcoran), the Hotel Washington (near the White House), the Capital Hilton (near the National Geographic Society), the Washington Hilton (near the Phillips Collection and Adams-Morgan restaurants), the Park Gourmet Washington (near the National Zoo), the National Cathedral, the Georgetown Park Mall, Arlington National Cemetery, the Lincoln Memorial, the Washington Monument/U.S. Holocaust Memorial Museum, the Holiday Inn Capitol Hill (near Mall museums), and the Library of Congress.

Tickets can be purchased at all stops except the Lincoln Memorial.

FAST WASHINGTON, D.C.

Airports/Airport Transportation See "Arriving" in "Orientation," earlier in this chapter.

Ambulances See "Emergencies," below.

American Express There's an American Express Travel Service office at 1150 Connecticut Ave. NW (tel. 457-1300).

Area Code Within the District of Columbia, it's 202. In suburban Virginia, it's 703. In suburban Maryland, it's 410 or 301.

Babysitters Most hotels provide child-care services. If yours does not, contact Mother's Aides Inc. (tel. 703/250-0700). In business since 1979, this company uses only licensed and bonded sitters whose qualifications and personal history are carefully checked. Rates are $8 per hour for one child, $1 per hour for each additional sibling, $2 per hour for any other child. There's a four-hour minimum, a one-time $15 booking fee, and a $5 round-trip transportation charge. Call weekdays between 9am and 4:30pm.

Car Rentals See "Getting Around," earlier in this chapter.

Climate See "When to Go," in Chapter 2.

Crime See "Safety," below.

Congresspersons To locate a senator or congressional representative, call the Capitol switchboard (tel. 224-3121).

Doctors and Dentists An organization called Prologue (tel. 362-8677) can refer you to any type of doctor or dentist you need. Its roster of close to 800 practitioners includes just about every specialty. Phones are answered 24 hours a day. You can also call the Dental Referral Service (tel. 547-7615 Monday through Friday from 8am to 4pm).

Drugstores Peoples, Washington's major drugstore chain (with about 40 stores), has two 24-hour locations: 14th Street and Thomas Circle NW, at Vermont Avenue (tel. 628-0720), and at Dupont Circle (tel. 785-1466), both with round-the-clock pharmacies. These drugstores also carry diversified merchandise ranging from frozen food and basic groceries to small appliances. Check your phone book for other convenient locations.

Embassies See "Fast Facts: The Foreign Traveler," in Chapter 3.

Emergencies Dial **911** to contact the police or fire department or to call an ambulance. See, also, "Hospital Emergency Wards," below.

Hairdressers/Barbers The Hair Cuttery, with five Washington locations—1645 Connecticut Ave. near Dupont Circle (tel. 232-9685) and 3209 M St. in Georgetown (tel. 965-8831) among them—is an inexpensive unisex hair salon offering trendy cuts and styling on a walk-in, no-appointment-necessary basis. The salons also do hair coloring, frostings, and reconditioning. The two above, and most other locations, are open seven days; call for hours.

Holidays See "When to Go," in Chapter 2.

Hospital Emergency Wards Georgetown University Hospital, 3800 Reservoir Rd. NW (make a left off Wisconsin Avenue; tel. 784-2118), and George Washington University Hospital, 901 23rd St. NW (entrance on Washington Circle; tel. 994-3884), are both excellent.

Hotel Tax In the District, in addition to your hotel rate, you pay 11% sales tax and $1.50 per room per night in occupancy tax. At Virginia hotels sales tax is 4.5%; hotel occupancy tax varies throughout the state. In Maryland, sales tax is 5%; hotel occupancy tax varies.

Libraries The Martin Luther King, Jr., Memorial Library, 901 G St. NW (tel. 727-1186), is an extensive facility. It's open daily; hours vary seasonally, so call ahead.

Liquor Laws Minimum drinking age is 21. Establishments can serve alcoholic beverages from 8am to 2am Monday through Thursday, until 2:30am on Friday and Saturday, and from 10am to 2am on Sunday. Liquor stores are closed on Sunday.

Newspapers/Magazines The major newspaper is, of course, the renowned *Washington Post*. The city's other daily is the *Washington Times*. Also informative are *Washingtonian* magazine and *The City Paper*, the latter a free newspaper available at restaurants, in bookstores, and other places around town.

Poison Control Center 625-3333 is a 24-hour emergency hotline.

Post Office The city's main post office (tel. 523-2628) is located opposite Union Station at 2 Massachusetts Ave. NE (at G and North Capitol Streets). It's open Monday through Friday from 7am to midnight, and on Saturday and Sunday until 8pm.

Religious Services Every hotel keeps a list of places of worship for all faiths. Inquire at the front desk.

Safety Whenever you're traveling in an unfamiliar city, stay alert. Be aware of your immediate surroundings. Wear a moneybelt— or better yet, check valuables in a safety-deposit box at your hotel. Keep a close eye on your possessions, and be sure to keep them in sight when you're seated in a restaurant, theater, or other public place. Don't leave valuables in your car—even in the trunk. Every city has its criminals. It's your responsibility to be aware and alert even in the most heavily touristed areas.

Taxis See "Getting Around," earlier in this chapter.

Tickets A service called TICKET place (tel. TICKETS [842-5387]) sells half-price tickets—on the day of performance only—to most major Washington-area theaters and concert halls. It also functions as a Ticketmaster outlet. See Chapter 9 for details.

Time Call 844-2525.

Tourist Information The Convention and Visitor Association's **Visitor Information Center,** Pennsylvania Avenue between 14th and 15th Streets NW (tel. 789-7038), knows all, tells all. It's open Monday through Saturday from 9am to 5pm. Dial 737-8866 for a recording of events of interest to tourists.

Also be sure to visit the superb **Smithsonian Information Center,** 1000 Jefferson Dr. SW (tel. 357-2700). Open daily except December 25 from 9am to 5:30pm, it's a must, especially for first-time visitors to the Smithsonian.

You can also call **Dial-a-Museum** (tel. 357-2020), the Smithsonian's number for recorded daily information on all its museum programs and activities, and **Dial-a-Park** (tel. 619-PARK) to find out about events in the National Capital Region parks.

Transit Information See "Getting There," in Chapter 2; and "Orientation" and "Getting Around," earlier in this chapter.

Weather Call 936-1212.

3. NETWORKS & RESOURCES

FOR ALL TRAVELERS

The **Travelers Aid Society** is a nationwide network of voluntary nonprofit social-service agencies providing help to travelers in difficulty. This might include anything from crisis counseling to straightening out ticket mix-ups, not to mention reuniting families accidentally separated while traveling, locating missing relatives (sometimes just at the wrong airport), and helping retrieve lost baggage (also sometimes at the wrong airport).

In Washington, Travelers Aid has a central office in the Capitol Hill area at 512 C St. NE (tel. 546-3120), where professional social workers are available to provide assistance. It's open only on weekdays from 9am to 5pm, but the phones are answered around the clock. There are also Travelers Aid desks at Washington National Airport (open Sunday through Friday from 9am to 9pm and on Saturday to 6pm; tel. 703/419-3972), on the lower concourse at the west end of Dulles International Airport (open Sunday through Friday from 10am to 9pm and on Saturday to 6pm; tel. 661-8636), and at Union Station (open daily from 9:30am to 5:30pm; tel. 546-3120); TTY or TDD (telecommunications device for the deaf) are provided at the above-mentioned locations.

FOR MILITARY PERSONNEL

If you're in a military service, you probably already know about **USO,** the congressionally chartered, nonprofit agency representing civilian concern for members of the armed forces and their families. You can stop by for assistance with accommodations, transportation, sightseeing, and other travel needs; find out about dozens of cultural events and recreational activities in the Washington area, many of them USO-sponsored for service families; pick up free tickets (when available) to theaters and sporting events; and learn about District discounts available on tours and travel, at hotels, restaurants, and elsewhere. Whatever your problems, USO tries to solve them. Call 703/696-2551 for information on theater/sporting events tickets.

You can also write to USO's Washington center at USO Metro, Post HQ, Bldg. 59, Rm. B-18, Fort Myer, VA 22211, or call 703/696-2628 weekdays from 9am to 5pm. They can answer questions and provide information.

There's also a USO center complete with TV lounge and free coffee on the first floor of the North Terminal of Washington National Airport (tel. 703/920-6990). At the same airport, also in the North Terminal, is a USO information booth (tel. 703/920-2705). They're staffed by volunteers, so hours vary occasionally, but they try to keep one or the other of these airport facilities open daily from 10am to 9pm.

FOR WOMEN

The **Women's Information Bank,** 3918 W St. NW, Washington, DC 20007 (tel. 202/338-8163), is a volunteer-staffed organization offering a number of services to women, among them help in finding safe, reasonably priced, long- and short-term accommodations. They often know of houses and apartments for rent, people who need roommates, and bed-and-breakfast places. Best of all, there's no fee, though donations are accepted. There's generally someone on hand daily from 10am to 10pm, but call first. Sometimes they're slow at answering phone messages. Persevere. In addition, WIB hosts a walk-in open house nightly from 7 to 9pm, sometimes with guest speakers.

FOR GAYS & LESBIANS

The complete source for the gay and lesbian community is *The Washington Blade,* a comprehensive weekly newspaper distributed free at about 400 locations in the District. Every issue contains an extensive events calendar and a list of about 300 resources, such as crisis centers, health facilities, switchboards, political groups, religious organizations, social clubs, and student activities; it puts you in touch with everything from groups of lesbian birdwatchers to the Asian Gay Men's Network. Gay restaurants and clubs are, of course, also listed and advertised. You can subscribe to the *Blade* for $30 a year or pick up a free copy at numerous locations, among them: in the Dupont Circle area, Olsson's Books/Records at 1307 19th St. NW, Annie's Paramount Steak House at 1609 17th St. NW, the Rock Creek Café at 2111 P St. NW, and Kramerbooks at 1517 Connecticut Ave. NW; in Georgetown, the Biograph Theatre at 29th and M Streets NW; in Capitol Hill, at Chesapeake Bagel Bakery, 215 Pennsylvania Ave. SE. Or call the *Blade* office at 797-7000.

CHAPTER 5

ACCOMMODATIONS IN WASHINGTON, D.C.

1. EXPENSIVE
- **FROMMER'S SMART TRAVELER: HOTELS**

2. MODERATE
- **FROMMER'S COOL FOR KIDS: HOTELS**

3. INEXPENSIVE

4. BUDGET

5. BED & BREAKFAST

Your first priority on a Washington visit is finding a place to stay. Luckily, with about 63,000 hotel and motel rooms in the District and surrounding metropolitan area, there's no shortage of rooms. They exist in every category, from luxurious accommodations to budget guesthouses—with many more, alas, in the upper bracket than in the lower. Presented below are those establishments in all price categories that offer the best value for your money.

PRICE CATEGORIES   Hotels listed as "expensive" charge $150 or more for a double room, those charging $100 to $149 are listed as "moderate," $65 to $99 as "inexpensive," and under $65 as "budget." B&Bs are in a section of their own. Most of the recommendations in all price categories are in the northwest section, where many major sightseeing attractions and good restaurants are located. However, within each price category hotels are listed by location.

TAXES   Whatever rate you end up with, keep in mind that the sales tax here is 11% of your total bill, and the occupancy tax is $1.50 per night. And if you have a car, look into the cost of parking when you reserve; some centrally located hotels charge as much as $22 a night!

GETTING THE MOST FOR YOUR DOLLAR

WEEKEND, OFF-SEASON & SPECIAL RATES   In Washington, the majority of hotels, from budget to expensive, slash prices by almost half during weekends, and sometimes, weekdays in off-season (generally July through August and late December through January). When making arrangements, be sure to verify that your reservation is at weekend rates before hanging up, and check on it again when you register. At many hotels, you have to register in advance to obtain weekend rates.

Write or call the **D.C. Committee to Promote Washington,** P.O. Box 27489, Washington, DC 20038-7489 (tel. 202/724-4091, or toll free 800/422-8644), and request a copy of "Washington Weekends." It lists weekend rates at over 90 hotels in all price ranges.

Taj International Hotels, 1315 16th St. NW, Washington, DC 20036 (tel. 202/462-7104, or toll free 800/DC-VISIT), owns four centrally located Washington, D.C. hotels—the Hampshire Hotel, the Canterbury, the Quality Hotel, and Howard Johnson's Hotel & Suites—all of which are described in this chapter. Their weekend rates, also available sometimes on weekdays November through February and during July and August, begin at just $59 per room per night. And they also offer marvelous weekend packages with extras such as champagne and chocolates upon arrival. Write or call for details.

Also inquire about special packages. Many hotels offer special rates as a matter of course to senior citizens, families, active-duty military personnel, and government workers.

A RESERVATIONS SERVICE   Make use of a free service offered by **Capitol Reservations,** 1730 Rhode Island Ave. NW, Suite 302, Washington, DC 20036 (tel. 202/452-1270, or toll free 800/VISIT-DC). They'll find you a hotel in the price bracket you desire that meets your specific requirements, and they'll do the bargaining for you. "Because of the high volume of room nights we book," explains owner Thom Hall, "many properties offer discounts available only through this service." Capitol Reservations listings begin at about $55 a night for a double. Hotels are screened for cleanliness and other desirability factors, and they're all in safe neighborhoods.

GROUPS   If you're planning a meeting, convention, or other group function requiring 10 rooms or more, you should know about a free service called **U.S.A. Groups** (tel. 202/861-1900, or toll free 800/872-4777). Representing hotel rooms at almost every hostelry in the Washington, D.C., and suburban Virginia/Maryland region—in categories from expensive to low cost—this organization works hard to locate accommodations that fit your group's needs perfectly. And it saves you dozens of phone calls seeking space, rate, and facility information.

1. EXPENSIVE

Whether they're old and grand or new and glamorous, all of these hostelries provide abundant luxuries and gracious service to guests. And they all feature beautiful gourmet restaurants, many of which merit a visit even if you stay at a less elegant address. Some proffer old-fashioned European-style services and traditions (shoeshine, bed turn-down, concierge, etc.). Others offer wide-ranging facilities.

Another feature you'll frequently find in the expensive category is the concierge floor. A special area of a hotel set aside for guests who pay a little bit more, it has larger rooms with additional amenities, special concierge and housekeeping services, a private lounge where complimentary continental breakfasts and cocktail-hour hors d'oeuvres are served, and, in most cases, daily newspaper delivery and nightly turn-down.

DOWNTOWN

HENLEY PARK, 926 Massachusetts Ave. NW (at 10th St.), Washington, DC 20001. Tel. 202/638-5200, or toll free 800/222-8474. Fax 202/638-6740. 90 rms, 6 suites. A/C MINIBAR TV TEL **Metro:** Metro Center or Gallery Place.

**FROMMER'S SMART TRAVELER:
HOTELS**

1. Use reservations services such as Capitol Reservations; they obtain lower rates by booking rooms in volume.
2. Take advantage of reduced rates, often offered Friday through Sunday and sometimes off-season weekdays as well. They may be as much as 50% lower.
3. Bargain with the reservations clerk. An unoccupied room nets a hotel zero dollars, and any reasonable offer is better than that. This works best on the afternoon of your arrival, when the desk knows there will be empty rooms.
4. Ask about special discounts for students, government or corporate employees, senior citizens, or military personnel.
5. Using toll-free numbers, compare rates at a wide variety of hotels. Sometimes even expensive hostelries, which list rates as high as $200, offer a rate as low as $75 on the phone.

$ Rates: Weekdays, $155–$215 single; $175–$235 double. Summer and weekends, $89 single or double (including parking). Children under 14 stay free in parents' room. AE, CB, DC, DISC, ER, MC, V. **Parking:** $15.

Named for the quaint British town Henley-on-Thames, this intimate, English-style hotel is housed in a converted 1918 seven-story Tudor-style apartment house with 119 gargoyles on its facade. The lobby, with its exquisite Tudor ceiling, archways, and leaded windows, is particularly evocative of the period. Room decor is residential in the English country house mode. Furnishings are 18th-century styles—Hepplewhite, Chippendale, and Queen Anne—with lovely period beds (you might get a four-poster). Floral-print bedspreads and drapes are charming, walls are hung with framed botanical prints, and crown moldings harmonize with carpet hues. Baths offer phones, makeup mirrors, and luxury toiletries, and in-room amenities include remote-control cable TVs with pay-movie options and AM/FM clock radios.

Dining/Entertainment: The hotel's posh French restaurant is Coeur de Lion (for Richard the Lion-Hearted, an English king of French descent). It's a lovely dining room, with walls of weathered brick and mirrors adorned with English oil paintings and a bacchanal-themed mural, glass windows, and a crystal chandelier suspended from a skylight. The menu features French cuisine, highlighting seafood, and the wine list is excellent. Adjoining the Coeur de Lion is Marley's, a delightful cocktail lounge, the setting for piano bar entertainment (and complimentary hors d'oeuvres) on weekdays from 5 to 8pm and live jazz on weekend nights. Afternoon tea (with scones, finger sandwiches, and pastries) is served daily in the octagonal Wilkes Room, a charming and comfortably furnished parlor with a working fireplace.

Services: 24-hour concierge and room service, *Washington*

Map legend:

Adams Inn **3A**	Four Seasons **12**	Hotel Lombardy **26**
Canterbury Hotel **6**	Georgetown Dutch Inn **11**	Howard Johnson's Hotel
Capital Hilton **18**	Hampshire Hotel **7**	& Suites **4A**
Carlyle Suites **3**	Hay-Adams **27**	Howard Johnson's Lodge
Channel Inn **31**	Henley Park **22**	J. W. Marriott **29**
Comfort Inn **24**	Holiday Inn Central **10**	Jefferson **15**
Connecticut Avenue	Holiday Inn Thomas Circle **16**	Kalorama Guest House **2**
Days Inn **2**	Hostelling's International—	Marriott's Residence Inn
Days Inn Downtown **19**	Washington, D.C. **21**	Mayflower **14**
Embassy Inn **4**	Hotel Anthony **17**	Morrison Clark Inn **20**

Post delivery each weekday morning, complimentary shoeshine, nightly bed turn-down with gourmet chocolate, complimentary weekday limo service to downtown and Capitol Hill locations.

Facilities: Access to fully equipped health club a block away, which has a lap pool, treadmills, Stairmasters, full complement of exercise equipment, and more.

J. W. MARRIOTT, 1331 Pennsylvania Ave. NW (at E St.), Washington, DC 20004. Tel. 202/393-2000, or toll free

ACCOMMODATIONS IN WASHINGTON, D.C.

Metro Stop **M**

Information **ⓘ**

Normandy Inn **2**	State Plaza Hotel **28**
Omni Shoreham **2**	Walter Reed Hospitality
Quality Hotel Central **2**	House **6**
Quality Hotel	Washington, D.C.,
Downtown **9**	Renaissance Hotel **23**
The Reeds' Bed &	Washington Hilton
Breakfast **5**	and Towers **2**
Ritz-Carlton **2**	Willard Inter-
Savoy Suites	Continental **30**
Georgetown **1**	Windsor Inn **4**

800/228-9290. Fax 202/626-6991. 721 rms, 51 suites. A/C
MINIBAR TV TEL **Metro:** Metro Center.

$ Rates: Weekdays, $189–$209 single or double; $219–$229
concierge level single or double. Weekend $129 single or double
with full breakfast. Additional person free. AE, DC, DISC, ER,
JCB, MC, V. **Parking:** $16.

⭐ This flagship property, opened in 1984 as part of the
masterplan to renovate historic Pennsylvania Avenue, is adjacent to the National and Warner Theaters. It's stunning,

combining futuristic architecture with warm color schemes and lush plantings to create an exciting but very livable environment. The imposing lobby, with expanses of marble flooring and gigantic crystal chandeliers overhead, surrounds two levels of marquee-lit stairwells.

Rooms are decorated in muted earth tones and equipped with remote-control TVs with cable and HBO, in-room voice mail, clocks, and plants. The concierge level, on the 14th and 15th floors, features a private lounge with a gorgeous view. Frills here include complimentary continental breakfast and cocktail-hour hors d'oeuvres, additional toiletries, nightly turn-down with a Godiva chocolate, and an electric shoeshiner.

Dining/Entertainment: The hotel's most elegant facility is Celadon, wherein Chinese Chippendale chairs (like the walls, upholstered in celadon green) and Oriental vases and screens create an Eastern ambience. Taped music varies from Vivaldi to show tunes. Lunch and dinner menus offer American/continental options ranging from filet mignon to pine-nut swordfish. The very pretty National Cafe utilizes a pink-and-peach Victorian/art nouveau motif and, in warm weather, has outdoor seating at umbrella-shaded tables. Lunch or dinner, the fare ranges from simple burgers and salads to heartier entrées. An "early-bird" dinner (soup, salad, entrée, and dessert) costs under $15. Al fresco dining is also a feature of SRO (for Standing Room Only), a New York–style deli. And for piano entertainment and jazz bands nightly there's the skylit Garden Terrace.

Services: 24-hour room service.

Facilities: A connecting mall with 85 shops and restaurants, health club (with indoor swimming pool, Universal equipment, hydrotherapy pool, and sun deck), videogame arcade, full business center, gift shop.

WASHINGTON, D.C., RENAISSANCE HOTEL, 999 9th St. NW (at K St.), Washington, DC 20001. Tel. 202/898-9000, or toll free 800/228-9898. Fax 202/789-4213. 779 rms, 21 suites. A/C MINIBAR TV TEL **Metro:** Gallery Place.

$ Rates: Weekdays, $175–$205 single; $195–$225 double; club level, $225 single, $245 double. Weekends, $89 single or double. Additional person free. AE, CB, DC, DISC, MC, V. **Parking:** $14.

Opened in 1989 directly across the street from the D.C. Convention Center, this hotel is part of the $340-million World Technology Trade Center Complex. Though catering primarily to conventioneers and business travelers, it also delivers a lot of luxury and convenience to tourists.

For openers, the spiffy rooms are well equipped and attractive. Done up in teal/mauve or sage/sienna color schemes, with oak furnishings and Southwest-look bedspreads and drapes, they offer remote-control TVs (with cable stations, pay-movie options, and video message retrieval/checkout), alarm clocks, phones with voice mail and computer jacks, and AM/FM radios. An entire 15-story tower with 166 rooms constitutes the Renaissance Club, where guests are pampered with extra amenities such as three phones, hairdryers, and an extensive toiletries package. Club guests can also enjoy a private concierge-staffed lounge, a cozy domain where a lavish complimentary continental breakfast and afternoon hors d'oeuvres are served. Private registration/checkout is another plus.

Dining/Entertainment: The mahogany-paneled and crystal-chandeliered Floreale features American regional cuisine. Less formal is the Café Florentine, off the lobby, offering reasonably priced buffets and à la carte meals at breakfast, lunch, and dinner; it's cheerfully decorated with fruit- and vegetable-motif tiles. Surrounded by lush tropical plantings, the skylit Marco Polo piano bar resembles a Chinese pagoda. And the Plaza Gourmet & Pastry Shop offers take-out sandwiches, salads, and fresh-baked pastries.

Services: 24-hour room service, concierge.

Facilities: Gift shop, hairdresser, full business center, full health club (with lap pool, whirlpool, steam rooms, treadmills, Stairmasters, free weights, bikes, and rowing machines).

WILLARD INTER-CONTINENTAL, 1401 Pennsylvania Ave. NW, Washington, DC 20004. Tel. 202/628-9100, or toll free 800/327-0200. Fax 202/637-7326. 304 rms. 37 suites. A/C MINIBAR TV TEL **Metro:** Metro Center.

$ Rates: Weekdays, $245–$325 single; $275–$335 double. Weekends, $179 single or double. Suites $450–$2,700. Additional person $30 extra; children under 12 stay free in parents' room. AE, DC, DISC, ER, JCB, MC, SAISON, V. **Parking:** $15.75.

Billed as the "crown jewel of Pennsylvania Avenue," the Willard Inter-Continental is actually the crown jewel of all Washington hotels. Reopened in 1986, it was built in 1901 as the grandest of grand hotels on the site of an earlier hostelry built by Henry Willard in 1850.

The Willard's history is inextricably intertwined with the history of Washington. It flourished from pre–Civil War days (at one time there were separate entrances and floors for pro-Union and secessionist factions) through just after World War II. In the 1860s, Nathaniel Hawthorne said of the Willard, "You exchange nods with governors of sovereign States; you elbow illustrious men, and tread on the toes of generals. . . . You are mixed up with office seekers, wire pullers, inventors, artists, poets, prosers . . . until your identity is lost among them." Lincoln spent not only the eve of his inaugural here, but sometimes held staff meetings in front of the lobby fireplace. And it was at the Willard that Julia Ward Howe penned the words to the "Battle Hymn of the Republic."

In 1901, Henry Janeway Hardenbergh—architect of New York's Waldorf-Astoria and Plaza hotels—was hired to design the French Second Empire beaux arts palace that is still standing today. The hotel continued as a "residence of presidents." By the time the Willard closed its doors in 1968, however, the hotel had deteriorated considerably.

Saved as a national landmark in 1974, restoration began in the 1980s, and a new building, designed to harmonize with the old, was

---

IMPRESSIONS

Washington is a town where thousands of people never unpack entirely. It is a seat of the theoretically mighty, where the cocktail glass is one of the more powerful instruments of government.
—RUSSELL BAKER

constructed. In the original building, the exquisite plasterwork and scagliola marble were repaired or replicated, along with marble mosaic tile floors, carpeting, and chandeliers. The colonnaded main lobby today is again an awesome entranceway, with massive marble columns ascending to a lofty ceiling decorated with 48 state seals and hung with huge globe chandeliers. Also restored is Peacock Alley, a plush potted-palmed promenade lined with exclusive boutiques.

Rooms are suitably sumptuous, decorated in Egyptian earth tones or sea and sky blues. Furnishings are Edwardian and Federal-period reproductions, and walls are hung with beautiful gilt-framed French prints. Cable TVs (with remote control, pay-movie channels, video messaging, and video checkout) are concealed in armoires. And in the bath you'll find a hairdryer, scale, phone, TV speaker, and makeup mirror.

Dining/Entertainment: The Willard Room (the term "power lunch" originated here) is simply stunning. It's the setting for American regional cuisine meals, with piano music during dinner. (See Chapter 6 for details.) The circular Round Robin Bar is where Henry Clay mixed the first mint julep in Washington. The Café Espresso offers croissant sandwiches, pastas, pastries, and vintage wines by the glass, along with more substantial entrées. And the Round Robin Lounge offers afternoon tea daily from 3 to 5pm and jazz piano nightly.

Services: Twice-daily maid service, nightly bed turn-down, complimentary shoeshine, 24-hour room service, concierge, currency exchange, airline/train ticketing.

Facilities: Full business center, fitness center (with multistation machine, treadmills, Lifecycles, Stairmasters, and free weights.

NEAR THE WHITE HOUSE

THE CAPITAL HILTON, 16th St. NW (between K and L Sts.), Washington, DC 20036. Tel. 202/393-1000, or toll free 800/HILTONS. Fax 202/639-5784. 517 rms, 32 suites. A/C MINIBAR TV TEL **Metro:** Farragut West or McPherson Square.

$ Rates: Weekdays, $230–$270 single; $255–$295 double; tower, $300 single, $325 double. Weekends (including continental breakfast), $130 single or double. Additional person $25 extra; children of any age stay free in parents' room. AE, CB, DC, DISC, ER, JCB, MC, V. **Parking:** $22.

This longtime Washington resident has played host to every American president since FDR, including Truman, who lived here while the White House (two blocks away) was being remodeled. In the 1940s, big-name entertainers like Edith Piaf and Xavier Cugat played the Embassy Room. The Rat Pack took over a dozen connecting rooms during the Kennedy inaugural festivities. And the annual Gridiron Club Dinner and political roast is held in the ballroom each year.

During a five-year $55-million renovation in the late 1980s, public areas were upgraded (note the gorgeous cherrywood paneling in the lobby). And in 1993 the rooms were redecorated in Federal-period motif with Queen Anne– and Chippendale-style furnishings. Each contains three phones (desk, bath, bedside) equipped with call waiting, a digital alarm clock, an AM/FM radio, and a remote-control cable TV featuring pay-movie stations and account-review/message-retrieval options. In the bath you'll find a small TV and hairdryer. Floors 10 to 14 house the Towers accommodations, where guests enjoy nightly bed turn-down with gourmet chocolates, private registration/checkout, a personal concierge, and complimentary continental breakfast in a plush private lounge.

Dining/Entertainment: There's a Trader Vic's here with oak-paneled walls and plush red tufted-leather booths. Nautical art and ship models tastefully replace the usual Polynesian clutter associated with this chain. Its Asian/South Seas–influenced fare (Mandarin orange beef, pupu platters, Tahitian bouillabaisse) is excellent; stop by for the $12.95 Polynesian buffet lunch. Another fine Hilton dining room is Twigs, a sunny gardenlike setting with lots of plants, white trelliswork, and seating amid potted palms; the more elegant Twigs Grill adjoins. Fare is American regional. Complimentary hors d'oeuvres are served in The Bar, a plushly furnished lobby lounge, weekdays from 5 to 7pm, and a pianist entertains throughout the evening.

Services: 24-hour room service, 24-hour concierge, full business center, tour and ticket desk.

Facilities: Unisex hairdresser, gift shop, facial salon, shoeshine stand, jeweler, airline desks (American, Continental, Northwest), fitness center (with Nautilus equipment, treadmills, rowing machines, exercise bikes, Stairmasters, steam, and sauna).

HAY-ADAMS, 1 Lafayette Sq. (at 16th and H Sts. NW), Washington, DC 20006. Tel. 202/638-6600, or toll free 800/424-5054. Fax 202/638-3803. 125 rms, 18 suites. A/C MINIBAR TV TEL **Metro:** Farragut West or McPherson Square. **$ Rates:** Weekdays, $205–$365 single; $225–$390 double. Weekends (Fri–Sun), $175 per room. Additional person $25 extra; children under 12 stay free in parents' room. Also available: Eight smaller rooms. $175 single or double. AE, CB, DC, JCB, MC, V. **Parking:** $19.

Few hotels have a more aristocratic air than this one, overlooking Lafayette Square. In 1927, famed Washington builder Harry Wardman created the Hay-Adams "to provide for the socially elite as well as men who loom large in the country's life." Its architecture evokes an Italian Renaissance palazzo with Doric, Ionic, and Corinthian orders and intricate ceiling motifs. Among the early guests were Amelia Earhart, Sinclair Lewis, Ethel Barrymore, and Charles Lindbergh. In the 1990s, the hotel is as elegant as ever. The walnut-paneled lobby is festooned with French Empire candelabras, 19th-century Chinese gouaches, and Regency furnishings.

Rooms are individually furnished with antiques and appointments far superior to those usually found in today's hotels. Though each is different, a typical accommodation might feature 18th-century-style furnishings, silk-covered walls hung with botanical prints and fine art, a gorgeous molded plaster ceiling, and French silk floral-print bedspreads, upholstery, and curtains. Many have ornamental fireplaces and/or French doors that open onto views of Lafayette Square and the White House. Amenities include fine toiletries, hairdryers, cosmetic mirrors, and phones in the bathrooms; terrycloth robes and slippers; AM/FM clock radios; and remote-control TVs with HBO.

The eight smaller rooms were originally for servants traveling with guests. Today, they're delightfully decorated; if you want one, request it when making reservations.

Dining/Entertainment: The sunny Adams Room, overlooking

Lafayette Square and the White House, serves all meals (it's undergoing a renovation in decor and concept at this writing). The Tudor-style John Hays Lounge—its walls hung with reproductions of works by Hans Holbein the Younger and 17th-century French tapestries—offers drinks and light fare. It's also the setting for afternoon teas and nightly piano-bar entertainment.

Services: Limousine service, 24-hour butler/room/concierge service, chocolates and petits fours with nightly bed turn-down, complimentary shoeshine.

Facilities: Guest access to several local health clubs, secretarial and business services.

JEFFERSON, 1200 16th St. NW (at M St.), Washington, DC 20036. Tel. 202/347-2200, or toll free 800/368-5966. Fax 202/223-9039. 68 rms, 32 suites. A/C MINIBAR TV TEL **Metro:** Farragut North.

$ Rates: Weekdays, $210–$250 single; $225–$265 double. Weekends, $145 single; $160 double. Additional person $25 extra; children under 12 stay free in parents' room. AE, CB, DC, JCB, MC, OPT, V. **Parking:** $20.

Esquire magazine has called the Jefferson "one of the ten best hotels in the world." Opened in 1923 just four blocks from the White House, it has served as the Washington home of political personages, royalty, actors, writers, and other notables. Among those who've enjoyed the Jefferson's discreet small-hotel hospitality over the years are Edward R. Murrow, Helen Hayes, Robert Frost, Leonard Bernstein, and H. L. Mencken (his books are still in the room he occupied). With a very high staff-to-guest ratio, the Jefferson puts utmost emphasis on service: Staff members greet you by name, and, should you return, your preferences will be remembered. If you like, a butler will unpack your luggage and press clothes wrinkled in transit.

The Jefferson is impressive from the minute you set foot in the sedately elegant lobby. Beautiful Persian rugs adorn marble floors, Italian turn-of-the-century crystal chandeliers are suspended from a carved-plaster rosette-motif Adams ceiling, big bouquets of flowers adorn 18th-century tables, and moss-green velvet-covered Chippendale armchairs face a Georgian-reproduction fireplace. A Thomas Jefferson grandfather clock chimes the hours in dulcet tones. A very fine art collection graces public areas, rooms, and hallways. Each room is uniquely decorated. Yours might have a four-poster bed with plump eyelet-trimmed comforter and pillow shams (many are topped with canopies), a cherrywood bibliothèque from the Napoleonic period filled with rare books, a French Empire Louis XVI bureau, or a red lacquer Chinoiserie case filled with objets d'art. In-room amenities include multiline phones with speaker-phone option plus fax and computer jacks, remote-control cable TVs with VCRs, AM/FM clock radios, and CD players; and, in the baths, terry robes, hairdryers, and phones.

Dining/Entertainment: Off the lobby is one of the city's premier dining venues (see Chapter 6). A marvelous high tea is served daily from 3 to 5pm in the reading room, its walls hung with framed original Thomas Jefferson letters and documents. Classical music enhances the ambience. There's also a cozy bar/lounge with a working fireplace, the setting for live jazz on Saturday night.

Services: 24-hour butler service, overnight shoeshine, nightly bed turn-down with Godiva chocolate, morning newspaper delivery, 24-hour room and multilingual concierge service.

Facilities: Business/secretarial services; for a fee guests have access to full health club facilities at the University Club across the street (pool, Nautilus, sauna, whirlpool, and more).

DUPONT CIRCLE

MAYFLOWER, 1127 Connecticut Ave. NW (between L and M Sts.), Washington, DC 20036. Tel. 202/347-3000, or toll free 800/HOTELS-1. Fax 202/466-9082. 559 rms, 80 suites. A/C MINIBAR TV TEL **Metro:** Farragut North.

$ Rates: Weekdays, $230–$290 single; $260–$320 double. Weekends, $179 single or double. Additional person $25 extra; children under 18 stay free in parents' room. Inquire about "summer value rates." AE, CB, DC, DISC, ER, JCB, MC, V. **Parking:** $12.

Designed by the architectural firm whose masterpieces include Grand Central Terminal in New York, the Stouffer-owned Mayflower is the grande dame of Washington hotels. Every president from Coolidge to Reagan held his inaugural ball in the gilded Grand Ballroom. FDR penned the words "The only thing we have to fear is fear itself" in Suite 776. JFK called the hotel home as a young congressman. And for 20 years before his death, FBI chief J. Edgar Hoover ate the same lunch (chicken soup, grapefruit, cottage cheese) in the Grille Room every day. One day he spotted Public Enemy No. 3 at an adjoining table and nabbed him. One could go on forever with Mayflower lore.

A major restoration in the 1980s uncovered large skylights and renewed the lobby's pink marble bas-relief frieze and the spectacular block-long promenade. Ceilings and columns were regilded and Italianate murals rediscovered.

In the graciously appointed guest rooms, hardwood crown moldings adorn high ceilings. Cream moiré wall coverings are complemented by accents of claret and teal, mahogany furnishings are period reproductions (Queen Anne, Sheraton, Chippendale, Hepplewhite), 25-inch remote-control TVs are discreetly concealed in handsome armoires, and amenities include three phones (bath, desk, bedside) and AM/FM clock radios. In the bath you'll find a terry robe, hairdryer, fine toiletries, and a small color TV.

Dining/Entertainment: The hotel's much-acclaimed premier restaurant, Nicholas, features American regional cuisine in a gemlike setting—crystal chandeliers illuminate ecru-colored walls hung with gilt-framed French oil paintings and lush floral arrangements are reflected in gleaming beveled mirrors.

Washington lawyers and lobbyists gather for power breakfasts in the posh Café Promenade. Under a beautiful domed skylight, the restaurant is adorned with Edward Laning's murals, crystal chandeliers, ficus trees, marble columns, and lovely flower arrangements. A full English tea is served here every afternoon. The room originally was, in fact, used for the dansants (tea dances). In the evening the café is a romantic venue for dinner.

Services: Coffee and newspaper with wake-up call, 24-hour room service, twice-daily maid service, complimentary overnight shoeshine, complimentary limo within a three-mile radius of the hotel, concierge, no surcharge on local calls.

Facilities: Business center, full on-premises fitness center (with sauna and Vectra exercise equipment, treadmills, Lifecycles, and Stairmasters).

RITZ-CARLTON, 2100 Massachusetts Ave. NW, Washington, DC 20008. Tel. 202/293-2100, or toll free 800/241-3333. Fax 202/293-0641. 206 rms, 24 suites. A/C MINIBAR TV TEL **Metro:** Dupont Circle.

$ Rates: Weekdays, $215–$285 single or double; $295 club single or double. Weekends, $150 single or double. Additional person free. Inquire about packages. AE, CB, DC, ER, MC, V. **Parking:** $16 (valet only).

★ The Ritz-Carlton is a gem—from its richly paneled lobby to its pristine Oriental-carpeted hallways and lovely residential rooms. The latter, which have recently undergone a $21-million facelift, are decorated in muted earth tones (soft gray, beige, amber, celadon, and sienna), with traditional dark-wood furnishings. Windows are framed by elegant tassled draperies, the walls hung with French architectural watercolor renderings. In-room amenities include remote-control cable TVs, AM/FM clock radios, phones with fax capability, and terry robes; and the gorgeous marble baths are equipped with phones, hairdryers, and upscale toiletries (some also have small TVs). The seventh and eighth floors comprise a Club Level where guests have use of a beautiful lounge and a library containing travel books donated by ambassadors to Washington from all over the world. Rates here include, among other perks, services of a private concierge, complimentary breakfast, afternoon tea and cocktails, and evening coffee, liqueurs, and desserts.

Dining/Entertainment: The Jockey Club has been one of Washington's most prominent see-and-be-seen restaurants since it opened in 1961. Though the crowd and cuisine are haute, the setting is cheerful and pubby, with a random-plank oak floor, amber lanterns suspended from a low beamed ceiling, shelves of pewterware on display, and walls of stucco or aged oak hung with equestrian prints. The fare is California-influenced American; Jockey Club chicken salad (Nancy Reagan's favorite) and crabcakes are signature dishes. In the adjoining and equally cozy Fairfax Bar, you can sink into a plush sofa before a blazing fireplace. It's a convivial setting for cocktails, light lunches, English-style afternoon teas, and nightly piano bar entertainment. (*Note:* Michael Feinstein got his start playing piano at the Ritz-Carlton.)

Services: Complimentary morning newspaper delivery, nightly turn-down with imported chocolates, 24-hour concierge and room service, complimentary shoeshine.

Facilities: Fitness center (with saunas, Stairmasters, treadmills, Lifecycles, and free weights), business/secretarial center.

GEORGETOWN

THE FOUR SEASONS, 2800 Pennsylvania Ave. NW, Washington, DC 20007. Tel. 202/342-0444, or toll free 800/332-2442. Fax 202/944-2076. 166 rms, 30 suites. A/C MINIBAR TV TEL **Metro:** Foggy Bottom.

$ Rates: Weekdays, $250–$295 single; $275–$320 double. Weekends (Fri–Sun), $195–$215 single or double. Additional person $30 extra; children under 18 stay free in parents' room. AE, CB, DC, ER, JCB, MC, V. **Parking:** $20.

⭐ The Four Seasons is one of Washington's most glamorous hotels. Since its opening in 1979, guests have included everyone from rock legend Prince to King Hussein of Jordan. Marla Maples once stalked out of the lobby after flinging a shoe—and a 7.5-carat engagement ring—at Donald Trump! And President Clinton stopped by for afternoon tea with Chelsea one day. The hotel does everything possible to pamper guests with unparalleled can-do concierge service. When Michael Jackson stayed, they set up a special dance floor in his room. But celebrity gossip aside, this is a magnificent hotel. Open the front door and you enter a plush lobby where thousands of tropical plants and palm trees grow, and large floral arrangements further the gardenlike ambience. Classical music is played throughout the public areas.

Exceptionally pretty accommodations, many of them overlooking Rock Creek Park or the C&O Canal, contrast traditional dark-wood furnishings with charming print fabrics. Textured white walls are hung with gilt-framed antique prints, and bedding is embellished with dust ruffles and scalloped spreads. Large desks and plump cushioned armchairs with hassocks add to the residential tone. In-room amenities include remote-control cable TVs with free HBO, AM/FM clock radios, hairdryers, three phones (bedside, bath, and desk—one with two lines), bathrobes, and upscale toiletries.

Dining/Entertainment: The elegant plant-filled Seasons—Milan modern with hunter-green walls, a tiled quartz floor, and halogen pin lighting—serves contemporary cuisine that is international in scope. It's open for all meals. Dinner fare might run the gamut from broiled grouper with Thai seasonings to a corn blini with quail egg, caviar, and smoked salmon. Weather permitting, there's outdoor terrace seating. Paneled in Australian ash, the delightful Garden Terrace has floor-to-ceiling windows overlooking the canal and seating on plush sofas and armchairs. It's open for lunch, light fare throughout the day, lavish Sunday brunches, and classic English afternoon teas. And guests are given temporary membership at the swanky Desirée, a private on-premises nightclub.

Services: Twice-daily maid service, 24-hour concierge and room service, nightly turn-down, complimentary limousine service, gratis newspaper of your choice, car windows washed when you park overnight.

Facilities: Beauty salon, gift shop, jogging trail, business facilities; state-of-the-art fitness club with Lifecycles, Stairmasters, treadmills, and rowing machines (all equipped with TVs, VCRs, and Walkmans; movie, music, and workout tapes are available), Nautilus equipment, free weights, pool, massage, whirlpool, sauna for women, steam for men, exercise classes, fitness evaluation, juice bar, workout clothes, and more.

ADAMS-MORGAN

OMNI SHOREHAM, 2500 Calvert St. NW (at Connecticut Ave.), Washington, DC 20008. Tel. 202/234-0700, or toll free 800/228-2121. Fax 202/265-5333. 745 rms, 55 suites. A/C MINIBAR TV TEL **Metro:** Woodley Park-Zoo.
$ Rates: Weekdays, $205–$265 single; $225–$285 double. Off-season and weekends, $79 single or double. Additional person $20 extra; children under 18 stay free in parents' room. AE, CB, DC, DISC, ER, JCB, MC, V. **Parking:** $12.

Set on 14 acres adjacent to verdant Rock Creek Park, the Shoreham is a resort hotel right in the heart of the city. And what a hotel it is! Built in 1930, this deluxe hostelry has been the scene of inaugural balls for every president since FDR. In the early years, prominent socialites like Perle Mesta and Alice Roosevelt Longworth threw private parties here. Truman held private poker games in Room D-106 while his limousine waited outside. And the most ostentatious guest ever was King Saud who, traveling with a full complement of armed guards and 32 limos, dispensed solid-gold watches as tips. JFK courted Jackie over drinks at the Shoreham, and Richard Nixon introduced his cabinet-to-be over network television at a dinner here.

Some years back, the hotel's public areas were restored to their original grandeur. In the vast Renaissance lobby, Chinese carpets were laid on marble floors, exquisite stenciled artwork was restored on vaulted ceilings, clerestory windows were fitted with new glass, and opulent crystal chandeliers were cleaned. The spacious guest rooms—beautifully decorated in soft burgundies, subtle grays, and chalky blues—are equipped with remote-control cable TVs (with pay-movie options) and AM/FM clock radios.

Dining/Entertainment: The hotel's excellent restaurant, the Monique Café et Brasserie, is reminiscent of the famed La Coupole in Paris—a convivial enclave of polished brass, dark woodwork, simulated marble columns, potted palms, and Oriental mirrors. Traditional brasserie fare (such as choucroûte with saucisson and steak au poivre) is served along with a selection of traditional American choices. The delightful Garden Court, under a 35-foot vaulted ceiling, is lushly planted with ficus trees and tropical foliage, all of it reflected in beveled-mirror walls. Rock Creek Park provides a fitting backdrop for this popular cocktail lounge. The hotel's nightlife centers on the art deco Marquee Cabaret (details in Chapter 9).

Services: Room service, concierge.

Facilities: Shops; travel/sightseeing desk; business center; extensive children's activity programs; 10 miles of jogging, hiking, and bicycle trails (winding off into Rock Creek Park), plus a 1.5-mile Perrier parcourse with 18 exercise stations; three lighted Har-Tru tennis courts; two outdoor pools; on-premises health club (with a full complement of Nautilus and Lifecycle equipment, Stairmasters, treadmills, rowing machines, sauna, and more).

WASHINGTON HILTON AND TOWERS, 1919 Connecticut Ave. NW (at T St.), Washington, DC 20009. Tel. 202/483-3000, or toll free 800/HILTONS. Fax 202/797-5755. 1,023 rms, 82 suites. A/C MINIBAR TV TEL **Metro:** Dupont Circle.

$ Rates: Weekdays, $189–$229 single, $209–$249 double; tower, $259 single, $279 double. Weekends (and selected weekdays and holidays), $95 per room, including continental breakfast. Additional person $20 extra; children of any age stay free in parents' room. AE, CB, CH, DC, DISC, ER, JCB, MC, OPT, V. **Parking:** $12.

This is a kind of super-hotel/resort offering imaginable amenity. A recent $42-million renovation spiffed up its accommodations, restaurants, and public areas, and it's looking great! The Hilton hosts numerous conventions and functions—inaugural balls, debutante cotillions, state banquets, and society shindigs.

Rooms are cheerful and attractively furnished in colors like cinnamon, mauve, and sea-foam green. All have AM/FM clock radios and remote-control cable TVs with pay-movie stations, and many offer panoramic views of Washington. The 10th floor is called the Towers—a VIP hotel-within-a-hotel featuring a beautifully furnished private lounge (with a gorgeous view) and concierge service; it's the setting for complimentary continental breakfasts and afternoon hors d'oeuvres and cocktails. Special in-room amenities here include nightly bed turn-down service and bathroom scales.

Dining/Entertainment: The cheerful Capital Café, bordered by planters of flowers, has a wall of windows overlooking the pool. Open daily for all meals, it offers fancy coffee-shop fare—everything from croissant sandwiches to filet mignon. The Gazebo, an alfresco poolside eatery, serves light fare under a striped tent top. A plush new steak-and-seafood restaurant, with adjoining lounge, is in the works at this writing. And McClellan's (named for the Union general whose equestrian statue fronts the hotel) is a clubby lounge with a handsome brass-railed mahogany bar and commodious leather chairs—a comfortable place to imbibe.

Services: Room service during restaurant hours, transportation/sightseeing desk. Airport bus stops at the door.

Facilities: Extensive health club facilities (Stairmasters, treadmills, rowing machines, Lifecycles, Cybex equipment, weight rooms, sun room, and massage), a large nightlit heated outdoor pool, children's pool, three nightlit Har-Tru tennis courts, numerous classes (including tennis and aerobics), pro/swim shop, shuffle board, bike rental, and jogging path. Also, lobby shops, comprehensive business center, car-rental desk.

2. MODERATE

Establishments listed in the moderate category charge about $100 to $149 for a double room. Some accommodations feature fully equipped kitchens.

DOWNTOWN

COMFORT INN, 500 H St. NW, Washington, DC 20001. Tel. 202/289-5959, or toll free 800/221-2222. Fax 202/682-9152. 197 rms. A/C TV TEL **Metro:** Gallery Place.

$ Rates: Weekdays, $79–$99 single; $89–$139 double. Weekends from $59 single or double. Premier Plus Plan (includes upgraded room and amenities and full breakfast), $94 single; $104 double. Additional person $10 extra; children under 18 stay free in parents' room. 30% senior citizen discount with 30-day advance booking. AE, CB, DC, DISC, ER, JCB, MC, V. **Parking:** $10.

A lower-priced offshoot of the Quality Inn chain, this hotel is within walking distance of many attractions—including the Smithsonian museums. Recently renovated rooms are attractively decorated and offer cable TVs, digital alarm clocks, and AM/FM radios. The Comfort's Cafe Express offers buffet breakfasts and a reasonably priced salad bar and deli fare at lunch and dinner. On-premises facilities include a coin-op laundry and a sunny exercise room with

Universal equipment and a sauna. Reserve early. This popular hotel is close to Chinatown restaurants and just three blocks from the Convention Center.

STATE PLAZA HOTEL, 2117 E St. NW, Washington, DC 20037. Tel. 202/861-8200, or toll free 800/424-2859. Fax 202/659-8601. 218 suites. A/C MINIBAR TV TEL **Metro:** Foggy Bottom.

$ Rates: Weekdays, $110–$125 suite for one, $140–$165 suite for two; larger suites, $175–$225 for one, $225–$275 for two. Weekends (also, subject to availability, off-season weeknights), $59–$89 suite for one or two. Additional person $20 extra; children under 16 stay free in parents' room. AE, DC, ER, MC, V. **Parking:** $12.

I was charmed by the State Plaza from the moment I entered its antique-furnished lobby—a setting enhanced by beautiful floral arrangements and the soft strains of classical music. This all-suite hotel is deservedly popular with performers (including many ballet troupes) from the nearby Kennedy Center.

The spacious accommodations are just lovely, done up in pastel hues and pretty chintz fabrics, with Federal-style mahogany beds and Queen Anne chests. Framed botanical prints embellish the walls. Fully equipped kitchens have been fitted with shuttered windows and louver doors. Remote-control cable TVs offer Spectravision movie options. Amenities here include a coin-op laundry on the lower level, a fully equipped fitness center (treadmills, Lifecycles, Stairmasters, free weights, exercise machines), a grocery-shopping service (a Safeway and gourmet shops are close by), complimentary shoeshine, and complimentary newspapers at the front desk.

The pristinely pretty Garden is a fine on-premises restaurant with an adjoining awninged patio for alfresco dining. Light and cheerful during the day, at night it's elegantly candlelit. The menu features continental and American regional cuisine, highlighting market-fresh fare.

NEAR THE WHITE HOUSE

HOLIDAY INN THOMAS CIRCLE, 1155 14th St. NW (at Massachusetts Ave.), Washington, DC 20005. Tel. 202/737-1200, or toll free 800/HOLIDAY. Fax 202/783-5733. 208 rms. A/C TV TEL **Metro:** McPherson Square.

$ Rates: Weekdays, $108–$113 single; $128–$133 double. Weekends, $89 single; $109 double. Additional person $13 extra; children under 18 stay free in parents' room. (For discount information, see below.) AE, CB, DC, DISC, JCB, MC, OPT, V. **Parking:** $8 (valet only).

Just five blocks from the White House, this centrally located, 14-story Holiday Inn is a good choice in the moderately priced category. Spacious rooms, decorated in mauve and earth tones, are equipped with remote-control satellite TVs offering free HBO and Showtime plus pay-movie stations, phones with call waiting and modem jacks, and AM/FM clock radios. There's a fairly large rooftop swimming pool and sun deck offering nice city views.

The hotel's restaurant/lounge, Filibuster's, offers low-priced all-you-can-eat buffet meals at breakfast, lunch, and dinner. Other

Ⓕ FROMMER'S COOL FOR KIDS: HOTELS

Channel Inn (see p. 72) This lovely hotel has a swimming pool, and adults will love the rooms with views of the boat-filled Washington Channel.

Howard Johnson's Hotel & Suites (see p. 78) Close to sightseeing attractions, it has a rooftop pool and games room. And most accommodations have kitchens, so you can prepare meals in your room, a big money-saver. Coin-op laundry machines are here, too.

The OMNI Shoreham (see p. 67) Adjacent to Rock Creek Park, close to the zoo, and equipped with two outdoor pools—a large one for swimming laps and a kiddie pool—the Shoreham offers an extensive program of children's activities. Three lighted tennis courts are an additional lure.

Washington Hilton and Towers (see p. 68) A large heated outdoor pool, a wading pool, video games room, three tennis courts, shuffleboard, and bike rental. What more do you need?

on-premises amenities include a coin-op laundry and a special parking lot for oversize vehicles.

At this writing, all Holiday Inns are featuring a "Great Rates" promotion, offering discounts of 20% to 50%, depending on the season and space availability. Be sure to inquire via the above toll-free number.

HOTEL ANTHONY, 1823 L St. NW, Washington, DC 20036. Tel. 202/223-4320, or toll free 800/424-2970. Fax 202/223-8546. Telex 904059. 99 suites. A/C TV TEL **Metro:** Farragut North or Farragut West.

$ Rates: Weekdays, $99–$123 suite for one, $109–$133 suite for two. Weekends, $60–$70 suite for one or two. Additional person $10 extra; children under 16 stay free in parents' suite. AE, CB, DC, DISC, JCB, MC, V. **Parking:** $9 (at nearby garage).

Fronted by an elegant gray awning, the Anthony offers suite accommodations in the heart of the downtown business/shopping/restaurant area and just five blocks from the White House. The large, comfortable suites are done in period styles—contemporary, art deco, or colonial. Most have full kitchens (the rest contain refrigerators and coffee makers only), and all are equipped with cable TVs (offering free HBO), AM/FM clock radios, and Water Pik shower massages, among other amenities. Eleven suites offer wet bars.

There are dozens of restaurants in the surrounding streets, but adjoining the hotel itself is the cozy Samantha's, a plush Yuppie watering hole with a working fireplace. Reasonably priced deli sandwiches, burgers, quiches, salads, and omelets are featured, along with daily specials. Also on the premises is Beatrice, an Italian restaurant open for all meals.

Anthony extras include a copy of the *Washington Post* each weekday morning, room service, and gratis use of the nearby Bally's Holiday Spa, which has Nautilus and Universal exercise equipment, Lifecycles, treadmills, rowing machines, Stairmasters, whirlpool, sauna, steam, and an indoor jogging track. A unisex hairstyling salon (also offering manicures, facials, and pedicures) is on the premises.

SOUTH OF THE MALL

CHANNEL INN, 650 Water St. SW (at 7th St. and Maine Ave.), Washington, DC 20024. Tel. 202/554-2400, or toll free 800/368-5668. Fax 202/863-1164. 100 rms. A/C TV TEL **Metro:** Waterfront.

$ Rates: Weekdays, $100–$120 single; $110–$135 double. Weekends, $80 single or double. Children under 12 stay free in parents' room. AE, CB, DC, DISC, ER, JCB, MC, V. **Parking:** Free.

This is Washington's only waterfront hotel, built in 1973 as part of a redevelopment project that brought a marina and a row of seafood restaurants to the area. Its rooms, most offering wonderful views of the boat-filled Washington Channel, are beautifully decorated in rich shades of teal and mauve, with floral chintz bedspreads and drapes, 18th-century-style mahogany furnishings, brass lamps, and plush velvet-upholstered armchairs. Some have high cathedral ceilings; all have balconies. Amenities include prettily wallpapered dressing rooms and AM/FM clock radios.

Dining/Entertainment: The inn has a moderately priced seafood/continental restaurant, the mahogany-paneled Pier 7. Under a peaked, beamed ceiling—from which are suspended immense wrought-iron and rope chandeliers with ship-lantern fixtures—it offers seating in comfortable red leather chairs and banquettes, many with marina and park views. Across the way is a sunny glass-walled coffee shop serving cafeteria-style breakfasts. The immense Engine Room lounge, featuring a cozy nautical decor and beautiful water views, offers a happy hour buffet of free hors d'oeuvres and a low-priced raw bar; stop by for live jazz and dancing Monday through Saturday until 1am.

Services: Concierge, room service (during restaurant hours).

Facilities: A pool and sun deck are out front; a golf course and indoor/outdoor tennis courts are within walking distance; the waterfront is an ideal place for jogging.

DUPONT CIRCLE

CANTERBURY HOTEL, 1733 N St. NW, Washington, DC 20036. Tel. 202/393-3000, or toll free 800/424-2950. Fax 202/785-9581. 99 junior suites. A/C MINIBAR TV TEL **Metro:** Dupont Circle.

$ Rates (including continental breakfast): Weekdays, $125 suite for one, $135 suite for two. Weekends (Fri–Sun) and off-season weekdays, $89–$99 per room. Additional person $20 extra; children under 12 stay free in parents' room. AE, CB, DC, DISC, ER, JCB, MC, V. **Parking:** $8.75.

The Canterbury Hotel is a small, European-style hostelry. Its prestigious address was once the home of both Theodore Roosevelt and Franklin D. Roosevelt. And though the building housing the hotel is not the original town house the Roosevelts occupied, it does attempt to recapture the elegance of an earlier era. It's entered via a graciously appointed lobby where classical music is playing, a tranquil setting in which to plan your day's itinerary.

Each room is actually a junior suite, with a sofa/sitting area, dressing room, and kitchenette or full kitchen. Decorated in tone-on-tone color schemes (mauve/burgundy, muted blues, or sea green), these spacious accommodations offer 18th-century mahogany English-reproduction furnishings (a few have four-poster beds). The look is pleasingly residential. Among the amenities: remote-control cable TVs with HBO movies and AM/FM clock radios. Baths are supplied with cosmetic mirrors, hairdryers, phones, and baskets of fine toiletries.

Dining/Entertainment: Intimate and charming, Chaucer's offers superb continental fare, service, and ambience. It's richly oak-paneled, with a beamed ceiling, gilt-framed mirrors, and crystal wall sconces. And the Tudor-beamed Union Jack Pub, complete with dart board and a menu featuring fish and chips, is the perfect place to relax after a busy day on the town. English beers on tap are served in pint mugs.

Services: Nightly turn-down with fine chocolate, morning delivery of the *Washington Post,* complimentary *Wall Street Journal* available in lobby and restaurant.

Facilities: Guests enjoy gratis use of the YMCA/National Capital Health Center nearby, offering Universal equipment, basketball/racquetball/handball/volleyball courts, a weight and exercise room, a 25-meter indoor heated pool, jogging track, Stairmasters, treadmills, stationary bikes, steam room, whirlpool, and more.

HAMPSHIRE HOTEL, 1310 New Hampshire Ave. NW (at N St.), Washington, DC 20036. Tel. 202/296-7600, or toll free 800/368-5691. Fax 202/293-2476. 82 junior suites. A/C MINIBAR TV TEL **Metro:** Dupont Circle.
$ Rates: Weekdays, $109 suite for one, $110 suite for two. Weekends (Fri–Sun nights) and off-season weekdays, $79–$89 per suite. Inquire, too, about low summer rates. Additional person $15 extra; children under 12 stay free in parents' room. AE, CB, DC, DISC, ER, JCB, MC, V. **Parking:** $10.

This is an elegant hotel, with lovely rooms and a first-rate restaurant. And though it's on a quiet tree-lined street, the Hampshire is convenient to numerous nightspots and restaurants—it's within easy walking distance of Georgetown and two blocks from Dupont Circle. Classical music played in public areas is a plus.

Spacious accommodations, furnished with 18th-century mahogany reproductions, are decorated in ecru/teal color schemes with cinnamon or plum accents. They're very residential, with lots of closet space, big dressing rooms, couches and coffee tables, desks, and kitchenettes equipped with sinks, refrigerators, coffee makers, and stoves or microwave ovens. There's a hairdryer in the bath. You'll find packets of Godiva chocolates on arrival. AM/FM clock radios and remote-control TVs with HBO movies are additional amenities.

Dining/Entertainment: The acclaimed J. Sun Dynasty serves Manchurian/Chinese specialties; it's open for all meals.

Services: Nightly turn-down with gourmet chocolate, free cocktail first night of your stay, morning delivery of the *Washington Post*, room service (during restaurant hours).

Facilities: Guests enjoy gratis use of the YMCA/National Capital Health Center nearby (see the Canterbury Hotel, above, for a rundown of facilities). Business center.

HOLIDAY INN CENTRAL, 1501 Rhode Island Ave. NW, Washington, DC 20005. Tel. 202/483-2000, or toll free 800/248-0016 or 800/HOLIDAY. Fax 202/797-1078. 205 rms, 8 suites. A/C TV TEL **Metro:** McPherson Square or Dupont Circle.

$ Rates: Weekdays, $97–$120 single; $120–$150 double. Weekends, $79 single or double. Additional person $14 extra; children 18 and under stay free in parents' room. Note also Holiday Inns' "Great Rates" program (see the Holiday Inn Thomas Circle, above). AE, CB, DC, DISC, JCB, MC, V. **Parking:** $7.

This very well located hotel underwent a major renovation in 1991 and it sparkles. Built in the 1960s, it's the typical "no surprises" hotel the Holiday Inn chain prides itself on offering. You'll find a souvenir shop and video games room off the lobby and a pool and sun deck on the roof. A pleasant restaurant features competitively priced American fare, and guests also relax over cocktails in an adjoining lounge.

Rooms are decorated in shades of mauve and teal, with blond-wood furnishings and color-coordinated floral-motif drapes and bedspreads. All offer remote-control cable TVs with free movie stations and AM/FM clock radios. Other pluses here are a coin-op laundry, room service (from 6am to 11:30pm), and an exercise room with weights, treadmills, and Lifecycles.

QUALITY HOTEL CENTRAL, 1900 Connecticut Ave. NW (at Leroy Place), Washington, DC 20009. Tel. 202/332-9300, or toll free 800/842-4211. Fax 202/328-7039. 147 rms. A/C TV TEL **Metro:** Dupont Circle.

$ Rates: Weekdays, $85–$110 single; $110–$125 double. Weekends (Fri–Sun), $69 single or double. Additional person $15 extra; children under 18 stay free in parents' room. AE, CB, DC, DISC, ER, JCB, MC, V. **Parking:** $10.

The Quality has the well-heeled look of a much more expensive hostelry with the amenities to match. It's right across the street from the deluxe Washington Hilton, where you can pick up sightseeing tour buses. You'll be pleased from the minute you step into the chandeliered lobby, where classical music is always playing. Guest rooms—off charming hallways—are decorated in either of two attractive color schemes: muted green with peach and rose accents or soft blues. Residential furnishings include in-room sofas; concealed in mahogany armoires are remote-control cable TVs (with pay-movie options) and AM/FM clock radios; phones are equipped with modem jacks. Accommodations on higher floors offer panoramic views.

In addition to a rooftop pool and sun deck, facilities include Claret's, a rather elegant restaurant with linened tables and Waterford-crystal chandeliers overhead. It serves moderately priced American fare at all meals, including such upscale items as a croque monsieur at lunch and grilled swordfish with artichokes and hearts of palm at dinner. Bailey's, a clubby bar with tapestried banquettes and equestrian art on the walls, adjoins. Room service is offered during restaurant hours, *USA Today* is available gratis at the front desk, and guests can enjoy nightly bed turn-down on request. For a fee, Quality guests can also use the very well equipped Washington Sports Club just across the street—treadmills, Lifecycles, Stairmasters, rowing machines, Nautilus, Gravitron, and much more.

FOGGY BOTTOM/GEORGETOWN

HOTEL LOMBARDY, 2019 I St. NW, Washington, DC 20006. Tel. 202/828-2600, or toll free 800/424-5486. Fax 202/872-0503. 20 rms, 106 suites. A/C MINIBAR TV TEL **Metro:** Farragut West or Foggy Bottom.

$ **Rates:** Weekdays, $115 single; $130 double; $150 suite for one, $165 for two; additional person $20 extra. Weekends (and sometimes off-season weekdays), $59–$89 single or double; $89–$109 suite for one or two. Children under 16 stay free in parents' room. AE, CB, DC, ER, MC, V. **Parking:** $10 (subject to space availability).

From its rich wood-paneled lobby with carved Tudor ceiling to its appealing restaurant and rooms, the Lombardy offers a lot of luxury for the price—and the location, about six blocks west of the White House. Rooms are charmingly residential, all but 20 with fully equipped kitchens, large walk-in closets, and dining nooks. Entered via pedimented louver doors, they have fine cherrywood furnishings (including nice-size desks), cotton chintz floral bedspreads and drapes, dusty-rose carpeting, and Casablanca fans overhead. Cream-colored walls are hung with gilt-framed mirrors and well-chosen artworks. All offer AM/FM clock radios and remote-control cable TVs with pay-movie options. The *Washington Post* is free at the desk or in the café, shoes are shined gratis overnight, and a coin-op laundry is located in the basement.

The Café Lombardy, a sunny glass-enclosed restaurant/bar/lounge (with open-air seating, weather permitting), serves delicious and authentic northern Italian fare. Try the pasta pesto pancake. Yummy desserts here, too.

THE GEORGETOWN DUTCH INN, 1075 Thomas Jefferson St. NW (just below M St.), Washington, DC 20007. **Tel. 202/337-0900,** or toll free 800/388-2410. Fax 202/333-6526. 47 suites. A/C TV TEL **Metro:** Foggy Bottom. **Bus:** M Street buses go to all major Washington tourist attractions.

$ **Rates** (including continental breakfast): Weekdays, $105–$125 one-bedroom suite for one, $120–$140 for two; $195–$250 two-bedroom duplex penthouse quad (sleeps six). Weekends, $89–$99 one-bedroom suite for one or two; $170–$210 penthouse suite. Additional person $15 extra. AE, CB, DC, DISC, ER, MC, V. **Parking:** Free.

The Dutch Inn is superbly located in the heart of Georgetown, just half a block from the C&O Canal (many rooms offer water views), on a charming brick-paved street lined with maple trees. Thomas Jefferson once lived on this street. Accommodations are very spacious one- and two-bedroom suites, nine of them ultra-luxurious duplex penthouses; staying here is like having your own Georgetown apartment. You'll have a full living room with a comfy queen-size convertible sofa, dining area, and desk, plus a complete kitchen (the maid does your dishes, and the hotel offers food-shopping service). Decor is residential: Burgundy-accented earth-tone color schemes are complemented by Queen Anne–style mahogany furnishings with marquetry detail. Walls are hung with historic prints of Washington. Amenities include remote-control cable TVs with HBO, AM/FM clock radios, and, in the bath, cosmetic mirrors, Caswell-Massey toiletries, and hairdryers. The Dutch Inn's reputation as a comfortable home away from home draws a celebrity clientele. Nell Carter stayed here during *Ain't Misbehavin*'s revival at the National, as did many *Les Misérables* cast members. Ditto George Shearing, Dizzy Gillespie, Gene Hackman, and the Smothers Brothers when playing local engagements.

There's no on-premises restaurant. A limited room-service menu is available, however, and in the heart of Georgetown you have dozens of eating places within a block's radius. Gratis continental breakfast is served in the very charming lobby each morning, and free newspaper delivery is available on request. Guests also enjoy gratis use of a health club right across the street where aerobics classes are given throughout the day.

MARRIOTT'S RESIDENCE INN, 1000 29th St. NW (between K and M Sts.), Washington, DC 20007. Tel. 202/298-1600, or toll free 800/331-3131. Fax 202/333-2019. 78 suites. A/C TV TEL **Metro:** Foggy Bottom.

$ Rates (including extended continental breakfast): $145 studio suite (for one or two); $160 one-bedroom suite (for up to four). Weekends (Fri–Sun), $99 studio suite; $109 one-bedroom suite. Rollaways or sleep sofa $10 extra. Discounts for stays of seven days or more. AE, CB, DC, DISC, JCB, MC, V. **Parking:** $13.

This home-away-from-home concept was designed to meet the needs of business travelers making extended visits, but it's marvelous even if you're only spending a single night. Residence Inn accommodations are luxurious apartments, with fully equipped kitchens, living rooms, and dining areas. This particular inn, in the heart of Georgetown, is entered via a brick courtyard prettified by flowering plants in terra-cotta pots and Victorian white wooden benches. Inside, off the lobby, is a comfortable lounge equipped with a cable TV, games, books, magazines, and daily newspapers. Here, tea and coffee are available throughout the day, and a substantial continental breakfast (danish, muffins, bagels, hot and cold cereals, fresh fruit, juice, tea and coffee) is served daily. Monday through Thursday afternoons, complimentary beer, wine, and soft drinks are offered to guests between 5:30 and 7pm, along with snacks such as nachos or sloppy joes. Wednesday afternoon that snack is a full dinner—perhaps spaghetti and salad or barbecue.

Attractive resortlike accommodations are decorated in taupe/teal or ecru/mauve color schemes and equipped with large desks, remote-control cable TVs with HBO, AM/FM clock radios, hairdryers, and irons and ironing boards. On-premises facilities include an outdoor barbecue grill for guest use, occasional organized parties and activities, coin-op washers and dryers, and a small workout room with a Nautilus multistation machine, Stairmaster, treadmill, and Lifecycle. Hotel services include complimentary grocery shopping and food delivery from nearby restaurants. M Street buses (a block away) will take you to most major D.C. attractions.

3. INEXPENSIVE

The below-listed are all reputable hotels with double rooms priced from $65 to $99.

DOWNTOWN

DAYS INN DOWNTOWN, 1201 K St. NW, Washington, DC 20005. Tel. 202/842-1020, or toll free 800/562-3350 or 800/325-2525. Fax 202/289-0336. 220 rms. A/C TV TEL **Metro:** Metro Center.

$ Rates: Weekdays, $77–$87 single; $87–$97 double. Weekends, $75 single or double. Additional person $10 extra; children under 18 stay free in parents' room. Lower Super Saver rates (about $49) are sometimes available if you reserve at least 29 days in advance via the toll-free number, 800/325-2525—it's worth a try. AE, CB, DC, DISC, ER, MC, V. **Parking:** $8.

This hotel is conveniently located near the Convention Center. Rooms are cheerfully decorated in blue or rust color schemes and equipped with satellite TVs (with free movie channels). A big plus here is Buckley's Grill, a simpatico, nautically themed restaurant. Very competitively priced, it offers excellent New American fare plus Créole specialties, fresh seafood, baby back ribs, and gourmet pizzas—great desserts, too. The adjoining Buckley's Lounge is the scene of happy-hour buffets Monday through Friday from 5 to 7pm. And Buckley's Deli serves light fare (Philadelphia cheese-steak sandwiches and salads) weekdays. A small rooftop pool with a sun deck and a video games room makes this a good choice for families with young children. Additional amenities: room service (from 7am to 9pm); a fitness center (with workout equipment including a treadmill and exercise bikes) and car-rental agencies just across the street. Inquire about special packages when you reserve.

DUPONT CIRCLE

CARLYLE SUITES, 1731 New Hampshire Ave. NW (between R and S Sts.), Washington, DC 20009. Tel. 202/234-3200, or toll free 800/946-5377. Fax 202/387-0085. 176 suites. A/C TV TEL **Metro:** Dupont Circle.

$ Rates: Weekdays, $69–$119 studio suite for one; $79–$129 for two; $150 one-bedroom suite. Weekends, $64.50 suite for one or two. Additional person $10 extra; children under 18 stay free in parents' suite. AE, CB, DC, MC, V. **Parking:** Free but limited.

On a quiet residential street near Dupont Circle—the kind of street with a neat little garden and a shade tree in front of each house—Carlyle Suites occupies a converted landmark building. Its exterior art deco elements are complemented by similarly styled interior silver moldings, light fixtures, and cove ceilings.

Only the suites eschew the art deco motif. Cheerfully decorated in pastel shades (mauve, grape, and ice gray), they have oak beds, white stucco walls, gray drapes, charcoal carpeting, and cheerful print bedspreads with matching pillow cushions on the sofa. All accommodations are equipped with huge closets, remote-control TVs with pay-movie choices, AM/FM radios, small but complete kitchens (a huge Safeway is two blocks away), cozy seating areas with sofas, and dining nooks.

Dining/Entertainment: The Neon Cafe—decorated in shades of gray with purple neon tubing, glass-brick walls, and a black-and-white checkerboard floor—is one of the hotel's great assets. Its period ambience is enhanced by background music from the 1930s/1940s. Moderately priced American/continental fare is served; entrées run the gamut from tortellini pesto to deli sandwiches and salads. There's live music here (a singer and combo) weekend nights.

Services: Carry-out food available from the café.

Facilities: Coin-op laundry; gratis access to a nearby health club with Nautilus and Universal exercise equipment, Lifecycles, exercise bikes, treadmills, rowing machines, Stairmasters, whirlpool, sauna, steam room, and more.

HOWARD JOHNSON'S HOTEL & SUITES, 1430 Rhode Island Ave. NW, Washington, DC 20005. Tel. 202/462-7777, or toll free 800/368-5690. Fax 202/332-3519. 168 mini-suites, 18 one-bedroom suites. A/C MINIBAR TV TEL **Metro:** Dupont Circle.

$ Rates: Weekdays, $69–$89 mini-suite for one or two; $89–$109 one-bedroom suite. Weekends and off-season weekdays, $59 suite for one or two. AE, CB, DC, DISC, ER, MC, V. **Parking:** $7.

Set on a tranquil tree-lined street close to Mall attractions, Dupont Circle, and the White House, this hotel is popular with government employees, businesspeople, and families. It has a handsome art deco lobby and attractive rooms with faux silk-covered walls and floral-print bedspreads. There are dining areas and full kitchens in all but 20 of the units. In-room amenities include cable TVs (with HBO and Spectravision movies) and AM/FM radios. Eighteen one-bedroom suites additionally offer a full living room with a sofabed plus a bedroom with a king-size bed, with phones and TVs in each. Among the on-premises facilities are a coin-op laundry, a rooftop pool and sun deck. Guests enjoy complimentary use of the YMCA/National Capital Health Center nearby (see the Canterbury Hotel, in "Moderate," above, for a rundown of facilities).

Off the lobby is the Kitchen Cabinet, an unpretentious restaurant with lots of leafy green plants, tables adorned with fresh flowers, and lighting from brass candelabras and wall sconces. Open for all meals, it features moderately priced American fare and a special menu for children. Cocktails are served in the Civil Servant Lounge, a cozy low-ceilinged pub with shelves of books and sofas grouped around a fireplace.

NORMANDY INN, 2118 Wyoming Ave. NW (at Connecticut Ave.) Washington, DC 20008. Tel. 202/483-1350, or toll free 800/424-3729. Fax 202/387-8241. 75 rms. A/C TV TEL **Metro:** Dupont Circle.

$ Rates: Weekdays, $89 single; $99 double. Weekends (see below), $65 single or double. Children under 12 stay free in parents' room. AE, CB, DC, MC, V. **Parking:** $8.

This gracious small hotel blends in perfectly with neighboring embassies. Pristinely charming rooms have tapestry-upholstered mahogany furnishings in 18th-century styles. Hunter-green and white floral-print bedspreads harmonize nicely with lemon-colored walls hung with gilt-framed botanical prints.

Amenities include refrigerators, AM/FM clock radios, and remote-control cable TVs with pay-movie options.

Continental breakfast (juices, tea or coffee, croissants, English muffins, toast, and cold cereals) is available in your room or in the comfortable Tea Room off the lobby for $5. Coffee and tea are available throughout the day from an antique oak sideboard in the Tea Room, and cookies are put out at 3pm. In nice weather you can take these snacks outside to umbrella tables on a garden patio. Tuesday nights, complimentary wine and cheese are served to guests. Numerous restaurants are located nearby, and guests enjoy access to a large swimming pool a block away.

A weekend package includes continental breakfast; guests must stay both Friday and Saturday or Saturday and Sunday nights.

QUALITY HOTEL DOWNTOWN, 1315 16th St. NW, Washington, DC 20036. Tel. 202/232-8000, or toll free 800/368-5689. Fax 202/667-9827. 125 rms, 10 suites. A/C TV TEL **Metro:** Dupont Circle.

$ Rates: Weekdays, $79–$99 single or double; $99–$119 one-bedroom suites. Weekends, $59 single or double. Additional person $15 extra; children under 18 stay free in parents' room. AE, CB, DC, DISC, ER, JCB, MC, V. **Parking:** $6.75.

A few years back the Quality underwent a total renovation from a homey, family-style hotel to a rather luxurious property. The good news is that despite its plush new look, it's still charging very moderate rates. And, in fact, it's still a good bet for families.

For openers, each of the rooms here is actually a large suite, with a fully equipped kitchen. Done up in pastel shades of muted teal blue and pale rose/mauve, the rooms feature French country pine or Oriental-style dark-wood furnishings. Framed Chinese prints adorn ecru raw-silk-covered walls, and bedspreads are pretty cotton florals. Each room has a dining area, sofa, AM/FM clock radio, remote-control cable TV with free HBO (plus pay movies), a large walk-in closet, and a dressing room. Baths, with shiny brass fixtures, offer hairdryers and baskets of fine toiletries. Some rooms have handsome desks, and a few feature Murphy beds—an innovation appreciated by people who conduct business in their hotel rooms. Even the public areas of the hotel have been attractively upgraded.

The Quality's restaurant, Scott's Cafe, is pleasant and pretty, with flower-bedecked tables and numerous plants flourishing in the sunlight. At night Scott's is cozily candlelit. The reasonably priced American menu highlights regional specialities. Bleeker's Lounge, a cozy pub off the lobby, has a billiards table.

Guests have gratis use of the nearby YMCA/National Capital Health Center (see the Canterbury Hotel in "Moderate," above, for a rundown of facilities). Room service, a coin-op basement laundry, free use of the swimming pool at a nearby hotel, and a very central location are additional pluses. Gray Line tours depart from the lobby.

Note: Bill Clinton attends Sunday services at the Baptist church across the street and often greets guests outside the hotel.

FOGGY BOTTOM/GEORGETOWN

HOWARD JOHNSON'S LODGE, 2601 Virginia Ave. NW, Washington, DC 20037. Tel. 202/965-2700, or toll free 800/654-2000. Fax 202/965-2700, ext. 7910. 192 rms. A/C TV TEL **Metro:** Foggy Bottom.

$ Rates: Weekdays, $50–$89 single; $58–$97 double. Weekends (Fri–Sun), $57 single or double. Additional person $5 extra; children under 18 stay free in parents' room. AE, DC, DISC, ER, JCB, MC, V. **Parking:** Free (maximum height 6'2").

Just two blocks from the Kennedy Center is a HoJo with a nicely landscaped entrance where rose bushes bloom in season. Attractively furnished modern rooms have AM/FM radios, desks, small refrigerators, and VCRs (movies can be rented). Some rooms have sofas, and over half have balconies. A Bob's Big Boy on the premises offers typical American fare, including inexpensive all-you-can-eat buffets at lunch and dinner. A coin-op laundry, sightseeing bus tours, a large L-shaped rooftop pool with sun deck and Ping-Pong room, a gift/sundry shop, and video games are additional amenties.

NORTH WASHINGTON

CONNECTICUT AVENUE DAYS INN, 4400 Connecticut Ave. NW (between Yuma and Albermarle Sts.), Washington, DC 20008. Tel. 202/244-5600, or toll free 800/325-2525 or 800/952-3060. Fax 202/244-6794. 150 rms, 5 suites. A/C TV TEL **Metro:** Van Ness.

$ Rates (including continental breakfast): Weekdays, $59–$109 single; $59–$119 double; $99–$129 suites. Weekends, $59–$79 single or double. Additional person $10 extra; children under 18 stay free in parents' room. Inquire about senior-citizen rates. Lower "Super Saver" rates are sometimes available if you reserve at least 29 days in advance via the corporate toll-free number, 800/325-2525. AE, CB, DC, DISC, MC, V. **Parking:** $3.

If you don't mind a 10- to 15-minute Metro or bus ride into the heart of town, you can do very nicely here. This Days Inn is located in a very pleasant neighborhood, and its rooms are kept in tip-top condition. Furnished in teak Danish modern pieces, with brass-framed art prints on grass-cloth-covered walls, they offer remote-control cable TVs with HBO movies and AM/FM radios; refrigerators, VCRs, and movie tapes can be rented. Families can book a parlor suite that includes an extra room (and an extra TV). Complimentary continental breakfast is served in the lower lobby each morning—coffee, juice, herbal teas, cold cereals, danishes, muffins, and doughnuts. Room service is available from a number of nearby restaurants. There's a gift shop in the rather plush lobby. A coin-op laundry is close by.

SAVOY SUITES GEORGETOWN, 2505 Wisconsin Ave. NW (above Calvert St.) Washington, DC 20007. Tel. 202/337-9700, or toll free 800/944-5377. Fax 202/337-3644. 150 rms. A/C TV TEL **Bus:** Even-numbered buses stop in front of the hotel and connect to Georgetown, Dupont Circle, and the Mall.

$ Rates: Weekdays, $69–$119 single; $79–$129 double. Weekends, $64.50 single or double. Additional person $10 extra; children under 18 stay free in parents' room. AE, CB, DC, MC, V. **Parking:** Free.

This moderately priced luxury hotel is in a sedate embassy district, just five minutes from the heart of Georgetown by bus or car. Many restaurants are within walking distance, and the National Cathedral is just four blocks away.

The accommodations, half of them suites with fully stocked kitchens and dining areas, are traditionally decorated with French provincial pieces, marble-topped bureaus, and faux malachite desks with cabriole legs. Grasspaper-covered walls are hung with gilt-framed 18th-century color lithographs. All rooms offer remote-control cable TVs with pay-movie stations and AM/FM radios. Many have large walk-in closets and/or in-room steam baths, and about half offer panoramic city views over the treetops. Eighth-floor guests enjoy large in-room Jacuzzis.

The owner hired a set designer to liven up the hotel's public areas. A stunning art nouveau lobby is set against a garden-motif restaurant called On Wisconsin, with seating amid ficus trees, potted plants, and floral arrangements. Walls function as gallery space for exhibits by local artists. Popular with neighborhood residents, On Wisconsin features very reasonably priced American/continental fare—great chilis, foccacia pizzas, and entrées ranging from roast duck to couscous paella. In good weather the Savoy also operates a tree-shaded outdoor café serving light fare.

Other on-premises amenities include a room of food-vending machines, a small sun deck, and a laundry room with a TV and coin-op washers and dryers. The front desk proffers conciergelike hospitality, and there's a complimentary shuttle bus to and from the Woodley Park Metro stop. Guests also enjoy gratis use of a nearby health club featuring treadmills, Stairmasters, Nautilus and Universal equipment, rowing machines, and an Olympic-size swimming pool.

By the way, note the ornate fence fronting the Savoy Suites. Made in 1890, it's from the original lion's cage of the National Zoo.

4. BUDGET

The budget section is limited to two accommodations. For fancier accommodations that are still a great value, check out the bed-and-breakfasts in the next section of this chapter.

DOWNTOWN

HOSTELLING INTERNATIONAL—WASHINGTON, D.C., 1009 11th St. NW (at K St.), Washington, DC 20001. Tel. 202/737-2333. 250 beds. A/C **Metro:** Metro Center.
$ Rates: $15 for AYH members, $18 for nonmembers. MC, V.

S The best bet on the budget hotel scene is this spiffy youth hostel, which opened in late 1987. In a fully renovated eight-story brick building, it offers freshly painted dorm rooms (with 4 to 14 beds) and clean baths down the hall. Though the accommodations are basic, the facility itself provides a lot of features you won't find at a hotel. These include a huge self-service kitchen where you can cook your own meals (a supermarket is two blocks away), a dining room, a comfortable lounge, coin-op laundry machines, storage lockers, and indoor parking for bicycles. There's street parking.

Upon registering, you'll be given an information sheet detailing local services. HIW offers special activities for guests—volleyball games, cookouts, lectures, movies, travel seminars, and more. And near the entrance, knowledgeable volunteers staff a comprehensive information desk to help guests with sightseeing and other travel questions.

The hostel's location is excellent—just three blocks from the Metro, six blocks from the Mall. And the clientele is monitored, so it's a perfectly safe place to send your college-age kids or, for that matter, your mother.

Those in all age groups can stay, but since dorms are for men or women only, couples are, of course, separated. (Subject to availability, a limited number of rooms are offered to families and couples October to March; reserve them early.) Maximum stay is six nights, but that limit may be extended with permission, subject to available space. You must supply your own linens, towels, and soap (blankets and pillows are provided); sleeping bags are not allowed. You can rent the requisite sleep sheet here for $2 a night or buy one. Call as far in advance as possible to reserve (there are only 250 beds and they go fast), and guarantee your reservation with a 50% deposit.

NORTH WASHINGTON

WALTER REED HOSPITALITY HOUSE, 6711 Georgia Ave. NW (at Aspen St.), Washington, DC 20012. Tel. 202/722-1600, or toll free 800/222-8388. Fax 202/723-3979. 72 rms. A/C TV TEL **Metro:** Takoma Park.

$ Rates (including continental breakfast): $35–$45 single; $39–$49 double. Additional person $4 extra; children 14 and under stay free in parents' room. Weekend, $80 per room for a two-night stay. Weekly and monthly rates available. AE, CB, DC, DISC, ER, MC, V. **Parking:** Free.

This delightful hotel is a 15-minute Metro or bus ride from the center of the District. A bus stop is across the street, and the Metro station is about four blocks away.

The hotel's public areas—such as the plant-filled, oak-paneled lobby and well-lit hallways—are reassuringly spiffy. Rooms were recently refurnished; some have sofas or "cuddle couches" and/or balconies. All the expected amenities are present, including TVs with cable and movie stations. A Chinese-American restaurant on the premises offers a low-priced menu in a striking modern setting. Complimentary coffee/tea and doughnuts are served every morning in the lobby, and a gratis copy of the *Washington Post* is available at the desk. An outdoor swimming pool and sun deck make this a good bet for families, and proximity to Rock Creek Park is a lure for joggers.

5. BED & BREAKFAST

One of the most enjoyable ways to travel on a budget is to stay at B&B accommodations. Prices are reasonable, rooms are often charming, and you get an opportunity to meet local people.

In addition to specific B&B accommodations, I've listed two services that represent numerous homes renting out rooms on this basis. Reserve as early as possible to obtain the greatest selection of locations and the lowest rates, and do specify your needs and preferences: For instance, discuss children, pets, smoking policy, preferred locations (do you require convenient public transportation?), parking, availability of TV and/or phone, preferred breakfast, and choice of payment.

The **Bed and Breakfast League/Sweet Dreams and Toast,** P.O. Box 9490, Washington, DC 20016 (tel. 202/363-7767), is a reservation service representing more than 80 B&Bs in the District and adjoining Virginia suburbs. Through them, you might find a room in a mid-1800s Federal-style Capitol Hill mansion, a Georgetown home with a lovely garden, or a turn-of-the-century Dupont Circle town house filled with Victorian furnishings. Those are just a few of the many possibilities. Accommodations are all screened, and guest reports are given serious consideration. Hosts are encouraged, though not required, to offer such niceties as fresh-baked muffins at breakfast. All listings are convenient to public transportation. Rates for most range from $40 to $105 for a single, $55 to $125 for a double, and $10 to $25 per additional person. There's a two-night minimum-stay requirement and a booking fee of $10 (per reservation, not per night). AE, DC, MC, V.

A similar service, **Bed & Breakfast Accommodations Ltd.,** P.O. Box 12011, Washington, DC 20005 (tel. 202/328-3510; fax 202/332-3885), has about 80 homes, inns, guesthouses, and unhosted furnished apartments in its files. Some are in historic District homes. Its current roster offers, among many others, a Georgian-style colonial brick home on a tree-lined avenue in Tenley Circle; an 1899 Victorian home on Capitol Hill owned by a network news producer (a well-stocked library is a plus); and a Dupont Circle Victorian town house with a two-level deck. Rates are $50 to $100 single, $55 to $110 double, $15 for an extra person, and from $65 for a full apartment. At guesthouses and inns, rates run the gamut from $75 to $180 for a single, $85 to $225 for a double. AE, DC, MC, V.

DUPONT CIRCLE

EMBASSY INN, 1627 16th St. NW (between Q and R Sts.), Washington, DC 20009. Tel. 202/234-7800, or toll free 800/423-9111. Fax 202/234-3309. 38 rms (all with bath). A/C TV TEL **Metro:** Dupont Circle.

$ Rates (including continental breakfast): $69–$79 single; $79–$89 double. Weekends, $55 single or double. Additional person $10 extra; children 14 and under stay free in parents' room. AE, CB, DC, MC, V.

This four-story brick building, built in 1922 and an inn for two decades (1940–62), was rescued from demolition some years back, spruced up, and transformed once more into a quaintly charming small hotel. Its Federal-style architecture harmonizes with other town houses on the block, some of which were actually designed by Thomas Jefferson. The comfortably furnished pale-lemon lobby, with its plushly upholstered sofas and armchairs, doubles as a parlor. Breakfast (fresh-baked blueberry muffins, croissants, cold cereals, juice, and coffee) is served here daily, and fresh coffee brews all day; it's complimentary, along with tea, cocoa, and evening sherry. You can buy Tourmobile tickets here, too, pick up maps and brochures, read a complimentary *Washington Post*, or request sundries you may have forgotten (toothbrush, razor, and the like). Soft classical music is piped into the lobby, and brass planters grace every hallway. There's also a basement lounge with a color TV, ice machines, a small refrigerator, and a supply of books.

Rooms are furnished with 18th-century-style mahogany pieces. Bedspreads and curtains in attractive floral prints, pale-lemon walls hung with turn-of-the-century lithographs and historic prints of Washington, and new carpeting combine to create a homey atmosphere. Everything is freshly painted, pristine, and neat. All accommodations have AM/FM clock radios. Baths have showers only (no tubs). *Note:* There is no elevator, and there's street parking only.

THE REEDS' BED & BREAKFAST, P.O. Box 12011, Washington, DC 20005. Tel. 202/328-3510. 5 rms (with shared bath), 1 apt (with bath). A/C TV TEL **Metro:** McPherson Square or Dupont Circle (about six blocks from either).

$ Rates (including breakfast): $60–$80 single; $70–$80 double. Apt (no breakfast), $65–$80 for one, $75–$85 for two. Additional person $15 extra; children 18 and under $10; crib $5 extra. AE, DC, MC, V. **Parking:** $5.

Even by the most exacting standards, the Reeds' restored Victorian mansion is a masterpiece of good taste. Built in 1887 by notable Washington builder John Shipman, it had a long succession of subsequent owners. When Charles and Jackie Reed bought it in 1975, it was in such disrepair that they spent nine years on a renovation they say "took on the appearance of a Pentagon cost overrun." They combed antiques shops and auction houses for period/reproduction furnishings and art, landscaped the garden, and added fountains. Today, the house is a gorgeous Victorian/art nouveau showplace with carved fireplace mantels, shuttered bay windows, leaded glass, and rich oak and mahogany paneling. The living room is furnished with a velvet Chesterfield, a Jacobean oak armchair, Oriental carpet, and a turn-of-the-century player piano. Breakfast is served at a Victorian banquet table in a formal dining room complete with working fireplace.

Rooms, up a grand carved-oak staircase with intricate fretwork and a leaded-glass skylight above, are charmingly decorated in period styles. Yours might have a floral-print chaise, Eastlake Victorian bed, ornamental fireplace, white wicker daybed and rocker, Empire bureau, or Regency lady's writing desk. All are supplied with AM/FM clock radios and books and magazines. Completely separate from the main building is a one-bedroom apartment with a private bath and a fully equipped kitchen; it easily accommodates five people. There's no maid service, however, and you'll have to get your own breakfast.

Guests are encouraged to use the gorgeous Victorian-style lattice porch, fountained patio, and barbecue facilities. Breakfast is continental (featuring fresh-baked breads and muffins, cereals, fruit, and juice) on weekdays, a full bacon-and-eggs meal on weekends. A computer and a treadmill are available on request, and there's a washer and dryer for guest use. No charge for local calls here.

The Reeds' doesn't take walk-ins, hence you'll note the P.O. Box address above. You must call to reserve.

WINDSOR INN, 1842 16th St. NW (at T St.), Washington, DC 20009. Tel. 202/667-0300, or toll free 800/423-9111. Fax 202/667-4503. 37 rms (all with bath), 10 suites. A/C TV TEL **Metro:** Dupont Circle.

$ Rates (including continental breakfast): Weekdays, $69–$79 single; $89–$99 double; $125–$150 suite accommodating up to four people. Weekends, $55 single or double. Children under 14 stay free in parents' room. AE, CB, DC, MC, V.

⭐ 🆂 The Windsor Inn, a neat brick building on a tree-lined residential street, was built in the 1920s as a boarding house, then renovated and run as an inn through 1963. A wealthy owner subsequently let the property stand empty until the Windsor folks discovered and purchased it in 1985, along with an adjacent building fronted by a neoclassic portico. Accommodations are located in both. Some of the public areas are done up in art deco motif, and hallways are especially nice, lit by sconces and crystal chandeliers and hung with lovely gilt-framed lithographs. Rooms, neat as a pin and handsomely furnished with mahogany antique reproductions, utilize mauve or sea-green color schemes. Some have floral wall friezes, many are adorned with botanical prints or silk flower arrangements, and you may get a sofa and/or decorative fireplace. Suites are worthy of a first-class hotel—but much cheaper. Lower-level rooms face a skylit terrace with lawn furnishings and flower boxes, but I prefer the sunnier upstairs accommodations. All accommodations offer AM/FM clock radios. A continental breakfast—fresh-baked muffins, cold cereals, fruit juices, and tea or coffee—is served in the comfy lobby, or, upon request, in your room. During the day, complimentary coffee, tea, and hot chocolate are available, and sherry is offered evenings from 5 to 7pm. There are ice machines and a refrigerator for guest use. A very friendly multilingual staff is a big plus. Guests also enjoy gratis use of a beautiful small conference room that seats 10. *Note:* There is no elevator, and parking is on the street.

ADAMS-MORGAN/WOODLEY PARK

ADAMS INN, 1744 Lanier Place NW (between Calvert St. and Ontario Rd.), Washington, DC 20009. Tel. 202/745-3600. 25 rms (12 with bath). A/C **Metro:** Woodley Park–Zoo.

$ Rates (including continental breakfast and tax): $45 single without bath, $60 single with bath; $55 double without bath, $70 double with bath. Additional person $10 extra. AE, CB, DC, DISC, MC, V. **Parking:** $7.

While many B&B accommodations are decorator homey with rooms in *Architectural Digest* good taste, the Adams is down-to-earth, for-real homey. In a cozy parlor (with a floral-design carpet on oak floors, flowered wallpaper, and lace curtains), maps, books, games, and magazines are provided for guests. In the dining room, where you'll find a large mahogany table and wood-burning fireplace, a substantial continental breakfast (including fresh-baked breads and muffins) is served each morning (in good weather you can take this fare out to the front porch or the small flower-bordered garden patio). Tea and coffee with doughnuts are available throughout the day.

Like the public areas, the rooms have a kitschy charm, with furnishings selected from flea markets and auctions, matching ruffled curtains and bedspreads, and freshly painted or cheerfully papered walls. No TVs or phones here, but you do get a clock radio. One room has a decorative fireplace, and all have oak floors, some with carpets. Accommodations that share baths have in-room sinks.

A coin-op washer/dryer is available in the basement, there are pay phones in the lobby, and the desk takes incoming messages. Other pluses: a refrigerator, microwave oven, iron/ironing board, and TV lounge. The location is close to Adams-Morgan eateries and a Safeway supermarket. Gene and Nancy Thompson are your genial— and very helpful—hosts ably assisted by Anne Owens.

Note: No smoking is permitted on the premises. No pets, but children are welcome.

KALORAMA GUEST HOUSE, 1854 Mintwood Place NW (between 19th St. and Columbia Rd.), Washington, DC 20009. Tel. 202/667-6369. 31 rms (12 with bath). A/C **Metro:** Woodley Park–Zoo.
$ Rates (including continental breakfast): $45–$65 single with shared bath, $65–$90 single with bath; $45–$75 double with shared bath, $65–$95 double with bath; $95 two-room suite ($5 each additional occupant). AE, CB, DC, MC, V. **Parking:** $5 (limited).

This San Francisco–style B&B guesthouse was so successful it expanded in a short time from a six-bedroom Victorian town house (at 1854 Mintwood) to include four houses on Mintwood Place and two on Cathedral Avenue NW. A great effort is made throughout to create charming rooms and public areas. Owner Roberta Pieczenik regularly haunts antique stores, flea markets, and auctions to find beautiful furnishings.

Many rooms have brass beds, perhaps with lovely floral-print bedspreads and matching ruffled curtains. Other possibilities: Oriental throw rugs, a cane-backed rocking chair, an oak mirror shelf with a display of antique bottles, and walls hung with turn-of-the-century artwork or very old framed family photos. Whatever you find, it will be a delight. Live plants and/or fresh flowers grace the rooms, and you're likely to get a dish of candy, too. All rooms have AM/FM clock radios.

Over at 1854 is the cheerful breakfast room with plant-filled windows and park benches at marble tables. Breakfast consists of bagels, croissants, English muffins, orange juice, and tea or coffee. Adjoining amenities include a seldom-used TV, a phone (local calls are free), a phone for long-distance credit- or charge-card calls, a vending machine for soft drinks, a washing machine and dryer, and a refrigerator. Upstairs in the parlor, which has a working fireplace, there's a decanter of sherry on the buffet for complimentary afternoon lemonade or tea and evening apéritifs; magazines, games, and current newspapers are provided. There's a garden behind the house with umbrella tables, and a barbecue grill is provided for guest use. At 1859 Mintwood (also a Victorian town house) is another cozy parlor with two working fireplaces. A lower level here contains additional laundry-ironing facilities and a refrigerator. Though the rooms have no phones, incoming calls are answered around the clock, so people can leave messages for you. Maid service is provided daily.

The Mintwood Place location is very good—near Metro stations, dozens of restaurants, nightspots, and Connecticut Avenue shops. And the Cathedral Avenue houses (tel. 202/328-0860), even closer to the Metro, provide similarly wonderful amenities and facilities.

DOWNTOWN

MORRISON CLARK INN, Massachusetts Ave. NW (at 11th St.), Washington, DC 20001. Tel. 202/898-1200, or toll free 800/332-7898. Fax 202/289-8576. 40 rms (all with bath), 14 suites. A/C TV TEL **Metro:** Metro Center.

$ Rates (including continental breakfast): Weekdays, $115–$175 single; $125–$195 double. Weekends, $85 single or double. Additional person $20 extra; children under 12 stay free in parents' room. AE, CB, DC, DISC, MC, V. **Parking:** $10.

⭐ This magnificent inn, occupying twin 1865 Victorian brick town houses—with a newer wing in converted stables across an interior courtyard—is on the National Register of Historic Places. Its arresting Victorian/Chinois facade features Shanghai porches with Chinese Chippendale railings and a pagodalike mansard roof. Guests enter via a turn-of-the-century parlor, with velvet-upholstered Victorian furnishings, swag-curtained bay windows, and a large floral centerpiece on a piecrust table under a converted gaslight chandelier. Continental breakfast—oven-fresh cakes, muffins, danish, and croissants—is served in the adjoining Club Room with lace-curtained 13-foot windows flanking gold-leafed mahogany-framed pier mirrors on either side of the room. Ornate white marble fireplaces, large potted palms in Chinese cachepots, and a 19th-century carved rosewood screen with Chinese paintings on silk in glass panels are further adornments.

Exquisite, high-ceilinged guest rooms are individually decorated. Yours might be neoclassical in feel, with coffered ceilings and wall columns. Some are furnished in antique wicker pieces with floral chintz balloon shades on the windows and matching bed ruffles. Others have floral swag friezes and/or decorative fireplaces. Color schemes utilize delicate hues like rose, muted gray/blue, and cream. Artwork runs the gamut from Rajasthani paintings on silk to illuminated manuscripts of poems by Lord Byron, bibelots from Dresden figurines to antique Chinese vases. Four rooms have private porches, a few are octagonal with bay windows, and many have plant-filled balconies (with umbrella tables) overlooking a fountained courtyard garden with flower beds amid crepe myrtle and dogwood trees. In-room amenities include remote-control cable TVs housed in handsome armoires, VCRs (tapes are available at the front desk), and two phones (bed and bath) equipped with computer jacks. Baths are supplied with an array of Caswell-Massey toiletries.

Room service is available from the hotel's highly acclaimed American regional restaurant (see Chapter 6). Other amenities here include twice-daily maid service with Belgian chocolates at bed turn-down, complimentary daily newspapers, overnight shoeshine, concierge, many business services, and fresh flowers in every room.

CHAPTER 6

DINING IN WASHINGTON, D.C.

1. **VERY EXPENSIVE**
2. **EXPENSIVE**
3. **MODERATE**
• **FROMMER'S SMART TRAVELER: RESTAURANTS**
4. **INEXPENSIVE**
• **FROMMER'S COOL FOR KIDS: RESTAURANTS**
5. **RESTAURANTS AT SIGHTSEEING ATTRACTIONS**
6. **SPECIALTY DINING**

In the last decade, Washington, like many other American cities, discovered food. Once a culinary boondocks, it is today a great restaurant town on a par with major American and European capitals. The District supports dozens of first-rate restaurants, with chefs who are not only up-to-date on the latest culinary trends but in the vanguard. And in a city filled with foreign embassies, numerous eateries cater to the international contingent, offering authentic Afghan, Indian, Ethiopian, and other exotic menus. Here, too, you can join the rich and powerful at select spots where historic decisions are made over gravlax and champagne or perhaps rub elbows with a justice at the Supreme Court cafeteria or with your senator in a restaurant right in the Capitol. Fresh seafood comes in from Chesapeake Bay, hence crabcakes are a staple of Washington menus. And this is also a southern town, where biscuits are on every breakfast menu, and it's not too hard to find greens and grits. It all adds up to an excitingly diverse dining scene.

I have listed my restaurant choices first by price and then by geographical area, using four **price categories:** "Very Expensive" (dinner typically is more than $50 per person for a full meal, including a glass of wine, tip, and tax), "Expensive" (main courses at dinner average $12 to $16), "Moderate" (main courses at dinner average $7.50 to $11.95), and "Inexpensive" (main courses at dinner are under $7.50).

Keep in mind that the above categories refer to dinner prices, and some very expensive restaurants offer affordable lunches and/or early-bird dinners. Also, I'm going under the assumption that you're not stinting when you order. Some restaurants, for instance, have entrées ranging from $12 to $20. In most cases, you can dine for less if you order carefully.

Note: A Metro station is indicated when it's within walking distance of a restaurant. If you need bus-routing information, call 637-7000.

My very favorite restaurants are marked with a star. However, I must say that every restaurant listed here is actually a favorite of mine, and I wish I could star them all. I guarantee a marvelous dining experience at all of the below-listed establishments. Bon appétit!

1. VERY EXPENSIVE

These upper-bracket restaurants are distinguished by truly excellent food and beautiful settings.

DOWNTOWN

MORRISON CLARK INN, Massachusetts Ave. NW, at 11th St. Tel. 898-1200.
   Cuisine: AMERICAN REGIONAL. **Reservations:** Recommended. **Metro:** Metro Center.
$ Prices: Appetizers $5.25–$6.50 at lunch, $5.50–$9.50 at dinner; main courses $11.75–$14.25 at lunch, $15.75–$20 at dinner; three-course Sun brunch (including unlimited champagne) $19.50. AE, CB, DC, MC, V.
   Open: Lunch Mon–Fri 11:30am–2:30pm; dinner daily 6–9pm; brunch Sun 11:30am–2pm.

⭐ The dining room at the Morrison Clark, an exquisite upscale accommodation (see Chapter 5), is one of the District's most fashionable restaurants (Barbara Bush celebrated a birthday here). Its setting is a National Register Victorian town house, and the interior decor beautifully evokes that period. The dining room is symmetrical, with floor-to-ceiling mahogany- and gilt-valanced lace-curtained windows flanking pier mirrors at either end. Also paired are ornately carved white marble fireplaces. The room centers on a circular settee upholstered in a gorgeous floral print and crowned by a stunning flower arrangement. At night, soft lighting emanates from Victorian brass candelabras, crystal candelabra chandeliers suspended from intricate ceiling medallions, and the glow of candlelight. During the day, sunlight streams in through those massive windows. A smaller dining area adjoins, its trellised walls hung with plants, and you can also dine al fresco at courtyard umbrella tables.

Chef Susan Lindeborg's seasonally changing menus are elegant and inspired. At dinner you might begin with an appetizer of Maryland crab, glazed with cognac and crème fraîche and served in two lemon crêpe cornets with a green herbed-butter sauce. Entrées on my last visit included juicy grilled salmon on a bed of green lentils mixed with applewood-smoked bacon, the fish topped with creamed horseradish sauce; sautéed Catalan-style duck breast in a garlicky saffron-flavored tomato sauce, served with Spanish green olives, basmati rice, haricots verts, and a crunchy garnish of pickled red onions; and apple-stuffed pork loin served with spätzle and cardamom-glazed carrots. Everything is beautifully presented and accompanied by divine side dishes. Similar fare is available at lunch. A reasonably priced wine list offers a variety of premium wines by the glass, plus a good choice of champagnes and sparkling wines. Desserts—such as maple crème brûlée served in a pecan tulip with Grand Marnier-marinated strawberries—are fittingly fancy.

RED SAGE, 605 14th St. NW, at F St. Tel. 638-4444.
   Cuisine: SOUTHWESTERN. **Reservations:** Recommended. **Metro:** Metro Center.
$ Prices: Appetizers $7.50–$9.50 at lunch, $7.50–$11 at dinner;

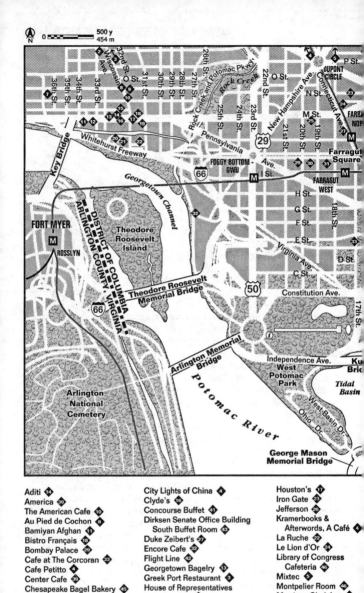

N 0 ⊨▬▬▬ 500 y
454 m

Map labels: 32nd St, Wisconsin Ave, 35th St, 36th St, 34th St, 33rd St, 31st St, 30th St, 29th St, 28th St, 27th St, 26th St, O St, N St, P St, DUPONT CIRCLE, Connecticut Ave, New Hampshire Ave, 22nd St, 21st St, 20th St, 19th St, 18th St, 17th St, M St, FARRAGUT NORTH, FARRAGUT WEST, Farragut Square, L St, K St, H St, G St, F St, E St, D St, C St, Virginia Ave, Constitution Ave, Independence Ave, Rock Creek and Potomac Pkwy, Rock Creek, Pennsylvania, (29), Whitehurst Freeway, Key Bridge, Georgetown Channel, FOGGY BOTTOM - GWU, I St, Georgetown, (66), FORT MYER, ROSSLYN, DISTRICT OF COLUMBIA, ARLINGTON COUNTY, VIRGINIA, Theodore Roosevelt Island, Theodore Roosevelt Memorial Bridge, (50), Arlington Memorial Bridge, Arlington National Cemetery, West Potomac Park, Tidal Basin, West Basin Dr, Ohio Dr, Potomac River, George Mason Memorial Bridge, Kutz Bridge

Aditi ⓮	City Lights of China ❹	Houston's ⓱
America ❸❾	Clyde's ⓰	Iron Gate ㉓
The American Cafe ❿	Concourse Buffet ㊹	Jefferson ㉖
Au Pied de Cochon ❻	Dirksen Senate Office Building	Kramerbooks &
Bamiyan Afghan ⓫	South Buffet Room ㊸	Afterwords, A Café ❹
Bistro Français ⓰	Duke Zeibert's ㉗	La Ruche ㉒
Bombay Palace ㉙	Encore Cafe ㉜	Le Lion d'Or ㉔
Cafe at The Corcoran ㉝	Flight Line ㊸	Library of Congress
Cafe Petitto ❹	Georgetown Bagelry ⓭	Cafeteria ㊻
Center Cafe ㊴	Greek Port Restaurant ❸	Mixtec ❺
Chesapeake Bagel Bakery ㊺	House of Representatives	Montpelier Room ㊵
Cities ❺	Restaurant ㊾	Morrison Clark Inn ㉘

main courses $8.75–$14.25 at lunch, $16–$27.50 at dinner. AE,
CB, DC, MC, V.
Open: Restaurant, lunch Mon–Fri 11:30am–2:15pm; dinner
Mon–Sat 5:30–10:30pm, Sun 5–10pm. Upstairs Chili Bar, Mon–
Sat 11:15am–11:30pm, Sun 4:30–11:30pm. Bar, Sun–Thurs to
2am, Fri–Sat to 3am.

★ One of the brightest stars in Washington's culinary galaxy, Red
Sage is the stunning creation of owner/distinguished chef
Mark Miller, who brings brilliant inspiration to traditional

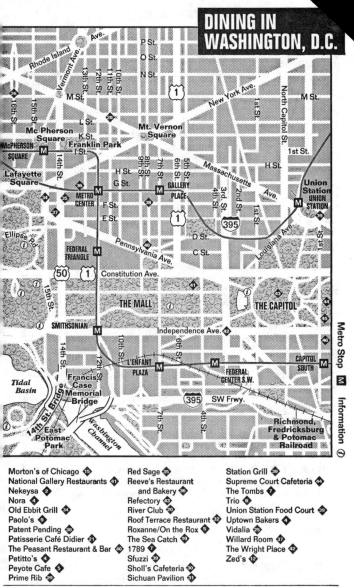

Ave. Rhode Island
P St.
O St.
N St.
Vermont Ave.
13th St.
12th St.
10th St.
M St.
New York Ave.
North Capitol St.
M St.
16th St.
15th St.
L St.
1st St.
Mc Pherson
Square
McPHERSON
SQUARE
K St.
Franklin Park
I St.
14th St.
Mt. Vernon
Square
1st St.
H St.
Union
Station
UNION
STATION
Lafayette
Square
H St.
G St.
8th St.
7th St.
6th St.
5th St.
GALLERY
PLACE
Massachusetts
Ave.
3rd St.
2nd St.
METRO
CENTER
F St.
E St.
4th St.
1st St.
Louisiana Ave.
Ellipse
Rd.
FEDERAL
TRIANGLE
Pennsylvania Ave.
D St.
C St.
395
THE CAPITOL
50 1
Constitution Ave.
15th St.
THE MALL
SMITHSONIAN
Independence Ave.
14th St.
10th St.
12th St.
L'ENFANT
PLAZA
6th St.
CAPITOL
SOUTH
Francis
Case
Memorial
Bridge
FEDERAL
CENTER S.W.
Tidal
Basin
14th St. Bridge
East
Potomac
Park
Washington Channel
395
SW Frwy.
7th St.
4th St.
Richmond,
Fredricksburg
& Potomac
Railroad

Metro Stop M   Information ⓘ

Morton's of Chicago 🔵
National Gallery Restaurants 🔵
Nekeysa 🔵
Nora 🔵
Old Ebbit Grill 🔵
Paolo's 🔵
Patent Pending 🔵
Patisserie Café Didier 🔵
The Peasant Restaurant & Bar 🔵
Petitto's 🔵
Peyote Cafe 🔵
Prime Rib 🔵

Red Sage 🔵
Reeve's Restaurant
   and Bakery 🔵
Refectory 🔵
River Club 🔵
Roof Terrace Restaurant 🔵
Roxanne/On the Rox 🔵
The Sea Catch 🔵
1789 🔵
Sfuzzi 🔵
Sholl's Cafeteria 🔵
Sichuan Pavilion 🔵

Station Grill 🔵
Supreme Court Cafeteria 🔵
The Tombs 🔵
Trio 🔵
Union Station Food Court 🔵
Uptown Bakers 🔵
Vidalia 🔵
Willard Room 🔵
The Wright Place 🔵
Zed's 🔵

southwestern cookery. His dynamic setting—in a stunning beaux arts building—is an elegantly whimsical Wild West fantasy. Down a curved stairway, the main dining area comprises a warren of cozy, candlelit dining nooks under a curved ponderosa log–beamed ceiling supported by hand-hewn trunklike pine columns. Native American (Zapotec) rugs are strewn on flagstone floors, adobe peach fresco walls are hand-rubbed to a sheen with beeswax, etched-glass panels by Santa Fe artist Kit Carson depict western motifs, and ring-of-fire chandeliers overhead are embellished with silver bullets and barbed

...ners are comfortably ensconced in butter-soft burgundy-...booths or roomy upholstered chairs. Special dining areas include an exhibition kitchen, a wine bar, a hogan (Native American hut), and a library where Persian rugs enhance century-old pine floors and "bookshelves" in arched niches are used to display wines. Upstairs, the more casual high-ceilinged Chili Bar—with its large white cloud (emitting bolts of blue lightning) overhead, western-landscape mural, and buffalo-hide upholstery and table lamps is a romantic venue for drinks and light fare. There's validated parking in a garage next door for $3.

The menu changes seasonally. On a recent visit, memorable appetizers included a buttermilk-corn pancake topped with large grilled shrimp in chipotle-butter sauce and a terrine of chorizo sausage and black beans with a creamy center of fresh goat cheese; topped with crunchy blue and yellow tortilla strips tossed in hot habañero chile vinaigrette, it was served on a tomatilla-avocado salsa. Among the entrées, I loved the fan of grilled tender duck breast, served with spicy duck/sun-dried cherry sausage with a garnish of shredded deep-fried yam "hay," and a red-chili-spiced potato custard layered with thin-sliced Idaho and sweet potatoes. Another notable choice was a pecan-crusted chile lamb chop, served with spicy smoked lamb sausage, goat cheese mashed potatoes atop a bed of spinach and mustard greens, and a garnish of yam chips to which molido chilies added piquancy. Red Sage desserts are sublime. Two standouts: a rich, moist warm chocolate-truffle cake surrounded by small mounds of malted vanilla ice cream and drenched in white-chocolate fudge sauce and a silky-smooth caramelized goat's-milk flan topped with crunchy crushed pralines and served with a scoop of chocolate ancho ice cream and chocolate sauce. The well-researched wine list is very extensive.

Note: If you can't afford the restaurant, patronize the upstairs Chili Bar, where items such as a chipotle barbecued-beef sandwich with grilled onions, various "bowls of red," and a hickory-roasted chicken enchilada in blackened-tomato salsa with black beans are under $10.

WILLARD ROOM, in the Willard Inter-Continental Hotel, 1401 Pennsylvania Ave. NW. Tel. 637-7440.

Cuisine: AMERICAN REGIONAL. **Reservations:** Required. **Metro:** Metro Center.

$ Prices: Appetizers $8.75–$11.50 at lunch, $8.50–$14.50 at dinner; main courses $5–$16 at breakfast, $18.50–$24 at lunch, $18.50–$32 at dinner; three-course fixed-price brunch $27.50–$38. AE, DC, DISC, ER, JCB, MC, SAISON, V.

Open: Breakfast Mon–Fri 7:30–10am; lunch Mon–Fri 11:30am–2pm; dinner daily 6–10pm; brunch Sun 11am–2pm.

Since the reopening of the magnificent Willard Inter-Continental Hotel in 1986, its restaurant has become Washington's most prestigious see-and-be-seen dining room. This is nothing new. An 1880 guidebook to the city described the Willard Room as "a most agreeable and pleasing spectacle where refined people enjoy an unequaled table." Today that "refined" clientele includes upper-crust Washingtonians, visiting presidents and premiers, movie and sports stars, and often a king or two. To ensure the continuance of an "unequaled table," the restaurant shops the markets of the world to stock its larders, from the pâtés of Strasbourg to West Virginia's finest

mountain brook trout. Award-winning chefs and sommeliers ha
been assembled. And the room itself has been re-created to reflect its
original turn-of-the-century splendor in every detail—the gorgeous
carved oak paneling, towering scagliola columns, brass and bronze
torchères and chandeliers, and faux-bois beamed ceiling have all
been restored or faithfully reproduced. "The Willard Room is so
elegant," said *Dossier* magazine, "that one could eat a hot dog here
and still think it was the dining experience of a lifetime."

The menus, highlighting East Coast cuisine, change frequently to
offer seasonal specialties. On a recent visit, dinner appetizers included
ravioli (filled with lobster, shrimp, and oysters in lobster-butter sauce
with a topping of caviar) and honey-roasted quail on green-bean
salad with cognac-marinated golden raisins. Fresh seafood entrées—
such as pecan-crusted rock fish filet with sautéed chanterelle mushrooms and bacon on herbed lentils—are a house specialty. But you
could opt, as well, for roast rack of lamb or pan-seared beef
tenderloin medallions with figs, apricots, prunes, and brandied cream
au jus. Desserts—such as poached baby apple charlotte atop a
buttery cinnamon-flavored biscuit, served on calvados crème anglaise
marbelized with chocolate—are superlative. Award-winning French
sommelier Bruno Bonnet oversees the wine cellars, which contain
over 250 varieties.

NEAR THE WHITE HOUSE

**DUKE ZEIBERT'S, in the Washington Square Building,
1050 Connecticut Ave. NW. Tel. 466-3730.**
  Cuisine: AMERICAN. **Reservations:** Recommended. **Metro:**
  Farragut North.
$ Prices: Appetizers $4.95–$9.95; main courses $9–$16 at lunch,
  $16–$24 at dinner. AE, CB, DC, MC, V.
  Open: Mon–Sat 11:30am–11:30pm, Sun 5–10pm. **Closed:**
  Sun July–Aug.

Duke Zeibert's is a reincarnated venerable on the D.C. dining scene.
Opened in 1950, it closed in 1980 when the building it occupied was
torn down, then reopened in 1983 in the new building that went up
on the same spot. Washington legend and lore abound at Duke's. In
the old days it was a Runyonesque hangout into which few women
ventured. ("Ladies go to Georgetown," said the *Washington Star.*
"Macho Washington dines at Duke Zeibert's.") Both Jimmy Hoffa
and J. Edgar Hoover frequented the old Duke's.

Though the new Duke's is less macho (he's selling 10 times more
white wine), the old gang is still here in force. It's not unusual to note
Howard Cosell, Peter Jennings, David Brinkley, Art Buchwald,
Redskins owner Jack Kent Cooke, or Tip O'Neill among the
lunchtime crowd. It was at Duke's that Jimmy the Greek wrecked his
TV career with an infamous remark about the breeding of black
athletes. And it certainly caused a stir when President Clinton dined
here with his chief congressional adversary, Sen. Bob Dole. The main
dining room is under an eight-story atrium skylight. The ambience is
light and airy opulence; it feels like you're dining in a crystal.
Adornments include art deco lighting fixtures and numerous photos
of sports figures and famous guests lining mahogany-paneled walls.
Food is also served in the bar, and cocktails and light fare are offered
on a tree-lined terrace. Duke and his son, Randy, are always on hand
to greet customers.

able is a basket of assorted rolls and a silver bowl of
ckles—a Zeibert trademark. The latter go well with
deli sandwiches made with fresh-cooked meats and
ich—for example, a combo of breast of turkey, smoked
tongue, iss cheese, onion, homemade coleslaw, and Russian
dressing. In fact, you'll note many New York deli characteristics at
Duke's, not the least of them the red-jacketed waiters who would fit
in at any Gotham pastrami house. Furthermore, appetizers include
matzoh-ball soup, chopped liver, and creamed herring. However, you
could also—and wisely—begin your meal with a bluepoint oyster
cocktail and follow up with feathery-light crabcakes served with
mashed potatoes (heaven) and coleslaw. For dessert, strawberry
cheesecake—the rich Lindy's variety—is recommended.

JEFFERSON, 1200 16th St. NW, at M St. Tel. 347-2200.
   Cuisine: AMERICAN REGIONAL. **Reservations:** Recommended. **Metro:** Farragut North.
$ Prices: Appetizers $4.75–$5.50 at lunch, $4.75–$9.75 at din-
   ner; main courses $12.50–$19.50 at lunch, $16.50–$24 at dinner;
   Sun jazz brunch $21–$23 for appetizer, entrée, dessert, and
   coffee. AE, CB, DC, JCB, MC, OPT, V.
   Open: Breakfast daily 6:30–10am; lunch Mon–Sat 11:30am–
   2:30pm; dinner daily 6–10:30pm; brunch Sun 11:30am–2:30pm.
Built in 1923 as a residence for Washington's society elite, the
Jefferson remains the city's most exclusive hotel, discreetly catering
to royalty and other distinguished visitors. Its dining room is, of
course, fittingly elegant, offering the kind of exquisite fare and
impeccable service you'd expect in such a prestigious establishment.
Cozy, rather than intimidatingly plush, it has bare oak floors and
flower-bedecked tables covered with brown-and-cream tattersall-
plaid cloths. Walls and ceiling are handsomely painted in faux
tortoiseshell, the former adorned with intricately carved moldings
and hung with 1830s hand-colored lithographs by Charles Bird King,
James Otto Lewis, and other notable American artists. Seating is in
deep-brown tufted-leather banquettes.
   Award-winning chef William C. Greenwood offers a seasonally
changing menu of American regional dishes. Virginia cuisine is
highlighted, but his wide-ranging food sources are international—
from a farm in Maryland that supplies organically raised free-range
game birds to fresh salmon flown in from Scandinavia. A delectable
appetizer from a recent menu was spinach soufflé with sautéed lobster
in tomato-garlic butter. Another excellent starter was a plantation
corncake topped with smoked salmon and chive cream. Typical
entrées from the same day's menu included braised breast of
pheasant in spiced rum (served with onion, cranberry, and walnut
relish and butternut squash purée) and juniper-marinated venison and
cabbage served with chanterelles and chestnut pancakes. For dessert:
whiskey almond pound cake with Southern Comfort sauce. An
extensive wine list, predominantly French and Californian and
including many by-the-glass selections, complements the menu.

**LE LION D'OR, 1150 Connecticut Ave. NW., at M St. Tel.
296-7972.**
   Cuisine: FRENCH. **Reservations:** Required. **Metro:** Farragut
   North.

$ Prices: Appetizers $6–$12 at lunch, $11–$22 at dinner; main courses $12–$22 at lunch, $20–$32 at dinner. AE, CB, DC, MC, V.

Open: Lunch Mon–Fri noon–2pm; dinner Mon–Sat 6–10pm.

Under the creative and skillful direction of owner/chef Jean-Pierre Goyenvalle, Le Lion d'Or is one of Washington's most highly esteemed bastions of haute cuisine. It opened in 1976 to immediate acclaim, Goyenvalle having previously garnered a loyal following in a decade of classic cookery at other noted area restaurants. This talented chef continues to excel; in the late 1980s he received the prestigious Toque d'Argent award from the Maître Cuisiniers de France—a rare honor for a chef in this country. Le Lion d'Or is patronized by visiting kings, presidents, and power brokers. You might overhear major policy decisions in the making over lunch.

Though the restaurant is down a flight of steps from the street, you'll quickly forget you're underground in a delightful French country setting with seating in dark-brown tufted-leather banquettes under tented silk canopies. Ecru silk walls are adorned with provincial French faïence platters, copper cooking implements, and gilt-framed oil paintings of pastoral scenes. Soft lighting emanates from brass chandeliers and shaded sconces. A single rose in a vase graces every pink-linened table.

The food is classic French cuisine at its best, beautifully presented and graciously served. A not-to-be-missed hors d'oeuvre is the petit soufflé de homard, a feather-light hot lobster mousse, delicately pink and lightly browned on top in lobster-cream sauce flavored with a soupçon of tarragon and parsley. Another excellent beginning: ravioli de foie gras—a large poached pasta pocket stuffed with fresh duck foie gras marinated in white port wine and served in a canard glaze with small diced vegetables. A red snapper entrée "aux senteurs de provence" (with the aroma of the provinces) comes lightly roasted in extra-virgin olive oil and served on a bed of fennel—a marvelously flavorful foil to the fish—with a side dish of new potatoes and a colorful garnish of julienned tomatoes and spinach. And tender, juicy roast rack of lamb is coated just before completion with a Dijon-mustard meringue, crushed green peppercorns, and herbed breadcrumbs; it's served with an array of fresh seasonal vegetables. Dessert options include hot soufflés (orange, raspberry, chocolate, and passionfruit), scrumptious pastry cart selections, or possibly a gratin of broiled seasonal fruits marinated in Cointreau and served in sabayon sauce. A dish of cookies or miniature pastries is complimentary. Le Lion d'Or offers an extensive wine list, primarily French and Californian, and house wines are bottled with the restaurant's own label.

PRIME RIB, 2020 K St. NW. Tel. 466-8811.

Cuisine: STEAK/CHOPS/SEAFOOD. **Reservations:** Recommended. **Metro:** Farragut West.

$ Prices: Appetizers $6–$12; main courses $10–$16.50 at lunch, $18–$24 at dinner. AE, CB, DC, MC, V. **Parking:** Free (valet) after 6pm.

Open: Lunch Mon–Fri 11:30am–3pm; dinner Mon–Thurs 5–11pm, Fri–Sat 5–11:30pm.

Washington Post restaurant critic Phyllis Richman calls the Prime Rib "Washington's most glamorous setting for plain old steak and roast beef." Modeled after Central Park South hotel restaurants, it is indeed glamorous—in a substantial, well-heeled fashion—with gold-trimmed black walls, comfortable black leather chairs and banquettes, white-linened tables softly lit by shaded brass lamps, swagged white curtains, and large floral displays. Waiters are in black tie, a pianist at the baby grand plays show tunes, and the art on the walls includes dozens of gilt-framed Louis Icart art deco lithographs.

As for that "plain old" steak and roast beef, they are thick, tender, juicy, and prepared from meat of the best grain-fed steers that has been aged for four to five weeks. And it's served exactly the way you ordered it. For less carnivorous diners there are about a dozen seafood entrées. A bountiful basket of fried potato skins with a big bowl of sour cream is a must. Lunch or dinner might begin with an appetizer of smoked fresh trout with Dijon-mustard sauce or creamy lobster bisque and end with a gorgeous hot-fudge sundae over amaretto pound cake. Bar drinks here, by the way, are made with fresh-squeezed juices and Evian water.

DUPONT CIRCLE

NORA, 2132 Florida Ave. NW, at R St. Tel. 462-5143.
   Cuisine: MULTI-ETHNIC/ORGANIC. **Reservations:** Recommended. **Metro:** Dupont Circle.
$ Prices: Appetizers $5.95–$8.95; main courses $16–$22. MC, V.
   Open: Dinner Mon–Thurs 6–10pm, Fri–Sat 6–10:30pm.
Nora features beautifully presented haute organic dishes in one of Washington's most charming settings. You enter through a cozy café-curtained bar where brick walls are hung with antique cooking utensils. In the main dining room, fresh flowers and paraffin lamps adorn tables clothed in pale gray and stark white walls display Amish patchwork crib quilts, ceramic dishes, and antique mirrors. Handmade Windsor chairs enhance the Early American feel, as does an immense coffee grinder from a turn-of-the-century Philadelphia general store in the center of the room. There's additional seating in a smaller elegant dining room upstairs and on a lovely brick-walled patio where plants flourish under a skylight ceiling.

The fare is extremely healthful, but not of the brown-rice-and-bean-sprout variety. Chemical-free and additive-free meats are used, vegetables and fruits are fresh and organically grown, and eggs are provided by a farm where the hens run free and their diet is pure. You'll taste the difference. The menu changes daily to take advantage of seasonal specialties and allow creative latitude to the chef. On one visit there were appetizers of Mount Walden smoked trout with creamed-horseradish sauce and Oriental shrimp-stuffed ravioli with sesame-lemon dressing. Typical entrées: grilled yellowfin tuna served with papaya-avocado relish, wild rice timbale, carrot purée, and broccoli; free-range chicken breast with duck sausage/juniperberry stuffing and calvados sauce; and fettuccine mixed with home-cured ham, asparagus, herbs, and shiitake mushrooms. A dessert of French bittersweet-chocolate mousse with hazelnut-cream sauce inspired rhapsodies.

VIDALIA, 1990 M St. NW. Tel. 659-1990.
   Cuisine: PROVINCIAL AMERICAN. **Reservations:** Recommended. **Metro:** Dupont Circle. **Parking:** Complimentary valet parking at dinner.

$ Prices: Appetizers $4.75–$6.50 at lunch, $5.50–$6.75 at dinner; main courses $9.25–$11.50 at lunch, $14.50–$19 at dinner. AE, DC, MC, V.
Open: Lunch Mon–Fri 11:30am–2:30pm; dinner Mon–Sat 5:30–10:30pm. Onion Bar, Mon–Sat to midnight.

Down a flight of steps from the street is one of Washington's finest new restaurants, the charmingly country-cozy Vidalia, named for a variety of sweet Georgia onion. It's entered via a watermelon-green foyer where an oak table is used to display baskets overflowing with fresh flowers, breads, and onions. The oak-floored bilevel dining room centers on a similar display table. Its cream stucco walls are hung with gorgeous dried-flower wreaths and works by local artists, soft lighting emanates from graceful Georgian-style brass chandeliers and sconces, family china is displayed in antique cabinets, and seating is in sturdy oak chairs or forest-green tapestried banquettes. It's a lovely setting, enhanced by exquisite flower arrangements, big terra-cotta pots of chrysanthemums, and bowls of fruit.

Talented chef Jeff Buben's "provincial American" menus (focusing on southern-accented regional specialties) change frequently, but his highly recommended crisp East Coast lump crabcakes (the lightest, fluffiest ever, with a piquant dash of capers and cayenne) are a constant among appetizer choices; they're served with a mound of celery seed–studded pepper slaw and coriander mayonnaise. Another signature appetizer is his magnificent wild-mushroom ragoût—a mix of exotic seasonal mushrooms and finely diced Smithfield Virginia ham served over a rosemary biscuit soaked with cream gravy. On a recent visit, entrée selections—aesthetically arranged on colorful fioriware platters—included a scrumptious fan of pan-roasted moularde duck sauced with saffron, honey, and lemon and served with seared cabbage and a creamy soufflé of cheese grits. At lunch, in addition to similar entrées there are hearty sandwiches such as smoked lamb with soft Vermont goat cheese and roasted onions on grilled olive bread, garnished with sun-dried tomatoes. Meals here include an assortment of fresh-baked breads such as wheatberry, onion foccacia, and moist cornbread studded with chewy creamed-corn niblets. Either meal, save room for a dessert of buttery-crusted lemon chess pie with strawberry sauce—or pig out over a dessert sampler plate. Tapas—such as warm lentil salad with duck sausage and smoked chicken quesadillas—are served in the very simpatico adjoining Onion Bar. A carefully chosen wine list highlights American vintages.

GEORGETOWN

MORTON'S OF CHICAGO, 3251 Prospect St. NW. Tel. 342-6258.
Cuisine: STEAKS/CHOPS/SEAFOOD. **Reservations:** Recommended.
$ Prices: Appetizers $7.50–$8.95; main courses mostly $15.95–$23.95. AE, CB, DC, JCB, MC, V. **Parking:** Free valet parking.
Open: Dinner only, Mon–Sat 5:30–11pm, Sun 5–10pm.

Part of a national restaurant empire created by Arnie Morton, a flamboyant former Playboy Enterprises executive, this is far and away the best steak house in town. It attracts a celebrity-studded clientele: You might spot James Carville and Mary Matalin,

Janet Reno, CNN's Larry King, Warren Christopher, or Ted Kennedy
among the beef eaters. It's also a favorite of athletes; the Washington
Redskins served as waiters for a Special Olympics fund-raiser here.
And National Symphony conductor Mstislav Rostropovich dined
here one night with a famous classical pianist, both wearing headphones! But, basically, one comes to eat, not gawk at the glitterati.

Huge portions of succulent midwestern beef and scrumptious
side dishes are the real attraction. Start off with an appetizer such as
smoked Pacific salmon or a lump-crabmeat cocktail served with
rémoulade sauce. Steaks (rib eye, double filet mignon, porterhouse, or
New York sirloin) are perfectly prepared to your specifications. Other
entrée choices include prime rib, lamb chops, fresh swordfish steak,
lemon-oregano chicken, and baked Maine lobster. Side orders of
flavorfully fresh al dente asparagus served with hollandaise or hash
browns are highly recommended. A loaf of onion bread on every
table is complimentary. Consider taking home a doggy bag if you
want to leave room for dessert—perhaps a soufflé Grand Marnier or
rich and creamy cheesecake.

Morton's plush interior is cozy and convivial. Large framed LeRoy
Neiman sports prints adorn wainscotted stucco walls. Seating is in
comfortable cream-colored leather booths at white-linened tables
adorned with flowers and lit by pewter oil lamps in the shape of
donkeys or elephants. The display kitchen is hung with gleaming
copper pots.

RIVER CLUB, 3223 K St. NW. Tel. 333-8118.
   Cuisine: ASIAN-INFLUENCED AMERICAN. **Reservations:**
   Recommended.
$ **Prices:** Appetizers $6–$12; main courses $16.50–$25.50; tast-
   ing portions $9.50–$13; four-course early-bird fixed-price meal
   (5:30–7pm) $33. AE, CB, DC, DISC, MC, V. **Parking:** Compli-
   mentary valet parking.
   Open: Dinner Mon–Thurs 5:30–11pm, Fri–Sat 5:30pm–
   midnight; late supper Mon–Thurs to midnight, Fri–Sat to 1am.
   Dancing is till 2am Mon–Thurs, 3am Fri–Sat.

It's not often that a restaurant can best be described as
glamorous—especially in an essentially bureaucratic town like
Washington. This is a setting evocative of old movies, a posh
supper club where elegantly attired men and women sip champagne,
dine, and dance to romantic music (to 2am Monday through
Thursday, to 3am on Friday and Saturday). The last word in art deco
elegance, its $1.3-million interior features graceful etched-glass
murals (one of them a marble-framed panel under a cascading
waterfall), gleaming silver and black-lacquer columns, a cove ceiling
subtly aglow in pink neon, and a 50-foot serpentine marble bar.
Seating is in comfy-cozy alcoves at tables ringing a sunken circular
dance floor.

The menu changes seasonally. On my last visit, appetizers
included a Moroccan-spiced lobster salad and a Napoleon layered
with crisp potato and smoked salmon served with lemon cream and
drizzled with chive oil. And entrées ran the gamut from sautéed loin
of lamb with goat-cheese ravioli and rosemary sauce to sesame-
seared tuna served pinkly rare with black-bean sauce, ginger, and
cucumber. Dessert was a banana-macadamia cheesecake with caramel sauce. A pianist plays show tunes weeknights from 7 to 10pm. Do
take advantage of the River Club's knowledgeable and friendly

sommelier, Mark Slater—the champagnes, wines, and dessert wines he recommends with ensuing courses will immensely enhance your meal. The River Club is the kind of place where you can manage to spend hundreds on caviar and champagne—or dine modestly at about $60 for two. Don your best duds and make a night of it (see Chapter 9 for further details).

THE SEA CATCH, 1054 31st St. NW, just below M St. Tel. 337-8855.

   Cuisine: SEAFOOD. **Reservations:** Recommended.

$ Prices: Appetizers $5.95–$8.95 at lunch, $6.75–$11.95 at dinner; main courses $7.75–$13.95 at lunch, $15.75–$19.95 at dinner. AE, CB, DC, MC, V.

   Open: Lunch Mon–Sat noon–3pm; dinner Mon–Sat 5:30–10:30pm.

I love the C&O Canal, so I was especially thrilled when this stunning restaurant opened in 1988 offering canalside seating. Outside on the long awninged wooden deck, mulberry and ailanthus trees form a verdant archway over the canal. The marble-topped tables are romantically candlelit in the evening; by day, watch ducks, punters, and mule-drawn barges glide by while you dine. But don't pass up Sea Catch on days that are less than ideal for alfresco meals; the restaurant, housed in a historic Georgetown stone-and-brick building, is as beautiful within as without. There's a white Carrara-marble raw bar adorned with exquisite floral and food displays and backed by a rustic stone wall. A deluxe brasserie under a low inn-style beamed ceiling adjoins; large windows overlook the canal, and there's a working fireplace. The rustic main dining room—with its rift-sawn white oak ceiling, random-plank oak floor, and rough-hewn walls made of fieldstone dug from Georgetown quarries is warmed by a working fireplace. Classic jazz tapes provide a fine acoustical background.

A dinner here might begin with an appetizer of lobster wrapped in grape leaves with a parsleyed white-bean-and-garlic flan. Of course, plump farm-raised oysters and other raw-bar offerings also merit consideration. The entrée focus is on daily-changing fresh fish and seafood specials, such as grilled hickory-smoked tuna on diced eggplant with fresh sage butter served with potato casserole and a melange of fresh corn and black-eyed peas. The kitchen willingly prepares fresh fish and seafood dishes to your specifications, including live lobster from the tanks. Don't miss the softshell crab when it's in season here. Lunch offerings include seafood salads and sandwiches on brioche. An extensive wine list highlights French, Italian, and American selections and features five premium wines by the glass each day.

1789, 1226 36th St. NW, at Prospect St. Tel. 965-1789.

   Cuisine: AMERICAN REGIONAL. **Reservations:** Recommended. **Parking:** Complimentary valet parking.

$ Prices: Appetizers $6–$10; main courses $21–$28; fixed-price pretheater menu $23. AE, CB, DC, DISC, V.

   Open: Dinner only, Sun–Thurs 6–10pm, Fri–Sat 6–11pm.

One of Washington's most elegantly charming restaurants, 1789 (its name commemorating not the French Revolution but the year the village of Georgetown was incorporated) is as cozy as a country inn. Housed in a Federal town house, its intimate dining areas include the John Carroll Room, where walls are hung with

Currier and Ives prints and old city maps, a log fire blazes in the hearth, and a gorgeous flower arrangement is displayed atop a hunting-themed oak sideboard. In the smaller Manassas Room, rough-hewn pine walls (siding from an 1860s Maryland barn) are covered with prints of the Civil War period. And the pubby bar area, with seating in oak-backed tufted-leather banquettes, has a stunning gas chandelier overhead and walls embellished with shelves of pewterware, hunting prints, and 18th-century hand-colored English caricatures. Throughout, silk-shaded brass oil lamps provide romantic lighting at crisply white-linened tables set with Limoges china. One could go on and on with interior detail here; 1789 is a virtual decorative arts museum of period furnishings and museum-quality paintings, prints, and objets d'art. It's also one of the city's prime see-and-be-seen dining venues, where you might spot anyone from Bill and Hillary Clinton to Stacy Keach at the next table.

Talented chef Michael Patton's menus change seasonally. A recent one offered appetizers of basil-potato stuffed dumplings (garnished with julienned Petrossian smoked salmon in a light and lemony cream sauce) and grilled Gulf Coast shrimp coated with bourbon-pecan barbecue sauce and served on a bed of fresh sweet corn purée. Do consider a salad here, such as sautéed artichoke bottoms served warm with roasted red- and yellow-pepper strips and crisp radicchio in herbed vinaigrette. An entrée of roast rack of lamb with garlicky Napa goat-cheese crust was served au jus on an array of sautéed mixed southern greens (mustard, turnip, spinach, and collard) with potatoes au gratin. Also notable were Patton's lumpmeat crabcakes (with zesty infusions of garlic, cayenne, and Dijon mustard) served with fire-roasted tomato sauce, grilled ratatouille, and Cheddar-cheese grits. Homemade breads such as basil parmesan and whole-wheat walnut accompany entrées, desserts might range from tiramisu to pecan-crusted lemon soufflé pie with raspberry sauce, and the wine list is long and distinguished. A great bargain here: the pretheater menu offered between 6 and 6:45pm, including appetizer, entrée, dessert, and coffee for just $23!

2. EXPENSIVE

Most of the restaurants in this category also offer options—such as pizzas, pastas, and sandwiches—in the moderate price range.

DOWNTOWN

OLD EBBITT GRILL, 675 15th St. NW, between F and G Sts. Tel. 347-4801.

Cuisine: AMERICAN. **Reservations:** Recommended. **Metro:** McPherson Square or Metro Center.

$ Prices: Appetizers $4.50–$6.50; main courses $7.95–$10.95 lunch, $9.95–$15.95 dinner; burgers and sandwiches $6.50–$7.95; breakfast/brunch $4.95–$6.95. AE, DC, DISC, MC, V.

Open: Breakfast Mon–Fri 7:30–11am, Sat 8–11:30am; lunch Mon–Fri 11am–5pm, Sat 11:30am–4pm; dinner Mon–Fri 5pm–midnight, Sat–Sun 4pm–midnight; brunch Sun 9:30am–4pm. Bar, Sun–Thurs to 2am, Fri–Sat to 3am.

Located two blocks from the White House is the city's oldest saloon, founded in 1856. Presidents Grant, Johnson, McKinley, Cleveland, Theodore Roosevelt, and Harding were patrons, and among its artifacts are Alexander Hamilton's wooden bears—one with a secret compartment in which it's said he hid whiskey bottles from his wife. However, don't go expecting to find a fusty old tavern. The existing facility is a plush reconstruction loosely based upon the original. Fronted by a grandiose beaux arts facade, it has Persian rugs on beautiful oak and marble floors, beveled mirrors, gas lighting, etched-glass panels, and other elements evocative of turn-of-the-century Washington saloons. Old Ebbitt heirlooms are scattered throughout—the Hamilton bears and animal trophies bagged by Teddy Roosevelt among them. The street level comprises a dining area and three bars, plus a glassed-in atrium dining room with umbrella tables amid much greenery. The main dining room, hung with period oil paintings, has lace-curtained windows and forest-green velvet banquettes and booths. Other areas include the Old Bar (where the Ebbitt's famed collection of antique beer steins is displayed), the Oyster Bar, and Grant's Bar, complete with a classic gilt-framed bar nude. The Ebbitt is a stunning setting for meals, cocktails, or a romantic rendezvous.

Menus change daily, but lunch entrées might include fettuccine tossed with spinach and walnuts in cream sauce or a fried-oyster sandwich. Typical dinner entrées: a half chicken (roasted with lemon, herbs, and honey, and served with rice and fresh vegetables) and straw and hay pasta tossed with prosciutto, peas, onions, mushrooms, olive oil, and fresh-grated parmesan. At either meal you can order a sandwich (perhaps a Reuben or turkey club), a hamburger, or a half a dozen raw oysters, thus enjoying the luxe ambience at low cost. Desserts range from a hot-fudge sundae made with homemade vanilla ice cream to toll house pie studded with chocolate morsels and walnuts, spiked with bourbon, and served warm with vanilla ice cream.

THE PEASANT RESTAURANT & BAR, 801 Pennsylvania Ave. NW. Tel. 638-2140.

Cuisine: AMERICAN/CONTINENTAL. **Reservations:** Recommended at dinner. **Metro:** Archives–Navy Memorial.

$ Prices: Appetizers $5.95–$7.95; main courses $6.95–$10.95 at lunch, $10.95–$22.95 at dinner. AE, CB, DC, DISC, MC, V.

Open: Lunch Mon–Fri 11am–3pm; dinner Mon 5:30–10pm, Tues–Sat 5:30–11pm, Sun 5–9pm.

Part of a first-rate Atlanta-based restaurant group, the Peasant belies its name with a plushly clubby interior. High ceilings are adorned by carved moldings, mahogany-wainscotted cream walls are hung with turn-of-the-century French silhouette portraits, crisply white-linened tables are graced by fresh flowers and lit by brass candle lamps, and additional muted lighting emanates from elegant chandeliers and sconces. It's a romantic setting, with seating amid potted palms and soothing classical background music. During the day, weather permitting, you can dine al fresco at café tables on the Navy Memorial Plaza.

Service is smooth and gracious, and the fare both original and delicious. A marvelous appetizer is herb-marinated warm goat cheese served with grilled French bread, roasted tomatoes, and big savory cloves of roasted elephant garlic. If you plan to kiss someone later, give this garlicky treat a miss and order the plump and fluffy scallion-studded crabcakes, zestily spiced with a little cumin and hot peppers; they're served with fresh tomato salsa. Entrées come with incredible fresh-baked parmesan bread, a salad, vegetables, and rice or potatoes du jour. Some examples: a fan of crisp-grilled pinkly juicy duckling in plum sauce, pan-sautéed gulf shrimp in ginger-orange glaze served with julienned vegetables and citrus rice, and grilled North Atlantic salmon with juniperberry-butter sauce. This is the kind of food that excites the senses, and dazzling desserts provide a fitting climax. Chocolate-toffee pie is a symphony of tastes and textures—a rich mocha mousse whipped into a chocolate wafer crust and smothered in whipped cream, hot caramel, and chocolate-covered toffee. And there's blackberry-peach cobbler with crunchy brown-sugary streusel topping served with cinnamon ice cream. The wine list is reasonably priced, with many premium wines available by the glass.

DUPONT CIRCLE

IRON GATE RESTAURANT & GARDEN, 1734 N St. NW. Tel. 737-1370.
  Cuisine: MEDITERRANEAN. **Reservations:** Recommended.
  Metro: Dupont Circle.
$ **Prices:** Appetizers $4.50–$6 at lunch, $5–$6.50 at dinner; main courses $9.50–$12.50 at lunch, $15.50–$19 at dinner. AE, MC, V.
  Open: Lunch Mon–Fri 11:30am–5pm; dinner Mon–Sat 5–10pm, Sun 5–9pm. **Closed:** Sun July–Aug.

Housed in a converted 19th-century stable, the Iron Gate is probably Washington's most romantic dining venue. In winter, it's the coziest place in town: A big fire blazes in an immense brick fireplace hung with gleaming copper pots, and the smell of burning wood is as alluring as the aromas emerging from the kitchen. Exposed brick walls are hung with exquisite dried flower arrangements and wreaths. There's additional seating upstairs in a room with another working fireplace. And fall through spring, you can dine al fresco under a grape-and-wisteria arbor in an enchanting brick-walled garden with a splashing fountain and lovingly tended flower beds.

With its superb ambience, the Iron Gate has always been a local favorite, all the more so since 1991 when Nabeel and Karen David took over and created a menu worthy of the setting. Everything is fresh (even herbs are grown out back) and prepared with finesse using the finest possible ingredients. An excellent beginning is a baked goat-cheese torte with charred-pepper coulis. There are fantastic soups such as potato-leek topped with lebne (rich, creamy drained yogurt) and parsley. And the mesclun salad is a refreshing mix of greens (radicchio, baby lettuces, endive, baby bok choy, frise) with chopped tomato and crumbled goat cheese in a tasty balsamic vinaigrette. Entrées are served with fresh-baked foccacia breads (herb, parmesan, walnut, sun-dried tomato) and coins of herbed butter. A totally satisfying pasta dish is fettuccine tossed with grilled shrimp, pancetta, and sugar peas. Crisp-skinned roast free-range chicken (you'll taste the difference) is served in a lemony jus de poulet with fresh veggies and wild-rice pilaf in golden raisin/pine nut vinaigrette. And there's also a savory vegetable tajine with couscous. Divine desserts include mint-garnished almond flan in caramel sauce and a chocolate-truffle pie with dark cookie crust on a raspberry coulis topped with fresh whipped cream. There's a full bar, a good choice of wines, even fresh-squeezed lemonade. Keep the Iron Gate in mind not only for meals, but as the perfect place for leisurely afternoon tea/espresso/cappuccino or cocktails.

GEORGETOWN

BISTRO FRANÇAIS, 3124-28 M St. NW. Tel. 338-3830.
   Cuisine: FRENCH. **Reservations:** Recommended.
$ Prices: Appetizers $3.95–$6.25 at lunch, $5.95–$7.95 at dinner; main courses $7.95–$13.95 at lunch, $12.95–$18.95 at dinner; fixed-price lunch $11.95; Early-Bird Special $14.95. AE, CB, DC, MC, V.
   Open: Sun–Thurs 11am–3am, Fri–Sat 11am–4am.

This charming restaurant authentically captures a certain air of excitement associated with Parisian bistros. Wainscotted walls are hung with mahogany-framed mirrors and French period posters from World Wars I and II. Seating areas are defined by wrought-iron and brass railings, ceilings are ornate pressed copper, and etched- and stained-glass panels add to the cozy clutter. Candlelit tables, set with white linen and adorned with fresh flowers, strike an elegant note.

The Bistro is actually a two-part affair, half of it a casual café, the other half a more serious dining room. Depending on where you sit, you have different menus to deal with, though the offerings are very similar. In either section, a good bet on weekdays from 5 to 7pm is the Early-Bird Special, offered once again from 10:30pm to 1am. It includes a glass of house wine, soup du jour (perhaps cream of vegetable) or an appetizer such as mussels niçois, an entrée (such as roast leg of lamb rubbed with rosemary and served with sautéed potatoes and haricots verts), and a selection from the pastry cart. A similar menu is offered weekdays at lunch (noon to 2pm). A la carte listings, also on both sides, include a selection of traditional French hors d'oeuvres: a seafood terrine with horseradish sauce, escargots with vegetables and garlic butter, sherried chicken-liver pâté. There are delicious salads (I like the tropiques—a mix of avocado, tomato, hearts of palm, and artichoke hearts), a classic French onion soup, and entrées like poulet rôti with tarragon, entrecôte au poivre, and coquilles St-Jacques with ginger and red-pepper sauce. Desserts also are the Paris café standbys—chocolate mousse, crème caramel, and pâtisseries maison (the raspberry tarte is first-rate)—unless you want to be fancy and order a pêche Melba. Numerous daily specials supplement the menu, as does an extensive, mostly French, wine list. Several selections are offered by the glass each day. Liqueurs, fancy drinks made with them, brandies, cognacs, and dessert wines are additionally featured.

PAOLO'S, 1303 Wisconsin Ave. NW, at N St. Tel. 333-7353.
   Cuisine: CALIFORNIA-STYLE ITALIAN. **Reservations:** Accepted at lunch only.
$ Prices: Appetizers $4.95–$7.95; pastas mostly $7.95–$11.95; pizzas $7.95–$8.95; main courses $13.95–$17.95; lunch specials $7.50–$11.95. AE, CB, DC, DISC, MC, MOST, V.

Open: Mon–Thurs 11:30am–midnight, Fri–Sat 11:30am–12:30am, Sun 11am–midnight. Bar, Sun–Thurs to 1:30am, Fri–Sat to 2:30am.

Under the same auspices as the River Club (see "Very Expensive," above), Paolo's is one of Georgetown's hottest restaurants. Restaurateur Paul Cohn is a virtuoso when it comes to creating a scene that crackles with excitement. "It's the closest thing to show business," he says. "You're on every night."

I never tire of the show at Paolo's. For one thing, the setting is *molto simpático*. Tables spill out onto the street from an open-air patio, and the front room, with a stunning peach-hued Italian marble floor and black marble bar, centers on the warm glow of a pizza-oven fire. Red peppers, dried herbs, and strings of garlic are suspended above the wood-burning brick oven, which is fronted by a colorful display of pizza toppings—creamy white bowls filled with pine nuts, peppers, sausage, sun-dried tomatoes, and more. Here diners can watch the chef preparing his luscious golden-crusted pies. The back room, richly paneled in cherrywood and agleam with copper mirrors, also centers on an open exhibition kitchen. Black Italian marble tables are adorned with fresh flowers, and, at night, candle lamps with frosted shades complement the subdued track lighting. Paolo's is a major D.C. see-and-be-seen celebrity haunt.

Young chef Steve Roberts applies subtle nouvelle principles to traditional Italian fare, but don't worry—he doesn't skimp on portion size. A delightful surprise arrives as soon as you're seated—a bowl of tapenade (a Mediterranean spread of puréed olives, chickpeas, and roasted red peppers) along with oven-fresh sesame-studded chewy breadsticks made from pizza dough. The same menu is offered all day. You can dine lightly on a pizza with toppings running the gamut from oak-grilled chicken to goat cheese. Pastas include such temptations as grilled garlic-fennel sausage served with peppers and onions over saffron fettuccine in marinara sauce. Among the nonpasta entrées is clay-pot-roasted chicken with peppers, potatoes, red onions, and roasted elephant garlic. Or you might select juicy grilled jumbo shrimp scampi stuffed with garlic, romano cheese, and herbed breadcrumbs, and served atop spinach and egg fettuccine. Wines, many available by the glass, are de rigueur with this food. Desserts include a white-chocolate banana-cream pie. Paolo's takes no reservations at dinner, so plan a before-dinner drink in the bar.

ADAMS-MORGAN

CITIES, 2424 18th St. NW. Tel. 328-7194.
   Cuisine: INTERNATIONAL. **Reservations:** Recommended.
$ Prices: Appetizers $3.95–$7.95; main courses $10–$18.95. AE, DC, MC, V.
   Open: Dinner only, Mon–Thurs 6–11pm, Fri–Sat 6–11:30pm. Bar, Sun–Thurs 5pm–2am, Fri–Sat 5pm–3am.

Housed in a century-old former five-and-dime store, Cities is a restaurant-cum-travelogue. Every six or seven months, following a comprehensive research expedition by the owner and chef, the restaurant is revamped to reflect the cuisine, character, and culture of a different city. Even the music reflects the city under consideration, and the waiters are in native dress or some facsimile thereof. When the city was Bangkok, for instance, vases were filled with large bird-of-paradise and bamboo arrangements, corrugated steel sheets overhead suggested Thai roofing, beautiful photographs of rickshaws and rice paddies lined the walls, and Thai sculpture, paper umbrellas, fans, tapestries, and other artifacts provided further evocation. On one visit, the highlighted city was Paris, and the decor replicated a Montparnasse-style brasserie, with French street lamps, flower boxes, murals of Parisian park and café scenes, and French bistro menus on the walls. My Parisian meal began with an appetizer of escargots served with shiitake mushrooms and sautéed spinach in a garlicky Pernod-flavored butter sauce with a gratinée of fresh Gruyère and parmesan. That was followed by an entrée of poulet grillé served in a fan of slices on a bed of leeks in butter-cream-chèvre reduction sauce with classic pommes frites. And dessert was chef Mary Richter's divine interpretation of a marquise au chocolat—layers of crunchy hazelnut meringue filled with hazelnut-butter cream on a crème anglaise marbelized with raspberry and garnished with fresh raspberries, mint, and crème chantilly. *Formidable!* Of course, by the time you read this, the cuisine and setting will be entirely different—that's part of the fun. Not to worry—Cities' fare is always excellent. There's a small but expertly conceived wine and champagne list enhanced by alcoholic beverages representing the city cuisine, and premium wines are offered by the glass.

The adjoining bar, open-air in summer and one of the most simpatico spots for imbibing in the Adams-Morgan district, is also redecorated with every city change. It offers a light-fare menu with items in the $4.50 to $7.50 range. For Paris, these included a croque monsieur, plat de fromages, and pâté served with cornichons, radishes, and bread. After dinner or drinks, check out the dance club upstairs (details in Chapter 9).

PETITTO'S, 2653 Connecticut Ave. NW, between Calvert St. and Woodley Rd. Tel. 667-5350.
Cuisine: ITALIAN. **Reservations:** Recommended. **Metro:** Woodley Park–Zoo.
$ Prices: Appetizers $3.75–$6.75 at lunch, $4.25–$7.50 at dinner; main courses $6.75–$10.75 at lunch, $11.25–$17.75 at dinner. AE, CB, CHOICE, DC, MC, V.
Open: Lunch Mon–Fri 11:30am–2:30pm; dinner Mon–Sat 6–10:30pm, Sun 6–9:30pm. Dolce Finale, Mon–Thurs 11:30–12:30am, Fri 11:30–1:30am, Sat 4pm–1:30am.

The superb Petitto's features the cuisine of Rome and Abruzzi—plus a few southern specialties—in a very charming setting. There are three dining rooms in this converted turn-of-the-century town house, each with its own working fireplace. Seating, in bentwood chairs at white linen-clothed tables, sets a traditionally elegant tone, and soft, suffused lighting is provided by hanging lamps wrapped in creamy silk scarves. Operatic arias make very appropriate background music. In good weather you can dine al fresco at umbrella tables on the street.

A shared pasta entrée makes a marvelous appetizer course—perhaps falasche alla Petitto (homemade spinach and egg noodles tossed with mushrooms, prosciutto, and peas in a cream sauce) or penne all' Amatriciana (a zitilike pasta with chunks of thickly sliced bacon and hot peppers in a lusty red sauce flavored with freshly grated romano cheese). Two exquisite pasta dishes available as entrées only are pappardelle (wide fettuccine) mixed with chunks of sautéed chicken breast, exotic mushrooms, and prosciutto in a sage-marjoram-rosemary–flavored butter-wine sauce and fettuccine primavera tutto giardino—with seasoned vegetables and a lemon-cream sauce; the recipe for the latter has appeared in *Bon Appétit*. A salad course here is a must. Light and refreshing is a harmonious arrangement of tomatoes (always bright red and delicious here; off-season they're imported from Holland or Mexico) and home-made mozzarella in an olive oil/basil dressing. Also noteworthy: an exquisite affair of marinated squid and seafood with red peppers, onions, and black olives vinaigrette.

Nonpasta entrées change weekly, but always include excellent fresh seafood dishes such as plump jumbo shrimp grilled in garlic, oil, and fresh oregano and cacciucco—an array of shellfish (lobster, scallops, mussels, clams, and squid) served with linguine in a sauce of olive oil, garlic, and fresh tomatoes. Entrées are served with flavorful al dente fresh vegetables and new potatoes prepared in various ways. Breads—pan-fried in olive oil, flavored with garlic and parmesan, or toasted with tomato, parmesan, and basil—are famed house special-ties, but you might forgo them in a good cause: leaving room for dessert. Recommended choices include a great tira misu, zuppa inglese (a sponge cake layered with custard, real whipped cream, and fresh raspberries, saturated with Chambord liqueur), and the creamiest-ever orange cheesecake topped with fresh fruit. A moder-ately priced and well-chosen list of Italian wines is augmented by more elite and costlier vintages (including French and California selections); a few premium wines are available by the glass each night.

Dolce Finale, in Petitto's cozily candlelit, brick-walled wine cellar, features a variety of cappuccinos, wines, grappas, liqueurs, fruits and cheeses, and an array of sumptuous desserts. It can be visited separately from the restaurant.

3. MODERATE

The following moderate selections are restaurants most of us prefer for everyday dining. They all offer excellent meals at reasonable prices, in many cases with a fair amount of ambience thrown in for good measure. Many ethnic eateries are included in this category.

NEAR THE WHITE HOUSE

BOMBAY PALACE, 2020 K St. NW. Tel. 331-0111.

   Cuisine: NORTH INDIAN. **Reservations:** Recommended. **Metro:** Farragut North or Farragut West.

$ Prices: Appetizers $3.50–$4.50; main courses mostly $7.95–$11; fixed-price three-course lunch (Mon–Fri) $10–$13; lunch buffet (Sat–Sun) $9.95; fixed-price four-course dinner $16.95. AE, MC, V.

   Open: Lunch daily noon–2:30pm; dinner Sun–Thurs 5:30–10pm, Fri–Sat 5:30–10:30pm; brunch Sat–Sun noon–2:30pm.

The Bombay Palace features the Mughlai cookery of northern India. Created by international restaurant "moghul" Sant Chatwal, this restaurant has served everyone from Princess Elizabeth of Yugoslavia to Sens. Bob Dole and Pat Moynihan. At this writing, the restaurant is undergoing a total interior renovation, so I can't describe it except to say that it will be elegant and softly lit. The menu will stay the same.

Throughout the day, your choice of appetizers includes vegetable samosas (crisp pastries stuffed with mildly spiced potatoes and peas), pakoras (vegetable fritters), chooza pakoras (chicken pieces marinated in yogurt, ginger, and garlic, and batter fried), and shammi kebabs (subtly spiced, minced lamb patties blended with egg, lentils, onions, nutmeg, and garlic). An assorted hors d'oeuvre platter obviates the decision-making process.

Tandoori specialties are featured (the restaurant has two clay ovens in operation at all times). Be sure to order one of the tandoor-baked breads, either a simple chewy and delicious nan or a more complex affair such as nan stuffed with chicken and almonds. With soup and an appetizer or salad, the latter could in itself make a meal. Recommended entrées include tandoori prawns or chicken, gosht patiala (mildly spiced boneless beef or lamb cooked with potatoes, onions, ginger, and garlic), and the Palace nawabi biryani (long-grain rice flavored with saffron and 21 exotic spices, cooked with pieces of lamb, nuts, and egg). There are vegetable entrées as well, such as tandoor-roasted eggplant, mashed and seasoned with herbs and roasted with sautéed onions. For dessert, try the home-made mango ice cream.

Weekend buffet brunches provide an excellent opportunity to sample a wide variety of dishes.

SICHUAN PAVILION, 1820 K St. NW. Tel. 466-7790.

Cuisine: SZECHUAN. **Reservations:** Recommended. **Metro:** Farragut North or Farragut West.

$ Prices: Appetizers $2–$4.50 at lunch, $2.50–$5 at dinner; main courses $6.95–$14.95 at lunch, $7.95–$15.95 at dinner; fixed-price brunch (Sat–Sun) $10.95. AE, DC, DISC, MC, V.

Open: Lunch Mon–Fri 11:30am–3pm; dinner daily 3–10:30pm; brunch Sat–Sun noon–4pm.

The Sichuan Pavilion is unique in several ways. Though it's American-owned, its chefs are recruited from the highest ranks of the People's Republic of China's Chengdu Service Bureau, which operates luxurious hotels and restaurants for visiting dignitaries and prepares sumptuous state banquets. These chefs, supplied from home with special seasonings and spices not otherwise available in the United States, are masters of Szechuan cuisine. The Chinese embassy sent its cook here for training, and when Premier Zhao Ziyang visited Washington, the Sichuan Pavilion prepared special meals for him. The setting is unpretentious but elegant, with white-linened tables, crystal chandeliers, and walls hung with paintings and calligraphy from the Chungking Institute of Fine Arts. And the food is beautifully presented (these chefs are also trained in food sculpture and adorn platters with exquisite carrot and leek flowers). It's also light—never greasy—low in salt, and prepared without MSG.

Do begin with an appetizer of tangy dumplings in spicy red hot sauce or crispy but feather-light spring rolls. And keep in mind that though some of the dishes sound familiar—moo shu pork, Kung Pao chicken, twice-cooked shredded duck—their subtle flavors distinguish them from Szechuan fare you've had elsewhere. The chef's specialties include tinkling bells with 10 ingredients (sliced shrimp, crab, beef, and chicken sautéed with vegetables and topped with Sichuan dumplings) and crispy fried sea bass in Sichuan sauce. Each dish is a revelation; dining here is like discovering new colors on the culinary spectrum. And as a concession to Western palates, there are dessert choices such as cheesecake—though you can also opt for almond tofu custard.

DUPONT CIRCLE

CAFE PETITTO, 1724 Connecticut Ave. NW. Tel. 462-8771.

Cuisine: ITALIAN. **Reservations:** Not accepted. **Metro:** Dupont Circle.

$ Prices: Appetizers $3.25–$5.75; main courses $5.25–$10 ($6.25–$6.95 at brunch); salad bar $6.25 a plate; pizzas from $5.25. AE, DC, MC, V.

Open: Mon–Thurs 11:30am–10:30pm, Fri–Sat 11:30am–11pm, Sun 11:30am–10pm; brunch Sat–Sun 11:30am–3pm.

Roger and Byron Petitto, original owners of the upscale Petitto's (see "Expensive," above), launched this exciting, moderately priced new venture in 1985. They lure diners inside with an exquisite antipasto display in the front window—about 50 items including stringbean and fava-bean salads, rice salads, marinated eggplant, snow peas with oil-cured olives, creamy egg salad, stuffed grape leaves, cold fried eggplant, pasta salads, escarole and pancetta (Italian bacon), homemade potato salad, rice/peas/pepper salad, and much more. It's always changing, always fabulous, and you can sample as much as you can stack on a plate. Then there are the scrumptious Calabrian pizzas, on flavorful bready dough that's lightly fried in olive oil before toppings are added and the entirety grilled. For $7.95 you'll get a pizza ample for two with Italian plum tomatoes, mozzarella, and fresh basil. Optional additions, priced from $1.25 to $2.50, include over 30 choices, among them hot sausage, pancetta, artichoke hearts, black olives, sun-dried tomatoes, eggplant, roasted peppers, mussels, baby clams, and smoked mozzarella. A third menu category is hoagies—sandwiches on hard rolls with fillings such as grilled chicken breast, fresh marinated tomatoes, basil, and olive oil—served with roasted potatoes. Or you might opt for foccacia—a doughy bread stuffed with ricotta, mushrooms, roasted red peppers, and fresh rosemary. An order of "slats"—toasted garlic bread, baked with fresh marinated tomatoes, basil, and olive oil—is most recommended, as is the chocolate-amaretto cheesecake for dessert. Daily specials always include great pasta dishes. Italian wines are reasonably priced and available by the glass.

Additional items are offered at brunch, among them frittatas and eggs Roman style (baked in cream and butter with chunks of smoked bacon and parmesan cheese); they're served with roast potatoes, fresh fruit, and Italian bread.

The setting is pleasant but unpretentious. Cafe Petitto has a black-and-white checkerboard floor, bare wood tables, and pine wainscotted cream stucco walls hung with a veritable Petitto family photo album—mom, dad, and brother Tony at nine months, among others. Arrive off-hours to avoid waiting in line.

CITY LIGHTS OF CHINA, 1731 Connecticut Ave. NW, between R and S Sts. Tel. 265-6688.

Cuisine: CHINESE. **Reservations:** Recommended. **Metro:** Dupont Circle.

$ Prices: Appetizers $2–$4.50 at lunch, $2–$4.95 at dinner; main courses mostly $5.95–$9.95 at lunch, $6.95–$11.95 at dinner (a few are pricier). AE, CB, DC, DISC, MC, V.

Open: Mon–Thurs 11:30am–10:30pm, Fri 11:30am–11pm, Sat noon–11pm, Sun noon–10:30pm (dinner from 3pm daily).

George McGovern, Jesse Jackson, former Attorney General Dick Thornburgh, Supreme Court Justices Sandra Day O'Connor and Antonin Scalia, and political commentator Martin Agronsky are just a few of the many Washington insiders who make City Lights a regular stop on their dining itinerary. Like myself, they're hooked on the irresistible Mandarin/Cantonese/Szechuan dishes prepared by talented Taiwanese chef (and part owner) Kuo-Tai Soug. The setting is pretty but unpretentious—a three-tiered dining room with much of the seating in comfortable pale-green leather booths and banquettes. Neat white-linened tables set with peach napkins, cloth flower arrangements in lighted niches, and green neon track lighting complete the picture.

There are wonderful appetizers like crisp-fried Cornish hen prepared in a cinnamon-soy marinade and served with a tasty dipping sauce, garlicky Chinese eggplant with a hot red-pepper tang, sesame noodles tossed with shreds of cucumber and scrambled eggs, and plump, delicious dumplings (steamed or pan-fried) stuffed with artfully seasoned pork, chives, scallions, and green peppers. As for entrées, the pièce de résistance (listed under "chef's specialties") is the crisp fried shredded beef—a delicate mix of finely julienned beef, carrot, scallion, and celery in a crunchy peppercorn hot-caramel sweet glaze (this is an occasion to forget about not eating beef). Also exemplary here: stir-fried spinach richly flavored with sesame and garlic and pan-fried noodles—a crunchy Chinese kugel topped with shrimps, scallops, and vegetables. There's a full bar.

KRAMERBOOKS & AFTERWORDS, A CAFÉ, 1517 Con-

Ⓕ FROMMER'S SMART TRAVELER: RESTAURANTS

1. Eat your main meal at lunch when prices are lower; you can enjoy gourmet entrées for a fraction of what they cost at dinner.
2. Washington abounds with parks and beautifully landscaped squares. You'll not only save money by occasionally buying food and lunching al fresco, you'll also probably find it more relaxing than a crowded museum cafeteria.
3. Note restaurants in the listings below offering early-bird and fixed-price dinners; they usually represent great values.
4. Some accommodations listed in Chapter 5 include breakfast in the rates or have rooms with fully equipped kitchens; for families, these can represent substantial savings.
5. Many bars in D.C. offer fairly extensive happy-hour buffets. If you're a light eater, or you've had a big lunch, this could suffice for a meal.

necticut Ave. NW, between Q St. and Dupont Circle.
Tel. 387-1462.
Cuisine: AMERICAN. **Reservations:** Not accepted. **Metro:**
Dupont Circle.
$ **Prices:** Appetizers $4.25–$5.75; main courses $7.75–$12.95.
AE, MC, V.
Open: Mon–Thurs 7:30am–1am, around the clock Fri 7:30am–
Sun 1am.

This schmoozy bookstore-cum-café is the kind of congenial place
you go for cappuccino after the movies, for an intense discussion of
your love life over a platter of fettuccine, or to linger over a good
book and a cognac (both of which can be purchased here) on a sunny
afternoon. There's cozy seating indoors at butcher-block tables
under a low beamed ceiling, at the bar, upstairs on a balcony, in a
two-story glassed-in solarium, and at outdoor café tables.

The café opens early serving items like cream cheese and Nova on
a bagel and fresh-baked muffins. At Sunday brunch—served from
9:30am to 3pm—a glass of champagne or a Bloody Mary is just
$1.25. Entrées at lunch or dinner might include anything from a salad
of sesame noodles tossed with sweet peppers, broccoli, snow peas,
and grated carrots in French sesame dressing to chicken Taos—
finished with smoked bacon, fresh cilantro, and tomatillo sauce and
served with black beans, seasoned rice, and a cheese quesadilla. Or
you could opt for a sandwich of sliced chicken breast with hickory
bacon, grilled sweet peppers, and onion on foccacia bread. Meats are
roasted fresh on the premises and fish are fresh. Then there are
margaritas ($17.50 for a large pitcherful) served with nachos, banana
splits and ice-cream sundaes, luscious desserts like chocolate/
coconut/sour cream blackout cake, and rum-spiked ice-cream
drinks, as well as a selection of premium wines offered by the glass.
Friday and Saturday nights there's live entertainment—piano, folk,
jazz, or blues.

GEORGETOWN

ADITI, 3299 M St. NW. Tel. 625-6825.
  Cuisine: INDIAN. **Reservations:** Recommended.
$ **Prices:** Appetizers $1.25–$4.95; main courses $5.95–$7.50 at
  lunch, $6.95–$13.95 at dinner. AE, DC, DISC, MC, V.
  Open: Lunch Mon–Sat 11:30am–2:30pm, Sun noon–2:30pm;
  dinner Sun–Thurs 5:30–10pm, Fri–Sat 5:30–10:30pm.

This pristinely charming restaurant provides a serene setting in
which to enjoy first-rate Indian cookery—the kind where
everything is made from scratch and each dish is uniquely
spiced and sauced. You enter a small, red-carpeted, cream-walled
front room, where tables are set with white linen, fresh flowers, and
candles. Above the bar is a display of Kathakali figurines, representing
the classic dance forms of India. A staircase spirals its way past niches
filled with plants to the larger second-level dining space. Soft Indian
music sets the tone for your meal.

A "must" here is the platter of assorted appetizers—bhajia (a
deep-fried vegetable fritter), deep-fried cheese and shrimp pakoras
lightly flavored with chili powder and dry-roasted herbs, and vegetable samosa (a crispy turnover stuffed with spiced potatoes and peas).
It comes with a tangy green cilantro chutney. Favorite entrées include

lamb biryani, an aromatic saffron- and rosewater-flavored basmati rice pilaf tossed with savory pieces of lamb, cilantro, raisins, and almonds. I also love the chicken pasanda (in a mild yogurt-cream sauce seasoned with onion, cumin, fresh cilantro, and almond paste) and the skewered jumbo tandoori prawns, chicken, lamb, or beef—all fresh and fork tender—barbecued in the tandoor (clay oven). Sauces are on the mild side, so if you like your food fiery, inform your waiter. A kachumber salad—diced cucumber, tomato, bell pepper, lettuce, and onion, topped with yogurt and spices—is a refreshing accompaniment to entrées. Excellent vegetable dishes like malai kofta (deep-fried croquettes in a creamy sauce) and fresh-from-the-tandoor-baked breads (like hot, chewy nan) also merit consideration. For dessert, try kheer, a cooling rice pudding garnished with chopped nuts. There's a full bar, including a good choice of wines. Do note that a $4.95 lunch is offered weekdays.

THE AMERICAN CAFE, 1211 Wisconsin Ave., between N and M Sts. Tel. 944-9464.
  Cuisine: AMERICAN. **Reservations:** Not required.
$ **Prices:** Appetizers $3.95–$5.95; main courses $5.95–$14.95; brunch $9.95. AE, CB, DC, DISC, MC, V.
  Open: Mon–Thurs 11am–midnight, Fri–Sat 11am–3am, Sun 10:30am–midnight. Upstairs market/carry-out, Mon–Fri 8am–6pm, Sat–Sun 10am–6pm.

This is one of Georgetown's most popular hangouts. Its angular modern interior, lit by track lighting, offers seating areas divided by oak-framed wire-mesh screens and railings. Brick and rough-hewn stone walls are hung with colorful prints of Washington scenes, exposed pipes overhead are painted in glossy white enamel, and red neon tubing and stars enhance the café's contemporary look. French doors open on a small patio offering a few tables for alfresco dining. The setting is attractive, service is friendly (never any problems about substitutions), and the food is really quite good.

Immense sandwiches, served with your choice of sesame noodles, coleslaw, or creamy potato salad, run the gamut from tarragon chicken tossed with almonds and water chestnuts on a croissant to avocado, Monterey jack, sprouts, and tomato on whole-wheat. There are also snack items such as small cheese pizzas, guacamole and chips, and spicy chicken wings with bleu cheese dip. Among the salad choices are chicken couscous in lemon vinaigrette and a traditional Cobb or Caesar salad. And full entrées, which vary seasonally, might include spicy sausage lasagne served with garlic sticks, a grilled fresh fish entrée, or Caribbean grilled chicken breast served with a baked potato and fresh vegetables. Premium wines are available by the glass, and the bar mixes up delicious specialty drinks—everything from frozen daiquiris to hot mulled cider to Irish cream with hazelnut liqueur, coffee, and whipped cream. For dessert, there's an immense hot-fudge sundae over a chocolate-chip cookie. A special Sunday brunch menu lists such items as eggs Benedict served with freshly squeezed orange juice, red potatoes (sautéed in their skins with basil, onions, and green peppers), muffins or danish, and tea or coffee. And you can also stop by for continental breakfast at the upstairs market—muffins, croissants, and the like.

There are additional American Cafe locations at 227 Massachusetts Ave. NE (tel. 547-8500) and at National Place, 1331 Pennsylva-

nia Ave. NW (tel. 626-0770). Smaller express branches are in Union
Station (tel. 682-0937) and at 1701 Pennsylvania Ave. NW (tel.
833-3434).

**AU PIED DE COCHON, 1335 Wisconsin Ave. NW, just
below O St. Tel. 333-5440.**

Cuisine: FRENCH. **Reservations:** Not accepted.

$ Prices: Appetizers $3–$5; most main courses $6–$11. AE, DC,
MC, V.

Open: Daily 24 hours.

Authentically Parisian in feel, this café/brasserie has been a Georgetown landmark since the 1940s. Its high-ceilinged interior is light and
airy, its walls aclutter with historic Georgetown photographs and
copper pots. Big windows overlook Wisconsin Avenue, and a
whimsical Gallic mural of a pig being led to slaughter by chefs graces
the back wall. Adjoining the main room is a glass-enclosed café with
marble-topped tables—a setting conducive to long Paris-style afternoons over pâtisseries and espresso. History was made here in 1985,
when KGB defector Col. Vitaly Yurchenko, after three months of
leaking sensitive information, eluded his CIA security guard and
slipped out the back door. A biographer claims that Yurchenko, a
cultured man, found the constant company of CIA operatives too
high a price to pay for freedom. A plaque commemorates his seat, and
every year on the anniversary of his escape the CIA agents involved in
the case meet here and quaff Yurchenko shooters (Stoly and Grand
Marnier).

On a more regular basis, joggers and Georgetown students drift in
for an early breakfast of fresh-baked croissants or perhaps eggs and
bacon with pommes frites. Later in the day you might order an
omelet fines herbes with pommes frites and ratatouille, a salade
niçoise, quiche Lorraine, or chicken-and-mushroom-filled crêpe
served with ratatouille and pommes frites, steamed or cold lobster (a
great bargain at just $10.95), or roast duck à l'orange (just $10.25).
Traditional café desserts include crème caramel and chocolate
mousse. There's a full bar, and wines are offered by the glass.

BAMIYAN AFGHAN, 3320 M St. NW. Tel. 338-1896.

Cuisine: AFGHAN. **Reservations:** Recommended.

$ Prices: Appetizers $2.75–$3.25; main courses $5.25–$5.95 at
lunch, $7.25–$13.95 at dinner; fixed-price meal for two $35. AE,
MC, V.

Open: Lunch Mon–Fri 11:30am–3pm; dinner daily 5:30–11pm.

When an ambassador from Afghanistan returned to his homeland,
his chef stayed behind to open this restaurant. Its cuisine is both
interesting—because it consists largely of dishes new to most
Americans—and delicious. Bamiyan Afghan is also quite an attractive place, with its dining room upstairs and a cozy bar/lounge on the
street level. White walls are hung with Afghan rugs and a large oil
painting depicting *booz keshi,* the wild national game played on
horseback and using a dead goat for the ball! Tablecloths of cheerful
Afghani geometric prints, hanging plants, curtained windows, and
candles in glass holders combine to create a cozy atmosphere, which
is enhanced by taped Afghani music.

The food is spicy but not hot unless you request it that way. A
multicourse fixed-price dinner for two includes a demi-carafe of
wine; noodle and vegetable soup with yogurt and ground beef;
deep-fried pastries stuffed with ground beef, chickpeas, and parsley;

chicken pieces marinated in herbs and spices on a skewer; scallion-filled dumplings topped with yogurt and meat sauce; rice; salad; Afghani bread; desserts of baklava, firni (custard), or fried pastry dusted with sugar, cardamom, and pistachio nuts; and coffee or Afghani tea. You can, of course, also order à la carte. The lunch menu highlights beef, chicken, and lamb kebabs served with brown rice, salad, homemade bread, and hot sauce.

CLYDE'S, 3236 M St. NW. Tel. 333-9180. = *Holidays smart casual*

   Cuisine: AMERICAN. **Reservations:** Recommended.
$ Prices: Appetizers $5–$6; burgers, ribs, omelets, salads, sandwiches $5.50–$10.95; dinner specials $8.95–$13.95. AE, DC, DISC, MC, V.
   Open: Mon–Thurs noon–2am, Fri noon–3am, Sat 9am–3am, Sun 9am–2am; brunch Sat–Sun 9am–4pm.

Clyde's has been a favorite watering hole for an eclectic mix of Washingtonians since 1963. You'll see university students, Capitol Hill types, affluent professionals, Washington Redskins, romantic duos, and well-heeled "ladies who lunch" bogged down with shopping bags from Georgetown's posh boutiques. Nancy Reagan's staff once treated her to a birthday lunch here.

   Clyde's is your classic New York–style saloon—a warren of pubby bars and cozy dining areas furnished with bentwood chairs at checkered-clothed tables. The Back Room has wide-plank oak floors, dark oak walls, and amber globe lamps overhead. Ornate brass filigree antique elevator doors divide this room from the Main Bar, which is always mobbed at night. The smaller Atrium Bar has a train theme, with railroad lamps flanking an 1880s mother-of-pearl-inlaid painting of the *Rocky Mountain Limited*. The sunnier Omelette Room, up front, lit by authentic gaslight sconces, features an exhibition kitchen under a copper hood and dark oak walls hung with gilt-framed turn-of-the-century French posters. And last, there's my favorite Clyde's precinct—the light and airy brick-walled Patio Room, a jungle setting with dozens of plants, trees, vines, and ferns flourishing under a skylight ceiling. Big papier-mâché toucans and parrots amid the lush foliage add to the tropical ambience.

   At weekend brunch you can get terrific omelets prepared to order or eggs Benedict with thinly sliced smoked salmon. Throughout the day the menu lists burgers, homemade soups, delicious Maryland lump crabmeat sandwiches, award-winning chili, hickory-smoked barbecued ribs, and salads—plus daily lunch specials such as fresh-made fettuccine tossed with Cajun andouille sausage, tomatoes, and herbs. At dinner, similar specials might include thin-sliced London broil served with roasted potatoes and a vegetable or broiled salmon in hot basil vinaigrette served with rice pilaf and wax-bean salad. A special snack menu offered from 4 to 7pm features "Afternoon Delights" ($2.50 to $4) such as beer-batter shrimp with orange-mustard sauce and hard smoked salmon with black bread and horseradish sauce. Beverage choices range from premium wines by the glass, to Clyde's famous lager, to a milkshake made with Ben & Jerry's ice cream. Desserts—such as a classic creamy cheesecake or a rich mousse made from Belgian Callebaut chocolate—also merit attention.

GREEK PORT RESTAURANT, 1736 Wisconsin Ave. NW, between R and S Sts. Tel. 333-0111.
   Cuisine: GREEK. **Reservations:** Recommended.

$ Prices: Appetizers mostly $3.95–$4.50; main courses $4.25–$12.50. MC, V.

Open: Lunch Mon–Fri 11:30am–2:30pm; dinner Mon–Sat 5:30–11pm.

Macedonian immigrants Moskos and Despina Nomikos opened this homey mom-and-pop restaurant in 1984. It's an unpretentious setting. Light-blue walls are hung with photographs of Greece, and diners sit at tables covered with plastic cloths. Eating here is like visiting a kindly aunt and uncle who delight in providing you with a good, filling meal. Regular customers (of which there are many) kiss Despina good-bye and shake hands with Moskos when they leave. Despina does all the cooking and marketing, somehow managing to procure the best tomatoes of the season for her delicious tomato salad layered with feta cheese and thin-sliced onions and garnished with black olives. Share an order of it along with her homemade taramasalata, soaking up the juices with chunks of French bread. Also worth sharing are entrées of vine leaves stuffed with rice and ground beef and, the pièce de résistance, roast lamb marinated in lemon and garlic, and served with roasted potatoes. Order up a bottle of Boutari (a Greek white wine), and save room for Despina's homemade baklava and a cup of rich Greek coffee. It's a totally satisfying meal. There's a full bar.

HOUSTON'S, 1065 Wisconsin Ave. NW, just below M St. Tel. 338-7760.

Cuisine: AMERICAN. **Reservations:** Not accepted.

$ Prices: Appetizers $1.25–$6.45; main courses $6.25–$15. AE, MC, V.

Open: Sun–Thurs 11:15am–11pm, Fri–Sat 11:15am–1am.

Arrive before or after peak lunch and dinner hours to avoid long lines at the very popular Houston's, where the barbecued ribs are tender and juicy enough to eat with a knife and fork, the large and delicious burgers are made from fresh-ground chuck, and the soups, salads, and desserts are prepared from scratch. A very simpatico ambience further enhances this restaurant's appeal. Exposed brick walls are hung with framed mirrors, an old American flag, and flickering gaslight sconces. Overhead are rough-hewn wood rafters. Most seating is in roomy red leather booths at oak tables, lighting—from dark-green enamel lamps with amber bulbs—is subdued, and the background music is mellow rock and country. An area in the back has many large plants growing under a skylight ceiling.

The same menu is offered throughout the day. A hickory-grilled cheeseburger is served with a choice of iron skillet beans, couscous, fresh-cut thick fries, or coleslaw. You can choose two of these side dishes with an order of barbecued chicken breast or ribs. If you're in the mood for something heartier, there's prime rib with a baked potato, creamed spinach, and house salad; something lighter might be a grilled chicken salad tossed with honey-lime vinaigrette and garnished with a light peanut sauce. The bar serves drinks made with premium liquor brands only and fresh-squeezed juices. And for dessert, an immense chewy brownie topped with vanilla ice cream and Kahlúa is hard to surpass.

LA RUCHE, 1039 31st St. NW, a block below M St. Tel. 965-2684.

Cuisine: COUNTRY FRENCH. **Reservations:** Recommended.
$ **Prices:** Appetizers $3–$5; main courses $6.50–$8.50 at lunch, $9–$14.50 at dinner; fixed-price brunch $9.95. AE, MC, V.
Open: Mon–Fri 11:30am–midnight, Sat 10am–1am, Sun 10am–11pm; brunch Sat–Sun 10am–3pm.

This is a pretty little plant-filled restaurant with cushioned wicker-seated chairs, flower-bedecked tables (candlelit at night), and white walls adorned with framed art posters, French street signs, and baskets. The French countryside ambience is furthered by an outdoor courtyard café with umbrella tables amid lots of plants.

Inside, your eye is likely to be caught by the pastry case filled with exquisite fresh-baked desserts—banana tart with custard and bitter-sweet chocolate, gâteau amande chocolat layered with meringue and whipped cream, a classic tarte aux pommes, and more. Many people take an afternoon break from Georgetown rambles just for dessert and coffee here. Throughout the day menu offerings include a hearty potage parisien with fresh chopped leeks, potatoes, and cream; salade niçoise; a wedge of Brie with apple and French bread; croque monsieur (toasted French bread with ham and cheese); and escargots aux champignons—all the traditional specialties of a Paris brasserie. In addition, there are daily "spécialités du chef Jean-Claude," which might include mussels niçois, bouillabaisse, Algerian couscous (a hearty dish replete with chunks of chicken, eggplant, zucchini, peppers, and chickpeas), and duck à l'orange served with tomato provençal, haricots verts, and sautéed potatoes. There's a full bar, and wines are offered by the bottle, glass, and carafe. The fixed-price brunch includes a mimosa, entrée, and pastry.

NEKEYSA, 1564 Wisconsin Ave., just below Q St. Tel. 337-6500.
Cuisine: PERSIAN. **Reservations:** Recommended.
$ **Prices:** Appetizers $3.95–$4.50; main courses $6.95–$11.95; complete dinner for two $32. DC, MC, V.
Open: Mon–Thurs noon–10pm, Fri–Sat noon–11pm, Sun noon–9pm.

This charming restaurant offers a tranquil setting enhanced by traditional Persian music. Exposed brick walls are hung with Iranian calligraphic art, there are brass urns and live plants, and a posy of fresh flowers adorns each table. More important than its ambience, however, is Nekeysa's delicious, moderately priced, and totally authentic fare, which will add new and exciting colors to your culinary palette.

Begin with an assortment of appetizers such as kashke bademjan (sautéed mashed eggplant in yogurt sauce with a crunchy contrast of mint-flavored crisp-fried onions), mirza ghasemi (eggplant charcoal-roasted to create a charred tang, sautéed with egg, tomatoes, and garlic, and puréed), and fresh grape leaves stuffed with a slightly honey-sweetened mixture of ground beef, rice, split peas, and herbs (mint, coriander, and tarragon). Excellent entrée choices include a kebab of lime-marinated charcoal-grilled boneless chicken breast, subtly spiced and served with basmati rice and grilled tomato; fesenjan (a piquant sweet-and-sour stew with chunks of tender chicken simmered in a spicy sauce of pomegranate, ground walnuts, and sun-dried tomatoes, also served with basmati rice); and shirin polo and murgh (a baked-chicken dish embellished with shredded almonds, candied orange peel, pistachios, and saffron over a bed of sweetened rice). A side dish of homemade yogurt with chopped cucumbers and crushed dried mint makes a perfect foil for these sweetish entrées, as do salad selections. A basket of homemade lavash bread accompanies all entrées. For dessert, I like the light and delicate rollet—a golden cake filled with homemade whipped cream. Nakeysa has no liquor license, so you might consider picking up a bottle of wine at the store across the street.

ADAMS-MORGAN

PEYOTE CAFE, 2319 18th St. NW, between Belmont and Kalorama Rds. Tel. 462-8330.
  Cuisine: SOUTHWEST/TEX-MEX. **Reservations:** Recommended. **Metro:** Woodley Park–Zoo.
$ Prices: Appetizers $3.25–$7.95; sandwiches, salads, burgers $3.50–$9.95; main courses $5.95–$14.95 at dinner, mostly $3.95–$5.95 at brunch. AE, CB, DC, MC, MOST, V.
  Open: Mon–Fri 5pm–1am, Sat–Sun noon–1am. Bar, Sun–Thurs to 2am, Fri–Sat to 3am.

Sharing an Adams-Morgan town house with Roxanne (see below), the Peyote Cafe, occupying the downstairs level, evokes a southwestern roadside eatery with Texas-themed lights (shaped like cowboy boots, lizards, cacti) over the bar, neon beer signs, Santa Fe peach walls decorated with coyotes and armadillos, and an authentic Wurlitzer jukebox stocked with country-western tunes. You can dine at the bar or seated on high chairs at round tables.

It's a casual place, but there's nothing casual about the kitchen. This is inspired cookin'. The café's chili is Lone Star State quality—thick and stewlike with tender chunks of sirloin, tomatoes, and pinto beans, its spicy sauce spiked with Dos Equis beer. Similarly spiked is the chili con queso, a melted-cheese-and-jalapeño dip you eat with tortilla chips. Another noteworthy appetizer: vegetable quesadillas—pan-crisped flour tortillas wrapped around finely minced vegetables spiced with chili peppers; they're served with fresh-made guacamole. Everything here is good, but two entrées are especially irresistible. One is the Tex-Mex mixed grill (pork chop, chicken breast, and chorizo sausage) served with skin-on mashed potatoes (the best ever, topped with ancho-chili gravy), corn on the cob, and chunky homemade applesauce. The other is tacos al carbon—flour tortillas stuffed with grilled pork, melted asadero cheese, shredded lettuce, homemade pico de gallo (made with the freshest market tomatoes), guacamole, and sour cream. At brunch, served weekends, the regular menu is supplemented by entrées like New Orleans pain perdu—rum-soaked French toast topped with pecans, fresh berries, whipped cream, and powdered sugar. There's a full bar, and specialty drinks run the gamut from frozen margaritas and daiquiris (made from scratch) to liqueur-coffee concoctions topped with fresh whipped cream. For dessert, cheesecake studded with chunks of dark and white chocolate and topped with dark cocoa, cherry sauce, chocolate fudge, and fresh strawberries makes an opulent finale.

ROXANNE/ON THE ROX, 2319 18th St. NW, between Belmont and Kalorama Rds. Tel. 462-8330.
  Cuisine: SOUTHWEST. **Reservations:** Recommended. **Metro:** Woodley Park–Zoo.
$ Prices: Appetizers $3.25–$7.95, sandwiches, salads, burgers

$3.95–$8.95; main courses $7.95–$14.95 at dinner, mostly $3.95–$5.95 at brunch. AE, CB, DC, MC, MOST, V.
Open: Mon–Fri 5pm–1am, Sat–Sun noon–1am. Bar, Sun–Thurs to 2am, Fri–Sat to 3am.

Up a flight of stairs from the Peyote Cafe (see above), Roxanne offers similar fare (some menu items are identical) in a somewhat more sophisticated setting, with a display kitchen and seating in tan leather-upholstered banquettes and booths. Though Roxanne is cozy, head to the candlelit rooftop deck area (called On the Rox), weather permitting. Warmed by big heaters, the Rox is open most of the year. It's a delightful setting for alfresco dinners.

The food is worthy of its romantic, starlit venue. There are two specially scrumptious appetizers: Spicy chicken wings are served with a celestial cilantro- and lime-flavored chunky peanut sauce. And plump poached shrimp and scallops, marinated in a mix of avocado, serrano chilies, lime, and cilantro, are served with grenadine-rimmed tequila-soaked orange slices; it all gets wrapped into warm flour tortillas. The mix of flavors is ambrosial. Entrées include the Tex-Mex grill described at Peyote Cafe, always a great choice. Crisp-skinned grilled Muscovy duck, moist and tender, is served over garlicky wilted spinach studded with roasted pumpkin seeds in a green mole (sauce); it comes with blue-corn crêpes. I also like Roxanne's thin-crust pizzas and a pasta dish called fettuccine Toluca, which is tossed with shrimp, chorizo sausage, plum tomatoes, poblano chilies, roasted red peppers, mushrooms, and fresh basil. Like the Peyote, Roxanne adds brunch items on weekends, like blue-cornmeal pancakes served with honey-maple butter. Drinks and desserts are also the same (see above). I usually don't want dessert after such filling fare. One exception is a refreshing gratin of lightly grilled fresh berries in sabayon sauce topped with powdered sugar. There's live music downstairs weekend nights—generally, R&B, jazz, or blues.

4. BUDGET

Washington is filled with budget restaurants. Actually, I often patronize those listed below for reasons other than monetary—the food is great or they're comfortable places to hang out. Many of the "Restaurants at Sightseeing Attractions," below, are also budget eateries.

CAPITOL HILL/UNION STATION

CHESAPEAKE BAGEL BAKERY, 215 Pennsylvania Ave. SE. Tel. 546-0994.
Cuisine: SANDWICHES/SALADS. **Metro:** Capitol South.
$ Prices: Salads $1.50–$4.50; bagel and croissant/sandwiches $1.35–$5. No credit cards.
Open: Mon–Fri 7am–8pm, Sat 7am–6pm, Sun 7am–5pm.
For a good quick meal near the Capitol, it's hard to beat this pleasant mini-cafeteria with impressionist art posters adorning gallery-white walls. The bagels are baked from scratch on the premises, and the aroma is divine. There are 10 varieties (plain, cinnamon raisin,

pumpernickel, whole wheat, poppy, sesame, onion, garlic, salt, and all of the above). Sandwich fillings include cream cheese, walnuts, raisins, and carrots; cream cheese and Nova; chicken salad; chopped liver; and hummus and sprouts, among others. In the same price range are sandwiches on fresh-baked croissants—for example, roast beef with lettuce and mayo or a ham, turkey, Swiss combo with sliced tomato and sprouts. A cup of coffee is 55¢, and for dessert there are brownies, blondies, carrot cake, and such.

There's a Dupont Circle location at 1636 Connecticut Ave. NW, between Q and R Streets (tel. 328-7985), and another at 818 18th St. NW (tel. 775-4690). The menus are the same.

NEAR THE WHITE HOUSE

SHOLL'S CAFETERIA, Esplanade Mall, 1990 K St. NW. Tel. 296-3065.

    Cuisine: AMERICAN. **Reservations:** Not accepted. **Metro:** Farragut West.

$ **Prices:** Appetizers 80¢–90¢; main courses $1.65–$4.95. No credit cards.

    Open: Breakfast Mon–Sat 7–10:30am; lunch 11am–2:30pm; dinner 4–8pm.

 In March 1928, Pennsylvania Dutchman Evan A. Sholl opened this Washington cafeteria, offering fresh, wholesome, inexpensive fare, prayers, and patriotism. Though Mr. Sholl died in 1984, the current owner, his nephew, upholds his uncle's traditions. On every table is a sheet announcing the weekly special (for example, baked ham with peach half), along with a biblical quote or prayer, the slogan "We pray together. . . . We stay together," Sholl's motto ("Live well for less money with quality food at more reasonable

---

Ⓕ FROMMER'S COOL FOR KIDS: RESTAURANTS

The Dirksen Senate Office Buffet (see p. 124) Getting here involves a subway ride through the belly of the Capitol, there's a reduced price for children, and desserts include a make-your-own-sundae bar.

Flight Line (see p. 127) At this airy, very pleasant cafeteria the kids can dig into burgers and pizza, while adults enjoy many other options, even wine. Before you get here, pick up astronaut freeze-dried ice cream for the kids at any museum shop, an intriguing dessert.

Union Station Food Court (see p. 130) Something for everyone, and the setting is very pleasant.

Houston's (see p. 114) Burgers, barbecue, and an ice-cream-topped brownie for dessert.

Chesapeake Bagel Bakery (see p. 117) Quick, easy, and very affordable.

prices"), and perhaps an inspirational poem as well. Sholl's is a homey environment, with soft lighting and carpeted floors. Photographs of the President and Pope John Paul II are prominently displayed on the cream-colored walls.

Everything served here is prepared on the premises. All vegetables are fresh, pies and cakes are homemade, and chopped meat is ground daily. And the prices are not to be believed. At breakfast, load up your tray with scrambled eggs, bacon, biscuits, coffee, orange juice, and home fries for under $3.50. Lunch or dinner entrées might include braised beef and rice, roast turkey and dressing, roast beef, or beef stew with potatoes, carrots, celery, and onions. Add corn or broccoli and a scoop of mashed potatoes for another $1.30, a piece of homemade peach or pumpkin pie for 95¢. It's cheaper than cooking yourself. Or, to quote a Sholl's flyer, "If you have problems with breakfast or dinner, just a meal at Sholl's and you'll be a winner."

DOWNTOWN

REEVE'S RESTAURANT AND BAKERY, 1306 G St. NW. Tel. 628-6350.
Cuisine: AMERICAN. **Reservations:** Not accepted. **Metro:** Metro Center.
$ Prices: Main courses $4.75–$6.05; sandwiches $2.95–$5.55; buffet breakfast $4.95 Mon–Fri, $5.95 Sat and holidays. No credit cards.
Open: Mon–Sat 7am–6pm.

There's no place like Reeve's, a Washington institution since 1886. J. Edgar Hoover used to send a G-man to pick up chicken sandwiches, Lady Bird Johnson and daughter Lynda Bird worked out the latter's wedding plans over lunch here, and the late Helen Hayes always stopped by when she was in town. Closed for a few years when its former building was demolished, Reeve's has reincarnated at a new address offering the identical famous fare and retaining something of its vintage ambience. It's still fronted by a long bakery counter filled with scrumptious pies and cakes. One exultant reviewer compared the strawberry pie—Bess Truman's favorite, by the way—to desserts at Maxim's in Paris. It's delicious, with enormous juicy berries atop a cakey crust. And the familiar brass-railed counter seating on both floors utilizes the original 19th-century wooden stools. The ambience is cheerful. Oak-wainscotted cream walls are hung with pictures of Washington, and soft lighting emanates from wall sconces. Much of the seating is in cozy booths and banquettes.

Reeve's has managed to reassemble most of the old staff, many of whom have been employees for three or four decades. Everything is homemade with top-quality ingredients—the turkeys, chickens, salads, breads, desserts, even the mayonnaise. At breakfast, you can't beat the all-you-can-eat buffet—scrambled eggs, home fries, French toast, pancakes, cinnamon and sticky buns, corned-beef hash, grits, bacon, sausage, stewed and fresh fruit, and biscuits with sausage gravy. At lunch, try a roast turkey sandwich on fresh-baked bread, perhaps with an order of homemade coleslaw or potato salad. Hot entrées run the gamut from golden-brown Maryland crabcakes with fries and coleslaw to Italian sausage subs, to country-fried chicken (three pieces) with mashed potatoes and gravy. And leave room for one of those fabulous pies—strawberry, peach, chocolate cream, key lime, coconut custard . . . you name it. Or, if you like, a butterscotch sundae. No alcoholic beverages are served.

DUPONT CIRCLE

TRIO, 1537 17th St. NW, at Q St. Tel. 232-6305.
Cuisine: AMERICAN. **Reservations:** Not accepted. **Metro:** Dupont Circle.
$ Prices: Appetizers $1–$3; main courses $1.95–$5.35 at breakfast, $4.25–$8.25 at lunch and dinner; burgers and sandwiches $1.55–$5. AE, MC, V.
Open: Daily 7:30am–midnight.

The Trio is a real find. Its comfortable and roomy burgundy leather booths (the kind with coathooks) are filled each morning with local folk checking out the *Washington Post* over big platters of bacon and eggs. Multipaned windows are hung with plants, there are fresh flowers on every table, and in good weather, the awninged outdoor café is always packed. The Trio has been around for four decades— originally Pete and Helen Mallios' mom-and-pop business, now run by son George—and it's on its way to becoming a Washington legend.

The food is fresh, and you can't beat the prices. At breakfast, a meal of fried eggs with bacon, toast, home fries, and coffee comes to about $3.95. The same menu is offered throughout the day, but there are very low priced lunch specials such as crabmeat cakes with tartar sauce, grilled pork chops with applesauce, turkey with cornbread dressing and cranberry sauce, and fried oysters—all served with two side dishes (perhaps baked macaroni au gratin and buttered fresh carrots) and a beverage. The same kind of specials are featured at dinner, when they also include an appetizer and dessert such as key lime pie. In addition, an extensive menu features such typical coffeeshop fare as a chef's salad, chili con carne, and a turkey-salad sandwich. There's a full bar, so a glass of wine with your meal is an option. In fact, there's a surprisingly extensive wine list. A soda fountain turns out hot-fudge sundaes and milkshakes. And that's not all—espresso drinks spiked with liqueurs like Grand Marnier and Frangelico and topped with whipped cream are also available at this eclectic eatery.

GEORGETOWN

GEORGETOWN BAGELRY, 3245 M St. NW. Tel. 965-1011.
Cuisine: SANDWICHES.
$ Prices: Sandwiches $3–$5. No credit cards.
Open: Mon–Sat 6am–9pm, Sun 6am–6pm.

Here, ex–New Yorker and bagel maven Erik Koefoed turns out about 5,000 bagels a day—plain, sesame, poppyseed, onion, garlic, salt, garlic-salt, caraway, rye, onion rye, pumpernickel, oatmeal-raisin, cinnamon-raisin, whole-wheat, and bran. And that's not to mention bialys. You can get them spread with cream cheese and lox or an array of other fillings such as homemade chicken salad, hummus and sprouts, even hot pastrami. Homemade brownies, carrot cakes, fruit salad, and other desserts are also inexpensive. Come by early in the morning to enjoy an oven-fresh bagel with fresh-squeezed orange juice and coffee over the morning paper (it's sold here too). It's nice to sit by the big windows and watch Georgetown coming to life.

PATISSERIE CAFE DIDIER, 3206 Grace St. NW, off Wisconsin Ave. just below M St. Tel. 342-9083.
Cuisine: CONTINENTAL/PATISSERIE. **Reservations:** Not accepted.
$ **Prices:** Main courses $4.50–$7.50; desserts $1–$3.75. DC, DISC, MC, V.
Open: Tues–Sun 8am–7pm.

This is the most delightful place in town for continental breakfasts, light lunches, and afternoon teas. Dieter Schorner, former pastry chef at New York's haute-cuisine bastions Le Cirque and La Côte Basque, came to D.C. in 1988 as pâtissier of restaurateur Warner LeRoy's Potomac. Potomac went under, but Schorner stayed behind and opened this Georgetown café specializing in classic European pastries. His marvelous creations have already graced many of Washington's most fashionable parties. For National Symphony Orchestra Director Mstislav Rostropovich's 60th birthday, he fashioned a cello-shaped birthday cake complete with bow and strings of pulled sugar—plus 800 miniature replicas for guests!

His café is charming—light and sunny, with 18th-century lithographs on pale-peach walls, fresh flowers adorning the tables, and exquisite larger floral arrangements here and there. The tempting pastries are displayed in a glass case—oven-fresh croissants worthy of Paris, classic tarte tatins, lemon tarts, strüdels, mini-fruit tartlets and eclairs, and sumptuous creations such as a rich Swiss chocolate cake lavishly iced and filled with chocolate ganache. And while you're decadently eating cake for breakfast, why not accompany it with real hot chocolate made from scratch with chunks of Belgian chocolate? Great coffee, cappuccino, espresso, freshly brewed tea, and café au lait are also options. At lunchtime, you can enjoy homemade soups (for example, saffron-flavored cream of mussel) served with a basket of fresh-baked breads, quiches, soufflés (shrimp, spinach, mushroom), a daily changing menu of sandwiches (perhaps Camembert or tarragon chicken salad on baguette or croissant), salads, cold platters (seafood, saucisson, chicken), cheese plates, and, occasionally, crabcakes.

THE TOMBS, 1226 36th St. NW, at Prospect St. Tel. 337-6668.
Cuisine: AMERICAN. **Reservations:** Not accepted.
$ **Prices:** Appetizers/light fare $4.25–$5.75; burgers, sandwiches, salads $3.95–$7.75; main courses mostly $6.50–$8.95. AE, DISC, MC, V.
Open: Mon–Thurs 11am–2am, Fri–Sat 11am–3am, Sun 10am–2am; brunch Sun 10am–3pm.

For good food, moderate prices, and simpatico ambience, you can't beat this classic college watering hole which occupies a converted 19th-century Federal-style home. Its name derives from a London pub in the T. S. Eliot poems, *Old Possum's Book of Practical Cats*. Innlike and cozy, with low ceilings, brick floors, and a working fireplace, it's a favorite hangout of both local residents and Georgetown University students (Bill Clinton was a frequent patron during his college years) and faculty. They congregate at the central bar and surrounding tables, where walls are hung with old sporting prints and lithographs from the original

Harper's, Spanish-American War recruiting posters, and brass lanterns. I prefer to sit in the less rambunctious room called "the Sweeps." Down a few steps, its exposed brick walls are hung with vintage rowing-motif prints, along with oars from Yale, Columbia, and other college teams. Seating is in comfortable red leather banquettes.

The menu offers a wide selection of burgers and sandwiches served with steak fries (Philadelphia cheese steak on a sub, Chesapeake crabcake on a roll with tartar sauce, roast turkey breast with cranberry sauce), chili, and salads, along with a few more serious entrées such as sliced London broil with a baked potato and vegetable. From 5pm on there are low-priced nightly specials—perhaps broiled salmon filet stuffed with spinach, topped with herbed cream sauce, and served with rice and vegetables. There are similar specials at lunch. Everything on the menu is fresh and delicious. Beer prices are low to accommodate the student crowd, and a few premium wines are offered by the glass each night. Lager, brewed to German standards with no additives or preservatives, is a specialty. And the fresh-baked desserts are stupendous. Try the toll-house pie or densely moist chocolate brownie topped with ice cream and a dollop of real whipped cream. A special brunch menu offering items such as eggs Maryland (spinach, crabmeat, and poached eggs on an English muffin topped with hollandaise) is featured on Sunday. Arrive at off-peak hours to avoid a wait for tables.

ZED'S, 3318 M St. NW. Tel. 333-4710.

Cuisine: ETHIOPIAN. **Reservations:** Accepted for large parties only.

$ Prices: Salads $3.75 at lunch, $4.75 at dinner; main courses $5.95–$7.75 at lunch, $6.50–$9.95 at dinner. AE, MC, V.

Open: Sun–Thurs 11am–11pm, Fri–Sat 11am–1:30am.

Though this spicy cuisine has long been popular in Washington, it's not always easy to find restaurants offering truly authentic, high-quality Ethiopian fare. Such a one is Zed's, a charming little place with Ethiopian paintings, posters, and artifacts adorning pine-paneled walls and coral-clothed tables set with fresh flowers. Ethiopian music enhances the ambience. Zed's two dining floors are particularly cozy at night by candlelight.

Everything here is made from scratch using spices imported from Ethiopia. This is a healthy cuisine, with a minimum of fat used in cooking. It's eaten *sans* utensils—a sourdough crêpelike bread called injera (made fresh daily from an African grain called teff) is used to scoop up food. Items listed as *watt* are hot and spicy; *alitchas* are milder and more delicately flavored. I love both the chicken dishes here. Doro watt is chicken stewed in a tangy hot red-chili-pepper sauce; it comes with a hard-boiled egg that has simmered in the sauce. I love that egg, but equally scrumptious is infillay—strips of tender chicken breast flavored with seasoned butter and honey wine and served with a delicious chopped spinach and rice side dish. Also highly recommended are the flavorful lamb dishes, a deep-fried whole fish, and steamed shrimp with sautéed onions, garlic, and red chili peppers. And vegetables have never been tastier. You get a choice of one with each entrée, but consider ordering extras such as garlicky chopped collard greens, red lentil purée in spicy red-pepper sauce, or a purée of roasted yellow split peas mixed with onions, peppers, and garlic (it's served cold, a refreshing taste contrast). Half-portions are available. Other marvelous side dishes are cooked bulgur wheat blended with herbed butter and marvelous lemony fresh-made tomato or potato salads spiked with hot green chili peppers. There's a full bar. Drink options include Ethiopian wines and beers as well as after-dinner coffees with liqueurs. And should you have the inclination, there are Italian pastries for dessert.

ADAMS-MORGAN

MIXTEC, 1792 Columbia Rd. Tel. 332-1011.
    Cuisine: MEXICAN. **Reservations:** Not accepted. **Metro:** Woodley Park–Zoo.
$ **Prices:** Appetizers $3.95–$5.25; main courses $4.75–$9.95. MC, V.
    Open: Sun–Thurs 11am–10:30pm, Fri–Sat 11am–midnight.

Having lived in Texas for a time, I'm real finicky about Mexican food. Mixtec lives up to my lofty Lone Star standards. This Adams-Morgan eatery serves up authentic regional cuisine in a cheerful setting, with an open kitchen and seating in gaily painted wicker-seat ladderback chairs at checker-clothed tables. Colorful paper lanterns are suspended overhead, and Mexican music provides south-of-the-border ambience.

Delicious corn tortillas, made fresh on the premises, enhance whatever they're stuffed with. Start out with an appetizer of queso fundido—a bubbling hot dish of broiled Chihuahua cheese topped with shredded spicy chorizo sausage and flavored with jalapeños and cilantro. The freshly prepared guacamole is also excellent. An interesting side dish is cebollitas al carbon—spring onions lightly grilled in olive oil and flavored with fresh lime juice. Tacos al carbon, pieces of spicy grilled beef, come wrapped in small corn tortillas with three sauces—a purée of green tomatillos flavored with onion and garlic, a hot red-chili sauce, and a salsa cruda of chopped tomatoes, onions, jalapeños, and cilantro. A similar dish, tacos al pastor, comprises small corn tortillas stuffed with pork that has been marinated overnight in mild guajillo peppers, fresh garlic, cumin, black pepper, and chicken broth. All these dishes are in the $3.95 to $5.25 range, and if you order a few of them you'll enjoy a hearty meal and diverse culinary thrills. Full entrées served with rice and beans include the house specialty, pollo en mole—broiled chicken in a rich sauce of five peppers (mulato, gaujillo, pasillo, ancho, and arbol), sunflower and sesame seeds, onions, garlic, almonds, cinnamon, and chocolate. There's a good choice of Mexican beers. For dessert, try homemade flan flavored with brandy and orange and lemon peel. And if you want to try your hand at Mexican cooking, there's a small grocery on the premises selling the requisite spices, mole pastes, sweet Mexican breads, and more.

5. RESTAURANTS AT SIGHTSEEING ATTRACTIONS

Given the hectic round of Washington sightseeing, you'll sometimes want to save time by eating at or near sightseeing attractions. Here's a rundown of restaurants right in the Smithsonian, the Capitol, the

Supreme Court, the Library of Congress, and the Kennedy Center. Check out other sections of this chapter to locate additional restaurants close to sights you'll be visiting.

THE CAPITOL

You can rub elbows with senators and congresspeople if you dine in the Capitol—a good choice when you're touring the building.

DIRKSEN SENATE OFFICE BUILDING SOUTH BUFFET ROOM, 1st and C Sts. NE. Tel. 224-4249.
  Cuisine: AMERICAN. **Reservations:** Not accepted. **Metro:** Capitol South or Union Station.
$ **Prices:** Fixed-price buffet $7.75 adults, $5.25 children under 12, plus 15% gratuity. MC, V.
  Open: Lunch only, Mon–Fri 11:30am–2:30pm.

This is a marvelous lunchtime option, featuring lavish all-you-can-eat meals. To get here, you can take a free subway that runs through the underbelly of the Capitol, a fun trip—ask Capitol police for directions. You can also go directly to the Dirksen Building, of course, in which case your closest Metro is Union Station. The marble-colonnaded art deco setting for these buffets is most attractive, with seating in comfortable dark-green leather chairs at white-linened, flower-bedecked tables. You can help yourself to unlimited viands from the carvery station (perhaps roast beef or leg of lamb), about eight additional hot entrées, vegetables, potatoes, rice, pasta, a full salad and fruit bar, a wide choice of desserts (including a make-your-own-sundae bar), soft drinks, and tea, coffee, or milk.

HOUSE OF REPRESENTATIVES RESTAURANT, Room H118, at the south end of the Capitol. Tel. 225-6300.
  Cuisine: AMERICAN REGIONAL. **Reservations:** Not accepted. **Metro:** Capitol South.
$ **Prices:** Appetizers $1.05–$5.95; main courses $4.20–$9.50. AE, DC, DISC, MC, V.
  Open: Breakfast Mon–Fri 9–11am; lunch Mon–Fri 1:30–2:30pm when Congress is in session, Mon–Fri 9am–2:30pm when Congress is not in session.

Most impressive of all Capitol eateries open to the public, the House Restaurant consists of two plush dining rooms. Both are beautifully appointed. In one, walls are hung with gilt-framed Federal mirrors, historic prints, and a Bierstadt landscape, and lighting emanates from crystal sconces and graceful Georgian chandeliers. The other has high ceilings with beautiful moldings, floor-to-ceiling windows framed by swagged satin draperies, and a large gilt-framed Brumidi fresco of George Washington receiving Cornwallis's letter of surrender at Yorktown. White-linened tables are adorned with fresh flowers.

Bean soup has been a featured item here since 1904, when Speaker of the House Joseph G. Cannon ordered it only to find that it had been omitted from the menu because the day was too hot for hearty soups. "Thunderation," roared Cannon, "I had my mouth set for bean soup. . . . From now on, hot or cold, rain, snow, or shine, I want it on the menu every day!" And so it has been ever since. Prices are very reasonable for such a lofty setting. A breakfast of two eggs, homemade biscuits, sausage patty, fresh-squeezed orange juice, and coffee is under $5. At lunch, the famous bean soup is $1.25. Other choices might include grilled Pacific salmon, Maryland crabcakes, or roast prime rib au jus. There are also deli sandwiches and burgers, and daily specials always include one low-cholesterol/low-salt entrée. Seven wines (representing various regions of the country) are offered by the glass daily. For dessert, a butterscotch sundae is a treat, though apple pie seems more appropriate. Who knows, you might even get to see your congressperson.

REFECTORY, first floor, Senate side of the Capitol. Tel. 224-4870.

    Cuisine: AMERICAN. **Reservations:** Not accepted. **Metro:** Capitol South.

$ **Prices:** Appetizers $1.45–$5.70; main courses $3.50–$9.95. MC, V.

    Open: Mon–Fri 8am–4pm (later if the Senate is in session).

Another good choice for Capitol meals, this charming dining room with vaulted ceilings and wainscotted gray walls offers light fare. A big breakfast—eggs, bacon, grits, juice, coffee, and toast—can be obtained here for just $3.25. Lunch items might include a roast-beef sandwich with mashed potatoes and gravy or a cold chunky chicken salad plate with seasonal fruits. There are also sandwiches, burgers, and salads. Try hot pecan pie or a hot-fudge sundae for dessert.

THE CORCORAN

CAFE AT THE CORCORAN, 17th St. NW, between E St. and New York Ave. Tel. 638-3211.

    Cuisine: AMERICAN/CONTINENTAL. **Reservations:** Not accepted. **Metro:** Farragut West or Farragut North.

$ **Prices:** Main courses $5.95–$9.95; afternoon tea sampler $5.95 for one, $9.95 for two; buffet jazz brunch $15.95 adults, $8.50 children under 12. No credit cards.

    Open: Mon and Wed–Sat 11am–4:30pm, Thurs 11am–8:30pm; brunch Sun 11:30am–3pm.

This museum café couldn't be more lovely. Under a lofty skylight ceiling, it's ensconced by fluted Doric columns and neoclassic marble statuary. Flower-bedecked tables are set amid tall palms in terra-cotta pots. The menu is quite "haute" for a museum eatery, featuring entrées like boneless breast of chicken with banana-curry sauce and wild-mushroom salad, a Caesar salad topped with grilled chicken, and paper-thin slices of smoked salmon served with herbed Neuchatel cheese, garden-fresh tomatoes, and foccacia bread. Fresh-baked desserts include key lime pie. Afternoon tea includes a selection of cheeses with tea biscuits, fresh fruit, a pot of tea, and freshly baked currant scones with Devonshire cream and strawberry preserves.

Do stop by on Sunday for a buffet brunch, with live jazz and gospel music. The fare highlights Créole and southern dishes—catfish étouffé, oyster-and-corn pudding, blackened redfish, andouille sausage, sticky chicken, grits, dirty rice, and more—along with a honey-baked ham or steamship of beef, potato dishes, salads, fresh fruits and vegetables, breads, desserts, coffee or tea, and a mimosa or orange juice.

KENNEDY CENTER

ENCORE CAFE, New Hampshire Ave. NW, at Rock Creek Pkwy. Tel. 416-8560.

Cuisine: AMERICAN. **Metro:** Foggy Bottom.
$ Prices: Most items $4.50–$6. No credit cards.
Open: Daily 11am–8pm.

An inexpensive choice is this attractive cafeteria with windows all around providing gorgeous city views. Typical entrées here: baked trout with mashed potatoes and a medley of fresh vegetables, Spanish paella, and chilled salmon filet with pecan-studded wild rice. Sandwiches, homemade soups, pizza, salads, wine, and beer are available, and there are fresh-baked pastries such as apple-cinnamon cobbler for dessert. From 5 to 8pm you can order a fresh-carved prime-rib dinner here, with baked potato and vegetable, for $10.95.

ROOF TERRACE RESTAURANT, New Hampshire Ave. NW, at Rock Creek Pkwy. Tel. 416-8555.

Cuisine: AMERICAN REGIONAL. **Reservations:** Recommended. **Metro:** Foggy Bottom.
$ Prices: Roof Terrace, appetizers $4–$5.50 at lunch, $6–$9 at dinner; main courses $9.95–$12.95 at lunch, $21–$24 at dinner; three-course fixed-price brunch $24.95, fixed-price dinner $33. Hors d'Oeuvrerie, light-fare items $8–$10. AE, CB, DC, MC, V.
Open: Roof Terrace, lunch daily 11:30am–3pm; dinner daily 5:30–9pm; brunch Sun 11:30am–3pm. Hors d'Oeuvrerie, daily 5pm to half an hour after the last show.

A meal in this fine dining room adds a glamorous note to an evening at the theater. It's extremely plush, with ornate chandeliers suspended from a lofty ceiling, immense windows providing panoramic views of the Potomac, and Louis XV–style chairs at white-linened tables. Potted palms and big floral arrangements further adorn the luxe ambience.

Menus change seasonally. On a recent visit, dinner appetizers included crabcakes in Dijon-mustard sauce and lamb sausage and a grilled vegetable and goat-cheese terrine. Among the entrées were walnut- and herb-roasted rack of lamb and grilled salmon steak with potato-leek crust. The signature dessert here is chocolate Concorde cake—chocolate meringue topped with chocolate ganache and chocolate mousse. At lunch, lighter fare is an option—such as a sandwich of smoked turkey, avocado, and grilled tomato with honey-mustard dressing on a sourdough-potato roll. Many premium wines are offered by the glass.

After-theater munchies and cocktails are served in the adjoining and equally plush **Hors d'Oeuvrerie.** I love to stop here after a show for a glass of wine and late supper—perhaps a wild-mushroom and eggplant strüdel or cold lobster salad on a chive-buckwheat pancake. It's gourmet snack fare. Desserts and coffee are also available.

LIBRARY OF CONGRESS

CAFETERIA, James Madison Memorial Building of the Library of Congress, 101 Independence Ave. SE. Tel. 707-8300.

Cuisine: AMERICAN. **Metro:** Capitol South.
$ Prices: Main courses $2–$3; sandwiches $2.60–$3.20. No credit cards.
Open: Breakfast Mon–Fri 9–10:30am; lunch, Mon–Fri 12:30–2pm; light fare Mon–Fri 2–3:30pm.

Ⓢ This facility has a classy sixth-floor cafeteria open to the public. The decor is tasteful (wall-to-wall carpeting, Breuer chairs at oak-framed white tables, a wall of windows for panoramic city views), the food fresh and homemade. Hot entrées change daily; they might include old-fashioned beef stew, Swedish meatballs over noodles, homemade pizza, or crabcakes with tartar sauce. A stir-fry station and special-event station (serving daily-changing fare—Mexican, pasta, Chinese, etc.) are options. Selections from the salad bar begin at 29¢ an ounce for such items as greens, tomatoes, pasta salads, Greek salad, Caesar salad, egg salad, mushrooms, chickpeas, beans, cheeses, and sprouts. Vegetables might include broccoli, noodles with mushrooms, mashed and au gratin potatoes, sautéed dilled tomatoes, and spinach soufflé. There are also sandwiches, fresh-baked pies and cakes, and a full array of breakfast items.

MONTPELIER ROOM, James Madison Memorial Building of the Library of Congress, 101 Independence Ave. SE. Tel. 707-8300.
   Cuisine: AMERICAN. **Reservations:** Recommended for parties of four or more. **Metro:** Capitol South.
$ **Prices:** Fixed-price lunch $8.50. MC, V.
   Open: Lunch Mon–Fri 11:30am–2pm. **Closed:** Aug to mid-Sept.

Ⓢ Adjoining the James Madison cafeteria (details above), the Montpelier Dining Room offers a marvelous fixed-price lunch buffet. It's a lovely carpeted room, with panoramic views (including the Capitol dome) from white-draped windows on two sides, tables adorned with fresh flowers, oak-paneled walls, and an elegant dessert display table with a floral centerpiece. The fixed-price lunch served here is one of the best deals in town. Menus change daily. On a recent visit it included cream of broccoli soup, prime rib, lyonnaise potatoes, honeyed carrots, bread and butter, beverage, and salad bar; desserts were $1.75 extra. Wine and beer are available by the glass. Friday is the Montpelier's prime-rib day.

NATIONAL AIR & SPACE MUSEUM

FLIGHT LINE, Independence Ave. at 4th St. SW. Tel. 371-8778.
   Cuisine: AMERICAN. **Metro:** L'Enfant Plaza.
$ **Prices:** Main courses, sandwiches, salads $3.25–$6. MC, V
   Open: Daily 10am–5pm.

This major Mall museum features a 39,400-square-foot restaurant complex consisting of Flight Line, an 800-seat cafeteria on the main level, and the Wright Place (see below), an elegant full-service dining room on the mezzanine. The two eateries occupy a conservatorylike glass building, with floor-to-ceiling windows on both levels offering panoramic views of the Mall and Capitol. Surrounding terraces are lushly planted and landscaped with seasonal flowers.

Flight Line, under a Tinker-Toy assemblage of white-steel tubing, is carpeted in forest green and handsomely furnished with marble-topped pine tables. Needless to say, with all those windows it's bright and sunny inside. The self-service fare is reasonably priced, fresh, and tasty. It's displayed on an immense octagonal food counter with buffet stations for salads, hot entrées (such as baked lasagne, meatloaf, and fried chicken), hot soups and chili, burgers, vegetables, fresh-baked breads and pastries, pastas and pizzas, fresh fruit, sandwiches, wine and beer, even bottled waters.

THE WRIGHT PLACE, Independence Ave. at 4th St. SW. Tel. 371-8777.

    Cuisine: AMERICAN. **Reservations:** Recommended (you must call between 9 and 11am). **Metro:** L'Enfant Plaza.

$ **Prices:** Main courses $6.25–$10.95; sandwiches and salads $5.95–$8.95. AE, MC, V.

    Open: Daily 11:30am–3pm.

Upstairs from Flight Line (see above), this is a plush, full-service restaurant enclosed by a chrome railing and planters of greenery. Tables are adorned with fresh flowers, and pale-gray walls are hung with vintage aviation photographs from the museum's collection. The city views here, being higher up, are especially great. The menu changes seasonally. Choices could include appetizers of crab gumbo and white pizza (topped with smoked provolone, parmesan, and goat cheeses with a julienne of fresh basil). And entrées run the gamut from sandwiches (such as marinated grilled breast of chicken with honey-mustard sauce) served with homemade french fries, to a hearty Brunswick stew served with salad and fresh-baked corn muffins. Wine and micro-brewery beers are available, and there's a low-priced children's menu with items such as a grilled-cheese sandwich, fries, and milk. Yummy fresh-baked desserts—like key lime pie and warm apple cobbler with a scoop of vanilla ice cream—change daily.

NATIONAL GALLERY OF ART

CONCOURSE BUFFET, on the Mall, between 3rd and 7th Sts. NW. Tel. 347-9401.

    Cuisine: AMERICAN. **Metro:** Archives or Judiciary Square.

$ **Prices:** Main courses $4–$5.50. AE, DISC, MC, V.

    Open: Mon–Sat 10am–3pm, Sun 11am–4pm; extended hours in summer.

Set in the concourse connecting the two wings of the National Gallery is this cheerful cafeteria with seating amid planters and potted palms. Good acoustics keep the noise level bearable, and efficient operation keeps the lines moving quickly. A good choice here is the create-your-own-salad bar—$2 for greens, 60¢ to $1 for such additional items as grated cheese, cucumbers, chopped egg, peas, pepperoni, cherry tomatoes, bacon, and mushrooms. Other choices are croissant sandwiches, pizza, frozen yogurts with varied toppings, burgers and hot dogs, a carvery for deli sandwiches, even a few hot entrées each day—perhaps roast beef with mashed potatoes, Idaho rainbow trout, or Italian vegetable quiche. There are fresh-baked desserts, and wine and beer are available.

NATIONAL GALLERY RESTAURANTS, on the Mall, between 3rd and 7th Sts. NW. Tel. 347-9401.

    Cuisine: INTERNATIONAL. **Reservations:** Not accepted. **Metro:** Archives or Judiciary Square.

$ **Prices:** Cascade Espresso Bar, menu items $2.95–$5.95. Terrace and Garden Cafés, main courses $5.25–$10. AE, DISC, MC, V.

    Open: Cascade Espresso Bar, Mon–Sat noon–4pm, Sun noon–5pm. Terrace Café, Mon–Sat 11am–3pm, Sun noon–6pm (extended hours in summer). Garden Café, Mon–Sat 11am–3pm, Sun noon–6:30pm (extended hours in summer).

There are three charming restaurants within the National Gallery itself, all of which provide restful settings and good food. And an attractive lunch spot with waiter service is nothing to scorn when you've been trudging around museums all day. The **Cascade Espresso Bar,** with marble tables amid potted palms, is the least secluded, since it adjoins the above-described cafeteria, though it does overlook a waterfall. The **Terrace Café,** in the East Building, overlooks the Mall, and the fern- and flower-bordered **Garden Café,** in the West Building, is under a skylight with tables around a marble fountain with a late Renaissance bronze *Venus and Cupid.*

The Terrace and Garden Cafés have similar menus listing about five items each day. They change from time to time (often reflecting current exhibits), but might typically include a plate of chilled poached salmon served on a bed of spinach pasta with a basket of bread; a salmagundi salad (greens with Cheddar cheese, eggs, black olives, anchovies, and Virginia ham); a cheese-and-fruit plate served with pâté and a glass of wine; a Caesar salad topped with grilled chicken; and English spring lamb stew. Fresh-baked pastries and delicious hot-fudge sundaes are among your dessert options at both eateries, as are wine, beer, and cappuccino/espresso.

The Cascade, an espresso/cappuccino/wine bar, features mini-croissant and tea sandwiches served with fresh fruit, fruit and cheese plates, and exquisite desserts.

NATIONAL PORTRAIT GALLERY

PATENT PENDING, 8th and F Sts. NW. Tel. 357-1571.
   Cuisine: AMERICAN. **Metro:** Gallery Place.
$ **Prices:** All items under $5; salad bar items 27¢ per ounce. No credit cards.
   Open: Continental breakfast Mon–Fri 10–10:30am; lunch daily 11am–3pm; coffee and desserts daily to 3:30pm.

Just off the courtyard that connects the Museum of American Art and the National Portrait Gallery is this tiny cafeteria. It's pristinely charming inside, with white marble floors and white walls hung with art posters, but the main lure of Patent Pending is its courtyard tables under the elms amid sculptures, flower beds, and splashing fountains. At lunch you can create a sandwich to order from an assemblage of breads (rye, pumpernickel, rolls, croissants, whole-wheat, white), meats (roast beef, ham, salami, and sliced turkey breast), cheeses, and other fillings such as egg, chicken salad, and tuna salad. Everything is fresh and prepared from scratch. A salad bar and homemade soups are additional options, and on Wednesday in summer there are barbecue specials such as sirloin or chicken served with corn on the cob. Add a glass of chablis and you've got a lovely picnic.

NEAR THE NATIONAL ZOO

UPTOWN BAKERS, 3313 Connecticut Ave. NW, just north of Macomb St. Tel. 362-6262.
   Cuisine: SANDWICHES/PASTRIES. **Metro:** Cleveland Park.
$ **Prices:** Sandwiches $3.75–$6.50; desserts $1.50–$3.50. No credit cards.
   Open: Daily 7am–8pm.

Though there are eateries in the zoo, their fast-food fare is less than inspiring. A better bet is an alfresco lunch at one of the zoo's very nice picnic areas. Get the fixings at Uptown Bakers—sandwiches on scrumptious fresh-baked breads (baguette, raisin-nut, sourdough, olive, herb, challah, and many more) with yummy fillings like country pâté and Brie with grainy mustard, lean roast beef with creamed horseradish, and fresh mozzarella with roasted red peppers, olive tapenade, and watercress. Foccacia pizzas, too. Uptown's coffee is a blend of Amazon and French roast beans. And oven-fresh desserts run the gamut from the world's best sticky buns to an apple tart topped with light calvados cream and caramel crunch.

SUPREME COURT

SUPREME COURT CAFETERIA, 1st St. NE, between East Capitol St. and Maryland Ave. Tel. 479-3246.
   Cuisine: AMERICAN. **Metro:** Capitol South.
$ Prices: Main courses and sandwiches $2.40–$3.95. No credit cards.
   Open: Breakfast Mon–Fri 7:30–10:30am; lunch Mon–Fri 11:30am–2pm (closed to public noon–12:15pm and 1–1:10pm).
Like the Capitol, the Supreme Court operates under the theory that lawmakers have to eat too, and can't always get out to do so. It's very likely you'll see a justice or two in the ground-floor cafeteria here, an attractive dining facility with appropriately Federalist blue-and-gold carpeting, red leather chairs, and brass chandeliers. The food is good and low priced, with daily soup-and-entrée specials such as New England clam chowder with fish and chips or navy bean soup followed by baked stuffed green pepper with whipped potatoes and broccoli. Sandwiches on fresh-baked croissants, stuffed with chicken salad or roast beef, are served with potato chips and pickles. Full breakfasts are available here as well (with fresh-baked muffins). There's a salad bar, and homemade pies and cakes are just 95¢ to $1.50.

UNION STATION

Since its renovation in the late 1980s, Union Station has become an extremely popular dining choice for both locals and tourists. It offers dozens of restaurants and food vendors in different price ranges, and when you're through dining you can browse the diverse shops (see Chapter 8) or take in a movie at the nine-screen cinema complex on the lower level. Other entertainments here might include strolling singers, orchestral performers, choral groups, and art exhibits. There's validated parking for 1,600 cars (entrance on H Street or Massachusetts Avenue), and of course, the Union Station Metro takes you right to the door.

   On the lower level is a vast **Food Court,** offering an incredible array of low- to medium-priced options. It's all cafeteria-style, with food vendors selling blintzes, falafel, stuffed baked potatoes, burgers, fresh seafood, enchiladas, sushi, fresh-squeezed juices, salad-bar items, fresh baked goods, homemade ice cream, chili, pastrami sandwiches, pizzas, fried-oyster po'boys, biriyani, barbecue, and much more. Ordinarily I tend to dislike food courts because they're big, noisy, and sterile-looking. This one, in line with the lofty quality of the station's renovation, is another story altogether. It's a very attractive facility, enhanced by extensive use of oak and pine, colorful canvas umbrellas over some tables, subtle lighting, live plants, and an exquisite marble floor. In addition, the vast space is divided into a number of seating areas, making for a more intimate ambience.

Pizzeria Uno, Mrs. Field's Cookies, McDonald's, Sbarro, and a branch of the **American Café** (detailed in the "Moderate" section) are also represented on the station's street level. Others to be noted are listed below.

AMERICA, Union Station, 50 Massachusetts Ave. NE. Tel. 682-9555.

Cuisine: AMERICAN. **Reservations:** Recommended. **Metro:** Union Station.

$ Prices: Appetizers $4.75–$6.25; main courses $5.95–$15.95 (most items are $10 or less). AE, DC, MC, V.

Open: Sun–Thurs 11:30am–midnight, Fri–Sat 11:30am–1am. Bar stays open a few hours later.

I always enjoy eating at this New York transplant, with seating on three levels and café tables sprawling out into the Main Hall. Its essentially art deco interior includes WPA-style murals, a large painting of the American West, and a whimsical frieze depicting surfers, athletes, astronauts, and superheroes in outer space. I especially like sitting by the balcony rail overlooking the action below. A vast American-classic menu consisting of hundreds of items is offered throughout the day. Some choices: delicious baked macaroni and cheese, Pecos red chili con carne, sandwiches (Philadelphia cheese steak, New Orleans po'boy, and a New York Reuben, among others), burgers, salads, egg dishes and omelets, and entrées running the gamut from crabcakes to New England roast turkey with stuffing, giblet gravy, and cranberry compote. A list of about 20 desserts includes white-chocolate macadamia-nut brownies, peanut butter pie with vanilla ice cream, and ultra-rich "death-by-chocolate" cake. All bar drinks are available, including a wide selection of domestic beers; nonalcoholic beverages range from milkshakes to lemonade.

CENTER CAFE, Union Station, 50 Massachusetts Ave. NE. Tel. 682-0143.

Cuisine: AMERICAN/MEXICAN/ASIAN. **Reservations:** Accepted for large parties only. **Metro:** Union Station.

$ Prices: Appetizers $4.75–$7.95; main courses $8.95–$14.95. AE, CB, DC, MC, V.

Open: Sun–Thurs 11:30am–10:30pm (bar, to 11:30pm), Fri–Sat 11:30am–midnight (bar, to 12:30am).

This handsome two-level oval mahogany restaurant, the hub of the Main Hall, offers a diverse menu of salads, sandwiches, quesadillas, and fancy pizzas. Entrées include crabmeat-filled lobster ravioli in herbed tomato-cream sauce, blue-corn enchiladas stuffed with chicken and chilies, and hacked roast Oriental chicken with peanut sauce and sesame noodles. The café is also an oyster bar. Good desserts here, too, such as key lime mousse and a "death by chocolate" flourless torte.

SFUZZI, Union Station, 50 Massachusetts Ave. NE. Tel. 842-4141.

Cuisine: ITALIAN. **Reservations:** Recommended. **Metro:** Union Station.

$ Prices: Appetizers $3.25–$5 at lunch, $4.50–$7.25 at dinner;

main courses $8.75–$11 at lunch, $11–$21.50 at dinner; brunch Sun $14.50. AE, CB, DC, MC, V.

Open: Lunch Mon–Tues 11:30am–2:30pm, Wed–Sat 11:30am–5:30pm; dinner Sun–Wed 5:30–9pm, Thurs–Sat 5:30–11pm; brunch Sun 11am–3pm.

An elegant multilevel restaurant in an alcove off the Main Hall, Sfuzzi serves California-influenced Italian fare. Entrées range from pizzas with gourmet toppings (smoked chicken, wild oregano, goat cheese) to citrus-glazed grilled salmon served with haricots verts and crispy new potatoes. There are also many pasta dishes such as spinach lasagne layered with grilled vegetables, portobello mushrooms, and asiago cheese. There's a full bar, and an extensive wine list includes many by-the-glass selections. A fixed-price Sunday brunch includes an extensive antipasto bar, an entrée, and dessert.

STATION GRILL, Union Station, 50 Massachusetts Ave. NE. Tel. 898-4745.

Cuisine: AMERICAN. **Reservations:** Not accepted. **Metro:** Union Station.

$ Prices: Appetizers $4.50–$7; main courses $8.95–$20 (most under $15); sandwiches and salads $5.50–$9.50. AE, MC, V.

Open: Mon–Thurs 8am–10pm, Fri 8am–11pm, Sat 9am–11pm, Sun 9am–10pm.

The Grill is a cozy pub in the West Hall with a gold-painted pressed-tin ceiling and a reproduction of Manet's *Odalisque* over the bar. The menu features classic grill-room fare such as a Reuben sandwich, charcoal-grilled London broil au jus, excellent crabcakes, pasta dishes, burgers, chili, sandwiches, and salads. A full breakfast menu is also offered.

6. SPECIALTY DINING

FOR BRUNCH

I love Sunday brunches, the kind that go on for hours fueled by free-flowing champagne. The following, all worthy choices for this leisurely repast, are described fully in earlier sections in this chapter (see the Restaurant Index at the back of this book for the page numbers).

The **Old Ebbitt Grill,** 675 15th St. NW (tel. 347-4801), a stunning reconstructed 19th-century saloon, serves Sunday brunch (à la carte) from 9:30am to 4pm. Entrées are $5 to $7. Very elegant. Reservations recommended.

Bombay Palace, 1835 K St. NW (tel. 331-0111), offers a marvelous brunch buffet for just $9.95—an opportunity to sample a variety of gourmet northern Indian dishes. The Palace is a deluxe restaurant that catered meals for the late Prime Minister Rajiv Gandhi. Brunch is served on Saturday and Sunday from noon to 2:30pm. Reservations recommended.

Or perhaps you'd like a Chinese brunch. Another elegant dining room, **Sichuan Pavilion,** 1820 K St. NW (tel. 466-7790), offers a $10.95 fixed-price brunch on Saturday and Sunday from noon to 4pm. It includes an appetizer, soup, entrée, a glass of wine or a mimosa, and tea.

LATE-NIGHT/24-HOUR DINING

Washington's not a late-night town unless you count the action at 5 or 6am when the workaholic population gets into gear for the workday ahead. In Georgetown, **Au Pied de Cochon,** 1335 Wisconsin Ave. NW (tel. 333-5440), is one place that never closes. Nearby and under the same ownership, **Aux Fruits de Mer** stays open till 4am on Thursday, 5am on Friday and Saturday. **Kramerbooks & Afterwords, A Café,** 1517 Connecticut Ave. NW, at Dupont Circle (tel. 387-1462), keeps late weekend hours too, staying open continuously from Friday at 7:30am through Sunday at 1am.

WHAT TO SEE & DO IN WASHINGTON, D.C.

People often come to Washington for a weekend expecting to see all the sights. Talk about life in the fast lane! The Smithsonian Institution alone consists of over a dozen museums plus the National Zoo. Then there are the monuments and memorials, the White House, the Capitol, the Supreme Court, the Library of Congress, the FBI, the Kennedy Center, the Holocaust Museum, the National Archives, and the National Cathedral—major sights one and all. About a dozen other very interesting attractions vie for your sightseeing time, and it's nice to get over to Georgetown, take a stroll on the canal, or visit nearby Mount Vernon, Arlington, and Alexandria.

There's so much to see that you should consider spending at least a week. Even then, remember that you can't see everything, and it's more rewarding to see a few attractions thoroughly than to race through dozens. To make the most of your time, read the following listings and plan a reasonably relaxed sightseeing itinerary focusing on the sights that interest you most. As you plan, keep in mind geographic proximity (don't waste energy zigzagging back and forth across town); days and hours attractions are open; and applicable warnings about arriving early to avoid long lines or secure necessary tickets. "Special Passes for VIP Tours" in "Before You Go," in Chapter 2, tells you how to obtain tickets ahead of time for VIP tours to some attractions.

Since even friends I've personally counseled to take it easy have exhausted themselves sightseeing in Washington, my advice to program relaxation into every touring day will no doubt go unheeded. For the record, I do suggest an occasional long leisurely lunch and visits to relaxing outdoor attractions. Tour the beautiful gardens at Dumbarton Oaks, take a river cruise, or plan a picnic at the Arboretum—anything that gets you off your museum-weary feet for a while. Speaking of those feet, you'll be on them a lot in Washington. Comfortable shoes are essential to bearing up under the rigors of sightseeing, and during sweltering summer days running shoes, shorts, and a T-shirt (or whatever little attire the shape you're in will tolerate) is the ideal costume.

Most museums offer highlight tours (call in advance for exact hours), a good way to get a meaningful overview in a limited time.

The good news: Almost everything is free.

SUGGESTED ITINERARIES

IF YOU HAVE ONE DAY   Make the Mall your destination, visiting whichever museums best suit your interests. Rest up, have a leisurely dinner (this advice pertains to every day's itinerary), and visit the Lincoln Memorial at night.

IF YOU HAVE TWO DAYS   Spend your first day as suggested above. Start your second day with a tour of the Capitol, followed by a tour of the Supreme Court. After a relaxing lunch, spend the afternoon visiting the Washington Monument, walking around the Tidal Basin, and seeing the Jefferson Memorial. If the weather makes this plan unfeasible, continue visiting Mall museums (you won't even have scratched the surface in one day). Have dinner in Georgetown and stroll the shops.

IF YOU HAVE THREE DAYS   Spend your first two days as outlined above.

In the morning of your third day, tour the White House and the National Archives. In the afternoon, visit the Vietnam Veterans Memorial, and, if you haven't already done so, the Lincoln Memorial. Or in bad weather, tour the National Cathedral or some of Washington's off-the-Mall art museums (Phillips Collection, National Portrait Gallery, Museum of American Art, or the Corcoran, for instance). See Chapter 9 for evening suggestions.

IF YOU HAVE FIVE DAYS OR MORE   Spend your first three days as suggested above.

On the fourth day, get an early start taking the FBI tour, and spend the rest of the morning at Ford's Theatre. Give over the afternoon to outdoor activities—the zoo, a hike along the C&O Canal, the museum and gardens at Dumbarton Oaks, or the Arboretum. Or in bad weather, visit the indoor U.S. Botanic Garden and Union Station. See Chapter 9 for evening suggestions.

On the fifth day, plan an entire day visiting Alexandria, Virginia. Or spend the morning touring Mount Vernon and the afternoon seeing the sights you've missed. See Chapter 9 for evening suggestions.

---

1. THE TOP ATTRACTIONS

These attractions may or may not strike you as major, and nowhere is it written that you must see them all. Give equal consideration to sights and outdoor activities listed later in this chapter when planning your itinerary. These are, however, the sights most tourists choose to visit on trips to Washington.

THE THREE MAJOR HOUSES OF GOVERNMENT

Three of the most visited sights in Washington are the buildings housing the executive, legislative, and judicial branches of the United

States government. All stunning edifices, they offer considerable insight into the workings of our system.

THE WHITE HOUSE, 1600 Pennsylvania Ave. NW (visitor entrance gate on East Executive Ave.). Tel. 456-7041.

⭐ "I never forget," said Franklin Delano Roosevelt in one of his fireside chats, "that I live in a house owned by all the American people." Not only do Americans own the White House, they're welcome to visit, making it almost unique among world residences of heads of state. The White House has been the scene of many great moments in American history. It is the central theater of government, where decisions on national and international policies are made. And, of course, it's also the private home of the president and his family, their personal doings and dramas as much a focus of national interest as any happenings in the political arena. Its interior is a repository of art and furnishings that showcases the tastes of our chief executives and first ladies from the early years of the American Republic. Highlights of the tour include the following rooms:

The gold-and-white **East Room,** scene of great and gala receptions, weddings of presidents' daughters (Lynda Bird Johnson, for one), and other dazzling events. Here, heads of state have been entertained, seven presidents who died in office lay in state, and Nixon delivered his resignation speech. The room is decorated in the early 20th-century style of the Theodore Roosevelt renovation, with parquet Fontainebleau oak floors and white-painted wood walls with fluted pilasters and relief inserts illustrating Aesop's fables. Note the famous Gilbert Stuart portrait of George Washington which Dolley Madison saved from the British torch during the War of 1812.

The **Green Room** (named in the 19th century for its green upholstery), today used as a sitting room, was Thomas Jefferson's

---

⭐ **FROMMER'S FAVORITE WASHINGTON EXPERIENCES**

A Picnic Along the C&O Canal   Hike the scenic canal towpath from Georgetown (about three miles) to Fletcher's Boat House where there are picnic tables and grills. Spend the day—bring kites, watercolors, whatever.

Afternoon Tea at the Four Seasons Hotel   It's served in the lushly planted Garden Terrace, with floor-to-ceiling windows offering canal views. Fresh-baked scones with homemade preserves and Devonshire cream, finger sandwiches, and pots of your favorite tea.

A Day in Alexandria   Just a short Metro ride from the District is George Washington's Virginia hometown. Roam the quaint cobblestone streets, browse charming boutiques and antiques stores, visit the boyhood home of Robert E. Lee and other historic attractions, and dine in one of Alexandria's fine restaurants.

dining room. He designed a revolving door with trays on one side, so servants could leave dishes on the kitchen side. Then he would twirl the door, take the food from the shelves, and serve his own guests. Thus his privacy was uninvaded. Walls here are covered in green watered-silk fabric, and some of the early 19th-century furnishings are attributed to the famous cabinetmaker Duncan Phyfe. There are notable paintings by Gilbert Stuart and John Singer Sargent.

The oval **Blue Room,** where presidents and first ladies have officially received guests since the Jefferson administration, is today decorated in the French Empire style chosen by James Monroe in 1817. It was, however, Van Buren's decor that began the "blue room" tradition. The walls, on which hang portraits of five presidents (including Rembrandt Peale's portrait of Thomas Jefferson and G. P. A. Healy's of Tyler), are covered in a reproduction of French Directoire paper from 1800, and a settee and seven of the original gilded armchairs Monroe ordered from French cabinetmaker Pierre-Antoine Bellangé remain. Grover Cleveland, the only president ever to wed in the White House, was married in the Blue Room; the Reagans, Nancy wearing symbolic yellow, greeted the 53 returned Iranian hostages here; and every year it's the setting for the White House Christmas tree.

Several portraits of past presidents—plus Albert Bierstadt's *View of the Rocky Mountains* and a Gilbert Stuart portrait of Dolley Madison—hang in the **Red Room.** It's used as a reception room, usually for small dinners. The satin-covered walls and most of the Empire furnishings are red, set off by white wainscotting and moldings.

The white-walled, gold-accented **State Dining Room** is a superb setting for state dinners and luncheons. Its architecture is modeled after late 18th-century neoclassical English houses. Theodore Roosevelt, a big-game hunter, had a large moose head over the fireplace and other trophies on the walls. Below G. P. A. Healy's portrait of a contemplative Lincoln is an inscription of words written by John Adams on his second night in the White House (FDR had them carved into the mantel): "I Pray Heaven to Bestow The Best of Blessings on THIS HOUSE and on All that shall hereafter Inhabit it. May none but Honest and Wise Men ever rule under This Roof."

History   Since its cornerstone was laid in 1792, the White House has gone through numerous changes. It was designed by Irishman James Hoban, so it isn't surprising that it's a lot like the house of the Duke of Leinster of Dublin. In 1824 the South Portico was added.

IMPRESSIONS

The President's mansion is more like an English clubhouse, both within and without, than any other kind of establishment with which I can compare it.
—CHARLES DICKENS

Washington . . . is the symbol of America. By its dignity and architectural inspiration . . . we encourage that elevation of thought and character which comes from great architecture.
—HERBERT HOOVER

Benjamin Henry Latrobe executed the design, as he did for the North Portico extending out over the front door and driveway (added in 1829). Electricity was first installed during Benjamin Harrison's presidency in 1891.

In 1902, repairs and refurnishings of the White House cost almost $500,000. No other great change came about until Harry Truman added his controversial "balcony" inside the columns of the South Portico. Also in 1948, after the leg of Margaret Truman's piano cut through the dining room ceiling, nearly $6 million was allotted for reconstruction of the building. The Trumans lived in Blair House across the street for four years while the White House interior was taken apart and put back together again, piece by piece. Steel girders and concrete shored up the place. It's as solid as Gibraltar now.

In 1961, Mrs. John F. Kennedy formed a Fine Arts Committee, and she and her group set about restoring the famous rooms to their original grandeur. Her artistic touch will be in evidence for generations to come.

Seeing the White House More than 1.2 million people line up annually to see the Executive Mansion. Best bet is to obtain tickets in advance from a congressperson or senator for the VIP tours at 8:15, 8:30, and 8:45am (see Chapter 2 for details). This ensures your entrance, even in tourist season when over 6,000 people try to squeeze in during the two hours each day the White House is open. It also entitles you to a more extensive—and guided—tour; on later visits there are guides on hand to answer questions, but no actual tour is given. A good idea, before you take any tour, is to pick up a book called *The White House: An Historic Guide,* available in bookstores here and at many other District sights. Then you'll know what to look for in each room, and your experience will be greatly enhanced. You can order it in advance (as well as another book, *The Living White House,* that gives more biographical information about the presidents and their families) from the **White House Historical Association,** 740 Jackson Place NW, Washington, DC 20503 (tel. 202/737-8292). Send $5.75 for a paperback or $7.50 for a hardcover edition of either book.

Most of the year, if you don't have VIP tour tickets, you just join the line at the East Gate before 10am (visitors enter in groups between 10am and noon). Arrive early to be sure you get in. *Note: Between Memorial Day and Labor Day tickets are required.* They are available (only one to a customer) at one of the kiosks on the Ellipse (at 15th Street and Constitution Avenue NW) beginning at 8am on the day of your visit only; lines begin forming even earlier. There's no charge. Once you've obtained your ticket (the tour time is stamped on it), you can go to a nearby hotel for breakfast, such as the Washington at 15th Street and Pennsylvania Avenue, or the classier, and pricier, Hay-Adams at 1200 16th St. Or you can sit and wait in the bleachers while glee clubs and bands entertain.

Admission: Free.

Open: Tues–Sat 10am–noon. **Closed:** Some days for official functions; check before leaving your hotel by calling the above 24-hour number. **Metro:** McPherson Square.

THE CAPITOL, at the east end of the Mall, entrance on East Capitol St. and 1st St. NW. Tel. 225-6827.

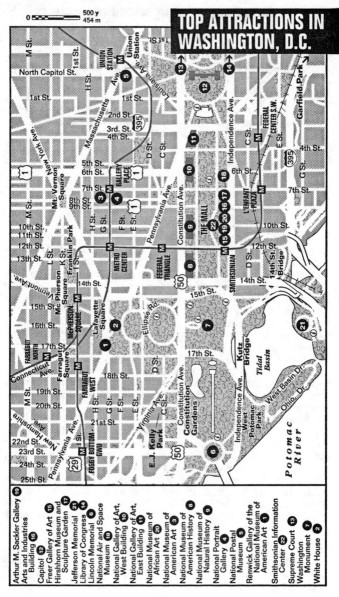

TOP ATTRACTIONS IN WASHINGTON, D.C.

As our most tangible national symbol since its first wing was completed in 1800, and the place where all our laws are debated, the Capitol is perhaps the most important edifice in the United States. It's also one of the most beautiful. Historian Allan Nevins called it "the spirit of America in stone." For 134 years it sheltered not only both houses of Congress but the Supreme Court, and for 97 years the Library of Congress as well.

IMPRESSIONS

The Capitol is the first temple dedicated to the sovereignty of the people, embellishing with Athenian taste the course of a nation looking far beyond the range of Athenian destinies.
—THOMAS JEFFERSON

It is our national center. It belongs to us, and whether it is mean or majestic, whether arrayed in glory or covered with shame, we cannot but share its character and its destiny.
—FREDERICK DOUGLASS

There is no greater spectator sport in America than watching Washington.
—MERRIMAN SMITH

On the massive bronze doors leading to the **Rotunda** are portrayals of events from the life of Columbus. The Rotunda—a huge circular hall some 97 feet across and under a 180-foot dome—is the hub of the Capitol. Nine presidents have lain in state here; when Kennedy's casket was displayed, the line of mourners stretched 40 blocks. On the circular walls are eight immense oil paintings of events in American history such as the reading of the Declaration of Independence and the surrender of Cornwallis at Yorktown. In the dome is an allegorical fresco masterpiece by Constantino Brumidi, *Apotheosis of Washington,* a symbolic portrayal of George Washington surrounded by Greek gods and goddesses watching over the progress of the nation. A trompe l'oeil frieze overhead depicts events in American history from Columbus through the Wright brothers' flight at Kitty Hawk. There's also a life-size marble statue of Lincoln.

National Statuary Hall was originally the chamber of the House of Representatives, but it was abandoned for that purpose because of its acoustics. Your guide will demonstrate that a whisper can be heard clear across the room. In 1864 it became Statuary Hall, and the states were invited to send two statues each of native sons to the hall. As the room filled up, statues spilled over into the Hall of Columns, corridors, and anywhere that might accommodate the bronze and marble artifacts. Many of the statues honor individuals who have had important roles in American history, such as Henry Clay, Ethan Allen, and Daniel Webster.

On congressional VIP tours (or with House and Senate visitors' passes) you'll also visit either the House or Senate chamber. The House of Representatives chamber is the largest legislative chamber in the world. The president delivers his annual State of the Union address here.

Seeing the Capitol As at the White House, VIP tour tickets from a congressperson or senator for the morning tours (between 8 and 9am) are a definite advantage (see Chapter 2 for details). Only on the longer VIP tours do you visit the House and Senate chambers. Also request visitors' passes for each member of your party to view a session of the House and/or Senate. If you don't get advance tickets, free 30-minute guided tours leave from the Rotunda every 15 minutes between 9am and 3:45pm. And if you don't receive visitors' passes in the mail (not every senator or representative sends them), they're obtainable at your senators' offices on the Constitution Avenue side of the building (for noncitizens it's even easier—you just present your passport at the first-floor appointment desk on the Senate side or at the third-floor House gallery and ask for a pass). You'll know when the House or Senate is in session when you see flags flying over their respective sides of the Capitol. Or you can check the "Today in Congress" column weekdays in the *Washington Post* for details on times of House and Senate committee meetings. This column also tells you which sessions are open to the public and allows you to pick a subject that interests you rather than attending, say, a hearing on official mail costs. If you're interested in a particular bill, call the above-listed number for information.

Admission: Free.

Open: Daily 9am–4:30pm (tours 9am–3:45pm). The Rotunda is open till 8pm Easter to Labor Day most years (it's determined annually). **Closed:** Jan 1, Thanksgiving Day, and Dec 25. **Metro:** Capitol South.

SUPREME COURT, east of the Capitol on 1st St. NE, between East Capitol St. and Maryland Ave. Tel. 479-3000.

In these oft-turbulent times, I find it reassuring to visit the massive Corinthian marble palace that houses the Supreme Court, its serene classical dignity reinforced by the pledge etched in a frieze over the colonnaded entrance: "Equal Justice Under Law." The Court's subtle excitement is well described by Justice Oliver Wendell Holmes, Jr., who wrote, "We are very quiet . . . but it is the quiet of a storm center." The highest tribunal in the nation, the Supreme Court is charged with deciding whether actions of Congress, the president, the states, and lower courts are in accord with the Constitution and with interpreting that document's enduring principles and applying them to new situations and changing conditions. It has the power of "judicial review"—authority to invalidate legislation or executive action that conflicts with the Constitution. Out of the 5,500 cases submitted to it, only about 150 cases are heard each year by the Supreme Court, many of them dealing with issues vital to the nation. The Court's rulings are final, reversible only by another Supreme Court decision or, in some cases, an Act of Congress or a Constitutional amendment.

Until 1935 the Supreme Court met in the Capitol. Architect Cass Gilbert designed the stately Corinthian marble palace that houses the Court today. The building was considered rather grandiose by early residents: One justice remarked that the justices ought to enter such pompous precincts on elephants.

If you're in town when the Court is in session, you should definitely see a case being argued. The Court meets Monday through Wednesday from 10am to 3pm (with a lunch-hour recess from noon to 1pm) from the first Monday in October through late April, alternating, in approximately two-week intervals, between "sittings" to hear cases and deliver opinions and "recesses" for consideration of business before the court. Mid-May to early July, you can attend brief sessions (about 15 minutes) at 10am on Monday, during which time the justices release orders and opinions. You can find out what cases are on the docket by checking the *Washington Post*'s "Supreme Court Calendar." Arrive at least an hour early—even earlier for a highly publicized case—to line up for seats, about 150 of which are allotted to the general public.

At 10am the entrance of the justices is announced by the marshal, and all present rise and remain standing while the justices are seated following the chant: "The Honorable, the Chief Justice and Associate Justices of the Supreme Court of the United States. Oyez! Oyez! [French for "Hear ye!"] All persons having business before the Honorable, the Supreme Court of the United States, are admonished to draw near and give their attention, for the Court is now sitting. God save the United States and this Honorable Court!" There are many rituals here. Unseen by the gallery is the "conference handshake"; following a 19th-century tradition symbolizing a "harmony of aims if not views," each Justice shakes hands with each of the other eight when they assemble to go to the bench. The Court has a record before it of prior proceedings and relevant briefs, so each side is allowed only a 30-minute argument.

If the Court is not in session during your visit, you can attend a free **lecture** in the courtroom about Court procedure and the building's architecture. Lectures are given from 9:30am to 3:30pm every hour on the half hour.

After the talk, explore the Great Hall and go down a flight of steps to see the 20-minute film on the workings of the Court. The ground floor is a good vantage point to view one of two grand spiral staircases here similar to those at the Vatican and the Paris Opera. There are also interesting exhibits and a gift shop on this level, and good meals are served at the adjoining cafeteria (see "Restaurants at Sightseeing Attractions," in Chapter 6, for details).

Admission: Free.

Open: Mon–Fri 9am–4:30pm. **Closed:** Weekends and all Federal holidays. **Metro:** Capitol South or Union Station.

TRIUMVIRATE OF PRESIDENTIAL MEMORIALS

Only three American presidents have been singled out for recognition with great monuments in Washington, D.C. They are George Washington, Abraham Lincoln, and Thomas Jefferson.

The first monument to be built (to Washington) was begun in 1848, the last (to Jefferson) was dedicated in 1943 during cherry-blossom time. There are wreath-laying ceremonies on (or close to) Lincoln's and Jefferson's birthdays at their respective monuments.

WASHINGTON MONUMENT, directly south of the White House at 15th St. and Constitution Ave. NW. Tel. 426-6839.

The 555-foot stark marble obelisk that shimmers in the sun and glows under floodlights at night is the city's most visible landmark. It is, like the Eiffel Tower in Paris or London's Big Ben, a symbol of the city.

The idea for a tribute to George Washington first arose 16 years before his death at the Continental Congress of 1783. An equestrian statue was planned, and Washington himself approved the site for it—on the Mall, west of the future Capitol and south of the "President's Palace." However, over a century was to elapse before a very different monument was completed. The new nation had more pressing problems, and funds were not readily available. It wasn't

IMPRESSIONS

May the spirit which animated the great founder of this city descend to future generations
—JOHN ADAMS

Every dedicated American could be proud that a dynamic experience of democracy in his nation's capital had been made visible to the world.
—MARTIN LUTHER KING, JR., AFTER THE 1963 MARCH ON WASHINGTON

---

until the early 1830s, with the 100th anniversary of Washington's birth approaching, that any action was taken. Then there were several fiascos. A mausoleum was provided for Washington's remains under the Capitol Rotunda, but a grandnephew, citing Washington's will, refused to allow the body to be moved from Mount Vernon. In 1830 Horatio Greenough was commissioned to create a memorial statue for the Rotunda. He came up with a barechested seated Washington, draped in classical Greek garb; a shocked public claimed he looked like he was "entering or leaving a bath," and the statue was relegated to the Smithsonian. Finally, in 1833 prominent citizens organized the Washington National Monument Society. Treasury Building architect Robert Mill's design (which originally contained a circular colonnaded Greek temple base, discarded later for lack of funds) was accepted. The cornerstone was laid on July 4, 1848, and for the next 37 years watching the monument grow—or not grow—was a local pastime. The Civil War and lagging funds brought construction to a halt at an awkward 150 feet. The unsightly stump remained until 1876 when President Grant approved federal monies to complete the project. Rejecting plans for ornate embellishment that ranged from English Gothic to Hindu pagoda designs, authorities put the U.S. Army Corps of Engineers to work on the obelisk. Dedicated in 1885, it was opened to the public in 1888.

The 360° views are spectacular. To the east are the Capitol and Smithsonian buildings; to the north, the White House; to the west, the Lincoln and Vietnam Memorials, and Arlington National Cemetery beyond; and to the south, the gleaming-white shrine to Thomas Jefferson and the Potomac River. It's a marvelous orientation to the city.

In tourist season, arrive before 8am to avoid long lines. Climbing the 897 steps is verboten, but a large elevator whisks visitors to the top in just 70 seconds. If, however, you're avid to see more of the interior, **"Down the Steps" tours** are given, subject to staff availability, weekends at 10am and 2pm (more frequently in summer). For details, call before you go or ask a ranger on duty. On this tour you'll learn more about the building of the monument and get to see the 193 carved stones inserted into the interior walls. They range from a piece of stone from the Parthenon to plaques presented by city fire departments.

Light snack fare is sold at a snack bar on the grounds; consider a picnic on the grass. There's free one-hour parking at 16th Street Oval.
Admission: Free.
Open: First Sun in Apr to Labor Day, daily 8am–midnight; the

rest of the year, daily 9am–5pm. **Closed:** July 4 and Dec 25. **Metro:** Smithsonian; then a 10-minute walk.

LINCOLN MEMORIAL, directly west of the Mall in Potomac Park, at 23rd St. NW, between Constitution and Independence Aves. Tel. 426-6895.

 The Lincoln Memorial attracts some six million visitors annually. It's a beautiful and moving testament to a great American, its marble walls seeming to embody not only the spirit and integrity of Lincoln, but all that has ever been good about America. Visitors are silently awed in its presence.

The monument was a long time in the making. Although it was planned as early as 1867, two years after Lincoln's death, it was not until 1912 that Henry Bacon's design was completed, and the memorial itself was dedicated in 1922.

A beautiful neoclassical templelike structure, similar in architectural design to the Parthenon in Greece, the memorial has 36 fluted Doric columns representing the states of the Union at the time of Lincoln's death, plus two at the entrance. On the attic parapet are 48 festoons symbolic of the number of states in 1922 when the monument was erected. Hawaii and Alaska are noted in an inscription on the terrace. To the west, the Arlington Memorial Bridge crossing the Potomac recalls the reunion of North and South. To the east is the beautiful Reflecting Pool, lined with American elms and stretching 2,000 feet toward the Washington Monument and the Capitol beyond.

The memorial chamber, under 60-foot ceilings, has limestone walls inscribed with the Gettysburg Address and Lincoln's Second Inaugural Address. Two 60-foot murals by Jules Guerin on the north and south walls depict, allegorically, Lincoln's principles and achievements. On the south wall, an Angel of Truth freeing a slave is flanked by groups of figures representing Justice and Immortality. The north-wall mural depicts the unity of North and South and is flanked by groups of figures symbolizing Fraternity and Charity. Most powerful, however, is Daniel Chester French's 19-foot-high seated statue of Lincoln in deep contemplation in the central chamber. Its effect is best evoked by these words of Walt Whitman: "He was a mountain in grandeur of soul, he was a sea in deep undervoice of mystic loneliness, he was a star in steadfast purity of purpose and service and he abides." It is appropriate to the heritage of Lincoln that on several occasions those who have been oppressed have expressed their plight to America and the world at the steps of his shrine. Most notable was a peaceful demonstration of 200,000 people on August 28, 1963, at which another freedom-loving American, Dr. Martin Luther King, Jr., said "I have a dream."

An information center and bookstore are on the lower lobby level. Ranger talks are given on request.

Admission: Free.

Open: Daily 24 hours; park staff on duty 8am–midnight. **Metro:** Foggy Bottom; then about a 15-minute walk.

JEFFERSON MEMORIAL, south of the Washington Monument on Ohio Dr., at the south shore of the Tidal Basin. Tel. 426-6822.

 President John F. Kennedy, at a 1962 dinner honoring 29 Nobel Prize winners, told his guests they were "the most extraordinary collection of talent, of human knowledge, that has ever been gathered together at the White House, with the possible exception of when Thomas Jefferson dined alone." Jefferson penned the Declaration of Independence, spoke out against slavery, and was George Washington's secretary of state, John Adams's vice president, and our third president. And he still found time to establish the University of Virginia and to pursue wide-ranging interests including architecture, astronomy, anthropology, music, and farming.

The site for the Jefferson Memorial, in relation to the Washington and Lincoln Memorials, was of extraordinary importance. The Capitol, the White House, and the Mall were already located in accordance with L'Enfant's plan, and there was no spot for such a project if the symmetry that guided L'Enfant was to be maintained. So the memorial was built on land reclaimed from the Potomac River, now known as the Tidal Basin. Franklin Delano Roosevelt had all the trees between the Jefferson Memorial and the White House cut down, so that he could see it every morning and draw inspiration from it.

It's a beautiful memorial, a columned rotunda in the style of the Pantheon in Rome, which Jefferson so admired. On the Tidal Basin side, the sculptural group above the entrance depicts Jefferson with Benjamin Franklin, John Adams, Roger Sherman, and Robert Livingston, who worked on drafting the Declaration of Independence. The domed interior of the memorial contains the 19-foot bronze statue of Jefferson standing on a 6-foot pedestal of black Minnesota granite. The sculpture is the work of Rudulph Evans, who was chosen from more than 100 artists in a nationwide competition. Jefferson is depicted wearing a fur-collared coat given to him by his close friend, the Polish general, Tadeusz Kościuszko. Inscriptions from Jefferson's writing engraved on the interior walls expand on Jefferson's philosophy, which is best expressed in the circular frieze quotation: "I have sworn upon the altar of God eternal hostility against every form of tyranny over the mind of man."

Park rangers give short talks to visitors on request. Spring through fall, a refreshment kiosk at the Tourmobile stop offers snack fare. There's free one-hour parking.

Admission: Free.

Open: Daily 8am–midnight. **Transportation:** Tourmobile.

SMITHSONIAN INSTITUTION

No longer referred to as "the nation's attic," which seemed somewhat musty, the Smithsonian Institution has been redubbed "the nation's showcase." That doesn't totally explain it either, for its collection of over 140 million objects deals with the entire world and its history, and the peoples and animals (past and present) that have inhabited the earth as well as our attempts to probe into the future. The sprawling institution employs in the neighborhood of 6,000 people, and they are assisted by an almost equal number of volunteers. Nine immense Smithsonian buildings are located between the Washington Monument and the Capitol on the Mall. Other buildings devoted to specialized exhibits are within walking distance of the Mall. And farther out, the National Zoological Park (the zoo) and the Anacostia Museum are also Smithsonian responsibilities. Thousands of scientific expeditions sponsored by the Smithsonian have pushed into remote frontiers in deserts, mountains, polar regions, and jungles. Traveling exhibits are sent to other museums, schools, and libraries. And all this is a mere hint of the Smithsonian's scope and involvement.

The Smithsonian Institution began with a $500,000 bequest from James Smithson, an English scientist who had never visited this country. When he died in 1829, he willed his entire fortune to the United States "to found at Washington an establishment for the increase and diffusion of knowledge. . . ." In 1846 Congress created a corporate entity to carry out Smithson's will, and the federal government agreed to pay 6% interest on the bequeathed funds in perpetuity.

Since then, other munificent private donations have swelled Smithson's original legacy many times over. Major gallery and museum construction through the years stands as testament to thoughtful donors. In 1987 the **Sackler Gallery** (Asian and Near Eastern art) and the **National Museum of African Art** were added to the Smithsonian's Mall attractions. The **National Postal Museum** opened in 1993. And future plans call for moving the **National Museum of the American Indian** (currently in New York) here by the end of the decade.

If you're here at lunchtime, or just want to rest your feet and refuel, flip back to "Restaurants at Sightseeing Attractions," in Chapter 6, for descriptions of the restaurants you'll find in the various museums here.

More Information, Please If you need to know what's happening at any of the Smithsonian museums, just get on the phone. A call to **Dial-a-Museum** (tel. 357-2020) brings you news of all special events.

SMITHSONIAN INFORMATION CENTER, 1000 Jefferson Dr. SW. Tel. 357-2700.

For years, visitors to the capital were left to explore the intimidatingly vast Smithsonian complex with the scantest of orientation. But that all changed with the 1989 opening of the high-tech Smithsonian Information Center, located in the "Castle" on the Mall. It is appropriately housed in the original Victorian red sandstone Smithsonian building, named for its resemblance to a Norman castle. Today the Castle is fronted by a lovely flower garden and entered via the ornate Oriental-motif Children's Room. Designed at the turn of the century for exhibits displayed at a child's eye level, this charming room has a gold-trimmed ceiling decorated to represent a grape arbor with brightly plumed birds and blue sky peeking through the trellising. Furnishings are peacock-themed, and large Chinese paintings adorn the walls.

The main information area, however, is the Great Hall, where a 20-minute video overview of the Institution runs throughout the day in two theaters. There are two large schematic models of the Mall (as well as a third in braille) detailing sights, Metro and Tourmobile stops, and major architectural structures. Interactive videos, some of them at children's heights, offer comprehensive information about Smithsonian and all other capital attractions and transportation (the menus seem infinite).

The entire facility is handicapped-accessible, and all information is available in a number of foreign languages. In addition, there's a large light-up map of Washington sights that allows visitors to electronically locate 70 popular attractions, daily Smithsonian events are displayed on monitors, and the information desk's multilingual staff can answer all your questions and help you plan a Smithsonian sightseeing itinerary. The crypt of James Smithson is also on the premises.

You can pick up brochures and parking maps here. A stop at the center is highly recommended, especially for first-time visitors to the Smithsonian. Most of the museums are within easy walking distance of the facility.

Open: Daily 9am–5:30pm. **Closed:** Dec 25. **Metro:** Smithsonian.

NATIONAL MUSEUM OF AMERICAN HISTORY, on the north side of the Mall between 12th and 14th Sts. NW, with entrances on Constitution Ave. and Madison Dr. Tel. 357-2700.

The National Museum of American History deals with "everyday life in the American past" and the external forces that have helped to shape our national character. Exhibits run the gamut from a Revolutionary War general's tent to Archie and Edith Bunker's chairs.

Exhibits on the **first floor** (enter on Constitution Avenue) explore the development of farm machines, power machinery, transportation, timekeeping, phonographs, and typewriters. The Palm Court on this level, a turn-of-the-century re-creation, includes the interior of Georgetown's Stohlman's Confectionery Shop as it appeared around 1900 and part of an actual 1902 Horn & Hardart Automat. You can have your mail stamped Smithsonian Station at a post office that was located in Headsville, West Virginia, from 1861 to 1971, when it was brought lock, stock, and barrel to the museum. An important first-floor exhibit, "A Material World," deals with the changing composition of artifacts—from predominantly natural materials such as wood and stone, to manufactured materials such as steel, to the vast range of synthetics that exist today. Also on this level is "Engines of Change: The American Industrial Revolution 1790–1860," which tells the story of America's transformation from an agricultural to an industrial society. And finally, "The Information Age: People & Technology," looks at the ways information technology has changed society over the last 150 years.

If you enter from the Mall, you'll find yourself on the **second**

floor facing the original Star-Spangled Banner, 30 by 42 feet, that inspired Francis Scott Key to write the U.S. national anthem in 1814. "After the Revolution," a major exhibition, focuses on the everyday activities of ordinary 18th-century Americans—their work, family life, and communities. "Field to Factory: Afro-American Migration, 1915–40," is an in-depth study of America's social and demographic history from an African-American perspective. And "American Encounters" on this level commemorates the Columbus quincentenary. But the most fascinating exhibit is the Foucault Pendulum, a copy of the original model exhibited in Paris in 1851 with the accompanying teaser, "You are invited to witness the earth revolve." The heavy pendulum, suspended from the roof, swings monotonously from one side to the other, never varying in its arc, yet knocking over, one by one, a series of red pointers that form a circle around it. How? The pendulum has an unvarying arc, but the earth revolves beneath it. On the second floor as well first ladies' gowns are displayed in an exhibit called "First Ladies: Political Role and Public Image."

A vast collection of ship models, uniforms, weapons, and other things military is found on the **third floor,** where major exhibits focus on the experiences of G.I.s in World War II (and the postwar world) as well as the internment of Japanese-Americans during that war. Other areas include Money and Medals, Textiles, Printing and Graphic Arts, and Ceramics. Here, too, is the first American flag to be called Old Glory (1824).

Inquire at the information desks about highlight tours, Demonstration Center hands-on activities for children and adults, films, lectures, and concerts. Holidays are especially event-filled times. There are several museum shops (most noteworthy is the Smithsonian bookstore, offering books and objects relating to all aspects of Americana), and a cheerful cafeteria is on the premises.

Admission: Free.

Open: Daily 10am–5:30pm. **Closed:** Dec 25. **Metro:** Smithsonian or Federal Triangle.

NATIONAL MUSEUM OF NATURAL HISTORY, on the north side of the Mall between 9th and 12th Sts. NW, with entrances on Madison Dr. and Constitution Ave. Tel. 357-2700.

The National Museum of Natural History contains over 120 million artifacts and specimens—everything from one of the largest African elephants ever bagged by a hunter in our time (it dominates the Rotunda on the Mall—entrance level) to the legendary Hope Diamond, the single most popular display in the museum (it rests on velvet in its own glass-faced vault in the Hall of Gems on the second floor).

Free highlight **tours** are given daily at 10:30am and 1:30pm, but if you have the time, the self-guided audio tour, narrated by Meryl Streep, provides the most comprehensive commentary on exhibits. It's available at the Rotunda information desk for a nominal fee. A **Discovery Room,** filled with creative hands-on exhibits and games for children, is on the first floor; it's open Monday through Thursday from noon to 2:30pm, and on Friday, Saturday, and Sunday from 10:30am to 3:30pm. One adult must accompany every three children, and tickets, obtained at the Rotunda information desk, are required on weekends and holidays. If you have kids, this is a "must."

On the **Mall level,** off the Rotunda, evolution is traced back billions of years in Fossils, comprising such exhibits as a 3.5-billion-year-old stromatolite (blue-green algae clump) fossil—one of the earliest evidences of life on earth—and a 70-million-year-old dinosaur egg. An animated film shows how the earliest forms of life on earth originated. "Life in the Ancient Seas" features a 100-foot-long mural depicting primitive whales, a life-size walk-around diorama of a 230-million-year-old coral reef, and over 2,000 fossils that chronicle the evolution of marine life. Dinosaurs, of course, loom large—giant skeletons of creatures that dominated the earth for 140 million years before their extinction about 65 million years ago. A glass-walled lab allows visitors to view museum workers unearthing dinosaur bones and other fossils from ancient rocks. On balconies over Dinosaur Hall are exhibits on ancient birds, including a life-size model of the pterosaur, which had a 40-foot wingspan. Also residing above this hall is an ancient shark—or at least the jaw of one, the carcharodon megalodon, that lived in our oceans five million years ago. A monstrous 40-foot-long predator, it had teeth five to six inches long and could have consumed a Volkswagen "bug" in one gulp! Here, too: the World of Mammals and Life in the Sea, the latter including a spectacular living coral reef in a 3,000-gallon tank. A second 3,000-gallon tank houses a subarctic sea environment typical of the Maine coast.

On the **second floor,** along with the Hope Diamond, are such dazzling gems as the 182-carat Star of Bombay sapphire that belonged to Mary Pickford, a rare red diamond (one of five in the world), and Marie Antoinette's diamond earrings. Nearby are geological specimens ranging from meteorites to moon rocks. Kids will enjoy the newly renovated Orkin Insect Zoo's Plexiglas cages housing tarantulas, centipedes, and the like—not to mention a crawl-through model of an African termite mound (many other fascinating entomological displays here range from cave insects to swamp bugs). Numerous skeletons—from the gigantic extinct Stellar sea cow to the tiny pocket mouse—are displayed in "Bones." Additional exhibits include "South America: Continent and Culture," with objects from the Inca civilization, among others, and "Western Civilization: Origins and Traditions"—from about 10,000 years ago to A.D. 500.

The **ground level** houses changing exhibits.

There's a plant-filled cafeteria off the Rotunda and an adjoining shop featuring books on natural history and anthropology for adults and children, jewelry, crafts, fossil reproduction kits, shells, and more. On the second floor are the Dinostore (all dinosaur merchandise) and a gem and mineral store.

Admission: Free.

Open: Daily 10am–5:30pm, with extended hours in summer some years. **Closed:** Dec 25. **Metro:** Smithsonian or Federal Triangle.

NATIONAL AIR AND SPACE MUSEUM, on the south side of the Mall between 4th and 7th Sts. SW, with entrances on Jefferson Dr. or Independence Ave. Tel. 357-2700, 357-1686 for IMAX ticket information.

The National Air and Space Museum chronicles the story of man's mastery of flight—from Kitty Hawk to outer space—in 23 galleries filled with exciting exhibits. Plan to devote at least three or four hours to exploring the exhibits and, especially during the tourist season and on holidays, arrive before 10am to make a rush for the film-ticket line when the doors open. The not-to-be-missed **IMAX films** shown in the Samuel P. Langley Theater here, on a screen five stories high and seven stories wide, are immensely popular; tickets tend to sell out quickly. There are usually four films playing each day, most with nature or space-exploration themes. See as many as you have time for. Tickets cost $3.25 for adults, $2 for children 2 to 16, students, and seniors over 55, and are free to children under 2. You can also see IMAX films most evenings after closing (call for details and ticket prices).

You'll also want to catch a show (same prices) at the **Albert Einstein Planetarium,** so after you've purchased IMAX tickets, make the planetarium ticket booth on the second floor your next stop.

In between shows, you can view the exhibits; free 1½-hour highlight **tours** are given daily at 10:15am and 1pm. Recorded tours, narrated by astronauts, are also available for rental. Interactive computers and slide and video shows enhance the exhibits throughout.

Highlights of the **first floor** include famous airplanes (such as *The Spirit of St. Louis*) and spacecraft (the *Apollo 11* command module); the world's only touchable moon rock; numerous exhibits on the history of aviation and air transportation; galleries in which you learn how a helicopter works, design your own jet plane, and study astronomy; and rockets, lunar exploration vehicles, manned spacecraft, guided missiles, even the U.S.S. *Enterprise*. A major exhibit on the *Enola Gay*, the plane that dropped the atomic bomb on Hiroshima, will open here in 1995. All the aircraft, by the way, are originals.

Kids love the "walk-through" Skylab orbital workshop on the **second floor.** Other galleries here highlight the solar system, U.S. manned space flights, sea-air operations, aviation during the World Wars, and artists' perceptions of flight. An important exhibit is "Beyond the Limits: Flight Enters the Computer Age." Occupying seven exhibit areas, it illustrates the primary applications of computer technology to aerospace.

A very attractive cafeteria and a rather elegant restaurant, **Flight Line** and the **Wright Place,** respectively, are on the premises (see "Restaurants at Sightseeing Attractions," in Chapter 6, for details). And the museum shop sells everything from model kits to freeze-dried astronaut ice cream.

Admission: Free.

Open: Daily 10am–5:30pm (some years the museum has extended hours in Easter week and in summer). **Closed:** Dec 25. **Metro:** L'Enfant Plaza (Smithsonian Museums exit).

NATIONAL MUSEUM OF AMERICAN ART, 8th and G Sts. NW. Tel. 357-2700.

The NMAA owns more than 35,000 works representing two centuries of our national art history. A rotating sampling of about 1,000 of these works are on display at any given time, along with special exhibitions highlighting various aspects of American art. The collection, along with the National Portrait Gallery (described below), is housed in the palatial quarters of the 19th-century Greek Revival Old Patent Office Building, partially designed by Washington Monument architect Robert Mills and Capitol dome architect

THE TOP ATTRACTIONS • 151

DID YOU KNOW . . . ?

- When the *Washington Post* sponsored a public music competition, John Philip Sousa was asked to compose a march for the awards ceremony; the result was *The Washington Post March*, for which Sousa earned the grand sum of $35.
- The only Presidential Inauguration Ceremony to be held in the White House was that of Franklin D. Roosevelt, in 1941.
- Herbert Hoover was the first president to have a telephone on his desk.
- The desk in the Oval Office, carved from the British ship *Resolute*, was a gift to Rutherford B. Hayes from Queen Victoria.
- The first first lady to fly to a foreign country was Eleanor Roosevelt in 1934.

Thomas U. Walter. Philip Johnson called it "the greatest building in the world." Fronted by a columned portico evocative of the Parthenon, it was originally a multi-purpose facility housing an eclectic mix of items ranging from the original Declaration of Independence to a collection of shrunken heads.

Twentieth-century art occupies the most exalted setting, the third-floor Lincoln Gallery, with vaulted ceilings and marble columns. In this room, 4,000 revelers celebrated Lincoln's second inaugural in 1865. On view are works of post–World War II artists (de Kooning, Kline, Noguchi, and others). Other 20th-century works on this floor include paintings commissioned during the New Deal era.

Mid- to late 19th-century artists—such as Winslow Homer, Mary Cassatt, Albert Pinkham Ryder, and John Singer Sargent—are on the second floor, as is the Hiram Powers Gallery housing the contents of the 19th-century neoclassic sculptor's Florence studio.

A unique work of folk art on the first floor is James Hampton's visionary religious piece (completely covered in aluminum and gold foil), *Throne of the Third Heaven of the Nation's Millennium General Assembly*. Here, too: works by such Early American masters as Charles Willson Peale, Benjamin West, and Samuel F.B. Morse; the $1.4-million Herbert Waide Hemphill, Jr., Folk Art Collection (19th and 20th centuries); and an Art of the West Gallery, featuring paintings by John Mix Stanley and Charles Bird King, along with George Catlin's Native American portraits from the collection he showed in Paris in the 1840s (the museum owns 445 of them).

Pick up a map and calendar of events, and ask about current temporary exhibits, at the information desk when you enter. Free walk-in tours are given at noon on weekdays and at 2pm on Saturday and Sunday. A lovely courtyard cafeteria is on the premises.

Admission: Free.

Open: Daily 10am–5:30pm. **Closed:** Dec 25. **Metro:** Gallery Place.

THE NATIONAL PORTRAIT GALLERY, 8th and F Sts. NW. Tel. 357-2700.

The "heroes and villains, thinkers and doers, conservatives and radicals" who have made "significant contributions to the history, development, and culture of the United States" are represented here in paintings, sculpture, photography, and other forms of portraiture. Though the museum didn't open until 1968, the concept of a national portrait gallery first evolved in the mid-19th century when Congress commissioned G. P. A. Healy to paint a series of presidential portraits for the White House. And American portraiture dates back even further, as evidenced by the Gilbert Stuart and Rembrandt Peale portraits of George and Martha Washington on display here, not to mention those predating the Revolution (of Pocahontas, among others). It's great fun to wander the corridors here, sometimes putting faces to famous names for the first time.

In addition to the Hall of Presidents (on the second floor), notable exhibits include Gilbert Stuart's famed "Lansdowne" portrait of George Washington, a portrait of Mary Cassatt by Degas, 19th-century silhouettes by French-born artist August Edouart, Jo Davidson's sculpture portraits (including a Buddha-like Gertrude Stein), and a self-portrait by John Singleton Copley. On the mezzanine, the Civil War is documented in portraiture, including one of the last photographs ever taken of Abraham Lincoln. Take a look at the magnificent Great Hall on the third floor. Originally designed as a showcase for patent models, it later became a Civil War hospital, where Walt Whitman came frequently to "soothe and relieve wounded troops."

Pick up a calendar of events at the information desk to find out about the museum's comprehensive schedule of temporary exhibits, lunchtime lectures, concerts, films, and dramatic presentations. Walk-in tours are given at varying hours—usually between 10am and 3pm (call 357-2920 for details).

Admission: Free.

Open: Daily 10am–5:30pm. **Closed:** Dec 25. **Metro:** Gallery Place.

RENWICK GALLERY OF THE NATIONAL MUSEUM OF AMERICAN ART, Pennsylvania Ave. and 17th St. NW. Tel. 357-2700.

A department of the National Museum of American Art, the Renwick is housed in a historic mid-1800s landmark building of the French Second Empire style. The original home of the Corcoran Gallery, it was saved from demolition by President Kennedy in 1963, when he recommended that it be renovated as part of the Lafayette Square restoration. In 1965 it became part of the Smithsonian and was renamed for its architect, James W. Renwick, who also designed the Smithsonian "Castle." Although the setting—especially the lavish Octagon Room and the magnificent Victorian Grand Salon with its wainscotted plum walls and 38-foot skylight ceiling—evokes another era, the museum's contents are mostly contemporary. The Renwick is a national showcase for American creativity in crafts. A rich and diverse display of objects here includes both changing exhibitions of contemporary works and pieces dating from 1900 to the present that are part of the museum's permanent collection. Typical exhibits run the gamut from "American Wicker: 1870–1930" to a Louis Comfort Tiffany show. The two above-mentioned Victorian galleries on the second floor are furnished in opulent 19th-century style, their walls hung with gilt-framed paintings by 18th- and 19th-century artists.

The Renwick has a comprehensive schedule of events, lectures, concerts, and films. Inquire at the information desk. And check out the museum shop near the entrance for books on crafts, design, and decorative arts, as well as craft items, many of them for children.

Admission: Free.
Open: Daily 10am–5:30pm. **Closed:** Dec 25. **Metro:** Farragut West or Farragut North.

HIRSHHORN MUSEUM AND SCULPTURE GARDEN, on the south side of the Mall at Independence Ave. and 7th St. SW. Tel. 357-2700.

⭐ Latvian-born immigrant Joseph H. Hirshhorn, the 12th of 13 children, came to America in 1905 at the age of 6 with his widowed mother. He dropped out of school at 13, and at the age of 15 got his first Wall Street job, earning $12 a week. In 1916 he invested his savings of $255, became a stock broker, and went on to amass a fortune in the market and in uranium mining. At age 18 he acquired his first works of art—two Dürer etchings—thus beginning a lifelong passion for collecting. Over the years, he amassed the world's most extensive private collection of 20th-century art. In 1966 he donated the entire collection—more than 4,000 drawings and paintings and some 2,000 pieces of sculpture—to the United States "as a small repayment for what this nation has done for me and others like me who arrived here as immigrants."

Constructed 14 feet above the ground on sculptured supports, the Hirshhorn's contemporary cylindrical concrete-and-granite building shelters a plaza courtyard where sculpture is displayed. The light and airy interior follows a simple circular route that makes it easy to see every exhibit without getting lost in a honeycomb of galleries. Natural light from floor-to-ceiling windows makes the inner galleries the perfect venue for viewing sculpture, second only, perhaps, to the magnificently beautiful tree-shaded sunken sculpture garden across the street (don't miss it). Paintings and drawings are installed in the outer galleries, artificially lit to prevent light damage.

A rotating show of about 600 pieces is on view at all times on the second and third floors. The collection features just about every well-known 20th-century artist and provides a comprehensive overview of major trends in Western art from the turn of the century to the present. Among the artists represented are Picasso, Brancusi, Arp, Rodin, de Kooning, Mondrian, Sargent, Eakins, Homer, Rothko, Warhol, Pollock, Nevelson, Noguchi, Giacometti, and Calder—and that's not the half of it. Among the best-known pieces are Rodin's *The Burghers of Calais,* four bas-reliefs by Matisse known as *The Backs,* and an important collection of the works of Henry Moore.

Pick up a free calendar when you come in to find out about free films, lectures, concerts, and temporary exhibits. Free docent **tours** are given mornings and early afternoons (call for schedule). Art books, posters, and prints are sold at the museum shop.
Admission: Free.
Open: Daily 10am–5:30pm. **Closed:** Dec 25. **Metro:** L'Enfant Plaza (Smithsonian Museums exit).

ARTHUR M. SACKLER GALLERY, 1050 Independence Ave. SW. Tel. 357-2700.

⭐ Opened in 1987, the Sackler, a museum of Asian art, presents traveling exhibitions from major cultural institutions in Asia, Europe, and the United States. In the recent past, these have focused on such wide-ranging areas as 15th-century Persian art and culture, ancient Buddhist and Hindu sculpture from Sri Lanka, Chinese porcelain, 19th-century Japanese woodblock prints, and the opulent court arts of Indonesia. Supplementing these exhibits are items from Arthur Sackler's original gift of close to 1,000 rare and valuable objects, including Chinese bronzes from the Shang (1700–1028 B.C.) through the Han (206 B.C.–A.D. 220) Dynasties; Chinese jade figures spanning the millennia from 3000 B.C. to the 20th century; Chinese paintings and lacqeurware (from the 10th through the 20th century); 20th-century Japanese ceramics and works on paper; ancient Near Eastern works in silver, gold, bronze, and clay; and stone and bronze sculptures from South and Southeast Asia. Since the museum's opening, Sackler's original gift has been enhanced by significant collections such as the Vever assemblage of 11th- to 19th-century Persian and Indian paintings, manuscripts, calligraphies, miniatures, and bookbindings.

Architecturally, but in no other way, the Sackler is linked to the adjoining National Museum of African Art in a pair-of-pavilions complex housing both facilities. Though 96% of the buildings' exhibition space is subterranean, there are two above-ground pavilions, both designed to harmonize with neighboring landmark buildings. The pyramidal silhouette of the Sackler is related to the Victorian Arts and Industries Building, and its exterior is faced with dark-beige Rockville granite. Subterranean areas are enlivened by dramatic descents, vast north-facing skylights, a spacious concourse, and lush plantings. Roofing material is copper, treated to oxidize green as it ages. The Sackler shares its staff and research facilities with the adjacent Freer Gallery; an underground exhibition space connects the two museums.

While visiting, be sure to browse the vast gallery shop on the premises, which offers a wide array of books on Asian art, posters, and art reproductions, along with marvelous gifts—Indian mirrorwork fabrics, Balinese masks, jade jewelry, Japanese kimonos, bonsai kits, and much more. For information about museum programs (including many wonderful experiences for children and families), highlight tours (highly recommended), films, events, and temporary exhibits, inquire at the information desk.

Admission: Free.

Open: Daily 10am–5:30pm. **Closed:** Dec 25. **Metro:** Smithsonian.

NATIONAL MUSEUM OF AFRICAN ART, 950 Independence Ave. SW. Tel. 357-2700 or 357-4600.

This is the only national art museum in the United States devoted to research in, and the collection and exhibition of, African art. Founded in 1964, and part of the Smithsonian since 1979, it moved to the Mall in 1987 to share a building (though not an entrance) with the Sackler Gallery (see above). Its domed pavilions reflect the arch motif of the neighboring Freer.

Though the museum collects and shows ancient and contemporary art from the entire African continent, its permanent collection of over 7,000 objects (shown in rotating exhibits) highlights the traditional arts of the vast sub-Saharan region. The majority of the collection dates from the 19th and 20th centuries, with works from the western part of Sudan and the Guinea Coast particularly well represented. Also among the museum's holdings are the Eliot Elisofon Photographic Archives, comprising 300,000 photographic prints and transparencies and 120,000 feet of film on African arts and culture. Permanent exhibits include a display of Royal Benin art from Nigeria, "The Art of the Personal Object" (everyday items such as

THE TOP ATTRACTIONS • 155

chairs, headrests, snuff boxes, bowls, and baskets), and "Purpose and Perfection: Pottery as a Woman's Art in Central Africa." Specific objects or themes are explored in depth in a small exhibition space called the Point of View Gallery.

Inquire at the desk about special exhibits, workshops (including excellent children's programs), storytelling, lectures, docent-led tours, films, and demonstrations. A very comprehensive events schedule here (in concert with exhibitions) provides a unique opportunity to learn about the diverse cultures and visual traditions of Africa.

Admission: Free.

Open: Daily 10am–5:30pm. **Closed:** Dec 25. **Metro:** Smithsonian.

ENID A. HAUPT GARDEN, 10th St. and Independence Ave. SW. Tel. 357-2700.

With its central parterre and 1870s cast-iron furnishings, elaborate flower beds and borders, plant-filled turn-of-the-century urns, and lush baskets hung from 19th-century-style lampposts, this tranquilly beautiful oasis on the Mall is named for its donor, a noted supporter of horticultural projects. Though on ground level, it's really a rooftop garden above the subterranean Sackler and African art museums. The magnolia-lined parterre has multicolored swags and ribbon beds adapted from the 1876 Philadelphia Centennial Exposition's horticultural hall. The swags are composed of 30,000 green and yellow Alternanthera, supplemented by seasonal displays of spring pansies, begonias, or cabbage and kale. A winter Oriental garden near the Sackler Gallery, entered via a nine-foot moongate, has benches backed by English boxwoods under the shade of weeping cherry trees; half-round pieces of granite in its still pool are meant to suggest ripples. A summer Islamic garden outside the African art museum provides granite seating walls shaded by hawthorn trees, with tiny water channels fed by fountains and a waterfall or "chadar" inspired by the gardens of Shalimar. Three small terraces, shaded by black sour gum trees, are located near the Arts and Industries Building. And five majestic linden trees shade a seating area around the Downing Urn, a memorial to American landscapist Andrew Jackson Downing. Additional features include wisteria-covered dome-shaped trellises, clusters of trees (Zumi crabapples, ginkos, and American hollies), a weeping European beech, and rose gardens. Elaborate cast-iron carriage gates made according to a 19th-century design by James Renwick, flanked by four pillars made from the same red Seneca sandstone used to construct the "castle," have been installed at the Independence Avenue entrance to the garden.

Admission: Free.

Open: Memorial Day–Labor Day, daily 7am–8pm; the rest of the year, daily 7am–5:45pm. **Closed:** Dec 25. **Metro:** Smithsonian.

NATIONAL POSTAL MUSEUM, 2 Massachusetts Ave. NE, at 1st St. Tel. 357-2700.

This newest addition to the Smithsonian complex (opened in 1993) appropriately occupies the palatial beaux arts quarters of the City Post Office Building designed by brilliant architect Daniel Burnham. Created to house and display the Smithsonian's national philatelic and postal history collection of more than 16 million objects, it is, somewhat surprisingly, a great deal of fun to visit.

Dozens of intriguing interactive exhibits throughout range from Nickelodeon "films" about train wrecks and robberies to a video game that challenges visitors to get 20 bags of mail from Philadelphia to New Orleans in the 1850s via train, boat, or stagecoach. The game is programmed so that 17,000 problems can arise en route! The museum documents America's postal history from 1673 (about 170 years before the advent of stamps, envelopes, and mailboxes) to the present.

In the central gallery, titled "Moving the Mail," three planes that carried mail in the early decades of the 20th century (including a converted World War I bomber) are suspended from a 90-foot atrium ceiling. Here, too: a railway mail car, an 1851 mail/passenger coach, a Ford Model A mail truck, and a replica of an airmail beacon tower atop an oil derrick. In "Binding the Nation," historic correspondence (letters from slaves and Native Americans, from a Revolutionary War soldier to his wife, from immigrants keeping in touch with folks back home, and from pioneers during America's westward expansion) illustrate how mail served to bind families together in the developing nation. Several exhibits deal with the famed Pony Express, a service which lasted less than two years but was romanticized to legendary proportions by Buffalo Bill and others. In the Civil War section you'll learn about Henry "Box" Brown, a slave who had himself "mailed" from Richmond to a Pennsylvania abolitionist in 1856. "Customers and Communities" explores how a growing America dealt with the vast increase in mail volume generated by an expanding population— via pneumatic tubes that carried mail underground, mail metering, ZIP Codes, and technological advances. Here you can find out how marketers view the demographics of your ZIP Code and try to decipher addresses on dead letters. Entertaining exhibits include whimsical folk art mailboxes on rural routes and an array of mail frauds such as an advertisement for a "solar clothes dryer" that turned out to be a clothespin! A nine-minute film features postal workers relating amusing anecdotes about their work. "The Art of Cards and Letters" gallery contains personal correspondence from World War I through Operation Desert Storm, as well as greeting cards, travel postcards, and disaster postcards documenting earth-quakes, fires, and floods; these were popular in the days before newspapers carried photographs. There are, of course, stamps on display here too, ranging from the rare and valuable to fakes and forgeries. In addition, the museum houses a vast research library for philatelic researchers and scholars, a stamp store, and a museum shop.

Admission: Free.

Open: Daily 10am–5:30pm. **Closed:** Dec 25. **Metro:** Union Station.

FREER GALLERY OF ART, on the south side of the Mall at Jefferson Dr. and 12th St. SW. Tel. 357-2700.

A gift to the nation of 9,000 works from Charles Lang Freer, a collector of Asian art and American works from the 19th and early 20th centuries, the Freer Gallery opened in 1923. Freer's original interest was, in fact, American art, but his good friend James McNeill Whistler encouraged him to collect Asian works as well. Eventually the latter became predominant. Freer's gift included funds to construct a museum and an endowment to add objects of the highest quality to the Asian collection only, which has been greatly augmented over the years. It includes Chinese and Japanese sculpture, painting, lacquer, metalwork, and ceramics; early Christian illuminated manuscripts; Japanese screens and woodblock prints; Chinese jades and bronzes; Korean ceramics; Near Eastern manuscripts, metalwork, and miniatures; ancient Near East metalware; and Indian sculpture, manuscripts, and paintings.

Among the American works, not surprisingly, are over 1,200 pieces by Whistler, including the famous Peacock Room permanently installed in Gallery XII. Originally a dining room designed by an architect named Thomas Jeckyll for the London mansion of F. R. Leyland, the Peacock Room contained a Whistler painting called *Rose and Silver, The Princess from the Land of Porcelain.* But after his painting was installed, Whistler was dissatisfied with the room as a setting for his work. When Leyland was away from home, Whistler painted over the very expensive gilded leather interior, embellishing it with paintings of golden peacocks. A permanent rift ensued between Whistler and Leyland. After Leyland's death, Freer purchased the painting and eventually shipped the entire room here from London. Other American painters represented in the collections are Childe Hassam, Thomas Wilmer Dewing, Dwight William Tryon, Abbott Henderson Thayer, and John Singer Sargent. (*Note:* Some 90% of the American works are in their original frames, many of them designed by Stanford White; Whistler designed all his own frames.)

Housed in an Italian Renaissance–style granite-and-marble building, the Freer is a very pleasant museum, with plants and trees adorning its skylit galleries. In 1993, a 4½-year, $26-million expansion and renovation project was completed. The main exhibit floor centers on a garden court open to the sky. There's a museum shop featuring books relating to the collection and reproductions from it; wonderful gifts here, too. An underground exhibition space connects the Freer to the neighboring Sackler Gallery. The museum's Meyer Auditorium is the setting for free chamber music concerts, dance performances, Asian feature films, and other programs. Inquire about these, as well as children's programs, at the information desk.

Admission: Free.

Open: Daily 10am–5:30pm. **Closed:** Dec 25. **Metro:** Smithsonian (Mall or Independence Avenue exit).

ARTS AND INDUSTRIES BUILDING, on the south side of the Mall at 900 Jefferson Dr. SW. Tel. 357-2700.

Completed in 1881 as the first national museum, this red-brick-and-sandstone structure was the scene of President Garfield's Inaugural Ball. Since 1976 it has housed exhibits from the 1876 United States International Exposition in Philadelphia—a celebration of America's 100th birthday that featured the latest advances in technology. The Exposition was re-created here in 1976 for the Bicentennial. The entrance floor is like a turn-of-the-century mall with display cases of Victorian furnishings, fashions, clocks, musical instruments, tools, photographic equipment, and medicines. In areas off the magnificent central Rotunda there's machinery that probably evoked oohs and ahs in the 19th century—steam and gas engines, printing presses, corn mills, refrigerator compresses, and tool builders, as well as a considerable display of weaponry and vehicles. Some are rather large, such as a steam locomotive. There are also state exhibits highlighting California wines, Kansas corn and wheat, Tennessee lumber, etc., as well as international displays.

An area called the Experimental Gallery, in the building's south hall, opened in 1991. It features innovative interactive exhibits from museums in the Smithsonian and around the world. Changing exhibits explore a wide range of topics. Some recent examples include "Kid's Bridge" (about overcoming racial stereotypes) and "Cartoons, Caricatures, and Comics" (exploring three centuries of graphic arts).

Singers, dancers, puppeteers, and mimes perform in the Discovery Theater (October to July, Tuesday through Saturday (call 357-1500 for show times and ticket information; admission is charged). Don't miss the charming Victorian-motif shop on the first floor selling books, jams and jellies, china, needlepoint patterns and samplers, antique reproduction dolls, and more. Most of the year, there's a carousel across the street.

Admission: Free.

Open: Daily 10am–5:30pm. **Closed:** Dec 25. **Metro:** Smithsonian.

NATIONAL ZOOLOGICAL PARK, adjacent to Rock Creek Park, main entrance in the 3000 block of Connecticut Ave. NW. Tel. 673-4800 or 673-4717.

Established in 1889, the National Zoo is home to more than 5,000 animals of some 500 species, many of them rare and/or endangered. A leader in the care, breeding, and exhibition of animals, it occupies 163 beautifully landscaped acres and is one of the country's most delightful zoos. Star resident is Hsing-Hsing, the giant panda donated by the People's Republic of China. The best time to catch him is at feeding time, 11am and 3pm.

It's best to enter the zoo at the Connecticut Avenue entrance, which puts you right by the Education Building. Here you can pick up a map and, on occasion, see films about animals and activities at the zoo's Conservation and Research Center. Friday through Sunday, you can also get tickets for **ZOOlab** (available on a first-come, first-served basis), a learning lab where visitors can handle and examine such objects as hummingbird eggs, read zoology texts, and peer at specimens through a microscope. Similar in concept is the **Reptile Discovery Center** (for the study of reptiles and amphibians; no tickets required). There's also a learning center at the birdhouse. ZOOlab is open Friday through Sunday from 10am to 2pm. The Reptile Discovery Center is open daily from 10am to 4:30pm. And the Bird Resource Center is open on Saturday and Sunday from 10am to 2pm.

Of course, the main reason to come to the zoo is to see the animals. They live in large open enclosures simulating their natural habitats on two easy-to-follow numbered paths, Olmstead Walk and the Valley Trail. You can't get lost, and you won't unintentionally miss anything. In total, there are 3½ miles of trails. Signs indicate the presence of baby animals born in captivity.

Lions, tigers, leopards, monkeys, apes, reptiles, and small animals live in proximity to one another on the Rock Creek side of the zoo. Nearby, in an immense glass-domed building, is **Amazonia,** an exhibit of fish, plants, and animals from the Amazon River region. Also grouped are the four largest land mammals—hippos, rhinos, giraffes, and elephants. Hsing-Hsing is bracketed with kangaroos, camels, and antelopes at the center of the park. Deer and Malayan tapirs coexist with abundant birdlife. Additional residents include North American mammals, otters, seals, and sea lions.

The invertebrate exhibit is the only one of its kind in the country. On display are starfish, sponges, giant crabs, anemones, insects, and other spineless creatures.

Zoo facilities include stroller-rental stations, a number of gift shops, a bookstore, and several paid-parking lots. These last fill up quickly, especially on weekends, so arrive early or take the Metro.

Snack bars and ice-cream kiosks are scattered throughout the park. Most notable is the **Panda Cafe,** with umbrella tables overlooking the outdoor habitat of Hsing-Hsing; fast food is featured. The largest facility is the **Mane Restaurant,** near the Beach Drive entrance. A pleasant alternative is an alfresco lunch at one of the zoo's very nice picnic areas. Buy picnic fare at **Uptown Bakers** (details in Chapter 6).

Admission: Free.

Open: Apr 15–Oct 15, daily (weather permitting): grounds, 8am–8pm; animal buildings, 9am–4:30pm. Oct 16–Apr 14, daily: grounds, 8am–6pm; animal buildings, 9am–4:30pm. **Closed:** Dec 25. **Metro:** Cleveland Park or Woodley Park–Zoo.

ANACOSTIA MUSEUM, 1901 Fort Place SE, off Martin Luther King Ave. Tel. 287-3382 or 357-2700.

This unique Smithsonian establishment was created in 1967 as a neighborhood museum, with major focus on the history and cultural interests of the predominantly black Anacostia community. Expanding its horizons over the years to include every aspect of black history, art, and culture, both American and worldwide, the permanent collection now includes about 5,000 items, ranging from videotapes of African-American church services to art, sheet music, and historic documents. In addition, the Anacostia produces a varying number of shows each year and offers a comprehensive schedule of free educational programs and activities in conjunction with exhibit themes. For instance, to complement an exhibition called "The African American Presence in American Quilts," the museum featured a video about artist/quiltmaker Faith Ringgold, quilting workshops for adults and children, talks by local quilting societies, and storytelling involving quilts.

Call for an events calendar (which always includes children's activities) or pick one up when you visit.

Admission: Free.

Open: Daily 10am–5pm. **Closed:** Dec 25. **Metro:** Anacostia; then take a W1 or W2 bus directly to the museum.

IMPRESSIONS

Take an umbrella, an overcoat, and a fan, and go forth.
—MARK TWAIN

It has a damp, wheezy, Dickensian sort of winter hardly equalled by London, and a steaming tropical summer not surpassed by the basin of the Nile.
—ALISTAIR COOKE

OTHER TOP ATTRACTIONS

**LIBRARY OF CONGRESS, 1st St. SE, between Indepen-
dence Ave. and E. Capitol St. Tel. 707-5458.**

⭐ *Note:* Due to renovations that will continue through some time in 1994, tours currently leave from the **James Madison Memorial Building**, 101 Independence Ave. SE. If you're using this book in 1994, call 707-8000 before you go for up-to-the-minute information.

This is the nation's library, established in 1800 "for the purchase of such books as may be necessary for the use of Congress," but over the years expanded to serve all Americans—from the blind, for whom books are recorded on cassette and/or translated into Braille, to research scholars and college students. Its first collection of books was destroyed when the British burned the Capitol (where the library was then housed) during the War of 1812. Thomas Jefferson then sold the institution his personal library of 6,487 books as a replacement, and this became the foundation of what would grow to be the world's largest library. Today the collection includes more than 101 million items (with new materials being acquired at the rate of 10 items per minute!) housed in three buildings. Its holdings include not only some 27 million books in all languages, but 4 million maps and atlases dating back to the middle of the 14th century; Stradivari violins; the letters of George Washington; more than 14 million prints and photographs; almost 2 million recordings; 691,000 motion picture reels, among them the earliest motion-picture print (made by Thomas Edison in 1893); Thomas Jefferson's rough draft of the Declaration of Independence; the papers of everyone from Freud to Houdini; sketches by Alexander Graham Bell; the magic books of Houdini; and the contents of Lincoln's pockets the night he died. The library also maintains the Dewey decimal system; offers a year-round program of concerts, lectures, and poetry readings; and houses the Copyright Office.

Almost as awesome as the scope of the library's effects and activities is its home, the ornate Italian Renaissance–style **Thomas Jefferson Building,** erected between 1888 and 1897 to contain the burgeoning collection and establish America as a cultured nation with magnificent institutions equal to anything in Europe. Fifty-two painters and sculptors worked for eight years on its interior, utilizing over 1,500 fully developed architectural drawings. There are floor mosaics from Italy, allegorical paintings on the overhead vaults, over 100 murals, and numerous ornamental cornucopias, ribbons, vines, and garlands within, as well as 42 granite sculptures and yards of bas-reliefs on the outside. Especially impressive are the exquisite marble Great Hall and the Main Reading Room, the latter under a 160-foot dome. Originally intended to hold the fruits of at least 150 years of collecting, the building was, in fact, filled up in 13. It is now supplemented by the **James Madison Memorial Building** and the **John Adams Building.**

Tours leave Monday through Friday at 10am and 1 and 3pm from the lobby of the James Madison Building (address above). A prelude to each tour is a 22-minute introductory slide-sound presentation called *America's Library,* shown weekdays every half hour from 9am to a half hour before closing.

Pick up a calendar of events at the ground-floor exit. The Madison Building offers interesting exhibits and features classic, rare, and unusual films in its Mary Pickford Theater. It also contains a noteworthy restaurant and cafeteria (see "Restaurants at Sightseeing Attractions," in Chapter 6, for details), though picnic tables out front here and at the Thomas Jefferson Building provide a tempting alternative.

Admission: Free.

Open: Mon and Wed–Thurs 8:30am–9:30pm, Tues and Fri–Sat 8:30am–5pm, Sun (exhibition areas of the Madison Building only) 8:30am–6pm. **Closed:** Jan 1 and Dec 25. **Metro:** Capitol South.

NATIONAL ARCHIVES, Constitution Ave., between 7th and 9th Sts. NW. Tel. 501-5000 for information on exhibits and films, 501-5400 for research information.

Keeper of America's documentary heritage, the National Archives displays our most cherished treasures in appropriately awe-inspiring surroundings. Housed in the Rotunda of the Exhibition Hall are the nation's three charter documents—the Declaration of Independence, the Constitution of the United States, and its Bill of Rights—which are on view daily to the public. Every night these three "Charters of Freedom" are lowered 20 feet into a 50-ton vault for safekeeping, and every morning they are raised for exhibition. During the day, armed guards stand on duty in the hall.

High above and flanking the documents are two larger-than-life murals painted by Barry Faulkner. One, entitled *The Declaration of Independence,* shows Thomas Jefferson presenting a draft of the Declaration to John Hancock, the presiding officer of the Continental Congress; the other, entitled *The Constitution,* shows James Madison submitting the Constitution to George Washington and the Constitutional Convention. In the display cases on either side of the Declaration of Independence are changing exhibits, such as the recent "Birth of Democracy," celebrating the 2,500th anniversary of Athenian democracy. The 1297 version of the Magna Carta, one of the bases for fundamental English privileges and rights, is on display in the Rotunda indefinitely. There are temporary exhibits in the Circular Gallery (at this writing, World War II propaganda posters).

The Archives serves as much more than a museum of cherished documents. Most famous as a center of genealogical research—Alex Haley began his work on *Roots* here—it is sometimes called the "nation's memory." This federal institution is charged with sifting through the accumulated papers of a nation's official life—billions of pieces a year—and determining what to save and what to destroy. The Archives' vast accumulation of census figures, military records, naturalization papers, immigrant passenger lists, federal documents, passport applications, ship manifests, maps, charts, photographs, and motion-picture film (and that's not the half of it) spans two centuries. And it's all available for the perusal of anyone 16 or over. All you have to do is get a research card; to apply, go to Room 207 with photo ID. If you're casually thinking about tracing your roots, stop in first at Room 400 where a staff member can tell you whether it's worth the effort and how to go about it.

But the National Archives merits a visit even if you have no research project in mind. The neoclassical building itself, designed by John Russell Pope in the 1930s (he was also the architect of the National Gallery and the Jefferson Memorial) is an impressive example of the beaux arts style. Seventy-two columns create a Corinthian colonnade on each of the four facades. Great bronze doors herald the Constitution Avenue entrance, and allegorical sculpture centered on *The Recorder of the Archives* adorns the pediment. On either side of the steps are male and female figures symbolizing guardianship and heritage, respectively. Guardians of the Portals at the Pennsylvania Avenue entrance represent the past and the future, and the theme of the pediment is destiny.

Free docent **tours** are given weekdays at 10:15am and 1:15pm by appointment only; call 501-5205 for details. Pick up a schedule of events such as lectures, films, and genealogy workshops when you visit.

Admission: Free.

Open: Exhibition Hall, Apr–Labor Day, daily 10am–9pm; day after Labor Day–Mar, daily 10am–5:30pm. Call for research hours. **Closed:** Dec 25. **Metro:** Archives.

NATIONAL GALLERY OF ART, on the north side of the Mall between 3rd and 7th Sts. NW (entrances at 6th St. and Constitution Ave. or Madison Dr., also at 4th and 7th Sts. between Madison Dr. and Constitution Ave.). Tel. 737-4215.

Most people don't realize it, but the National Gallery of Art is not really part of the Smithsonian complex (though it is, in some arcane way, related to it); hence its listing here apart from the other Mall museums.

Housing one of the world's foremost collections of Western painting, sculpture, and graphic arts from the Middle Ages through the 20th century, the National Gallery has a dual personality. The original West Building, designed by John Russell Pope (he was also the architect of the Jefferson Memorial and the National Archives), is a neoclassic marble masterpiece with a domed rotunda over a colonnaded pool and high-ceilinged corridors leading to delightful garden courts. It was a gift to the nation from Andrew W. Mellon, who also contributed the nucleus of the collection, including 21 masterpieces from the Hermitage—two Raphaels among them. The ultramodern honeycombed East Building, opened in 1978, is an asymmetrical trapezoid with glass walls and lofty tetrahedron skylights designed by I. M. Pei. The pink Tennessee marble from which both buildings are constructed was taken from the same quarry; it forms an architectural link between the two structures.

The East Building: Though the East Building primarily houses changing exhibits (many of them of major importance), a massive aluminum Calder mobile suspended from the skylight and an immense bronze sculpture by Henry Moore are among the works on permanent display. They were specifically commissioned for the museum.

The West Building: On the main floor of the West Building, about 800 paintings are shown at all times. Galleries to the right of the Rotunda (if you've entered from the Mall) feature 17th- to 19th-century French paintings, works of late 19th-century Americans such as Homer and Sargent, and of slightly earlier British artists such as Constable, Turner, and Gainsborough. To the left are the Italians (Renaissance, 17th and 18th centuries), including the only da Vinci outside Europe, *Ginerva De' Benci*. Paintings by El Greco, Goya, and Velázquez highlight the Spanish galleries; Grunewald, Dürer, Holbein, and Cranach can be seen in the German; Van Eyck, Rubens, and Bosch in the Flemish; and an excellent collection of Rembrandts in the Dutch. Room decor reflects the period and country of the art shown: For example, the Italian gallery walls are of Travertine marble, while the Dutch galleries are paneled in somber oak.

Down a flight are 17th- and 18th-century prints, 19th- and 20th-century sculpture (with many pieces by Daumier, Degas, and Renoir), American naïve 18th- and 19th-century paintings, Chinese porcelains, small Renaissance bronzes, 16th-century Flemish tapestries, decorative 18th-century arts, and an immense shop offering art books and prints—one of several.

In addition to its permanent collection, the National Gallery hosts a wide range of temporary exhibits. Some of the major shows require free passes, available on a first-come, first-served basis, with specified entry times.

Pick up a floor plan and calendar of events at an information desk to find out about exhibits, films, tours, lectures, and concerts. Highly recommended are the free highlight **tours** (call for exact times) and audio tours. There are several dining options here (see "Restaurants in Sightseeing Attractions," in Chapter 6, for details).

Admission: Free.

Open: Mon–Sat 10am–5pm, Sun 11am–6pm. **Closed:** Jan 1 and Dec 25. **Metro:** Archives or Judiciary Square.

FEDERAL BUREAU OF INVESTIGATION, J. Edgar Hoover FBI Building, E St. NW, between 9th and 10th Sts. Tel. 324-3447.

⭐ Over half a million annual visitors learn why crime doesn't pay by touring the headquarters of the FBI. The attraction is especially popular with kids. To beat the crowds, arrive for the one-hour **tour** before 8:45am or write to a senator or congressperson for a scheduled reservation as far in advance as possible (details in Chapter 2).

The tour begins with a short videotape presentation about the priorities of the bureau—organized crime, white-collar crime, terrorism, foreign counterintelligence, illicit drugs, and violent crimes. En route, you'll learn about this organization's history (it was established in 1908) and its activities over the years. You'll see some of the weapons used by big-time gangsters like Al Capone, Dillinger, Bonnie and Clyde, and "Pretty Boy" Floyd; an exhibit on counterintelligence operations; and photos of the 10 most wanted fugitives—435 of them (only 7 of them women) have made the list since its inception in 1950; 406 have been captured (127 apprehended through direct citizen cooperation), 2 were actually recognized at this exhibit by people on the tour, and 8 have been located via the FBI-assisted TV show, "America's Most Wanted."

Other exhibits deal with white-collar crime, the use of fingerprints for identification, terrorism, and agent training. On display are more than 4,200 weapons, most confiscated from criminals; they're used for reference purposes. And an illicit drug exhibit includes drug paraphernalia and shows how the FBI attempts to combat illicit drugs via educational as well as investigational methods.

You'll also visit the DNA lab, the Document Section (where fraudulent checks and holdup notes are examined), the Firearms Unit (where it's determined whether a bullet was fired from a given weapon), the Elemental and Metals Analysis Unit (where from a tiny piece of paint the FBI can determine the approximate make and model of a car), the unit where hairs and fibers are examined, and a

Forfeiture and Seizure Exhibit—a display of jewelry, furs, and other proceeds from illegal narcotics operations. The tour ends with a bang—lots of them in fact—when an agent gives a sharpshooting demonstration. He also talks about the FBI's firearms policy and gun safety.

Admission: Free.

Open: Mon–Fri 8:45am–4:15pm. **Closed:** Jan 1, Dec 25, and other federal holidays. **Metro:** Metro Center or Federal Triangle.

JOHN F. KENNEDY CENTER FOR THE PERFORMING ARTS, New Hampshire Ave. NW at Rock Creek Pkwy. Tel. 467-4600 or toll free 800/444-1324 for information or tickets.

Opened in 1971, the Kennedy Center is both our national performing arts center and a memorial to John F. Kennedy, whose administration was very enthusiastic about its development. Carved into the center's river facade are several Kennedy quotations, including ". . . the New Frontier for which I campaign in public life can also be a New Frontier for American art." Set on 17 acres overlooking the Potomac, the striking $73-million facility contains an opera house, a concert hall, two stage theaters, and a film theater. The best way to see the Kennedy Center—including areas you can't visit on your own—is to take a free 50-minute guided **tour,** given daily between 10am and 1pm. Once again, you can beat the crowds by writing in advance to a senator or congressperson for tickets for a 9:30am VIP tour (details in Chapter 2).

The tour begins in the Hall of Nations, where all flags of countries recognized diplomatically by the United States are displayed. Throughout the center you'll see gifts from more than 40 nations, including all the marble used in the building (3,700 tons), which was donated by Italy. First stop is the Grand Foyer—scene of many free concerts and programs and reception area for all three theaters on the main level; the 18 crystal chandeliers are a gift from Sweden. You'll also visit the Israeli Lounge (where 40 painted and gilded panels depict scenes mentioned in the Bible); the Concert Hall, home of the National Symphony Orchestra; the Opera House, with its Matisse tapestries; the African room (decorated with beautiful tapestries from various African nations); the Eisenhower Theater; the Hall of States, where flags of the 50 states and four territories are hung in the order they joined the Union; the Performing Arts Library; and the Terrace Theater, a Bicentennial gift from Japan. Your guide will point out many notable works of art along the way, such as a Barbara Hepworth sculpture (a gift of England), Henri Matisse tapestries (gifts of France), and an alabaster vase from 2600 B.C. found in a pyramid (a gift of Egypt). If rehearsals are going on, visits to the theaters are omitted.

If you'd like to attend performances during your visit, call the toll-free number above and request the current issue of *Kennedy Center News,* a free publication that describes all Kennedy Center happenings and prices.

After the tour, walk around the building's terrace for a panoramic 360° view of Washington and plan a meal in one of the Kennedy Center restaurants (details in "Restaurants in Sightseeing Attractions," in Chapter 6). See Chapter 9 for specifics on theater, concert, and film offerings. There is parking below the Kennedy Center during the day at $2.50 for the first hour, $1.50 for each additional hour,

IMPRESSIONS

*I went to Washington as everybody goes there prepared to see
everything done with some furtive intention, but I was
disappointed—pleasantly disappointed.*
—WALT WHITMAN

---

with a maximum of five hours and $7; nighttime parking (after 5pm)
is a flat $5.

Admission: Free.

Open: Daily 10am–midnight. **Metro:** Foggy Bottom. **Bus:** 46
down New Hampshire Avenue from Dupont Circle or 81 from
Metro Center.

THE WASHINGTON NATIONAL CATHEDRAL, Mount St. Alban, Massachusetts and Wisconsin Aves. NW (entrance on Wisconsin Ave.). Tel. 537-6200.

Pierre L'Enfant's 1791 plan for the capital city included "a
great church for national purposes," but possibly because of
early America's fear of mingling church and state, over a
century elapsed before the foundation for the National Cathedral
was laid. Its actual name is the Cathedral Church of Saint Peter and
Saint Paul. Though it's Episcopalian in denomination, it has no local
congregation and seeks to serve the entire nation as a house of prayer
for all people. It has been the setting for every kind of religious
observance from Jewish to Serbian Orthodox.

A church of this magnitude (it's the sixth-largest cathedral in the
world!) is a long time in the building. Its principal (but not original)
architect, Philip Hubert Frohman, worked on the project from 1921
until his death in 1972. The foundation stone (a stone from a field in
Bethlehem set into a larger piece of American granite) was laid 1907,
using the mallet with which George Washington set the Capitol
cornerstone. Construction was interrupted by two World Wars and
periods of financial difficulty. It was completed with the placement of
a final stone atop a pinnacle on the west front towers on September
29, 1990—83 years to the day of its inception.

English Gothic in style (with several distinctly 20th-century
innovations, such as a stained-glass window commemorating the
flight of *Apollo 11* and containing a piece of moon rock), the
cathedral is built in the shape of a cross, complete with flying
buttresses and gargoyles. It is, along with the Capitol and the
Washington Monument, one of the most dominant structures on the
Washington skyline. Its 57-acre landscaped grounds contain two
lovely gardens; five schools, including the College of Preachers; and a
herb garden, a greenhouse, and a shop called Herb Cottage (buy
seeds and start your own).

Over the years the cathedral has seen a lot of history. Services to
celebrate the end of World Wars I and II were held here. It was the
scene of President Wilson's funeral (he and his wife are buried here),
as well as President Eisenhower's. Helen Keller and her companion,
Anne Sullivan, are buried in the cathedral at her request. Martin
Luther King, Jr., preached his last sermon here. And during the
Iranian crisis, a round-the-clock prayer vigil was held in the Holy
Spirit Chapel throughout the hostages' captivity. When they were
released, the hostages came to a service here, and tears flowed at Col.

Thomas Shaefer's poignant greeting, "Good morning, my fellow Americans. You don't know how long I've been waiting to say those words."

The best way to explore the cathedral and see its abundance of art, architectural carvings, and statuary is to take a free one-hour **tour.** They leave continually—from the west end of the nave—Monday through Saturday from 10am to 3:15pm and on Sunday from 12:30 to 2:45pm. Among the highlights are dozens of stained-glass windows with themes ranging from the lives of Civil War Generals Lee and Jackson to the miracles of Christ; three exquisite rose windows; the nave, stretching a tenth of a mile to the high altar; Wilson's tomb; the delightful children's chapel; St. John's Chapel, where needlepoint kneelers memorialize great Americans; the Holy Spirit Chapel, painted by Andrew Wyeth's father, N. C. Wyeth; and crypt chambers like the Bethlehem Chapel, first section of the cathedral to be constructed.

Allow time to tour the grounds or "close," and to visit the Observation Gallery where 70 windows provide panoramic views. Tuesday- and Wednesday-afternoon tours are followed by a high tea in the Observation Gallery; reservations are required and a fee is charged. And you can, of course, attend **services** at the cathedral (Monday through Saturday at 7:30am, noon, and 4pm; on Sunday at 8, 9, and 11am and 4pm). September to June there's a folk guitar mass on Sunday at 10am.

The cathedral hosts numerous events: organ recitals, choir performances, flower markets, films and slide lectures, calligraphy workshops, and jazz, folk, and classical concerts. Past performances have ranged from Ravi Shankar playing sitar at a memorial for Gandhi to a Stravinsky Centennial with Leonard Bernstein conducting. The 53-bell carillon is played on Saturday at 5pm during spring and summer, 12:30pm in winter and fall. Organ recitals are usually given on the great organ following Sunday-evening services at 5pm. The Cathedral Choir of Men and Boys can be heard on Sunday at 11am and 4pm; the boys alone (during the school year only), Monday through Wednesday at 4pm.

A large gift shop on the premises sells replicas of cathedral statuary, religious books and art, Christmas cards, and more.

Admission: Free.

Open: Mon–Sat 10am–4:30pm, Sun 7:30am–4:30pm. **Metro:** Tenleytown; then about a 20-minute walk. **Bus:** Any N bus up Massachusetts Avenue from Dupont Circle.

BUREAU OF ENGRAVING AND PRINTING, 14th and C Sts. SW. Tel. 874-3187.

This is where they make the money—over \$103 *billion* of it each year. A staff of 2,300 works around the clock churning it out at the rate of 2.25 million notes a day. Everyone's eyes pop as they walk past rooms overflowing with money, the kind of rooms that Scrooge McDuck cavorted in. Though the money is the big draw, it's not the whole story. The bureau manufactures many different products, including 30.5 billion postage stamps per year, Treasury bonds, and White House invitations.

As many as 5,000 people line up each day to get a peek at all that moolah, so early arrival—especially in peak tourist season—is essential (though you can obviate the need if you secure VIP tickets from your senator or congressperson; details in Chapter 2). Memorial

Day through Labor Day, when you have to secure a ticket which specifies a tour time, the ticket booth opens at 8am. Be there! The rest of the year no ticket is needed; you just have to line up.

The 25-minute **self-guided tour** (there are audiovisual aids, and bureau personnel are on hand to answer questions) begins with a short introductory film. Then you'll see, through large windows, all the processes that go into the making of paper money—the inking, stacking (each stack of dollar bills contains $320,000), cutting, and examination for defects. Most printing here is done from engraved steel plates in a process known as "intaglio"—the hardest to counterfeit, because the slightest alteration will cause a noticeable change in the portrait in use. Additional exhibits include bills no longer in use, counterfeit money, and an enlarged photo of a $100,000 bill designed for official transactions (since 1969, the largest denomination printed for general consumption is $100).

Upon completion of the tour, leave time to explore the **Visitor Center** (open from 8:30am to 3:30pm), where the history of money is examined from "picces of eight" to current currency. Other exhibits include informative videos, money-related electronic games, and a display of $1 million. Here, too, you can buy unique gifts ranging from bags of shredded money to copies of documents such as the Gettysburg Address.

Admission: Free.

Open: Mon–Fri 9am–2pm. **Closed:** Dec 25–Jan 1 and Federal holidays. **Metro:** Smithsonian (Independence Avenue exit).

THE VIETNAM VETERANS MEMORIAL, just across from the Lincoln Memorial, east of Henry Bacon Dr. between 21st and 22nd Sts. NW. Tel. 634-1568.

To my mind, the saddest sight in Washington is the Vietnam Veterans Memorial—two long, black granite walls inscribed with the names of the men and women who gave their lives, or remain missing, in the longest war in our nation's history. Even if no one close to you died in Vietnam, it's emotionally wrenching watching visitors grimly studying the directories at either end to find out where their husbands, sons, and loved ones are listed. The slow walk along the 492-foot wall of names—close to 60,000 people, many of whom died very young—is a powerful evocation of the tragedy of all wars. And whatever your views on the war, it's also affecting to see how much the monument means to Vietnam vets who visit it. Because of the raging conflict over U.S. involvement in the war, its veterans had received virtually no previous recognition of their service.

The memorial was conceived by Vietnam veteran Jan Scruggs and built by the Vietnam Veterans Memorial Fund, a nonprofit organization that raised $7 million for the project. The VVMF was granted a site of two acres in tranquil Constitution Gardens to erect a memorial that would make no political statement about the war and would harmonize with neighboring memorials. By separating the issue of the wartime service of individuals from the issue of U.S. policy in Vietnam, VVMF hoped to begin a process of national reconciliation.

Yale senior Maya Ying Lin's design was chosen in a national competition open to all citizens over 18 years of age. It consists of two walls in a quiet, protected park setting, angled at 125 degrees to point to the Washington Monument and the Lincoln Memorial. The walls' mirrorlike surface reflects surrounding trees, lawn, and monuments. Names are inscribed in chronological order, documenting an epoch in American history as a series of individual sacrifices from the date of the first casualty in 1959 to the date of the last death in 1975.

The wall was erected in 1982. In 1984 a life-size sculpture of three Vietnam soldiers by Frederick Hart was installed at the entrance plaza. He describes his work this way: "They wear the uniform and carry the equipment of war; they are young. The contrast between the innocence of their youth and the weapons of war underscores the poignancy of their sacrifice. . . . Their strength and their vulnerability are both evident." Near the statue a flag flies from a 60-foot staff. Another sculpture, the Vietnam Veterans Women's Memorial was installed on Veteran's Day of 1993.

Admission: Free.

Open: Daily 24 hours, with rangers on duty 8am–midnight.
Metro: Foggy Bottom.

UNITED STATES HOLOCAUST MEMORIAL MUSEUM, 100 Raoul Wallenberg Pl. (formerly 15th St. SW), near Independence Ave., just off the Mall. Tel. 488-0400.

"Out of our memory . . . of the Holocaust we must forge an unshakable oath with all civilized people that never again will the world stand silent, never again will the world . . . fail to act in time to prevent the terrible crime of genocide. . . ." These words of Jimmy Carter are inscribed on a wall outside the museum.

Washington's multitude of museums celebrate the knowledge, the glory, and the creative achievements of human civilization. This museum, mandated by an Act of Congress in 1980 and opened in 1993, reminds us of what can happen when civilization goes awry. It serves the dual purpose of commemorating the dead and educating the living to the dangers of prejudice and fanatacism and the fragility of freedom.

Only a little over 50 years ago, a seemingly civilized Western nation legalized racism, brutally trampled on human rights, and engaged in the genocide of millions. Here the story is told in full. Even the building housing the museum is designed to reflect the bleakness of the Nazi era—to disorient the visitor with false perspectives and eerily somber spaces. An outer wall is reminiscent of an extermination camp's exterior brickwork, and towers evoke the guard towers of Auschwitz.

Upon entering, you will be issued an identity card of an actual victim (of your same age and sex) of the Holocaust. By 1945, 66% of those whose lives are documented on these cards were dead. As you ascend to the fourth floor (where events from 1933 to 1939 are portrayed), a video in the elevator features an American soldier describing his experiences liberating a camp. The Holocaust story begins with the rise of Nazism—book burnings, the Nuremburg Laws of 1935 that isolated Jews from German society, and the terror of "Kristallnacht" in 1938, when hundreds of Jewish synagogues and businesses were destroyed. A winding path takes you to a border crossing where the near impossibility of escape is dramatized. No countries will admit you; you're forced to return to the horror. Also highlighted are the non-Jewish victims of the Nazis—Gypsies, the physically and mentally handicapped, homosexuals, political and religious dissidents.

On the third floor (documenting the years 1940 to 1944), constricting walls symbolize the narrowing choices of people caught up in the Nazi machine. You'll board a German freightcar used to transport Jews from the Warsaw ghetto to Treblinka and hear recordings of survivors telling what life in the camps was like. A reconstructed Auschwitz barracks, the yellow stars Jews were forced to wear, instruments of genocide, and a gas-chamber door are among the thousands of artifacts bearing silent witness to this grim era. Like your identity card, displays foster identification with individuals who perished. In one of the towers, a montage of 1,500 family photographs documents the beauty and vitality of everyday lives of people in the Jewish town of Ejszyszki, Lithuania, before the Holocaust; later you'll learn that 90% of them were murdered by Nazi death squads in two days in 1941.

On the second floor, the focus turns to a more heartening story: how non-Jews throughout Europe saved Jews at great personal risk. In Denmark, 90% of the Jews were hidden and saved. The saga continues with exhibits on the liberation of the camps, life in D.P. camps, emigration to Israel and America, and the Nuremburg trials. The tour ends in the hexagonal (to commemorate the six million Jews slain) Hall of Remembrance—a place to meditate on what you've experienced and light a candle for the victims.

Dozens of educational interactive videos further promote understanding, as do films, lectures, cultural events, and temporary exhibits. Exhibits are designed so you can shield children (or yourself) from the most graphic material. This is not like any other museum you've ever visited. It's a deeply affecting encounter with evil—an opportunity to learn the lessons of history and the role of individual responsibility in protecting freedom and preserving human rights.

Allow at least four or five hours to tour the museum. I don't recommend bringing children under 12 to this facility, and even then, it's advisable to prepare them for what they'll see. There's a cafeteria on the premises.

Note: At this writing, because so many people wish to visit the museum, advance tickets are required. Reserve them via Ticketmaster (tel. 202/432-SEAT, or toll free 800/551-SEAT). There's a small service charge. You can also get them at the museum box office, which opens at 9:30am daily. However, this advance-ticket policy may change; call ahead for up-to-the-minute details.

Admission: Free.

Open: Daily 10am–5:30pm. **Closed:** Yom Kippur and Dec 25. **Metro:** Smithsonian.

UNION STATION, 40 Massachusetts Ave. NE. Tel. 371-9441.

⭐ In Washington, D.C., the very train station you pull into is in itself a noteworthy sightseeing attraction. Union Station, a monument to the great age of rail travel built between 1903 and 1907, was painstakingly restored in the late 1980s to its original grandeur at a cost of $180 million. The station was designed by noted architect Daniel H. Burnham, an enthusiast of French beaux arts neoclassicism and a member of the McMillan Commission—an illustrious task force assembled in 1900 to beautify the Mall and make the city an appropriately imposing world capital. The committee's philosophy was summed up by Burnham, who counseled, "Make no little plans. They have no magic to stir men's blood, and probably themselves will not be realized." The committee's "big plans" included Union Station, modeled after the Baths of Diocletian and Arch of Constantine in Rome.

When it opened in 1907, this was the largest train station in the world. Its Ionic-colonnaded exterior is of white granite, and 100 eagles are portrayed in the facade. Out front are a replica of the Liberty Bell and a monumental statue of Columbus. Six carved allegorical figures in niches over the entranceway represent Fire, Electricity, Freedom, Imagination, Agriculture, and Mechanics. The station's interior, entered through graceful 50-foot Constantinian arches, is finished with extravagant materials—acres of white marble flooring with red "Champlain dots," bronze grilles, elaborate coffered ceilings (embellished with a half-million dollars' worth of 22-carat gold leaf!), and rich Honduran mahogany. The Main Hall is a massive rectangular room with a 96-foot barrel-vault ceiling, its balcony adorned with 36 Augustus Saint-Gaudens sculptures of Roman legionnaires. Off the Main Hall is the East Hall, one of the most beautiful areas of the station, with scagliola marble walls and columns, a gorgeous hand-stenciled skylight ceiling, and stunning murals of classical scenes inspired by ancient Pompeiian art. Today it's the station's plushest shopping venue.

In its heyday, many important events took place at this "temple of transport." President Wilson welcomed General Pershing here in 1918 on his return from France. South Pole explorer Rear Admiral Byrd was also feted at Union Station on his homecoming. Franklin D. Roosevelt's funeral train, bearing his casket, was met by thousands of mourners in 1945. And in the 1960s, the Kennedys greeted King Hassan II of Morocco and Ethiopian Emperor Haile Selassie here.

But soon after, with the decline of rail travel, the station fell on hard times. Rain damage caused parts of the roof to cave in, and the entire building—with floors buckling, rats running about, and mushrooms sprouting in damp rooms—was sealed in 1981. That same year, Congress enacted legislation to preserve and faithfully restore this national treasure.

Today, Union Station is once again a vibrant entity—a transportation/dining/shopping/entertainment center patronized by locals and visitors alike. Every square inch of the facility has been cleaned, repaired, and/or replaced according to original designs. An elliptical mahogany kiosk has been erected in the center of the Main Hall, inspired by a Renaissance baldacchino, to contain a bilevel café and a visitor information center. About 100 retail shops on three levels offer a wide array of merchandise. The skylit Main Concourse, extending the entire length of the station, has become the primary shopping area as well as a ticketing and baggage facility. And a nine-screen cinema complex and beautiful food court have been installed on the lower level. The remarkable restoration, which involved hundreds of European and American artisans utilizing historical research, bygone craft techniques, and modern technology, is meticulous in every detail. I'm sure Burnham would be greatly pleased could he walk the majestic corridors of Union Station today. His own 1907 declaration foretells the spirit of the renovation: ". . . a noble, logical diagram once recorded will never die, but long after we are gone will be a living thing, asserting itself with ever-growing insistency. . . . Let your watchword be order and your beacon beauty."

For information on Union Station restaurants and shops, see "Restaurants in Sightseeing Attractions," Chapter 6, and Chapter 8.

MORE ATTRACTIONS • 171

Admission: Free.
Open: Daily 24 hours. Shops, Mon–Sat 10am–9pm, Sun noon–6pm. **Metro:** Union Station.

FORD'S THEATRE AND LINCOLN MUSEUM, 511 10th St. NW, between E and F Sts. Tel. 426-6924.

On April 14, 1865, President Lincoln was in the audience of Ford's Theatre, one of the most popular playhouses in Washington. Everyone was laughing at a funny line from Tom Taylor's celebrated comedy, *Our American Cousin,* when actor John Wilkes Booth grabbed center stage by shooting the president. Booth escaped by jumping to the stage, mounting his horse in the back alley, and galloping off. Doctors carried Lincoln to the house of William Petersen, across the street, and the president died there the next morning. (See below for details.)

After Lincoln's assassination, the theater was closed by order of Secretary of War Stanton. For many years afterward it was used by the War Department for clerical work. In 1893, 22 clerks were killed when three floors of the building collapsed. It remained in disuse until the 1960s, when it was remodeled and restored to its appearance on the night of the tragedy. Except when rehearsals or matinees are in progress (call before you go), visitors can see the theater and trace Booth's movements on that fateful night. Free 15-minute talks on the history of the theater and the story of the assassination are given throughout the day (call for exact hours). Be sure to visit the **Lincoln Museum** in the basement, which contains exhibits on Lincoln's life and times. In addition to Lincoln memorabilia, the museum displays the clothes Lincoln was wearing the night he was killed, the Deringer pistol used by Booth, the killer's diary outlining his rationalization for the deed, and other artifacts. See Chapter 9 for information on theatrical presentations here.
Admission: Free.
Open: Daily 9am–5pm. **Closed:** Dec 25. **Metro:** Metro Center.

THE HOUSE WHERE LINCOLN DIED, 516 10th St. NW. Tel. 426-6830.

This is where Lincoln was carried after the shooting. Furnished with period pieces, it looks much as it did on that fateful April night. You'll see the front parlor where an anguished Mary Todd Lincoln spent the night with her son, Robert. Her emotional state was such that she was banned from the bedroom because she was creating havoc. In the back parlor Secretary of War Edwin M. Stanton held a Cabinet meeting and began questioning witnesses. The room where Lincoln died contains a bed of the same design as the original, complete with the actual bloodstained pillow on which he rested. From this room, Stanton announced at 7:22am on April 15, 1865, "Now he belongs to the ages."

Six years after Lincoln's death, the house was sold to Louis Schade, who published a newspaper called the *Washington Sentinel* in its basement for many years. In 1896 the government bought the house for $30,000, and it is now maintained by the National Park Service.
Admission: Free.
Open: Daily 9am–5pm. **Closed:** Dec 25. **Metro:** Metro Center.

2. MORE ATTRACTIONS

PHILLIPS COLLECTION, 1600 21st St. NW, at Q St. Tel. 387-0961.

⭐ Conceived as "a museum of modern art and its sources," this intimate establishment houses—in an elegant 1890s Georgian Revival mansion and a wing added later—the exquisite collection of Duncan and Marjorie Phillips, avid collectors and proselytizers of modernism. Carpeted rooms, with leaded- and stained-glass windows, oak paneling, plush chairs and sofas, and, frequently, fireplaces create a comfortable, homelike setting for viewing art. The original building was once the Phillipses' elegant home, though always doubling as a museum. When their collection totaled 600 paintings, they moved out and had it renovated entirely as a museum. Today it contains over 2,500 works. Among the highlights are superb examples of Daumier, Dove, and Bonnard paintings; some splendid small Vuillards; three Van Goghs; Renoir's *Luncheon of the Boating Party;* five Cézannes; and five works by Georgia O'Keeffe. Ingres, Delacroix, Manet, El Greco, Goya, Corot, Constable, Courbet, Giorgione, and Chardin are among the "sources" or forerunners of modernism represented. Modern notables include Rothko, Hopper, Kandinsky, Matisse, Klee, Degas, Rouault, Picasso, and many others. It's a collection no art lover should miss. An ongoing series of temporary shows is presented, with works from the Phillips supplemented by loans from other museums and private collections.

Free **tours** are given on Wednesday and Saturday at 2pm, and a full schedule of events includes gallery talks, lectures, and free concerts in the ornate music room (every Sunday at 5pm, September to May; early arrival is advised at these popular performances).

On the lower level are a charming little restaurant serving light fare and a comprehensive museum shop.

Admission: Sat–Sun, $6.50 adults, $3.25 seniors and students, free for children under 18; Mon–Fri, contribution suggested.

Open: Mon–Sat 10am–5pm, Sun noon–7pm. **Closed:** Jan 1, July 4, Thanksgiving Day, and Dec 25. **Metro:** Dupont Circle (Q Street exit).

CORCORAN GALLERY OF ART, 17th St., NW, between E St. and New York Ave. Tel. 638-3211 or 638-1439.

The first art museum in Washington, and one of the first in the country, the Corcoran Gallery was housed from 1874 to 1896 in the red-brick and brownstone building that is now the Renwick. The collection outgrew its quarters and was transferred in 1897 to its present beaux arts building, designed by Ernest Flagg. It features a double atrium with two levels of fluted columns and a grand staircase.

The collection itself—shown in rotating exhibits—focuses chiefly on American art. A prominent Washington banker, William Wilson Corcoran was among the first wealthy American collectors to realize the importance of encouraging and supporting his country's artists. Enhanced by further gifts and bequests, the collection comprehensively spans American art from 18th-century portraiture to 20th-century moderns like Nevelson, Warhol, and Rothko. Nineteenth-century works include Bierstadt's and Remington's imagery of the American West; Hudson River School artists like Cole,

Church, and Durand; genre paintings; expatriates like Whistler, Sargent, and Mary Cassatt; and two giants of the late 19th century, Homer and Eakins. Displayed on the second floor is the white marble female nude, *The Greek Slave,* by Hiram Powers, considered so daring in its day that it was shown on alternate days to men and women.

The Corcoran is not, however, an exclusively American art museum. On the first floor is the collection from the estate of Sen. William Andrews Clark—an eclectic grouping of Dutch and Flemish masters, European painters, French impressionists, Barbizon landscapes, Delft porcelains, a Louis XVI salon doré transported in toto from Paris, and more. Clark's will stated that this diverse collection—which any curator must long to disperse among various museum departments—must be shown as a unit. He left money for a wing to house it which opened in 1928. Other non-American aspects of the museum's collection include a room of exquisite Corot landscapes, another of medieval Renaissance tapestries, and numerous Daumier lithographs donated by Dr. Armand Hammer.

Free 30-minute **tours** are given at 12:30pm and evenings at 7pm. The museum shop has a terrific selection of art reproductions, books, jewelry, and art nouveau glassware, among other things. And do pick up a schedule of events—temporary exhibits, gallery talks, concerts, art auctions, and more. There's a charming restaurant on the premises (details in "Restaurants in Sightseeing Attractions," in Chapter 6).

Admission: Free.

Open: Fri–Mon and Wed 10:30am–5pm, Thurs 10:30am–9pm. **Closed:** Jan 1 and Dec 25. **Metro:** Farragut West or Farragut North.

NATIONAL MUSEUM OF WOMEN IN THE ARTS, 1250 New York Ave. NW, at 13th St. Tel. 783-5000.

Celebrating "the contribution of women to the history of art," this relatively new museum (opened 1987) is Washington's 72nd but a national first. Founders Wilhelmina and Wallace Holladay, who donated the core of the permanent collection—more than 200 works by 115 women spanning the 16th through the 20th century—became interested in women's art in the 1960s. After discovering that no women were included in H. W. Janson's *History of Art,* a standard text (this, by the way, did not change until 1986!), the Holladays began collecting women's art, and the concept of a women's art museum to begin correcting the inequities of underrepresentation soon evolved. (Though women make up close to 50% of the working artists in the United States, over 95% of the works hanging in museums are by men!).

Artists represented in the collection include Rosa Bonheur, Frida Kahlo, Helen Frankenthaler, Barbara Hepworth, Georgia O'Keeffe, Lee Krasner, Nancy Graves, Mary Cassatt, Elaine de Kooning, and Käthe Kollwitz, along with many other lesser-known but notable artists from previous centuries. I was interested to discover here, for instance, that the famed Peale family of 19th-century portrait painters included a very talented sister, Sarah Miriam Peale. The collection is complemented by an ongoing series of changing exhibits.

The museum is housed in a magnificent Renaissance Revival landmark building designed in 1907 as a Masonic temple by noted architect Waddy Wood. It's entered via an opulent Great Hall with

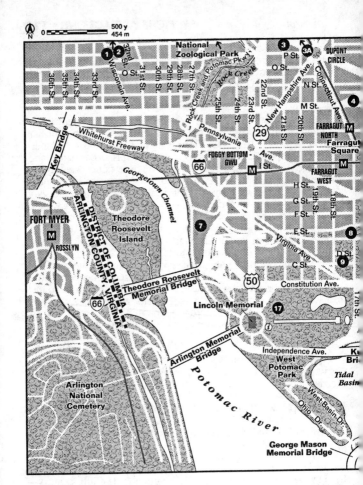

Turkish white marble floors, silk-brocaded walls, gilded moldings, and Belgian crystal chandeliers suspended from an ornately detailed ceiling. The museum's library contains over 8,000 volumes. The charming and sunny Mezzanine Cafe serves light lunches Monday through Saturday—soups, salads, and sandwiches.

Admission: Suggested contribution, $3 adults, $2 children.

Open: Mon–Sat 10am–5pm, Sun noon–5pm. **Closed:** Jan 1, Thanksgiving Day, and Dec 25. **Metro:** Metro Center.

MORE ATTRACTIONS IN WASHINGTON, D.C.

UNITED STATES BOTANIC GARDEN, 100 Maryland Ave., at the east end of the Mall. Tel. 225-8333.

Originally conceived by Washington, Jefferson, and Madison, and opened in 1820, the Botanic Garden is a lovely oasis—a series of connected glass-and-stone buildings and greenhouses (they call it a "living museum under glass") filled with pots of brightly colored flowers, rock beds of ferns, Spanish moss, palms, and shrubs. Tropical, subtropical, and desert plants are the highlights of the collection. There's a section filled with cactus; while other areas suggest a lush tropical jungle with tranquil pools and cascading fountains. Benches in shady corners create the illusion of a carefully tended woods. Poinsettias bloom at Christmas, chrysanthemums in fall; spring is heralded by lilies, tulips, hyacinths, and daffodils; and a large collection of orchids is on display year-round. The complex also includes Bartholdi Park, centering on a stunning cast-iron fountain created by Frédéric Auguste Bartholdi, designer of the Statue of Liberty. The park contains a rose garden and other themed areas. Of topical interest is the Dinosaur Garden of cycods (primitive conifers that resemble palms), mosses, and liverworts that existed in the Jurassic era—an age that predated flowering plants. The Summer Terrace, with umbrella tables amid plants and flower beds overlooking the Capitol's reflecting pool, is a lovely spot for a picnic lunch. For information on special shows (perhaps a rose show or a Japanese flower-arrangement display), tours, lectures, and classes such as "Growing Begonias and African Violets," call the above number. You can also call 225-7099 for a recording of events and to find out what's in bloom.

Admission: Free.
Open: Daily 9am–5pm. **Metro:** Federal Center SW.

DUMBARTON OAKS, 1703 32nd St. NW. (entrance to the collections on 32nd St., between R and S Sts.; garden entrance at 31st and R Sts.). Tel. 338-8278 or 342-3200.

Many people associate Dumbarton Oaks, a 19th-century Georgetown mansion named for a Scottish castle, with the 1944 international conference that led to the formation of the United Nations. Today the 16-acre estate is a research center for studies in Byzantine and pre-Columbian art and archeology, and landscape architecture. Its gardens, which wind gently down to Rock Creek Ravine, are magical, modeled after European gardens. The pre-Columbian museum, designed by Philip Johnson, is a small gem, and the Byzantine collection is a rich one.

This unusual combination of offerings dates to the occupancy of Robert Woods Bliss and his wife, Mildred. In 1940 they turned over the estate, their extensive Byzantine collection, a library of works on Byzantine civilization, and 16 acres (including 10 acres of exquisite formal gardens) to Mr. Bliss's alma mater, Harvard, and provided endowment funds for continuing research in Byzantine studies. In the early 1960s they also donated their pre-Columbian collection and financed the building of two wings—one to house it, the other to contain Mrs. Bliss's collection of rare books on landscape gardening. The Byzantine collection is one of the world's finest; it includes illuminated manuscripts, a 13th-century icon of St. Peter, mosaics, ivory carvings, a 4th-century sarcophagus, jewelry, and more. The pre-Columbian works, displayed chronologically in eight marble- and oak-floored glass pavilions, feature Olmec jade and serpentine figures, Mayan relief panels, textiles from 900 B.C. to the Spanish Conquest, funerary pottery, gold necklaces made by the lost-wax process, and sculptures of Aztec gods and goddesses.

The historic music room, furnished in French, Italian, and Spanish antiques, was the setting for the 1944 Dumbarton Oaks Conversations about the United Nations. It has a beamed, painted 16th-century French-style ceiling and an immense 16th-century stone fireplace. Among its notable artworks is El Greco's *The Visitation*.

Don't miss the formal gardens. They contain an Orangery, a Rose Garden (final resting place of the Blisses amid 1,000 rose bushes), wisteria-covered arbors, herbaceous borders, groves of cherry trees, and magnolias. You can picnic nearby, in Montrose Park.

Admission: Garden, $2 adults, $1 children under 12 and senior citizens; collections, free.

Open: Garden (weather permitting), Nov–Mar, daily 2–5pm; Apr–Oct, daily 2–6pm. Collections, Tues–Sun 2–5pm. **Closed:** Federal holidays and Dec 24.

NATIONAL GEOGRAPHIC SOCIETY'S EXPLORERS HALL, 17th and M Sts. NW. Tel. 857-7588.

The National Geographic Society, formed in 1888, exists to further "the increase and diffusion of geographic knowledge." At Explorers Hall, dozens of fascinating displays—a majority of them utilizing interactive videos—put that geographic knowledge literally at your fingertips. In Geographica, on the north side of the hall, you can touch a tornado, find out what it's like inside the earth, learn how caves are formed, study the origin of humankind, or explore other planets. A seven-minute video presentation narrated by Leonard Nimoy introduces visitors to the National Geographic Society. After hearing "Spock" speak, you can test your geographic knowledge at computer trivia games. The major exhibit here is Earth Station One, an interactive amphitheater (centered on an immense free-floating globe) that simulates an orbital flight. My favorite exhibit is a video microscope that zooms in clearly on slides containing such specimens as a hydra (a simple multicellular animal) or mosquito larva. Many of the video exhibits have overtones of environmental awareness.

Also on display: a scale model of Jacques Cousteau's diving saucer in which he descended to 25,000 feet; the flag and dog sledge, among other equipment, of Adm. Robert E. Peary, first man to reach the North Pole, along with a recording he made (his 1909 expedition was funded by the National Geographic Society); an *Aepyornis maximus* egg from Madagascar's extinct 1,000-pound flightless "elephant bird"; and the world's largest freestanding globe (34 feet around the equator, with a scale of one inch for every 60 miles). There's a full-size replica of a giant Olmec stone head dating to 32 B.C. from La Venta, Mexico. A 3.9-billion-year-old moon rock is on view in a small planetarium, and video excerpts from the society's TV specials are shown in the National Geographic Television Room. In addition, there's an ongoing program of temporary exhibits, and a display of oversize photographs from the magazine is backlit, so it can be viewed even after museum hours.

An on-premises shop sells all National Geographic publications, plus maps, globes, games, and videos. Within walking distance of the White House, this is a great place to take the kids, but they should be at least 9 or 10 years old. Younger children will not understand most of the exhibits.

Admission: Free.

Open: Mon–Sat 9am–5pm, Sun 10am–5pm. **Closed:** Dec 25. **Metro:** Farragut North (Connecticut Avenue and L Street exit) or Farragut West.

THE FOLGER SHAKESPEARE LIBRARY, 201 E. Capitol St. SE. Tel. 544-7077.

"Shakespeare taught us that the little world of the heart is vaster, deeper, and richer than the spaces of astronomy," wrote Ralph Waldo Emerson in 1864. A decade later, in 1879, Amherst student Henry Clay Folger was profoundly affected upon hearing a lecture by Emerson similarly extolling the Bard. Folger purchased an inexpensive set of Shakespeare's plays and went on to amass the world's largest collection of his printed works, today housed in the Folger Shakespeare Library. By 1930, when Folger, and his wife, Emily (whose literary enthusiasms matched his own), laid the cornerstone of a building to house the collection, it contained 93,000 books, 50,000 prints and engravings, and thousands of manuscripts. The Folgers made it all a gift to the American people.

The building itself is classical in style, its Georgian marble facade decorated with nine bas-relief scenes from Shakespeare's plays. A statue of Puck stands in the west garden, and quotations from the Bard and from contemporaries like Ben Jonson adorn the exterior walls. An Elizabethan garden on the east side of the building is planted with flowers and herbs of the period, many of them mentioned in the plays.

The facility, today containing some 250,000 books, 100,000 of which are rare, is an important research center not only for Shakespearean scholars, but for those studying any aspect of the English and continental Renaissance. And the oak-paneled Great Hall, reminiscent of a Tudor long gallery, is a popular attraction for the general public. It has an intricate plaster ceiling decorated with Shakespeare's coat of arms, fleurs-de-lis, and other motifs. On display are rotating exhibits from the permanent collection—costumes, playbills, Renaissance musical instruments, and more.

At the end of the Great Hall is a theater designed to suggest an Elizabethan innyard theater where concerts, readings, and Shakespeare-related events take place (see Chapter 9 for details). The timber and plaster walls are adorned with painted decorations; the gallery is triple-tiered and supported by oak columns with hand-carved satyrs.

Free walk-in **tours** are given at 11am.

Admission: Free.

Open: Mon–Sat 10am–4pm. **Closed:** Federal holidays. **Metro:** Capitol South.

UNITED STATES NAVY MEMORIAL, 701 Pennsylvania Ave. NW. Tel. 737-2300, or toll free 800/821-8892.

Authorized by Congress in 1980 to honor the men and women of the United States Navy, this memorial centers on a 100-foot-diameter circular plaza bearing a granite world map flanked by fountains and waterfalls salted with waters from the seven seas. In summer, military bands perform on the plaza. A statue of *The Lone Sailor* watching over the map represents all who have served in the navy. And two sculpture walls adorned with bronze bas-reliefs commemorate navy history and related maritime services.

Inside, in the "Quarterdeck" entrance area, a wall frieze commemorates battles from Yorktown to Operation Desert Storm, and a statue called *The Homecoming* depicts the joyous reunion of a navy family. Along a spiral staircase, a timeline of ship development spanning 200 years of naval history is etched into a glass wave-motif wall. Museum highlights include interactive video kiosks (with beautiful color graphics) proferring a wealth of information about navy ships, aircraft, and history; the Navy Memorial Log Room, a computerized record of past and present navy personnel; the Presidents Room, honoring six U.S. presidents who served in the navy and two who were secretaries of the navy; the Ship's Store, filled with nautical and maritime merchandise; and a wide-screen 70mm Surroundsound film called *At Sea* (by the makers of *To Fly*), which lets viewers experience the grandeur of the ocean and the adventure of going to sea on a navy ship. The 30-minute film plays continuously throughout the day; admission is $3 ($2.50 for seniors and children under 12).

Guided **tours** are available from the front desk, subject to staff availability. Free concerts take place Memorial Day through Labor Day on selected evenings at 8pm; call for details.

Admission: Free.

Open: Mon–Sat 10am–5:30pm, Sun noon–5pm. **Closed:** Dec 25. **Metro:** Archives/Navy Memorial.

---

3. COOL FOR KIDS

Visiting the capital with parents or classmates is as intrinsic a part of American childhood as baseball, hot dogs, and apple pie. Washington is a great place for family vacations, but how much fun you have depends on your approach and planning. Let the kids help in working out daily itineraries, a project that allows everyone to become acquainted with the sights and build up excitement over what you'll be seeing. The more you know about each place, the easier it is to communicate and create enthusiasm; it's also very helpful when taking tours if you can complement the guide's patter with child-oriented explanations. Kids tend to stay alert and interested when you discuss with them what you're seeing; leave them to their own devices and boredom—quickly followed by whining—sets in. This might mean doing a wee bit of homework (reading up a bit on the various attractions), but your efforts will enhance everyone's trip.

FAVORITE CHILDREN'S SIGHTS

Check for special children's events at museum information desks when you enter; better yet, call the day before to find out what's available. Here's a rundown of the biggest kid-pleasers in town (for details, see the full entries earlier in this chapter):

National Air and Space Museum: Spectacular IMAX films (don't miss), missiles, rockets, and a walk-through orbital workshop.

National Museum of Natural History: A Discovery Room just for youngsters, an insect zoo, shrunken heads, and dinosaurs.

National Museum of American History: The Foucault Pendulum, locomotives, atom smashers, and an old-fashioned ice-cream parlor.

Federal Bureau of Investigation: Gangster memorabilia, crime-solving methods, espionage devices, and a sharpshooting demonstration. You can't miss.

Bureau of Engraving and Printing: Kids like looking at immense piles of money as much as you do.

Capital Children's Museum (see below): All of it's for kids, with sound-and-light shows, hands-on exhibits, and educational computer games.

National Zoological Park: Kids always love a zoo, and this is an especially nice one.

Ford's Theatre and Lincoln Museum and the **House Where Lincoln Died:** Booth's gun and diary, Lincoln's blood-stained pillowcase, the clothes Lincoln was wearing the night he was assassinated; need I say more? Kids adore the whole business.

National Geographic Society's Explorers Hall: A moon rock, the egg of an extinct "elephant bird" (if it hatched it would weigh 1,000 pounds), numerous interactive videos. The magazine comes alive.

Washington Monument: Easy to get them up there, hard to get them down. If only they could use the steps, they'd be in heaven.

Lincoln Memorial: Kids know a lot about Lincoln and enjoy visiting his memorial. A special treat is visiting after dark (same for the Washington Monument and Jefferson Memorial).

Arts and Industries Building: 19th-century steam engines, ship models, farm machinery, old clocks, and performances just for children in the Discovery Theater.

National Archives: See the original Declaration of Independence, Constitution, and Bill of Rights.

White House, Capitol, and Supreme Court: Kids enjoy learning how our government works.

CAPITAL CHILDREN'S MUSEUM, 800 3rd St. NE, at H St. Tel. 543-8600.

Kids are, of necessity, rather restrained at most Washington sightseeing attractions; here's their chance to let loose on three floors of child-oriented hands-on exhibits. They can pet a resident goat, grind Mexican chocolate and prepare tortillas, send a message on a teletype machine, make slides and film shows, create shadow art on a wall (one of my favorite activities), and send messages—by a Greek torch system that dates to A.D. 300, by Morse code using naval lamps, and by African drums. A more serious exhibit called "Remember the Children" explores the Holocaust from a child's point of view. At U-TV, an interactive television studio, children can experiment with special-effects equipment, create animation, and broadcast on station WCCM, which is heard in other parts of the museum. Games involving light, shadows, and mirrors teach kids about optics in Science Hall. And a replica of a 30,000-year-old cave, complete with water dripping and the howling of distant beasts, illustrates the use of cave drawings and rituals as Ice Age means of communication. An exhibit about animator Chuck Jones features original cels, drawings, and film of Bugs Bunny, Daffy Duck, and the rest of the gang. There's also a maze with optical illusions to wander through, a talking (in 22 languages) Tower of Language staircase, and a telecommunications area with an old-fashioned operable switchboard and telephones of the future.

Inquire about ongoing workshops, demonstrations, and theater presentations for children.

Admission: $6 per person.

Open: Daily 10am–5pm. **Closed:** Jan 1, Easter, Thanksgiving Day, and Dec 25. **Metro:** Union Station.

ADDITIONAL TIPS

As to the rest, plan with your children's ages and interests in mind.

An occasional purchase at a museum shop can quickly revive flagging interest, and most of the museums have wonderful toys and children's books, not to mention items like freeze-dried astronaut ice cream.

The Friday "Weekend" section of the *Washington Post* lists numerous activities (mostly free) for kids: special museum events, children's theater, storytelling programs, puppet shows, video-game competitions, etc.

A hotel with a swimming pool is the best child-refresher known to man; it also means some time alone for adults. Consider this when making reservations; it may be worth a few extra bucks.

Ride the Metro, and let the kids purchase the tickets and insert their own farecards. It will be a high point, especially if they've never been on a subway before.

Take in some of the outdoor attractions listed in "Recreation in the Parks" later in this chapter, go bicycling, rowing, on a guided nature hike, or a Potomac boat ride.

Have fun!

4. ORGANIZED TOURS

BY BUS

On the whole, if you have even a few days to spend in Washington, I think you can do better on your own. However, a guided motorcoach tour can provide a good city overview.

The **Gray Line** (tel. 289-1995) offers a variety of tours: "Washington After Dark" (3½ hours), focusing on nightlit national monuments and federal buildings plus Georgetown; the "Washington, D.C., All-Day Combination Tour," which includes major Washington sights plus Arlington National Cemetery, Mount Vernon, and Alexandria; the four-hour "Interiors of Public Buildings," a morning tour visiting Ford's Theatre, the Jefferson Memorial, Museum of American History, and other important edifices, or a similar afternoon tour taking in the Capitol, Library of Congress, Supreme Court, National Air and Space Museum, and National Archives (a nine-hour tour combines both of these); and a "Two-Day Grand Tour." There are also trips as far afield as Colonial Williamsburg, Harper's Ferry, Gettysburg, and Charlottesville. Tours depart from Gray Line's Union Station terminal, with pickups at all major hotels. Headsets and tour tapes in foreign languages are available. For details, call the above number or inquire at your hotel desk.

A local company, **All About Town, Inc.,** 519 6th St. NW (tel. 393-3696), offers a similar range of tours. Pickup is offered at major hotels. Call for details or, once again, inquire at your hotel desk.

Consider, too, **Tourmobile** and **Old Town Trolley** tours (see "Getting Around," in Chapter 4, for details).

BY BOAT

Since Washington is a river city, why not see it by boat. **Spirit of Washington Cruises,** Pier 4 at 6th and Water Streets SW (tel. 554-8000), offers a variety of such trips daily from early March through December. Lunch and dinner cruises include a 20-minute high-energy musical revue. Call for departure times and make reservations in advance. The following trips are offered at this writing; check when you arrive, because they tend to change with some frequency.

Evening Dinner Cruises (7 to 10pm daily) include dancing to live music and a lavish buffet meal. The fare is $37.50 Sunday through Friday, $45 on Saturday.

Lunch and Brunch Cruises are two-hour narrated excursions on the Washington Channel. The meal consists of a seafood buffet, dessert, and tea or coffee. The fare is $21.75 Tuesday through Friday, $24.95 Saturday and Sunday.

Moonlight Dance Cruises feature dance music, complimentary hors d'oeuvres, cocktails (a cash bar), and dancing under the stars. Music is 1940s to Top 40, geared to adults, not teens (you must be at least 21 to participate). The boat heads to Alexandria. Cost for this 2½-hour late-night cruise is $19.95.

The Mount Vernon Cruise, a popular half-day excursion, takes in D.C. sights en route to Mount Vernon plantation, George Washington's beautiful estate on the Potomac. The trip is about 1½ hours each way. The round-trip fare is $20.25 for adults, $18 for seniors, $11.75 for children 6 to 11, free for children 5 and under. Prices include entrance to Mount Vernon. Book in advance.

The *Spirit of Washington* is a luxury ship with climate-controlled carpeted decks and huge panoramic windows designed for sightseeing. There are three well-stocked bars on board. Mount Vernon cruises are aboard an equally luxurious sister ship, the *Potomac Spirit.*

SCANDAL TOURS

You've seen the Smithsonian and the Lincoln Memorial. Now it's time to bypass the monuments and head right into the gutter. Scandal Tours, the creation of a brilliantly talented D.C. political-comedy group called Gross National Product, is a guided bus tour of Washington's sleaziest sites. ABC News anchor Peter Jennings called it "a worm's-eye view of Washington."

Highlights include visits to the Old Executive Office Building, where Ollie North and Fawn Hall shredded their way into history; the Tidal Basin, where former Congressman Wilbur Mills and "Argentine firecracker" Fannie Fox cavorted in the moonlight (she fell into the water, he got in hot water); the Capitol steps, scene of a night of passion for John and Rita Jenrette (Congressman Jenrette was later entrapped by Abscam and, still later, caught shoplifting in a department store); the Vista Hotel, where former mayor Marion Barry still claims "bitch set me up"; Watergate (of course); and Gary Hart's town house, from which he emerged with Donna Rice one morning to find himself at the evening of his political career. Tour participants are greeted by a GNP troupe member in the guise of a political figure (perhaps "Nancy Reagan" in signature red dress), while other GNP actors aboard the bus portray Clinton, Gennifer

Flowers, Sen. Bob Packwood, and other players in the forefront of the political arena. Historical figures are not spared—the company even has some dish on George Washington! "The great thing is the constant source of material," says GNP creator John Simmons. "You have power, money, and sex all along the Potomac. It's an unbeatable product—bad things happening to people it's hard to feel sorry for."

The 90-minute tours depart every Saturday at 1pm from the Transportation and Sightseeing Desk on the Terrace level of the Washington Hilton. Reservations are required. The cost is $27 per person. Or you can buy "Scandal Tour In-A-Box" for $12.95 and take the tour yourself by car. To order or make tour reservations, call 301/587-4291. *Note:* you can also see GNP perform Saturday night at the Bayou in Georgetown (details in Chapter 9).

5. RECREATION IN THE PARKS

Like most cities, Washington has manicured pockets of green amid its high-rise office buildings and superhighways. Unlike most cities, it's also extensively endowed with vast natural areas—thousands of parkland acres; two rivers; a 185-mile-long, tree-lined canalside trail; an untamed wilderness area; and a few thousand cherry trees—all centrally located within the District. And there's much more just a stone's throw away. This section explores D.C.'s wealth of outdoor facilities.

ROCK CREEK PARK

Created in 1890, Rock Creek Park was purchased by Congress for its "pleasant valleys and ravines, primeval forests and open fields, its running waters, its rocks clothed with rich ferns and mosses, its repose and tranquility, its light and shade, its ever-varying shrubbery, its beautiful and extensive views." A 1,750-acre valley within the District of Columbia, extending 12 miles from the Potomac River to the Maryland border (another 2,700 acres), it's one of the biggest and finest city parks in the nation. Parts of it are still wild; it's not unusual to see a deer scurrying through the woods in more remote sections.

The park's offerings include the Carter Barron Amphitheatre (see Chapter 9), playgrounds, an extensive system of beautiful wooded hiking trails, old forts to explore, and sports facilities.

For full information on the wide range of park programs and activities, visit the **Rock Creek Nature Center,** 5200 Glover Rd. NW (tel. 426-6829), Wednesday through Sunday from 9am to 5pm; or **Park Headquarters,** 5000 Glover Rd. (tel. 426-6832), Monday through Friday from 7:45am to 4:15pm. The Nature Center itself is the scene of numerous activities—weekend planetarium shows for kids (minimum age 4) and adults, nature films, crafts demonstrations, live animal demonstrations, and guided nature walks, plus a daily mix of lectures, films, puppet shows, concerts, and other events. A calendar is available on request. Self-guided nature trails begin here. All activities are free, but for planetarium shows you need to pick up tickets a half hour in advance. There are also nature exhibits on the premises. The Nature Center is closed on federal holidays.

You can see a water-powered 19th-century gristmill (one of over 20 mills that operated along Rock Creek from 1664 to 1925) grinding corn and wheat into flour at Tilden Street and Beach Drive (tel. 426-6908). It's called **Pierce Mill** (a man named Isaac Pierce built it), and it's open to visitors Wednesday through Sunday from 8am to 4:30pm. Pierce's old carriage house is today the **Art Barn** (tel. 244-2482), where works of local artists are exhibited; it's open Wednesday through Saturday from 10am to 5pm, and on Sunday from noon to 5pm (closed federal holidays).

Call 673-7646 or 673-7647 for details, locations, and group reservations at any of the park's 30 **picnic areas,** some with fireplaces. A brochure available at Park Headquarters or the Nature Center also provides details on picnic locations.

There are 15 soft-surface (clay) and 10 hard-surface **tennis courts** (five enclosed for indoor play October through May 1) at 16th and Kennedy Streets NW (tel. 722-5949). April through mid-November you must make a reservation in person at Guest Services on the premises to use them. Fees vary with court surface and time of play; call for details. Six additional clay courts are located off Park Road just east of Pierce Mill.

Poetry readings and workshops are held during the summer at the one-time residence of High Sierra poet Joaquin Miller, Beach Drive north of Military Road. Call 426-6832 for information.

The 18-hole **Rock Creek Golf Course** and clubhouse, 16th and Rittenhouse Streets NW (tel. 723-9832 or 882-7332), are open year-round, daily from dawn to dusk. A fee is charged. Clubs, lockers, and carts can be rented.

There are stables at the **Rock Creek Park Horse Center,** near the Nature Center on Glover Road NW (tel. 362-0117). Trail rides are offered Tuesday through Friday from 1:30 to 3pm and on Saturday and Sunday between noon and 3:15pm. Call for rates and information on riding instruction.

You have to rent bikes elsewhere, but there's an 11-mile **bike path** from the Lincoln Memorial through the park into Maryland, all of it paved. On weekends and holidays a large part of it is closed to vehicular traffic.

Joggers will enjoy the 1.5 mile **Perrier Parcourse** with 18 calisthenic stations en route. It begins near the intersection of Cathedral Avenue and Rock Creek Parkway.

There's another Perrier Parcourse, this one with only four stations, at 16th and Kennedy Streets NW.

Finally, 15 miles of **hiking trails,** from easy to strenuous, traverse the park. You can go on your own or participate in guided hikes. Details and maps are available at Park Headquarters or the Nature Center.

There's convenient **free parking** throughout the park. **Buses** E2, E3, E4, and E5 stop at Military Road and Oregon Avenue/Glover Road right in the center of things.

POTOMAC PARK

West and East Potomac Parks, their 720 riverside acres divided by the Tidal Basin, are most famous for their spring display of **cherry blossoms** and all the hoopla that goes with it.

West Potomac Park contains 1,300 trees bordering the Tidal Basin, 10% of them Akebonos with delicate pink blossoms, the rest

Yoshinos with white cloudlike flower clusters. It's the focal point of many of the week-long celebrations, which include the lighting of the 300-year-old **Japanese Stone Lantern** near Kutz Bridge, presented to the city by the governor of Tokyo in 1954; a Cherry Blossom Parade with floats, bands, clowns, Clydesdale horses, and Cherry Blossom princesses; dancers, entertainers, a black-tie ball with celebrity guests; and much, much more. If you manage to be in town for Cherry Blossom Week, details on all events and activities are available from the Washington, D.C., Convention and Visitors Association (tel. 789-7038), the National Park Service (tel. 619-7222), and in the *Washington Post*. The parade and ball require advance tickets. You can buy them through Ticketmaster or from the Downtown Jaycees (tel. 728-1135). Of course, unless you're planning a long vacation, arriving the right week is a matter of luck or flexibility. The trees bloom for a little less than two weeks beginning somewhere between March 20 and April 17; April 7 is the average date.

Though West Potomac Park gets more cherry blossom publicity, East Potomac Park has more trees (1,800 of them) and more varieties (11). Here, too, are **picnic grounds;** 24 **tennis courts,** including five indoors and three lit for night play (tel. 554-5962); one 18-hole and two 9-hole **golf courses** (tel. 863-9007); a large **swimming pool** (tel. 727-6523); and **biking** and **hiking** paths by the water.

West Potomac Park encompasses Constitution Gardens; the Vietnam, Lincoln, and Jefferson Memorials; a small island where ducks live; and the Reflecting Pool.

CHESAPEAKE & OHIO NATIONAL HISTORICAL PARK [C&O CANAL]

⭐ Paralleling the Potomac for 184½ miles, from Georgetown to Cumberland, Maryland, the C&O Canal, with its adjacent towpath, is a prime D.C. recreation area. It was built in the 1800s, when water routes were considered vital to transportation, but even before it was completed, the B&O Railroad, which was constructed at about the same time and along the same route, had begun to render it obsolete. Today, perhaps, it serves an even more important purpose as an urban refuge for jogging, hiking, biking, and boating in a lush, natural setting.

Headquarters for canal activities is the **Office of the Superintendent,** C&O Canal National Historical Park, P.O. Box 4, Sharpsburg, MD 21782 (tel. 301/948-5641). Also knowledgeable is the National Park Service office at **Great Falls Tavern Visitor Center,** 11710 MacArthur Blvd., Potomac, MD 20854 (tel. 301/299-3613). At this 1831 tavern you can see museum exhibits and a film about the canal; there's also a bookstore on the premises. And in summer, Wednesday through Sunday, the **Georgetown Information Center,** 1055 Thomas Jefferson St. NW (tel. 202/472-4376 or 653-5844), can also provide maps and information. Call ahead for hours at all the above.

Hiking any section of the flat dirt towpath—or its more rugged side paths—is a pleasure. There are **picnic tables** (at **camping areas**), some with fire grills, about every 5 miles from Fletcher's Boat House (about 3.2 miles out of Georgetown) to Cumberland. Use of campsites is on a first-come, first-served basis. Enter the towpath in Georgetown below M Street via Thomas Jefferson Street. If you hike

14 miles, you'll reach **Great Falls,** a point where the Potomac becomes a stunning waterfall plunging 76 feet. You'll have to drive to Great Falls Park on the Virginia side of the Potomac.

Stop at **Fletcher's Boat House,** described in "Sports," below (tel. 244-0461), to rent **bikes** or **boats** or purchase bait and tackle (or a license) for **fishing.** A snack bar and picnic area are on the premises. It's also accessible by car.

Much less strenuous than hiking is a **mule-drawn 19th-century canal boat trip** led by Park Service rangers in period dress. They regale passengers with canal legend and lore and sing period songs. These boats depart Wednesday through Sunday from mid-April to mid-October; call 202/653-5844 or 301/299-3613 for departure times. Tickets are available at the Georgetown Information Center or the Great Falls Tavern (address and phone for both above). The fare is $5 for adults, $3.50 for children under 12 and seniors over 62.

Call any of the above information numbers for details on riding, rock climbing, fishing, birdwatching, concerts, ranger-guided tours, ice skating, camping, and other canal activities.

UNITED STATES NATIONAL ARBORETUM

A research and educational center focusing on trees and shrubs, the U.S. National Arboretum, 3501 New York Ave. NE (tel. 475-4815), is one of the great joys of Washington. Its 9½ miles of paved roads meander through 444 hilly acres of rhododendrons, azaleas (the most extensive plantings in the nation), crab apples, magnolias, hollies, peonies, irises, dogwoods, day lilies, boxwoods, cherry trees, aquatic plants, and dwarf conifers. The highlight for me is the **National Bonsai and Penjing Museum**—a $4.5-million Bicentennial gift from Japan of 53 beautiful miniature trees, some of them over three centuries old. Each one is an exquisite work of art. The exhibit was augmented by a gift of 35 Chinese Penjing trees in 1986, and again in 1990 by the American Bonsai Collection of 56 North American plants. This area also includes a **Japanese Garden** and a garden of plants of American origin. The **Herbarium** contains 600,000 dried plants for reference purposes. The **Herb Garden,** another highlight, includes a historic rose garden (100 old-fashioned fragrant varieties), a contemporary interpretation of a 16th-century English-style "knot" garden, and 10 specialty gardens—a dye garden, a medicinal garden, and a culinary garden among them. The **National Bird Garden** features berrying shrubs that attract feathered friends. Along Fern Valley Trail is the Franklin Tree—a species now extinct in the wild—discovered in 1765 by a botanist friend of Benjamin Franklin. And a magnificent sight is the Arboretum's **acropolis**—22 of the original U.S. Capitol columns designed by Benjamin Latrobe in a setting created by the noted English landscape artist Russell Page. The columns, the sole remaining elements of Capitol architect Latrobe's original facade, were removed a few decades ago when they were deemed too fragile to support the building's new marble construction. They couldn't have found a more beautiful home. The **New American Garden,** opened in 1990, is a collection of ornamental grasses—reminiscent of prairie landscapes—and perennials, with brick walkways, terrraces, and a statue of Demeter, the Greek goddess of agriculture.

Its colorful spring bulb plants comprise a wide variety of narcissi, tulips, irises, and crocuses enhanced by small flowering and fruiting trees and interesting shrubs. Carefully placed teak benches provide a place for quiet contemplation. The **American Friendship Garden** also features an extensive collection of perennials and bulb plants. Magnolias and early bulbs bloom in late March or early April; rhododendrons, daffodils, and flowering cherry trees in mid-April; azaleas and peonies in May; lilies and hibiscus in summer. In autumn the Arboretum is ablaze in reds and oranges as the leaves change color.

The Arboretum is open Monday through Friday from 8am to 5pm, and on Saturday, Sunday and holidays from 10am to 5pm; the Bonsai Collection, 10am to 2:30pm daily. Everything is closed December 25. Take bus B2, B4, or B5 from the Stadium Armory Metro station to Bladensburg Road and R Street NE. Or hop in a taxi; it's only a few dollars. If you drive, **parking** is free (you can drive through if you wish). Frequent tours, lectures, and workshops (including bonsai classes) are offered, and a comprehensive guide-book is available in the gift shop.

THEODORE ROOSEVELT ISLAND

A serene 88-acre wilderness preserve, Theodore Roosevelt Island is a memorial to our 26th president, in recognition of his contributions to conservation. An outdoor enthusiast and expert field naturalist, Roosevelt once threw away a prepared speech and roared, "I hate a man who would skin the land!" During his administration the U.S. Forest Service created 150 national forests, five national parks, 51 bird refuges, and four game refuges. Forty-one states created their own conservation agencies to carry on the work begun by the national government during his term.

Theodore Roosevelt Island was inhabited as far back as the 1600s by Native Americans. Over the years it passed through many owners before becoming what it is today—an island preserve of swamp, marsh, and upland forest that's a haven for rabbits, chipmunks, great owls, fox, muskrat, turtles, and groundhogs. It's a complex ecosystem in which cattails, arrowarum, and pickerelweed growing in the marshes create a hospitable habitat for abundant bird life. And willow, ash, and maple trees rooted on the mudflats create the swamp environment favored by the raccoon in its search for crayfish. You can observe these flora and fauna in their natural environs on 2½ miles of foot trails.

In the northern center of the island, overlooking an oval terrace encircled by a water-filled moat, stands a 17-foot bronze **statue** of Roosevelt. From the terrace rise four 21-foot granite tablets inscribed with the tenets of his philosophy: "There are no words that can tell the hidden spirit of the wilderness, that can reveal its mystery, its melancholy, and its charm. The Nation behaves well if it treats the natural resources as assets which it must turn over to the next generation increased and not impaired in value." **Picnicking** is permitted on the grounds near the memorial.

To get to the island, take the George Washington Memorial Parkway exit north from the Theodore Roosevelt Bridge. The **parking** area is accessible only from the northbound lane; from there, a pedestrian bridge connects the island with the Virginia shore. You can also rent a canoe at Thompson's Boat Center (see "Boating" in "Active Sports," in "Sports," below) and paddle over, or walk across the pedestrian bridge at Rosslyn Circle, two blocks from the Rosslyn **Metro** station.

For further information, contact the District Ranger, Theodore Roosevelt Island, George Washington Memorial Parkway, c/o Turkey Run Park, McLean, VA 22101 (tel. 703/285-2598).

6. SPORTS

Too much museum-going and sightseeing can do you in. A change of pace is the answer and Washington has a lot to offer here, too. Catch a Redskins, Hoyas, or Baltimore Orioles game. Or get out there and bike, hike, ride horseback, swim, or play tennis. All this and more is described below. In addition, check the Friday "Weekend" section of the *Washington Post* for information on these and other activities from volleyball to river rafting.

SPECTATOR SPORTS

USAIR ARENA The **Washington Bullets** (NBA) and the **Washington Capitals** (NHL) play home games at the USAir Arena, Exit 15A or 17A off the Capital Beltway in Landover, Md. (tel. 301/350-3400). The 19,000-seat arena is also used for Georgetown University basketball games (the Hoyas), Harlem Globetrotter games, wrestling, and annual events like the Washington International Horse Show, the Ice Capades, and the World Professional Figure Skating Championships. Also big-name concerts. For tickets, call 202/432-SEAT, or toll free 800/551-SEAT.

ROBERT F. KENNEDY MEMORIAL STADIUM/D.C. ARMORY The 55,000-seat Robert F. Kennedy Memorial Stadium (and the 10,000-seat D.C. Armory complex), East Capitol Street between 19th and 20th Streets SE (tel. 547-9077 or 546-3337), is the D.C. home of the **Washington Redskins** (NFL). Events here also include wrestling, nationally televised boxing, roller derby, the circus, soccer games, and rodeos. To charge tickets call 202/432-SEAT, or toll free 800/551-SEAT.

ORIOLE PARK AT CAMDEN YARDS The 48,000-seat Oriole Park at Camden Yards, 333 W. Camden St., between Howard and Conway Streets, in Baltimore, Md. (tel. 410/685-9800), opened in 1992. It's the home of baseball's **Baltimore Orioles.** Unlike recent ultramodern sports stadiums, Oriole Park incorporates features of its urban environment, such as the old B&O Railroad yards near downtown Baltimore. A renovated brick warehouse serves as a striking visual backdrop beyond the right-field fence. For tickets, call 410/481-SEAT, or toll free 800/551-SEAT. From Union Station in Washington, take a MARC train to Baltimore, which lets you off right at the ballpark. By car, take I-95 N to Exit 53.

BALTIMORE ARENA The 13,500-seat Baltimore Arena, 201 W. Baltimore St., a few blocks from the Inner Harbor in Baltimore (tel. 410/347-2020), is home to the **Baltimore Thunder** (indoor lacrosse). The **Washington Bullets** (NBA) play at least four games here each year, and the facility also hosts the Ice Capades every February, Harlem Globetrotter games, tractor pulls, and more. For tickets, call 410/481-SEAT, or toll free 800/551-SEAT. Once again, take the MARC train from Union Station.

THE PATRIOT CENTER   The Patriot Center, 4400 University Dr. in Fairfax, Va. (tel. 703/993-3000), opened in late 1985 on the campus of nearby George Mason University. A 10,000-seat facility, it's used for college basketball games, gymnastic competitions, horse shows, and other events. To get here, take the Wilson Bridge to Braddock Road West (Route 623) and proceed for about eight miles to University Drive. For tickets, call 703/573-SEAT.

ACTIVE SPORTS

BICYCLING   Both **Fletcher's Boat House** and **Thompson's Boat Center** (see "Boating," below, for addresses and hours) rent bikes, as does **Big Wheel Bikes,** 1034 33rd St. NW, right near the C&O Canal just below M Street (tel. 337-0254). Hours are from 10am to 6pm daily, and till 8pm weekdays from April through September. There's another Big Wheel shop on Capitol Hill at 315 7th St. SE (tel. 543-1600), open Tuesday through Friday from 11am to 7pm, on Saturday from 10am to 6pm, and on Sunday from 11am to 5pm. Photo ID and a major credit card are required to rent bicycles.

The *Washington Post* Friday "Weekend" section lists cycling trips. See also Rock Creek Park, the C&O Canal, and the Potomac Parks in "Recreation in the Parks," earlier in this chapter, for details on their biking facilities.

BOATING   **Thompson's Boat Center,** Virginia Avenue at Rock Creek Parkway NW (tel. 333-4861 or 333-9543), rents canoes, sailboats, rowing shells, and rowboats. They also offer sculling and sweep-rowing lessons. Photo ID and a $20 deposit are required. They're open mid-April to early October, daily from 8am to 5pm. You can't rent a boat after 5pm. For bike rentals ($10 deposit required) the shop is open March to mid-November, same hours.

Fletcher's Boat House, Reservoir and Canal Roads (tel. 244-0461), is right on the C&O Canal, about a 3.2-mile wonderfully scenic walk from Georgetown. Open March to mid-November, daily from 7:30am to dusk, Fletcher's rents canoes and rowboats and sells fishing licenses, bait, and tackle. ID is required (a driver's license or major credit card). A snack bar and restrooms here are welcome after that hike. And there are picnic tables (with barbecue grills) overlooking the Potomac. You don't have to walk to Fletcher's; it's accessible by car (west on M Street to Canal Road) and has plenty of free parking.

CAMPING   See the C&O Canal in "Recreation in the Parks," earlier in this chapter.

FISHING   The Potomac River around Washington provides an abundant variety of fish—some 40 species, all perfectly safe to eat. Good fishing is possible from late February to November, but mid-March through June (spawning season) is peak. Perch and catfish are the most common catch, but during bass season a haul of 20 to 40 is not unusual. The Washington Channel offers good bass and carp fishing year-round.

A **fishing license** is required. You can obtain one at various locations around the city, among them **Fletcher's Boat House** (address and telephone number above) and the **Chinatown Coffee**

House, 616 H St. NW (tel. 783-6212). Cost is $7.50 for a year, $3 for a 14-day permit.

GOLF There are dozens of public courses within easy driving distance of the D.C. area, but in the District itself East Potomac Park and Rock Creek Park contain the only public courses. The 18-hole **Rock Creek Golf Course** and clubhouse, at 16th and Rittenhouse Streets NW (tel. 882-7332 or 723-9832), are open to the public daily year-round from dawn to dusk. A snack bar and lockers are on the premises, and clubs and carts can be rented. A fee is charged.

East Potomac Park has one 18-hole, par-72 and two 9-hole courses. For details, call 863-9007.

HIKING If you prefer group hikes, the **Sierra Club** (tel. 547-2326 or 547-5551) organizes guided hikes of varying length and ruggedness just about every weekend of the year. These include backpack trips to local wilderness areas, day hikes to nearby national parks and forests, also bike trips and white-water and flat-water canoe trips. There's an optional charge of $1 per person for each hiking trip, and people sharing rides chip in for gas. A calendar of events is available for $5 a year; call the above phone number for information or write to Sierra Club Calendar, 1863 Kalorama Rd. NW, Apt. 1B, Washington, DC 20009.

Also check the *Washington Post* Friday "Weekend" section for listings of hiking clubs; almost all are open to the public for a small fee. And inquire as to the difficulty of any hike you join and the speed with which the club proceeds; some don't stop to smell the flowers.

On your own, there are numerous hiking paths. The **C&O Canal** offers 184½ miles alone; it would be hard to find a more scenic setting than the 9½ miles of road at the **Arboretum** (see "Recreation in the Parks," earlier in this chapter); **Theodore Roosevelt Island** has 88 wilderness acres to explore, including a 2½-mile nature trail (short but rugged); and in **Rock Creek Park** there are 15 miles of hiking trails for which maps are available at the Visitor Information Center or Park Headquarters.

HORSEBACK RIDING The **Rock Creek Park Horse Center,** near the Nature Center on Glover Road NW (tel. 362-0117), offers rental horses for trail rides and riding instruction. There are 14 miles of woodland bridle paths to explore. Call for ride times. No riding experience is required.

ICE SKATING My favorite place for winter skating is on the **C&O Canal,** its banks always dotted with cozy fires at which one can warm frozen extremities. You might find it inspiring to skate on the **Reflecting Pool** between the Lincoln Memorial and the Washington Monument, especially by night when it's dramatically lit. Guest Services, Inc., operates the **National Sculpture Garden Ice Rink** on the Mall at 7th Street and Constitution Avenue NW (tel. 371-5342), the **Pershing Park** outdoor rink at 14th Street and Pennsylvania Avenue NW (tel. 737-6938), and a huge hockey-size indoor facility, the **Fort Dupont Ice Arena,** at 3779 Ely Place SE, at Minnesota Avenue in the Fort Dupont Park (tel. 581-0199). All three offer skate rentals. The Sculpture Garden and Pershing Park rinks are open approximately from December (some years earlier) to February, weather permitting; Fort Dupont, from Labor Day to the end of April. Call for hours and admission prices.

JOGGING A **Parcourse jogging path,** a gift from Perrier, opened in Rock Creek Park in 1978. Its 1½-mile oval route, beginning near the intersection of Cathedral Avenue and Rock Creek Parkway, includes 18 calisthenics stations with instructions on prescribed exercises. There's another Perrier Parcourse, this one with only four stations, at 16th and Kennedy Streets NW. Other popular jogging areas are the **C&O Canal** and the **Mall.**

SWIMMING There are 45 swimming pools in the District run by the **D.C. Department of Recreation Aquatic Program** (tel. 576-6436). Among the nicest are the Capitol East Natatorium, an indoor/outdoor pool with sun deck and adjoining baby pool at 635 North Carolina Ave. SE (tel. 724-4495 or 724-4496); the outdoor pool in East Potomac Park (tel. 727-0347); and the Georgetown outdoor pool at 34th Street and Volta Place NW (tel. 282-2366). Indoor pools are open year-round; outdoor pools, from Memorial Day to Labor Day. Call for hours and details on other locations.

TENNIS There are 144 outdoor courts in the District (60 of them lighted for night play) at 45 locations. Court use is on a first-come, first-served basis. For a list of locations, call or write the **D.C. Department of Recreation,** 3149 16th St. NW, Washington, DC 20010 (tel. 202/673-7646). Most courts are open year-round, weather permitting. In addition, there are courts in **Rock Creek** and **East Potomac Parks** (see "Recreation in the Parks," earlier in this chapter, for details).

CHAPTER 8

SHOPPING IN WASHINGTON, D.C.

- **1. SHOPPING A TO Z**
- • **SHOPPING TOUR— GEORGETOWN**

The city's most delightful shopping area is historic Georgetown, with hundreds of boutiques, antique shops, and a Neo-Victorian mall providing excellent browsing. Its highlights are detailed in a walking tour. But first I've covered the most interesting and/or budget-oriented shops throughout the District, malls, in D.C. and the suburbs, and major department stores. Check the Georgetown shopping tour for additional shops in each category.

Nearby Alexandria contains even more quaint and varied shops to explore than Georgetown. And there are marvelous high-quality selections at all the Smithsonian museum shops—unique toys, craft items, educational games for children, posters, art reproductions, books, jewelry, etc.—and at many other museums and attractions as well.

1. SHOPPING A TO Z

ART REPRODUCTIONS, PRINTS & ENGRAVINGS

All the art museums detailed in Chapter 7 have noteworthy shops. Of special interest are the following:

BUREAU OF ENGRAVING AND PRINTING, 14th and C Sts. SW. Tel. 874-3187.

Good engravings here, including presidential portraits, portraits of Supreme Court justices, scenes of Washington landmarks, and government seals, plus prints of the Gettysburg Address; the list goes on and on. The bureau also sells sheets of uncut currency. Write for a free catalog or stop by the on-premises store. It's open Monday through Friday from 8:30am to 3:30pm. Metro: Smithsonian.

NATIONAL GALLERY OF ART, north side of the Mall, between 3rd and 7th Sts. NW. Tel. 737-4215.

The shops here feature a wide choice of prints, posters, art reproductions, Christmas cards, and art books. The West Building shop is the largest; the special exhibition desk in the East Building deals with current exhibit-related books and art. It's open Monday through Saturday from 10am to 5pm and on Sunday from 11am to 6pm. Metro: Archives or Judiciary Square.

BOOKS/RECORDS/CDs/VIDEO CASSETTES

In addition to the stores listed here, you'll find others mentioned in "Malls" (below) and described in the Georgetown shopping tour later in this chapter.

GOVERNMENT PRINTING OFFICE BOOKSTORE, 710 N. Capitol St. NW, between G and H Sts. Tel. 512-0132.

The GPO, founded in 1861, is now the world's largest printer, with close to 16,000 titles (books and pamphlets) in print. Every conceivable area is covered, from *Starting and Managing a Small Business on Your Own* to the *Everglades Wildguide.* If you're probing any new hobby, interest, or activity—or writing a term paper, trying to understand a medical problem, looking for a new career, or considering a major purchase—you'll probably find some helpful literature here. The collection makes for fascinating browsing. The GPO bookstore also sells books of photographs (like *A Century of Photographs: 1846–1946,* selections from the Library of Congress) and sets of actual photographs (like a set of seven photos portraying marines in combat situations, suitable for framing); also prints, lithographs, and posters. It's open Monday through Friday from 8am to 4pm. Metro: Union Station.

The GPO operates another bookstore at 1510 H St. NW (tel. 653-5075), open Monday through Friday from 9am to 5pm. Metro: Farragut West.

KRAMERBOOKS & AFTERWORDS, 1517 Connecticut Ave. NW, between Q St. and Dupont Circle. Tel. 387-1400.

Ask 100 Washingtonians to name their favorite bookstore, and at least half will say Kramerbooks. This San Francisco–style bookstore combines with a popular restaurant (see Chapter 6 for details), so you can buy a book and read it over lunch. Employees here are all avid readers who display their current favorites on the counter and discuss literature with customers. It's also one of the few places anywhere you can buy a book at 8am—or midnight for that matter. Kramerbooks carries quality paperbacks—fiction and nonfiction—as well as European and other foreign works of major importance. The store recently expanded, adding 50% more space and large children's, gardening, and travel-book sections. "I look for books of real and substantial quality," says owner David Tenney. Quality books must have their audience, because Kramerbooks is one of the highest-grossing bookstores per square foot in the country. It's open Monday through Thursday from 7:30am to 1am, and around the clock from Friday at 7:30am to Sunday at 1am. Metro: Dupont Circle.

MELODY RECORD SHOP, 1623 Connecticut Ave. NW. Tel. 232-4002.

CDs, cassettes, and tapes are discounted 10% to 20% here, new releases 20% to 40%. There's a wide variety of rock, classical, jazz, pop, show, and folk music, as well as a vast number of international selections. This is also a good place to shop for discounted electronic equipment such as cassette and CD players, as well as blank tapes and cassettes. A knowledgeable staff is a plus. Open Monday through

Thursday from 10am to 10pm, on Friday and Saturday from 10am to 11pm, and on Sunday from noon to 8pm. Metro: Dupont Circle (Q Street exit).

OLSSON'S BOOKS & RECORDS, 1307 19th St. NW, just off Dupont Circle. Tel. 785-2662 for records, 785-1133 for books.

This independent quality bookstore chain offers discounts of 10% to 20% on many tapes and CDs (of which they stock an immense variety) and has about 60,000 to 70,000 books on its shelves focusing on every possible area except romance and porn. *Washington Post* hardcover bestsellers are reduced 25%; other books are sold at regular prices. However, if you buy three Penguin books here at one time, you get 20% off on any other Penguin paperback forever. At all Olsson's stores, book signings are frequent events (past ones have included P. D. James, Garrison Keillor, and Anthony Burgess), and there are even occasional signings of recordings. Metro: Dupont Circle.

Additional locations include 1200 F St. at Metro Center (tel. 393-1853 for recordings, 347-3686 for books), and 1239 Wisconsin Ave. NW, between M and N Streets (tel. 338-6712 for recordings, 338-9544 for books). All locations are open daily; call for hours.

SIDNEY KRAMER BOOKS, 1825 I St. NW. Tel. 293-2685.

This unique and very attractive bookstore specializes "in the business of Washington"—politics, economics, defense, area studies, and business management. Its clientele includes foreign ambassadors, generals, congresspeople, White House staffers, and other major governmental players. The people-watching is almost as good as the browsing. Kramer also offers comprehensive travel-book, fiction, and children's-book sections. Open Monday through Friday from 9am to 6:30pm and on Saturday from 10am to 5pm. Metro: Farragut West.

SUPER CROWN, 11 Dupont Circle NW, between New Hampshire Ave. and P St., on the northeast side of the Circle. Tel. 319-1374.

With locations throughout the District and in suburbia, Crown Books offers 40% off *New York Times* hardcover bestsellers and 25% off paperbacks. Other books and magazines are discounted 10% to 20%. Its largest outlet is this 12,000-square-foot "super" store, which has expanded sections for biographies, audio (books on tape), remaindered books, new authors, magazines (including many foreign periodicals), and children's books—the latter area equipped with little chairs and tables and playthings. Super Crown can special-order titles for you at its usual discounts. It has wider aisles with benches where people can sit and read. And there's an on-premises eatery, Ferrara's (a branch of New York's famed Little Italy establishment) offering sandwiches, Italian pastries, espresso, and cappuccino. Check the phone book for other Crown Book store locations. It's open Monday through Saturday from 9am to midnight and on Sunday from 10am to midnight. Ferrara's is open to 11pm nightly. Metro: Dupont Circle.

TOWER RECORDS, 2000 Pennsylvania Ave. NW, at the corner of 21st and I Sts. Tel. 331-2400.

Without a doubt, this 18,000-square-foot store houses the largest selection of cassettes and CDs in town. There are large departments for jazz, rock, soul, classical, and any other type of music you might favor, plus a vast inventory of video cassettes (for sale and rental). The store also functions as a **Ticketmaster** outlet. A trendy ambience is created by flashing lights, ultramodern decor, and about 20 monitors showing rock videos, cartoons, and movies. All merchandise is sold below list, with substantial discounts on sale items. Ongoing contests—drawings for trips to reggae festivals in Jamaica, stereo equipment, concert tickets—add to the fun. It's open daily from 9am to midnight. Metro: Foggy Bottom.

CLOTHING

Don't forget to check out "Department Stores" and "Malls" (below) for more places to shop for clothes.

LANE BRYANT, 10th and F Sts. NW. Tel. 347-1500.

This is a branch of Lane Bryant that carries large sizes (14 to 28) in women's clothing. It's open Monday through Friday from 10am to 7pm, Saturday from 10am to 6pm, and on Sunday from noon to 5pm. Metro: Metro Center.

SUNNY'S SURPLUS, 1416 H St. NW. Tel. 347-2774.

If you favor the "M*A*S*H" look, this is the place. They carry a full line of military surplus (mostly new, some used), including jeans, T-shirts, work shoes and clothing, insulated underwear, heavy thermal socks, rainwear and winter garments, pea coats, camouflage fatigues, army blankets, navy wool insignia middy blouses, all camping accessories (tents, sleeping bags, mess kits, rubber rafts, canteens), even World War I Snoopy helmets. Metro: McPherson Square.

Other branches are at 917 F St. NW (tel. 737-2032) and 3342 M St. NW (tel. 333-8550). All locations are open from October to early spring, Monday through Saturday from 8am to 6pm; the rest of the year, Monday through Saturday from 9am to 7pm; call for Sunday hours.

CRAFTS

INDIAN CRAFTS SHOP, Department of the Interior, 18th and C Sts. NW. Tel. 208-4056.

Work here is generally of a higher quality than those items sold at the Grand Canyon and other locations closer to Native American reservations. The price range is wide: I found many lovely small Navajo weavings for $15 to $18 (larger rugs can go up to $3,000), squash-blossom necklaces for $300 to $3,000, and many attractive pieces of jewelry—Navajo, Zuni, and Hopi—in varied price ranges. The store also offers Navajo sand paintings, a large selection of Eskimo soapstone and walrus ivory carvings, and an outstanding selection of Hopi, Santa Clara, San Ildefonso, Jemez, Acoma, Taos, Cochiti, and Navajo pottery. *Note:* You need a photo ID to enter the building. It's open Monday through Friday from 8:30am to 4:30pm. Metro: Farragut West.

There's another location in Georgetown Park Mall, 3222 M St. NW, at Wisconsin (tel. 342-3918), open Monday through Saturday from 10am to 6pm and on Sunday from noon to 6pm.

Map labels:

N

0 ——— 500 y
454 m

26th St. and Potomac Pkwy.

P St.
O St.

26th St.
27th St.
28th St.
29th St.
30th St.
31st St.
32nd St./Wisconsin Ave.
33rd St.
34th St.
35th St.
36th St.

Rock Creek and Potomac Pkwy.
Rock Creek

25th St.
24th St.
23rd St.
22nd St.

New Hampshire Ave.

N St.
M St.

Connecticut Ave.

DUPONT CIRCLE

① ② ③ ④ ⑤ ⑥

FARRA NOR

21st St.
20th St.
19th St.

⑦

⑧

Farragut Square

M

Pennsylvania Ave.

Whitehurst Freeway

Ker Bridge

Georgetown Channel

29

FOGGY BOTTOM - GWU

66

M St.

M

⑩

⑪

FARRAGUT WEST

H St.
G St.
F St.
E St.

18th St.

FORT MYER

M

ROSSLYN

DISTRICT OF COLUMBIA
ARLINGTON COUNTY, VIRGINIA

Virginia Ave.

D St.

㉒

17th St.

Theodore Roosevelt Memorial Bridge

66

50

Constitution Ave.

i

Arlington Memorial Bridge

Independence Ave.

West Potomac Park

Ku Brid

Tidal Basin

Arlington National Cemetery

Potomac River

West Basin Dr.

Ohio Dr.

George Mason Memorial Bridge

WASHINGTON, D.C.

Washington, D.C. Shopping

Better Buys ③
Bureau of Engraving & Printing ⑨
Calvert Woodley ③
Central Liquor ⑲
Four Eyes Optical ⑥
Ginns ⑦
Government Printing Office Bookstore ⑳

Hecht's ⑬
Indian Crafts Shop ㉒
Kid's Stuff ③
Kramerbooks & Afterwords ③
Lane Bryant ⑱
Mazza Gallerie ②
Melody Record Shop ④
National Gallery of Art ㉔

DEPARTMENT STORES

In addition to the below-listed, Washington boasts branches of prestigious New York and West Coast stores. **Lord & Taylor** is at 5255 Western Ave. NW (tel. 362-9600); **Saks Fifth Avenue** can be found at 5555 Wisconsin Ave. NW in Chevy Chase, Md. (tel. 301/657-9000); and **Neiman-Marcus** is located in Mazza Gallerie on upper Wisconsin Avenue (tel. 966-9700). You'll find a branch of **Bloomingdale's** at Tysons Corner Center in McLean, Va. (tel.

SHOPPING IN WASHINGTON, D.C.

Red Sage General Store ⑭
Shops at National Place ⑮
Sidney Kramer Books ⑪
Southwest Waterfront Fish Market ⑯
Sunny's Surplus ⑫
Once Is Not Enough ❶
Pavilion at the Old Post Office ㉓
Super Crown ❻

Tower Records ⑩
Union Station ㉑
Woodward & Lothrop ⑰

703/556-4600). And **Sears Roebuck & Co.** has a branch at 4500 Wisconsin Ave. NW (tel. 364-6066). See also the stores listed under "Malls" (below).

HECHT'S, 12th and G Sts. NW. Tel. 628-6661.

Hecht's stores have been in Washington for about a century. But this much newer branch (built in 1985) is not fusty. It's a fun store with five floors of moderate- to higher-priced merchandise and lots going on. You might happen on cooking and merchandise demonstrations here, a contest (win a trip to Paris or a Jaguar XJ6), or an in-store personality appearance (in the past these have included Jim Palmer, Leslie Uggams, Robin Leach for Giorgio, Kenneth Jay Lane showing Barbara Bush's pearls, and Bart Simpson). It's a full-service department store, featuring brand names in clothing and footwear for the whole family and contemporary and traditional home furnishings. In addition, all Hecht's stores house **Ticketmaster** outlets selling tickets to most major shows, concerts, and sports events in town; you get the best available seats for the price at the time you buy. There are 16 Hecht's stores in the D.C. area; check the phone book for additional locations. This branch is open Monday through Saturday from 10am to 8pm and on Sunday from 11:30am to 7pm. Metro: Metro Center.

WOODWARD & LOTHROP, 11th and F Sts. NW. Tel. 347-5300.

This store specializes in clothing for the whole family, plus gifts, shoes, housewares, and furniture. There's a large bridal department on the fifth floor. Woodies—that's how this store is known among Washington families, who have been coming here for several generations—has an excellent reputation for fine service and quality merchandise at reasonable prices. There are several eating places, including the archetypical department store tearoom, on the premises. Designer showrooms here include Calvin Klein, Donna Karan, Anne Klein, Anne Klein II, Ellen Tracy, and Ralph Lauren/Polo for men. Celebrity promotions—such as Elizabeth Taylor or Baryshnikov for their fragrances, Greg Louganis for Speedo, and Paloma Picasso for her handbag line—are part of the fun. Altogether, there are 16 Woodward & Lothrop stores in the D.C. area; check the phone book for additional locations. This branch is open Monday through Saturday from 10am to 8pm and on Sunday from 11am to 5pm. Metro: Metro Center.

DRUGSTORES

Washington's major drugstore chain, carrying diversified merchandise that ranges from frozen foods to charcoal briquettes to appliances, is **Peoples** (with about 40 stores). Check the phone book for the most convenient locations.

EYEGLASSES

FOUR EYES OPTICAL, 2021 L St. NW. Tel. 659-0077.

This company offers hefty discounts on lenses, designer frames (Pierre Cardin, Elizabeth Arden, Armani, Gucci, Ralph Lauren/Polo, Dior), and designer sunglasses (Bausch & Lomb and others).

There are additional locations at 1725 K St. NW (tel. 463-8860) and 700 13th St. NW (tel. 737-2222). All stores are open Monday through Friday 9:30am to 6pm and on Saturday from 10am to 5pm.

FISH & SEAFOOD

SOUTHWEST WATERFRONT FISH MARKET, between 11th and 12th Sts. SW, along Maine Ave. No phone.

The best home-cooked meal I ever had in Washington was fresh-caught red snapper from this fabulous fish market. About half a dozen merchants offer a wide selection of just-off-the-boat fish and seafood—shrimp, softshell crabs, crabmeat, lobster, red snapper, bluefish, and whatever else the day's catch brings. Some merchants cook up seafood specialties and sell them here as well. It's a picturesque outdoor market, and there's usually a boat selling produce as well. The market is open daily from 7:30am to 9:30pm. Metro: Waterfront.

GOURMET GROCERIES & UPSCALE GIFTS

RED SAGE GENERAL STORE, at 14th and F Sts. NW. Tel. 638-3276.

This beautiful retail adjunct to one of Washington's most highly acclaimed restaurants sells a wide range of southwestern and other gourmet grocery items. You can stock up on hard-to-find chilies, salsas, and spices here, along with fancy olive oils, coffees and teas, southwestern cookbooks (including famed Red Sage chef Mark Miller's *Coyote Cafe* and *The Great Chili Book*), and fresh-baked breads and desserts. Also on sale here: custom rugs, china dinner-ware, southwestern-look furnishings, great T-shirts, and posters. It's a great place to find innovative upscale gifts, including gift baskets. Red Sage is open Monday through Thursday from 8am to 7pm, on Friday from 8am to 9pm, and on Saturday from 10am to 8pm. Metro: Metro Center.

MALLS

THE FASHION CENTRE AT PENTAGON CITY, 1100 S. Hayes St., at Army-Navy Dr. and I-395. Tel. 703/415-2400.

This Arlington, Virginia, mall has nothing to do with America's defense program. It's a plush four-level shopping complex with more than 160 shops, restaurants, and services adjoining a Ritz-Carlton hotel. Anchored by Macy's and Nordstrom, it also features branches of Ann Taylor, Abercrombie & Fitch, the Museum Company (for museum art reproductions), Banana Republic, Brentano's, Scribner's, Disney Store, Record World, Pucci (shoes for men), Crabtree & Evelyn, Godiva Chocolatier, Laura Ashley, Villeroy & Boch (exquisite china), Victoria's Secret, Nature Company, Lane Bryant, The Limited, Body Shop, Charter Club, Sam Goody, Britches (men, women, and outdoor shops), and The Gap (also Gap Kids). There are numerous clothing and shoe stores for the whole family, jewelers, and retailers of photographic equipment, bridal wear, beach wear, maternity clothes, luggage, gifts, toys, eyeglasses, whatever. Dining choices include several restaurants plus 13 food-court eateries. There are six movie theaters, the Metro stops right in the mall, and parking is provided for 4,500 cars. The mall is open Monday through Saturday from 10am to 9:30pm and on Sunday from 11am to 6pm. Metro: Pentagon City.

THE GALLERIA AT TYSONS II, 2001 International Dr. in McLean, Va. Tel. 703/827-7700.

This plush three-level mall, adjoining a Ritz-Carlton hotel, offers 110 shops, galleries, restaurants, and services. Its lushly planted interior is an indoor park setting, with skylights, gleaming-white Carrara marble, and cascading multilevel fountains. Anchored by three fine department stores—Macy's, Saks, and Neiman-Marcus—the Galleria also houses The Sharper Image, Victoria's Secret, The Limited and Limited Express, Monsoon (a London upscale women's apparel shop), Hobbes (more upscale women's apparel), Godiva Chocolatier, Pottery Barn, H₂O (exquisite bath/beauty products), and a two-level Conran's Habitat. Your whole shopping spectrum is well covered here—shoes and clothing for the entire family, eight jewelers, electronics, home furnishings, gifts, maternity, etc. There are five full-service restaurants, as well as a lovely Garden Food Court complete with trellises and ivy plantings. There's parking for 3,200 cars. By the way, Tysons Corner Center (see below) is right across the street. The Galleria is open Monday through Saturday from 10am to 9pm and on Sunday from noon to 6pm. Metro: West Falls Church stop; from there you can catch a shuttle that runs every half hour in both directions.

MAZZA GALLERIE, 5300 Wisconsin Ave. NW, between Western Ave. and Jenifer St. Tel. 686-9515.

Billing itself as "Washington's answer to Rodeo Drive," this *très chic,* four-level mall has 48 boutiques under a skylit atrium, including a branch of Neiman-Marcus, a multilevel Ann Taylor, and Filene's Basement (discount designer labels). And though it's not part of the mall, a Lord & Taylor adjoins and Saks is two blocks north. Other classy boutiques here are Stephene Kelian (very upscale women's shoes), Laura Ashley (home furnishings), the Forgotten Woman (elegant clothes in large sizes), Pea in the Pod (gorgeous maternity wear), Pampillonia Jewelers (estate jewelry and one-of-a-kind creations), Kron Chocolatier, and Williams-Sonoma (gourmet cookware and foods). There's an excellent on-premises restaurant called Pleasant Peasant, plus three movie theaters, a Brentano's bookstore, numerous other clothing and shoe stores, jewelers, gourmet food shops, home furnishing stores, and an exclusive hair salon. The mall, located at the D.C./Maryland border, is open Monday through Friday from 10am to 8pm, on Saturday from 10am to 6pm, and on Sunday from noon to 5pm. There's two-hour free indoor parking. Metro: Friendship Heights.

THE PAVILION AT THE OLD POST OFFICE, 1100 Pennsylvania Ave. NW. Tel. 289-4224.

This is as much of a tourist attraction as a retail complex. Certainly no mall offers a more exquisite setting. Opened in 1983 in one of the capital's oldest federal buildings—an actual 1899 government postal department—it's a vital part of the renovation of the entire Pennsylvania Avenue area. The tallest structure in the city, after the Washington Monument, its 10 floors soar 196 feet to a skylight ceiling and are crowned by a 315-foot clock tower. The atrium is lined with balconied corridors reminiscent of an Italian palazzo, the arched galleries of the upper floors overlook a magnificent inner court 99 feet wide and 184 feet long, and the exterior stonework, turrets, and massive arches were inspired by the Romanesque cathedrals of 12th-century France. In the tower are 10 great bells (a Bicentennial gift from England, they duplicate those at Westminster Abbey) that ring out from time to time.

Today the building—along with an adjoining three-level, 100,000-square-foot addition of commercial and retail space—houses about 90 boutiques and restaurants, and its hub is a performing-arts stage, the scene of daily lunchtime, afternoon, and early-evening free entertainment. You can take a break from shopping to enjoy clowns, symphony orchestras, jazz ensembles, bluegrass groups, dance performances, or whatever else might be going on. On most Saturdays the entertainment is specially geared to children. (Call the phone number above to find out the entertainment on a given day.) Also on the premises is an indoor miniature golf course. While you're here, ride the glass elevator to the tower observation deck for a lofty 360° vista. You can climb down a flight and see the bells themselves. If you'd like to hear them, the bellringers practice on Thursday evenings between 6:30 and 9:30pm; otherwise they're played only for state occasions.

Most of the shops carry whimsical merchandise, ranging from Stars and Stripes (all red, white, and blue items) to Juggling Capitol for juggler's paraphernalia. Others offer African fashions for men and women, jewelry, souvenirs, and accessories.

Plan a meal here, too—your options range from every kind of fast food to New American cuisine. There's a much-acclaimed Chinese restaurant, Hunan at the Pavilion; Blossoms features a gorgeous brick-terraced café and immense salads, among other American/continental entrées; and the brass-railed Enrico's Trattoria offers noteworthy Italian fare. Some restaurants have outdoor cafés.

The East Atrium, a 50,000-square-foot expansion, houses additional retail shops, cafés, and a multimedia theater.

The Pavilion is open March to September, Monday through Saturday from 10am to 8pm (the restaurants stay open to 9:30pm) and on Sunday from noon to 6pm; the rest of the year, Monday through Saturday from 10am to 6pm (the restaurants stay open until 8pm) and on Sunday from noon to 6pm. Metro: Federal Triangle.

THE SHOPS AT NATIONAL PLACE, entrance on F St. NW, between 13th and 14th Sts., or via the J. W. Marriott at 1331 Pennsylvania Ave. NW. Tel. 783-9090.

A Rouse Company project (like Baltimore Harbor and New York's South Street Seaport), this four-tiered, 125,000-square-foot retail complex houses over 100 stores and eateries in the renovated National Press Building. With its terra-cotta floors, balconies, columns, and fountains, it's a most attractive setting for serious shopping. All the mall regulars are here—B. Dalton, The Sharper Image, The Limited, Banana Republic, Victoria's Secret, and Benetton—to name a few. You can also shop for candy, leather goods, lingerie, clothing and shoes for the entire family, gifts, and records and tapes. Pushcarts vending specialty items are a Rouse tradition, as is the upper-level Food Hall, with plenty of seating and walls lined with fast-food vendors of everything from sushi to subs. Also here: Au Bon Pain (croissant sandwiches and homemade desserts) and two branches of the American Café (see Chapter 6). And if you really want to get down to some serious eating, there are excellent restaurants in the adjoining Marriott (see Chapter 5). The mall is open Monday through Saturday from 10am to 7pm and on Sunday from noon to 5pm. Metro: Metro Center.

SPRINGFIELD MALL, just off I-95 at Exit 57 (Franconia Rd.). Tel. 703/971-3000.

This major shopping complex is about 10 miles from the downtown D.C. area in Springfield, Va. It has 280 shops and restaurants (including a food court) and 10 movie theaters. Major stores here include branches of Macy's, J.C. Penney, and Montgomery Ward. Ann Taylor, Britches of Georgetown, The Limited, The Gap, Disney Store, Raleighs, and Victoria's Secret are represented. There are over a dozen shoe stores; other shops and boutiques carry clothing for the entire family, athletic footwear, audio equipment, telephones, bicycles, books (Brentano's, B. Dalton, Super Crown, and Waldenbooks), toys, jewelry, health foods, gourmet foods, sporting goods (Herman's, among others), maternity wear, records and tapes, and just about anything else you might need or desire. While you're here you can have your hair done (several salons vie for your patronage) or even have your eyes examined. There's free parking for 8,000 cars. And you can park the kids at the movies or either of two video-games arcades while you shop. The mall is open Monday through Saturday from 10am to 9:30pm and on Sunday from noon to 5pm. Metro: Huntington Station; then take bus no. 109 or 110.

TYSONS CORNER CENTER, 1961 Chain Bridge Rd., at Rte. 7. Tel. 703/893-9400.

This well-known mall is about 15 minutes from town in McLean, Va. (take the Beltway, I-495, to Exit 11B and follow the signs). Among the 230 shops here are five major department stores—Bloomingdale's, Nordstrom, Lord & Taylor, Hecht's, and Woodward & Lothrop. Other notable emporia include Laura Ashley, Nature Company, Williams Sonoma (kitchenware), The Limited, Disney Store, Banana Republic, Brooks Brothers, F. A. O. Schwarz, Waldenbooks, Britches of Georgetown, Ann Taylor, Crabtree & Evelyn, Woolworth's, and The Gap. Once again, there are more than a dozen shoe stores, hair salons, a spa, and a bank. Over 30 eateries run the gamut from Magic Pan to California Pizza Kitchen, and eight movie theaters make this a good choice for an afternoon shopping spree followed by a relaxing dinner and a film. There's free parking for 10,000 cars. The mall is open Monday through Saturday from 10am to 9:30pm and on Sunday from noon to 5pm. Metro: West Falls Church; from there you can catch a shuttle that runs every half hour in both directions.

UNION STATION, 40 Massachusetts Ave. Tel. 371-9441.

Union Station, with about 100 high-quality shops, has become one of Washington's most frequented retail complexes. The setting is magnificent, there are lots of great on-premises eateries (details in Chapter 6), and the stores here offer a wide array of unique and high-quality merchandise.

The plushest emporia are in the **East Hall,** with wares displayed in handsome brass-trimmed mahogany kiosks amid tall palm trees, or in alcoves flanked by scagliola marble columns. Here you'll find, among others, Pacifica (handcrafted jewelry and wood carvings from Bali), Skazi И Mechti (Russian children's books, coins, military pins, stackable dolls, and more), Post Impressions (collector stamps—everything from Civil War to Elvis stamps), Appalachian Spring (for items handcrafted in America—patchwork quilts, pottery, exquisite jewelry, and an incredible collection of kaleidoscopes), Initial Impressions (an engraver), and Washington Pen (fine pens and accessories).

Notable **West Hall** shops include Tavros Leatherwear, Made in America (American-made and U.S.-related items, from military accessories to western sculpture), Political Americana (historic and political memorabilia), and, one of my favorite shops in the complex, the Nature Company, carrying all nature-environmental-themed items, including books, cassettes, artwork, toys, kites, leaf-collecting kits, bird feeders, backpacks, telescopes, and more.

The **Main Floor Level** of the Concourse is home to branches of

B. Dalton, Victoria's Secret, Crabtree & Evelyn, and The Limited. Also here: The Great Train Store (model trains, books, cassettes, and numerous other railroad-motif items); Emerald Isle, featuring Irish linen and crystal, Aran sweaters, Claddagh friendship rings, and Celtic jewelry (they play delightful Irish music here); a toy store called Flights of Fancy; Brookstone, a kind of adult toy store selling upscale gadgetry; and Parfumerie Douglas, for international fragrances.

Women's clothing boutiques predominate on the **Concourse Mezzanine Level,** among them Putumayo, Jones of New York, Ann Taylor, and an interesting shop called White House, which specializes in all-white clothing and accessory items. There are men's clothing stores here, too. And don't miss Imposters for fine jewelry reproductions (most are between $30 and $95, and it all looks real!).

There's quite a bit more, including electronics stores, a branch of Sam Goody, additional jewelry shops, accessory stores, nine movie theaters, and a variety of services (car and limousine rental, tour desks, post office, shoe repair, shoeshine, currency exchange, and so on).

Union Station is open Monday through Saturday from 10am to 9pm and on Sunday from noon to 6pm. Metro: Union Station.

OFFICE SUPPLIES/STATIONERY

GINNS, 1208 18th St. NW, at M St. Tel. 833-6112.
Ginns offers a very extensive selection of supplies—all you'd expect, plus office furniture, lamps, globes, leather portfolios, photo albums, reference books, maps, magazines, calendars, datebooks, and greeting cards. In addition, there's a large giftware section stocked with malachite boxes, elegant bird cages, fine crystal, and more. Check the phone book for other Ginns locations. This Ginns is open Monday through Friday from 8:30am to 6pm and on Saturday from 9am to 6pm. Metro: Dupont Circle.

PHOTOGRAPHIC EQUIPMENT

PENN CAMERA EXCHANGE, 915 E St. NW. Tel. 347-5777, or toll free 800/347-5770.
Penn offers big discounts (up to 40%) on all major brand-name equipment—such as Olympus, Canon, Minolta, Pentax, Leica, Vivitar, and Nikon. The store has been owned and operated by the camera-buff Zweig family since 1953; their staff is very knowledgeable, their inventory wide-ranging. Many professional Washington photographers shop at Penn. Most of the merchandise is new and comes with a U.S. warranty, but you'll also find good buys on used equipment here. Check the Friday *Washington Post* ("Weekend" section) for announcements of special sales. Penn is open Monday through Friday from 9am to 6pm and on Saturday from 10am to 5pm. Metro: Metro Center.

RESALE & THRIFT SHOPS

In addition to those listed below, stop by **Christ Child Opportunity Shop** and **Secondhand Rose,** detailed in the Georgetown shopping tour later in this chapter.

BETTER BUYS, 3512 Connecticut Ave. NW, between Porter and Ordway Sts. Tel. 363-4165.
This is the kind of thrift shop where you can wade through an

eclectic mix of merchandise searching out treasures. The pickings always include men's, women's, and children's clothing (some of it designer labels) and jewelry, but you also might come across a pair of ski boots, a set of barbells, an African sculpture, glassware, china, toys, even a toaster oven. Better Buys is run by the National Council of Jewish Women, and profits go to various charities they support. It's open Monday through Saturday from 10am to 5pm. Metro: Cleveland Park.

KIDS' STUFF, 5615 39th St. NW, between McKinley and Northampton Sts., just off Connecticut Ave. Tel. 244-2221.

Big families are no longer in fashion, but children still outgrow clothes at the alarming rate they did in hand-me-down days. That's why a store like this is such a find. This is no junk shop. The owners take on consignment only quality merchandise in excellent condition, and they display it attractively. You'll always find major brand and designer name clothing—Oshkosh B'Gosh, Levi, Laura Ashley—as well as toys, children's furniture, strollers, cribs, and even maternity clothes. And because Washington houses every foreign embassy, you'll also find wonderful European items. Open September to June, Monday through Saturday from 10am to 5pm; August, Monday through Friday from 10am to 5pm; closed July. Metro: Friendship Heights.

ONCE IS NOT ENOUGH, 4830 MacArthur Blvd. NW, near Reservoir Rd. Tel. 337-3072.

Washington society women must change their wardrobes frequently: What do they do with the lovely clothes they've worn only once or twice? Some of them find their way to this resale shop, which specializes in top-quality women's clothing. I've seen names here like Gloria Sachs, Ellen Tracy, Nippon, Perry Ellis, Anne Klein, and Calvin Klein, to mention just a few. On my last visit I noted a black voile Chanel gown for $150 (it retailed for $2,500), a Perry Ellis sweater for $40, and a four-piece Valentino outfit worth thousands for $450. Many items were much less. The store sometimes scoops up brand-new clothing too, and sells it at unfancy prices, averaging 40% off regular store tabs. You'll also find new clothing from top stores for children here at 30% to 60% off. And there are terrific bargains in used men's clothing; some examples: a $400 camel's-hair coat for $75, an $800 sheepskin coat for $150, and a Polo raw-silk blazer for $75. Brooks Brothers and Armani suits, Sulka shirts, tuxedos, and Liberty ties are other frequent finds. Open Monday through Wednesday and on Friday and Saturday from 10am to 4:30pm, and on Thursday from 10am to 8pm.

WINES & LIQUORS

CALVERT WOODLEY, 4339 Connecticut Ave. NW, between Van Ness and Wyndam Sts. Tel. 966-4400.

This is a major discount wine and liquor store. In addition to an immense selection (66 feet of wines alone), Calvert Woodley has a complete gourmet food store offering hundreds of cheeses, charcuterie meats and pâtés, smoked salmon and whitefish, fresh halvah, an extensive selection of fine coffees (beans are ground to order), pastries and breads, caviars, and salads. It's open Monday through Saturday from 10am to 8:30pm. Metro: Van Ness.

CENTRAL LIQUOR, 726 9th St. NW, between G and H Sts. Tel. 737-2800.

Central Liquor abounds in bottled booze—over 35,000 items on display, including thousands of wines ranging from Gallo to Château Mouton Rothschild. Not just wines, but liquors, cordials, and other alcoholic potables are all discounted 10% to 25%, with special sales on loss leaders. Good deals are also offered when you buy by the case. It's open Monday through Thursday from 10am to 9pm, on Friday from 10am to 10pm, and on Saturday from 10am to midnight. Metro: Gallery Place.

SHOPPING TOUR — GEORGETOWN

Start: M and 29th Streets NW.
Finish: Wisconsin Avenue NW, between Q Street and Reservoir Road.
Time: Allow one to three hours, depending on how much time you spend browsing—or actually shopping.
Best Times: During store hours.

In Georgetown you can combine shopping and browsing (there are hundreds of stores) with a meal at a good restaurant, crowd-watching over cappuccino at a café, even a little sightseeing. The hub is at Wisconsin Avenue and M Street, and most of the stores are on those two arteries. In addition to shops, you'll encounter numerous street vendors hawking T-shirts and handmade jewelry.

If you drive into Georgetown—definitely not advised because parking is almost impossible—check out the side streets off Wisconsin Avenue above M Street for possible spots. The Georgetown Park Mall (see below) offers validated parking. There's also public transportation (by bus) to Georgetown.

ALONG M STREET NW   For the first part of this Shopping Tour, we'll head generally along M Street NW from 29th to 33rd Streets. Start at the:

1. **Spectrum Gallery,** at 1132 29th St. NW, just below M Street (tel. 333-0954), a cooperative venture in which 28 professional Washington-area artists—painters, potters, sculptors, collagists, and printmakers—share in shaping gallery policy, maintenance, and operation. The art is reasonably priced. Open Tuesday through Saturday from 11am to 6pm and on Sunday from noon to 5pm.
   Walk around the corner onto M Street to:
2. **Grafix,** 2904 M St. NW (tel. 342-0610), which carries a noteworthy collection of vintage posters (from 1895 on), 16th- to 20th-century maps, and 19th-century prints. Open Monday through Friday from 11am to 6pm and on Saturday from 11am to 5pm.

3. American Hand, 2906 M St. NW (tel. 965-3273), features exquisite contemporary handcrafted American ceramics and jewelry, plus international objets d'art. Open Monday through Saturday from 11am to 6pm and on Sunday from 1 to 5pm.

4. Georgetown Antiques Center, 2918 M St. NW (tel. 338-3811), houses the Cherub Antiques Gallery (art nouveau, art deco, art glass, Louis Icart etchings) and Michael Getz Antiques, offering American and English silver and a vast selection of fireplace accessories. Open Monday through Saturday from 11am to 6pm and on Sunday from noon to 5pm; closed July and August.

5. Ashburner Beargie Antiques, just next door at 2920 M St. NW (tel. 337-4513), specializes in 17th-, 18th-, and early 19th-century European antiques and old master paintings. Open Monday through Saturday from 11am to 6pm.

6. Junior League Shop of Washington, at 3066 M St. NW (tel. 337-6120), is a secondhand clothing shop that sells goods donated or consigned by some very upper-crust Washingtonians. You can pick up designer gowns, furs, formal wear, preppy wear, and good costume jewelry for a song. I've seen designer wear by Victor Costa, Oscar de la Renta, Chanel, Chloë, and Ungaro here. Children's and men's clothing, too. The proceeds all go to charity. Open Monday through Saturday from 10am to 7pm.

Turn left on 31st Street NW to the:

7. Yes! Bookshop, at 1035 31st St. NW (tel. 338-7874, or toll free 800/YES-1516 for a free catalog). A wealth of literature (both books and books on tape) on personal-growth and -tranformation subjects can be found on the shelves of this rather unique store, along with books on health, natural medicine, men's and women's studies, mythology, creative writing, Jungian psychology, how to save the planet, ancient history, and Native American traditions. CDs and cassettes include non-Western music, instrumental music, new-age music, and instruction in everything from quitting smoking to astral projection and hypnosis. They also sell a large number of instructional videocassettes here. Open Monday through Thursday from 10am to 7pm, on Friday and Saturday from 10am to 10pm, and on Sunday from noon to 7pm.

8. Central Periodicals, at 3109 M St. NW (no phone). If you're looking for out-of-state newspapers, you'll find them here, along with dozens of magazines on subjects like needlework, cars, guns, computers, cooking, health, new age, woodworking, photography, fishing, boating, muscle building, and food and wine. There are magazines in Arabic, Italian, French, and German; comic books; baseball and other sports trading cards. Open daily from noon to 8pm.

9. Irish Corner at the Threepenny Bit, at 3122 M St. NW (tel. 338-1338), sells Irish imports—beautiful mohair scarves, linen clothing, ladies' wool tweeds, Irish records and tapes, shamrock-motif clothing, hand-knit fishermen's sweaters, delicate hand-painted Belleek china, Galway crystal, hand-painted coats-of-arms on parchment, Claddagh rings, 100% wool tartan blankets, and Irish jams, jellies, biscuits, and fruitcakes. It's worth stopping in just to hear the wonderful Irish music that's always playing. Open Monday through Saturday from 10am to 6pm and on Sunday from noon to 5pm; and from St. Patrick's Day through

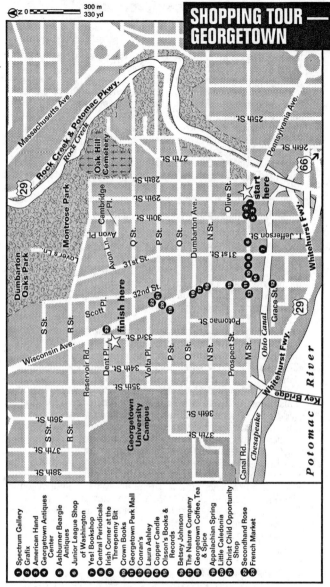

September and in the Christmas season, it's open Thursday through Saturday until 9pm.

10. Crown Books, at 3131 M St. NW (tel. 333-4493), is a sizable link in this bookstore chain. It offers 40% off *New York Times* hardcover bestsellers, 25% off paperbacks. Other books and magazines are discounted 10% to 20%. Stop in and browse. Open Monday through Thursday from 10am to 10pm, on Friday and Saturday from 10am to midnight, and on Sunday from 11am to 8pm.

11. **Georgetown Park Mall,** 3222 M St. NW, at Wisconsin Avenue (tel. 298-5577). This four-story complex of about 100 shops belongs, architecturally, to two worlds: outside, quietly Federal, in keeping with the character of the neighborhood; inside, flamboyantly Victorian, with a huge skylight, fountains, and ornate chandeliers. You could spend hours here exploring branches of the nation's most exclusive specialty stores. Represented are Ann Taylor, Caché, J. Crew, Polo/Ralph Lauren, Ports International (upscale women's apparel), and Abercrombie & Fitch. Also featured are many gift/lifestyle boutiques such as Dezzenio Futon, Impulse, Dapy, The Sharper Image, Crabtree & Evelyn, and the fascinating Gallery of History (framed collector historical documents). If you have kids take them to see the adorable stuffed animals at Georgetown Zoo, F. A. O. Schwarz, and Learningsmith (billing itself as "the general store for the curious mind, it has many interactive facilities for children"). There's a Thomas Cook foreign exchange (open daily) and an Old Town Trolley ticket booth (see Chapter 4). There are several restaurants, including Clyde's (details in Chapter 6) and a branch of the haute gourmet emporium/eatery Dean & Deluca (like a museum of food). An archeological exhibit of artifacts found during the complex's excavation is on display on Level 2. And Georgetown Park maintains a full-service Concierge Center offering gift wrapping, worldwide shipping, postal/fax/photocopy services, gift certificates, even sightseeing information. Validated parking is available in an underground 650-car facility. Open Monday through Saturday from 10am to 9pm and on Sunday from noon to 6pm.

12. **Conran's** is in (actually it's sort of behind) the Georgetown Park Mall, but since its main entrance is over at 3227 Grace St. NW, across the C&O Canal (tel. 298-8300), it's easy to miss. This London-based home-furnishings chain carries beautiful bedding and linens, a full line of furniture for the entire house and the outdoors (striking canvas beach chairs and umbrellas), kitchenware, china, lighting fixtures, shelving, Indian dhurrie rugs, and much more. It's open mall hours (see above).

13. **Laura Ashley,** at 3213 M St. NW. (tel. 338-5481). You probably need no introduction to Laura Ashley's romantic-look 100% cotton clothing and very feminine lingerie; luggage, china, stationery, perfume, and floral-design fabrics and wallpapers here, too. Open Monday through Saturday from 10am to 6pm and on Sunday from noon to 6pm.

Now go back to Wisconsin Avenue to continue shopping or for:

A REFUELING STOP At 1065 Wisconsin Ave. NW, just below M Street, **Houston's** is a very comfortable place specializing in barbecued chicken and ribs and hickory-grilled burgers; fabulous salads and desserts, too. Details in Chapter 6.

ALONG WISCONSIN AVENUE NW From your Refueling Stop, walk back up Wisconsin Avenue NW toward M Street to:

14. **The Copper Candle,** 1071 Wisconsin Ave. NW (tel. 337-7804). This Kennebunkport, Maine, transplant has some of the

most unique and exquisite candles I've ever seen, plus candle-sticks, Christmas ornaments and bells, and other lovely gift items. You can do all your holiday shopping here. Open spring to fall, Monday through Saturday from 10am to 10pm and on Sunday from 11am to 7pm; in winter, Monday through Wednesday from 10am to 7pm, Thursday through Saturday from 10am to 10pm, and on Sunday from 11am to 7pm.

Continue along Wisconsin Avenue NW, past M Street, to:

15. Olsson's Books & Records, 1239 Wisconsin Ave. NW, between M and N streets (tel. 338-6712). Open: Mon–Thurs 10am–10:45pm, Fri–Sat 10am–midnight, Sun noon–7pm. See details in Section 1 under "Books."

16. Betsey Johnson, 1319 Wisconsin Ave. NW (tel. 338-4090). New York's flamboyant flower-child designer has a Georgetown shop. She personally decorated the walls. Her sexy, offbeat play-dress-up styles are great party and club clothes for the young and the still-skinny young at heart. Open Monday through Friday from 11am to 7pm, on Saturday from 11am to 8pm, and on Sunday from noon to 6pm.

17. The Nature Company, 1323 Wisconsin Ave. NW (tel. 333-4100), my favorite mall emporium, has a branch here. These ecologically themed stores sell bird feeders, decorative mineral specimens, cassettes of whale songs, beautiful T-shirts, wonderful books (many for kids) and toys, sundials, delightful novelties, and much more. Open Monday through Thursday from 10am to 9pm, on Friday and Saturday from 10am to 10pm, and on Sunday from noon to 6pm.

18. Georgetown Coffee, Tea & Spice, 1330 Wisconsin Ave. NW, between N and O Streets (tel. 338-3801), features a collection of more than 80 different coffees—everything from Jamaican Peaberry to Ethiopian Harrar, plus a choice of about 20 decafs. Then there are some 85 varieties of tea—plum from Sri Lanka, Japanese basket-fired green, China Black, Assam, Kenyan broken-leaf orange pekoe, and many less exotic varieties. Also decaffeinated teas. The spice selection is equally wide-ranging, and in addition, this gourmet emporium sells fancy chocolates, and French candies made with real fruit. They mail purchases all over the world. Open Monday through Saturday from 10am to 9pm and on Sunday from noon to 6pm.

19. Appalachian Spring, 1415 Wisconsin Ave. NW, at P Street (tel. 337-5780), brings country crafts to citified Georgetown. They sell pottery, jewelry, newly made pieced and appliqué quilts in traditional and contemporary patterns, stuffed dolls and animals, candles, rag rugs, hand-blown glassware, an incredible collection of kaleidoscopes, glorious weavings, and simple country toys. Everything in the store is made by hand in the U.S.A. There's another branch in Union Station. Open Monday through Friday from 10am to 8pm, on Saturday from 10am to 6pm, and on Sunday from noon to 6pm.

20. Little Caledonia, at 1419 Wisconsin Ave. NW (tel. 333-4700), is a rabbit warren of tiny rooms filled with indoor and outdoor furnishings (18th- and 19th-century mahogany reproductions are featured), dolls, Beatrix Potter ceramic figures, stuffed animals, children's books and toys, exquisite fabrics, housewares (copperware, cookbooks, cookie jars, baking molds, etc.), candles, fancy gift wrappings, Indian dhurrie rugs, tablecloths, wallpapers, lamps, and much much more. A delight. Open Monday through Saturday from 10am to 6pm, and from Thanksgiving through Christmas, also on Sunday from noon to 5pm.

21. Christ Child Opportunity Shop, 1427 Wisconsin Ave. NW (tel. 333-6635). Proceeds from merchandise bought here go to various children's charities. Among the first-floor items (donations all), I saw a wicker trunk for $5 and the usual thriftshop jumble of jewelry, clothes, shoes, hats, and odds and ends. Upstairs, higher-quality merchandise is left on a consignment basis; it's considerably more expensive, but if you know antiques you might find bargains in jewelry, silver, china, quilts, paintings, and other items. Good browsing. Open Monday through Saturday from 10am to 3:45pm; closed in August.

22. Secondhand Rose, 1516 Wisconsin Ave. NW, at P Street (tel. 337-3378). This upscale second-floor consignment shop specializes in designer merchandise. Creations by Norma Kamali, Armani, Donna Karan, Calvin Klein, Yves St. Laurent, Ungaro, Ralph Lauren, and others are sold at about a third of the original value. Everything is in style, in season, and in excellent condition. On a recent visit I saw a gorgeous Scaasi black velvet and yellow satin ball gown for $400 (it was $1,200 new) and Yves St. Laurent pumps in perfect condition for $45. Secondhand Rose is also a great place to shop for gorgeous furs, designer shoes and bags, and costume jewelry. Open Monday through Saturday from 10am to 6pm.

23. The French Market, at 1626-32 Wisconsin Ave. NW, between Q Street and Reservoir Road (tel. 338-4828), has been supplying Washingtonians with French fare for over half a century—long before most Americans knew pâtés from potatoes. Run by three French brothers, Georges, Robert, and Jean Jacob, the market contains a *boucherie* carrying game (pheasant, quail, partridge, guinea hens, and mallards) in addition to less exotic European-cut meats. Other departments include a *charcuterie* (homemade pâtés en croûte and in loaf, superb salads, escargots); a *boulangerie* for baguettes, croissants, and pastries; and a *fromagerie* offering over 50 French cheeses. You can also get imported oils and vinegars, mustards, crème de marrons, canned pâtés, and other fine French groceries here as well as wines, champagnes, and French-roast coffees. *C'est merveilleux!* There's free parking behind the store on 33rd Street. Open Monday, Tuesday, Thursday, and Friday from 8:30am to 6pm, on Wednesday from 8:30am to 1pm, and on Saturday from 7:30am to 6pm.

CHAPTER 9

NIGHTS IN WASHINGTON, D.C.

Not so many years ago, Washington rolled up the sidewalks at an early hour. But today the city offers a wealth of nighttime activities. Don't go to bed early just because you're worn out from traipsing around museums and monuments all day. Take a nap before dinner and catch your second wind. In addition to the listings below, check out the Friday "Weekend" section of the *Washington Post,* which will also tell you about children's theater, sports events, flower shows, and all else. *Washingtonian* magazine and *The City Paper* are other good sources.

TICKETS

TICKETplace (call for location, because a move is scheduled shortly after we go to press; tel: TICKETS) is a service of the Cultural Alliance of Greater Washington. Here—on the day of performance only (except Sunday and Monday, see below)—you can pick up half-price tickets to productions at most major Washington-area theaters and concert halls, not only for dramatic productions, but for opera, ballet, and other performances as well. If half-price tickets aren't available, you can purchase full-price tickets in advance at this centrally located box office, not only for pop and cultural, but also for sports events. The outlet doubles as a **Ticketmaster** outlet. You must pay in cash for all tickets, and there's a 10% service charge. TICKETplace is open Tuesday through Friday from noon to 4pm and on Saturday from 11am to 5pm; half-price tickets to Sunday and Monday shows are sold on Saturday.

Full-price tickets for most performances in town can also be purchased through **Ticketmaster** (tel. 432-SEAT) or at **Hecht's Department Store,** 12th and G Streets NW. You can purchase tickets to Washington entertainments before you leave home by calling toll free 800/551-SEAT.

1. THEATER

Except for New York, I can't think of another U.S. city that offers more first-rate theatrical productions than D.C. Almost anything on

Broadway will eventually come to—or have previewed in—Washington. There are also several nationally acclaimed repertory companies here and an excellent theater specializing in Shakespearean productions. Additional theater offerings, including at the **Kennedy Center,** are listed under "Accent on Entertainment," later in this chapter.

ARENA STAGE, 6th St. and Maine Ave. SW. Tel. 488-3300.

Founded by the very brilliant Zelda Fichandler, the Arena Stage, now in its fifth decade, is the home of one of the longest-standing acting ensembles in the nation. Several works nurtured here have moved to Broadway, and many graduates—among them "L.A. Law"'s Jill Eikenberry and Michael Tucker, Ned Beatty, James Earl Jones, Robert Prosky, Jane Alexander, and George Grizzard—have gone on to commercial stardom.

The Arena's subscription-season productions (there are eight annually) are presented on three stages—the **Fichandler,** a theater-in-the-round; the smaller, fan-shaped **Kreeger;** and the **Old Vat Room,** a space used for new play readings and productions.

A recent September-to-June season (sometimes shows are extended into summer) included productions of *Twelfth Night, Long Day's Journey into Night, Hedda Gabler, The Revenger's Comedies* Parts I and II (a farce by Alan Ayckbourn), Brian Friel's *Dancing at Lughnasa,* and *A Community Carol,* an adaptation of the famous Dickens story set in present-day Anacostia. The theater has always championed new plays and playwrights and is committed to producing works of playwrights from diverse cultures. Douglas Wagner is the Arena Stage's artistic director. Metro: Waterfront.

Admission: Tickets, $22–$39; discounts available for students, the disabled, military, and senior citizens. And HOTTIX, a limited number of half-price tickets, are available 90 minutes before most performances (call for details).

NATIONAL THEATRE, 1321 Pennsylvania Ave. NW. Tel. 628-6161, or toll free 800/447-7400.

The luxurious, Federal-style National Theatre, elegantly renovated to the tune of $6.5 million in 1983, is the oldest continuously operating theater in Washington (since 1835) and the third-oldest in the nation. It's exciting just to see this stage on which Sarah Bernhardt, John Barrymore, Helen Hayes, and so many other notables have performed. The National is the closest thing Washington has to a Broadway-style playhouse. Managed by New York's Shubert Organization, the National presents star-studded hits—often pre- or post-Broadway—all year round. A recent season included productions of *Annie Get Your Gun* starring Kathy Rigby, *My Fair Lady* starring Richard Chamberlain, *A Chorus Line, Six Degrees of Separation* starring Marlo Thomas, and *A Tuna Christmas* (a sequel to *Greater Tuna*).

The National also offers free public-service programs: Saturday-morning children's theater (puppets, clowns, magicians, dancers, and singers), free summer films, and Monday-night showcases of local groups and performers. Call 783-3370 for details. Metro: Metro Center.

Admission: Tickets, $22.50–$60; discounts available for students, senior citizens, military personnel, and the handicapped.

MAJOR CONCERT & PERFORMANCE HALL BOX OFFICES

Arena Stage, 6th Street and Maine Avenue SW (tel. 488-3300).

Constitution Hall, 18th and D Streets NW (tel. 638-2661).

Ford's Theatre, 511 10th St. NW, between E and F Streets (tel. 347-4833).

John F. Kennedy Center for the Performing Arts, New Hampshire Avenue NW and Rock Creek Parkway (tel. 467-4600).

National Theater, 1321 Pennsylvania Ave. NW (tel. 628-2121).

Shakespeare Theatre, 450 7th St. NW, between D and E Streets (tel. 393-2700).

Wolf Trap Farm Park for the Performing Arts, 1551 Trap Rd., Vienna, Va. (tel. 703/255-1900).

FORD'S THEATRE, 511 10th St. NW, between E and F Sts. Tel. 347-4833 for listings, 432-SEAT to charge tickets.

This is the actual theater where, on the evening of April 14, 1865, actor John Wilkes Booth shot President Lincoln. The assassination marked the end of what had been John T. Ford's very popular theater—it remained closed for over a century. In 1968 Ford's reopened, completely restored to its 1865 appearance, based on photographs, sketches, newspaper articles, and samples of wallpaper and curtain material from museum collections. The presidential box is decorated and furnished as it was on the fateful night, including the original crimson damask sofa and framed engraving of George Washington.

Ford's season is more or less year-round (in August and September it's dark). Past productions have included several shows that went on to Broadway and off-Broadway. Some recent shows here were *Five Guys Named Moe* and cartoonist Lynda Barry's delightful foray into drama, *The Good Times Are Killing Me.*

A big event here is the nationally televised A Festival at Fords, always a celebrity-studded bash. Metro: Metro Center or Gallery Place.

Admission: Tickets, $23–$32; discounts available for families, also for senior citizens at matinee performances; both seniors and students with ID can get "rush" tickets a half hour before performances.

SOURCE THEATRE COMPANY, 1835 14th St. NW, between S and T Sts. Tel. 462-1073.

Washington's major producer of new plays, the Source also mounts works of established playwrights. It presents top local artists in a year-round schedule of dramatic and comedic plays, both at the above address and, during the summer, at various spaces around town. Recent productions here have included the Helen Hayes Award–nominated musical, *Executive Leverage* (a political satire about a future presidential election) and the Washington première of

Charles Bush's *Red Scare at Sunset.* The theater is also used for an OFF HOURS series of one-act productions geared to a contemporary urban audience. Annual events here include the Washington Theatre Festival each July, a four-week showcase of 50 or so new plays. The Source produces many African-American works and welcomes original scripts from unknowns.

Admission: Tickets, $16–$18; OFF HOURS shows, $10; July Festival shows, $5–$10.

STUDIO THEATRE, 1333 P St. NW. Tel. 332-3300.

Under artistic director Joy Zinoman, the Studio has consistently produced interesting plays, nurtured Washington acting talent, and garnered numerous Helen Hayes Awards for outstanding achievement. Many plays come here from off Broadway. Recent productions have included Caryl Churchill's *Hot Fudge,* Daniel McIvor's *2-2-Tango,* Frank Manley's *The Rain of Terror,* Tom Stoppard's *Rosencranz and Guildenstern Are Dead,* and Terrence McNally's *The Lisbon Traviata.* The Studio also houses **Secondstage,** a 50-seat space on the third floor where emerging artists, directors, and actors can showcase their work. The season runs from September through June (some productions run longer). Street parking is easy to find. Metro: Dupont Circle or McPherson Square.

Admission: Tickets, $16.50–$28.50; Secondstage shows, $12. Discounts available for students and senior citizens.

SHAKESPEARE THEATRE, 450 7th St. NW, between D and E Sts. Tel. 393-2700.

This internationally renowned classical ensemble company, which for two decades performed at the Folger Shakespeare Library, moved in 1992 to larger precincts at the above address. Under the direction of Michael Kahn, it offers three Shakespearean productions and one other classical work (last year it was Edmond Rostand's *Cyrano de Bergerac*) each September-to-June season. Well-known actors like Stacy Keach, Kelly McGillis, Tom Hulce, Richard Thomas, and Pat Carroll have joined the company for specific productions. This is top-level theater. In addition, the company offers admission-free summer Shakespearean productions in Rock Creek Park, usually for two to three weeks in June. Tickets are available the day of performance only, on a first-come, first-served basis. Call for details. Metro: Archives or Gallery Place.

Admission: Tickets, $20–$45, $10 for standing-room tickets sold two hours prior to sold-out performances; discounts available for students and senior citizens.

WOOLLY MAMMOTH THEATRE COMPANY, 1401 Church St. NW. Tel. 393-3939.

Established in 1980, the Woolly Mammoth offers four or five productions each year-long season, specializing, according to a publicist, in "new, offbeat, and quirky plays." "I'm not interested in theater where people sit back and say, 'That was nice. I enjoyed that,'" says artistic director Howard Shalwitz. "I only look for plays that directly challenge the audience in some important way." Hence shows here have included Wallace Shawn's *The Fever,* which radically confronts America's materialist lifestyle in the face of massive suffering throughout the world (audience discussion followed); *Kvetch* by Steven Borkoff (a wild comedy about anxiety, sex, and the nagging inner voices that plague us all); and Harry Kondoleon's

Obie-winning *Half Off* (two alcoholic aunts arrive to care for two teenagers whose bohemian parents have just died in a car crash). This company has garnered eight Helen Hayes Awards, among other accolades.

Metro: Dupont Circle, about five blocks away. You might consider taking a cab from there, since the neighborhood is kind of deserted and spooky at night; on request, they'll call a cab for you after the show as well.

Admission: Tickets, $16.50–$22.50. They offer a range of ticket discounts, from two-for-the-price-of-one admissions to pay-what-you-can nights; inquire at the box office. An hour prior to performances, a limited number of "stamped seats" are offered for $10.

2. ACCENT ON ENTERTAINMENT

The following listings are a potpourri of places offering a mixed bag of theater, opera, classical music, headliners, jazz, rock, dance, and comedy. Here you'll find some of the top entertainment choices in the District.

WASHINGTON'S MAJOR PERFORMANCE FACILITY

JOHN F. KENNEDY CENTER FOR THE PERFORMING ARTS, at the southern end of New Hampshire Ave. NW and Rock Creek Pkwy. Tel. 467-4600, or toll free 800/444-1324.

Our national performing arts center, the hub of Washington's cultural and entertainment scene, is actually a composite of five facilities. You can find out what will be on during your stay before leaving home (and charge tickets) by calling the above toll-free number. Half-price tickets are available for full-time students, senior citizens, enlisted personnel, and the disabled (call 416-8340 for details).

Opera House This plush red-and-gilt 2,300-seat theater is designed for ballet, modern dance, and musical comedy, as well as opera, and it's also the setting for occasional gala events such as the Kennedy Center Honors, which you've probably seen on TV (Lillian Gish, Cary Grant, Katharine Hepburn, and Gregory Peck have been honorees). Other offerings have included performances by the Joffrey Ballet, the Bolshoi Ballet, the Kirov Ballet, the Royal Ballet, the American Ballet Theatre, and the Metropolitan Opera. Recent theater productions here have included *Miss Saigon, Phantom of the Opera, Guys and Dolls,* and *The Will Rogers Follies* starring Mac Davis.

Concert Hall The National Symphony Orchestra under the direction of Mstislav Rostropovich has its home here and presents concerts from September to June. Tickets are available by subscription and single sales; some are free. Guest artists have included Itzhak Perlman, Vladimir Ashkenazy, Zubin Mehta, Pinchas Zuckerman, André Previn, Jean-Pierre Rampal, and Isaac Stern. In addition, chamber music societies, orchestras, and choral groups from all over the world have performed in this space; there's an annual free

Christmas concert, the *Messiah* sing-along; and rounding things out are headliner entertainers such as Johnny Mathis, Joel Grey, Dionne Warwick, Marvin Hamlisch, and Harry Belafonte.

Terrace Theatre   Small chamber works, operas, choral recitals, musicals, comedy revues, cabarets, and theatrical and modern-dance performances are among the varied provinces of the 500-seat Terrace Theatre, a Bicentennial gift from Japan. It's been the setting for solo performances by violinist Eugene Fodor, pianists Santiago Rodriguez and Peter Serkin, soprano Dawn Upshaw, and jazz singer Barbara Cook. Performance artists Laurie Anderson and Michael Moschen have performed here, and jazz evenings have included tributes to Count Basie, Louis Armstrong, and Duke Ellington. Every spring the Terrace hosts productions of six finalists in the American College Theatre Festival competition.

Eisenhower Theatre   A wide range of dramatic productions can be seen here. Some recent examples: *Marvin's Room*, David Mamet's controversial *Oleanna*, *And the World Goes Round* (a revue of Kander and Ebb songs), and Johnathan Tolin's *Twilight of the Gods*. The Eisenhower is also the setting for smaller productions of the **Washington Opera** from December to February. Tickets for most theatrical productions are in the $18 to $40 range. Opera seats soar higher.

Theatre Lab and More   Many Kennedy Center events and performances are free, including the Theatre Lab's schedule of children's shows such as *The Tale of Peter Rabbit*. In the evening, Theatre Lab becomes a cabaret, now in a long run of *Shear Madness*, a comedy whodunit, though this isn't gratis (tickets are $19 to $23). Elsewhere at the center, there are family concerts by the National Symphony Orchestra several times each year, not to mention clowns, jugglers, dance troupes, improvisational theater, storytellers, and films. Christmas, Easter, and the annual Kennedy Center Open House Arts Festival every September are especially event-filled times.

See also "Cinema," below, for details on the **American Film Institute,** yet another Kennedy Center facility.

Underground parking at the Kennedy Center is $5 for the entire evening after 5pm. Metro: Foggy Bottom. Bus: 46 from Dupont Circle.

OTHER MULTICULTURAL FACILITIES

THE FOLGER, 201 E. Capitol St. SE. Tel. 544-7077.

The **Folger Consort,** a medieval and Renaissance music ensemble, performs secular and sacred music, troubadour songs, Gregorian chants, and court ensembles in 30 concerts given over seven weekends between September and May. Tickets are $14 to $28.

The Folger also presents more than a dozen **theatrical programs** annually relating to Shakespeare and other literary greats. Some recent examples: Irish actor Donald Donnelly in *My Astonishing Self* (a one-man show as George Bernard Shaw), *Stand-up Shakespeare* (a show of music from Shakespearean plays), a production of *Macbeth* by the Traveling Shakespeare Company, and *The Joyicity*, a one-man show in which Irish actor Vincent O'Neill portrays 40 different characters from the life and works of James Joyce. Tickets are $12 to $20. Workshops related to these performances are open to the public.

In addition, there are sometimes **evening lectures** on Renaissance-related subjects (tickets: $10). On selected evenings, **readings** (tickets: $6) feature poets such as Joseph Brodsky, Octavio Paz, Czeslaw Milosz, Adrienne Rich, and Allen Ginsberg. Another exciting program is the Friday-night PEN/Faulkner series of fiction readings by noted authors; Arthur Miller, Nadine Gordimer, Margaret Atwood, J. P. Donleavy, Pat Conroy, and John Irving have participated. And September to May, the Folger offers Saturday morning **programs for children** ranging from medieval treasure hunts to preparing an Elizabethan feast. Admission is $7.50 per child. Metro: Capitol South.

WARNER THEATRE, 1299 Pennsylvania Ave. NW (entrance on 13th St., between E and F Sts.) Tel. 783-4000, or 432-SEAT to charge tickets.

Opened in 1924 as the Earle Theatre (a movie/vaudeville palace)—and recently renovated to its original appearance at a cost of $10 million—this stunning neoclassical-style theater features a gold-leafed grand lobby and auditorium. Everything is plush and magnificent, from the glittering crystal chandeliers to the gold-tasseled swagged-velvet draperies. It's worth coming by just to view its ornately detailed interior. The Warner offers year-round entertainment, alternating dance performances (Twyla Tharp, Baryshnikov, Alvin Ailey, the Washington Ballet's Christmas performance of *The Nutcracker*) and Broadway shows (Robert Goulet in *Camelot*, a 25th-anniversary production of *Jesus Christ Superstar, Annie, Falsettos*) with headliner entertainment (Liza Minnelli, Frank Sinatra, Shirley MacLaine, Kenny Rogers, Charles Aznavour, Tony Bennett). Call to find out what's on during your visit. Metro: Metro Center.

Admission: Play tickets, $32.50–$50; concert tickets, prices vary according to the performer.

WOLF TRAP FARM PARK FOR THE PERFORMING ARTS, 1551 Trap Rd., Vienna, Va. Tel. 703/255-1900, or 703/218-6500 to charge tickets.

The country's only national park devoted to the performing arts, Wolf Trap, just 30 minutes by car from downtown D.C., offers a star-studded **Summer Festival Season** from late May to mid-September. Recent seasons have featured performances by the New York City Opera and the National Symphony Orchestra, jazz trumpeter Wynton Marsalis, the Kirov Ballet, the Bolshoi Ballet, Ray Charles, Mary Chapin Carpenter, Gordon Lightfoot, Emmylou Harris, John Denver, Bill Cosby, the Joffrey Ballet, Willie Nelson, the Modern Jazz Quartet, Bonnie Raitt, and Jay Leno. Talk about eclectic! Performances are held in the 7,000-seat **Filene Center,** about half of which is under the open sky. You can also buy cheaper lawn seats on the hill, in some ways the nicest way to go. If you do, arrive early (the lawn opens 90 minutes prior to the performance), and bring a blanket and a picnic dinner; it's a tradition.

October to May is Wolf Trap's **Barn Season,** featuring jazz, pop, country, and bluegrass performers, chamber music, and more in the pre-Revolutionary, 350-seat German Barn at 1635 Trap Rd. Call 703/938-2404 for information.

Metro: West Falls Church; in summer only, the Wolf Trap Express Shuttle ($3.50 round-trip) runs from the Metro every 20 minutes starting two hours prior to performance time and (return trip) 20 minutes after the performance ends or 11pm (whichever comes first).

By car, take I-495 to Exit 12W (Dulles Toll Road); stay on the local exit road (you'll see a sign) until you come to Wolf Trap.

Admission: Tickets, Summer Festival, $18–$39 seats, $9–$16 lawn; Barn season, tickets average $15.

MOSTLY HEADLINERS

The following facilities offer primarily big-name entertainers—they're large spaces only headliners can fill.

BALTIMORE ARENA, 201 W. Baltimore St., Baltimore, Md. Tel. 410/347-2020, or 410/481-SEAT or toll free 800/551-SEAT for tickets.

This 13,500-seat arena, a few blocks from Baltimore's Inner Harbor, is home to a few local sports teams. When they're not playing, there are big-name concerts here. The Arena hosted the Beatles back in the 1960s. More recently, headliners have included Vanilla Ice, Neil Diamond, Conway Twitty, Randy Travis, Paul Simon, Hank Williams, Jr., Little Feat, and New Kids on the Block. Other events here have run the gamut from the Ringling Brothers and Barnum & Bailey Circus to the Ninja Turtles to *Disney on Ice*.

To get here by car, take I-95 north to I-395 (stay in the left lane) to the Inner Harbor exit and follow Howard Street to the Arena. You can also take a MARC train from Union Station.

Admission: Ticket prices vary according to the performer.

USAIR ARENA, Exit 15A or 17A off the Capital Beltway in Landover, Md. Tel. 301/350-3400.

This 19,000-seat arena hosts a variety of concerts and headliner entertainment in between sporting events. Bruce Springsteen, Pavarotti, Michael Jackson, Janet Jackson, Van Halen, George Michael, Madonna, Elton John, Eric Clapton, Paul McCartney, Prince, Neil Diamond, Bill Cosby, and the Rolling Stones have all played here.

Admission: Ticket prices vary according to the performer.

CONSTITUTION HALL, 18th and D Sts. NW. Tel. 638-2661 or 628-4780.

Somehow I don't associate people like Richard Pryor and Eddie Murphy with the Daughters of the American Revolution. Nevertheless, they've both appeared at this beautiful 3,746-seat Federal-style auditorium at the DAR's national headquarters. Others who've headlined here include Lee Greenwood, the Washington Civic Symphony, Patti LaBelle, Diana Ross, Jay Leno, Ray Charles, and Marilyn Horne. Metro: Farragut West.

Admission: Tickets, $15–$50, depending on the performer.

MERRIWEATHER POST PAVILION, 10475 Little Patuxent Pkwy., just off Rte. 29 in Columbia, Md. Tel. 410/730-2424.

During the summer there's celebrity entertainment almost nightly at the Merriweather Post Pavilion, about 40 minutes by car from downtown D.C. There's reserved seating in the open-air pavilion (roofed in case of rain) and general-admission seating on the lawn (no refunds for rain) to see such performers as James Taylor, Tina Turner, Van Halen, the Beach Boys, Frank Sinatra, Liza Minnelli, Sting, John Cougar Mellencamp, Julio Iglesias, Joan Rivers, Willie Nelson, Jimmy Buffett, Elton John, Al Jarreau, and Barry Manilow. If you opt

for lawn seating, bring blankets and picnic fare (you have to buy beverages on the premises).
Admission: Tickets, $17–$30 pavilion, $13.50–$18.50 lawn.

THE PATRIOT CENTER, George Mason University, 4400 University Dr., Fairfax, Va. Tel. 703/993-3000, 703/573-SEAT to charge tickets.
This 10,000-seat facility hosts major headliners. Performers here have included Prince, Randy Travis, David Copperfield, Hank Williams, Jr., Tom Petty, Wayne Newton, Miami Sound Machine, Chicago, Natalie Cole, Sting, Billy Idol, and Kenny Rogers. There are family events such as *Sesame Street Live* here, too. To get here by car, take the Wilson Bridge to Braddock Road West, and continue for about eight miles to University Drive.
Admission: Ticket prices vary according to the performer.

ROBERT F. KENNEDY MEMORIAL STADIUM, 2400 E. Capitol St. SE. Tel. 547-9077 or 546-3337, 432-SEAT to charge tickets.
It takes superstars to pack this 55,000-plus-seat facility. Michael Jackson, Bruce Springsteen, the Rolling Stones, U-2, Pink Floyd, Paul McCartney, the Grateful Dead, New Kids on the Block, Bob Dylan, and Madonna are a few of those who've played here. Metro: Stadium-Armory.
Admission: Ticket prices vary according to the performer.

3. THE MUSIC, BAR & CLUB SCENE

In addition to the big concert spaces detailed in "Accent on Entertainment," above, and the free concerts listed in "Free Shows," below, Washington has many more intimate places where great rock and jazz artists play. It also has lively bars, dance clubs (the latter offering some of the best singles action), and comedy clubs. There's even big-band music, square and folk dancing, and more, in a park. What else could you ask for?

By the way, some of these places could also fit under another category on occasion, so read all sections and then call the ones that interest you to see what's happening that night before setting out.

ROCK & JAZZ

THE BAYOU, 3135 K St. NW, under the Whitehurst Freeway near Wisconsin Ave. Tel. 333-2897.
This lively nightclub, located on the Georgetown waterfront, features a mixed bag of live musical entertainment—mostly progressive, reggae, and alternative sounds. Performers are up-and-coming national groups, with occasional big names playing the club for old time's sake. Show times vary.

Every Saturday night at 7:30pm (doors open at 6:30pm), a very funny comedy group called **Gross National Product** takes the stage. Their satirical show targets the foibles and frailties of the current administration—its pundits, policymakers, and hangers-on. Part of the show includes a mock town meeting in which the audience bombards "President Clinton" with irreverent questions on topics ranging from the nanny fiascos to the "First Brother." This ever-changing show (today's scandal is tomorrow's skit) is so popular that advance reservations are required (call 783-7212).

The Bayou is a funky, cavelike club, with exposed brick and stone walls and seating on two levels. Sandwiches and pizza are available during the show. Drinks average $3; most food items are $5 or less. No one under 18 is admitted.

Admission: $5–$17, $15 for Gross National Product.

BLUES ALLEY, 1073 Wisconsin Ave. NW, in an alley behind M St. Tel. 337-4141.

Blues Alley, in Georgetown, has been Washington's top jazz club since 1965, featuring such artists as Nancy Wilson, McCoy Tyner, Phyllis Hyman, Sonny Rollins, Flora Purim, Herbie Mann, Wynton Marsalis, Charlie Byrd, Ramsey Lewis, Dr. John, and Maynard Ferguson. There are usually two shows nightly. Reservations are essential (call after noon), and since seating is on a first-come, first-served basis it's best to arrive no later than 7pm and have dinner. Entrées on the steak and Créole-seafood menu (for example, jambalaya, chicken Créole, and crabcakes) are in the $14 to $19 range; snacks and sandwiches are $5.25 to $9, and drinks are $4 to $6. The decor is of the classic jazz club genre—exposed brick walls, beamed ceiling, and small candlelit tables. Sometimes well-known visiting musicians get up and jam with performers, and one night, when Jerry Lewis was in the audience, he got up on stage and told a few jokes.

Blues Alley will open a new adjoining club offering a wider spectrum of entertainers in the near future.

Admission: $13–$35, plus $7 food or drink minimum.

PUBS & BARS

BOTTOM LINE, 1716 I St. NW. Tel. 298-8488.

The Bottom Line is a popular sports bar, owned by Dick Heidenberger and Jack Million, both former PAC rugby team players. Consequently, lots of ruggers and other athletes hang out here. Monday night, sporting events are televised at the bar, and free hot dogs are given out to customers. Tuesday through Saturday, there's dancing to music (Top-40 tunes, progressive rock, reggae) provided by a DJ from 9pm to closing. Some people describe the Bottom Line as a place to come and go nuts. There's a definite anything-goes attitude, enhanced by frequent zany promotions. On a recent Unknown Customer Night, everyone who came in got a bag with eye-holes and a funny face to put over their heads; there were also numbers on the bags called out during the evening for prizes. Another night, anyone who could sit on a block of ice for an hour had $100 donated to a charity of his or her choice—plus unlimited free drinks while ice-sitting. And, of course, there's a big holiday bash on Christmas, New Year's, Valentine's Day, St. Patrick's Day, etc.—let's just say the party never stops. A reasonably priced menu—salads, omelets, pita sandwiches, deli sandwiches, and burgers, mostly under $6—is offered until 10 or 11pm. Drinks run $2.50 to $3.50. The Bottom Line is open Monday through Thursday to 1:30am, to 2:30am on Friday and Saturday. Metro: Farragut West.

CHAMPIONS, 1206 Wisconsin Ave. NW, just north of M St. Tel. 965-4005.

This Georgetown spot is D.C.'s premier hangout for athletes and sports groupies. *Playboy* has called it "Washington's best singles bar" and *Cosmopolitan* "the best place to meet jocks." Champions occupies two floors—the heaviest singles action is at the first-floor bar; the upstairs bar and glassed-in deck are more laid-back. The attractive interior is choc-a-bloc with autographed sports photos, posters, and artifacts such as Carl Lewis's running shoes, Sugar Ray Leonard's boxing gloves, Joe Louis's headgear, and O. J. Simpson's football jersey. And many TV monitors air nonstop sporting events. Of course, you're likely to see your favorite sports stars (particularly of Washington area teams) at the bars or tables, and entertainment-world celebrities also drop by with some frequency. Pat Sajak has been here a number of times; in fact, he met his wife at another Champions in California. And I once glimpsed Ryan O'Neal at the bar cheering the Celtics. Champions is always packed, and they don't take reservations, so unless you arrive early, you'll likely wait for a table. If you do get a seat, you might order such fare as nachos, burgers, a steak-and-cheese sandwich, or buffalo wings. And should you make your way through the crowd to the bar, you'll see that it's pasted over with $15,000 worth of baseball cards. Drinks average $3. A DJ is on hand nightly playing oldies and Top-40 tunes. Open Sunday through Thursday until 2am, on Friday and Saturday until 3am.

CLYDE'S, 3236 M St. NW. Tel. 333-9180.

Located in Georgetown, this New York–style bar complete with checkered tablecloths, gaslight sconces, and white tile floors is mobbed every evening with an upscale crowd of young professionals, college students, political types, and Old Line Washingtonians. Should you desire solid rather than liquid refreshment, there are several dining areas, my favorite being the candlelit patio with numerous plants and a skylight ceiling. Or you can adjourn to the Omelette Room where a chef working in an open copper-canopied kitchen turns out such omelets as the Bonne Femme—stuffed with bacon, sautéed potatoes, onions, sour cream, and chives—until the wee hours. (See further details on the food here in Chapter 6.) Clyde's opens at 11am and drinks are served until 2am Sunday through Thursday, to 3am on Friday and Saturday. Drinks average $3.20.

OLD EBBITT GRILL, 675 15th St. NW, between F and G Sts. Tel. 347-4801.

While I'm on the subject of simpatico hangouts, the Old Ebbitt, described in detail in Chapter 6, offers a good bit of glamour in its sumptuous turn-of-the-century bars and dining areas. A scene from Clint Eastwood's movie *In the Line of Fire* was shot here. Drinks average $3.20. Metro: McPherson Square or Metro Center.

SAMANTHA'S, 1823 L St. NW. Tel. 223-1823.

This is an exceptionally cozy hangout with oak-paneled and exposed brick walls hung with French posters from the 1920s, stained-glass panels, art nouveau wall sconces, tufted-leather banquettes, and a working fireplace (filled with plants and flowers in summer). A DJ is on hand Wednesday through Saturday playing Top-40 tunes. The menu features moderately priced American fare (eight-ounce burgers, omelets, spinach salad, and quiches, along with more ambitious daily specials such as hickory-smoked chicken breast with rotini pesto). Drinks average $2.85 to $4.25. Open Monday through Thursday until 2am, on Friday and Saturday until 3am. Metro: Farragut North.

DANCE CLUBS

DEJA VU, 2119 M St. NW. Tel. 452-1966.

This 10-room Victorian extravaganza, with two dance floors, eight bars, and two restaurants on the premises, is one of the liveliest places in D.C. Both dance floors have wood-burning fireplaces, which, along with stained-glass paneling, lots of plants, fountains, and plush furnishings, make for a cozy setting. A DJ plays "greatest hits of yesterday and today." Every Thursday, there's a dance contest at midnight, and there are frequent theme parties such as Christmas in July. You can dine here (reservations advised) at Blackie's House of Beef (steaks, prime rib, fresh seafood) or Lulu's New Orleans Cafe, offering Créole-Cajun and seafood entrées as well as indoor and outdoor seating. Drinks average $3.25. Open Sunday through Thursday to 2am, on Friday and Saturday to 3am. Metro: Dupont Circle or Foggy Bottom.

Admission: $2 cover Fri–Sat, no cover or drink minimum Sun–Thurs.

FIFTH COLUMN, 915 F St. NW. Tel. 393-3632.

The 900 block of F Street, traditionally kind of a ghost town at night, is turning into something of a club district (see also Nightclub 9:30, below). Fronted by massive neoclassical columns, the Fifth Column isn't decorator fancy, but it does have a rather grand interior—a former Equitable Bank with a soaring 45-foot arched ceiling over the dance floor. Especially plush is the upstairs VIP room with comfortable sofas, a working fireplace, aquariums, and water bubbling through blue neon-lit mirrored walls. Guests are admitted to the latter at the discretion of the guy behind the velvet rope; bar prices are higher in this elevated precinct, but it's a cozy setting for sipping champagne. Also simpatico is the open-air patio out back. The music (mostly DJ/occasional live entertainment, till 2am Monday through Thursday, to 3am on Friday and Saturday) is a mix of progressive house, European house, acid jazz, techno, and underground. The club stays on top of trends, keeps an ear to New York and London, and often plays pre-release recordings. There are changing art shows on the walls. The crowd is 25 to 30, upwardly mobile with a sprinkling of Arab princes and the occasional visiting celeb (Cher, Prince, Julia Roberts, Sylvester Stallone). You must be 21 to get in (18 Monday and Wednesday nights). No drink minimum; the average drink is about $3.75. Metro: Metro Center.

Admission: $5–$8.

KILIMANJARO, 1724 California St. NW, between 18th St. and Florida Ave. Tel. 328-3838 or 328-3839.

This popular reggae/calypso/African-music club, owned by a Kenyan and a Bajan, is the hub of Washington's Caribbean music scene. The setting is fittingly exotic—dimly lit, with candles aglow in red-glass holders and zebra skins adorning the walls. There are two separate dance areas; on weekends, a different band plays in each (good acoustics here; there's no cacaphony). Some of the artists who've played Kilimanjaro are Shabba Ranks (from Jamaica), Hugh Masekela (South Africa), Arrow (Trinidad), and Gregory Isaacs (Jamaica). There are live bands most Thursday, Friday, and Saturday nights, a DJ the rest of the week. You can dine here on menu items like nyama ya mbuzi—East African-style charcoal-grilled goat. Drinks average $3.75. Open 2am Sunday through Thursday, to 3am on Friday and Saturday. Best way to get here is by taxi. You must be 21 to get in.

Admission: Free Mon–Wed, $5 Thurs and Sun, $10 Fri–Sat; there's always a two-drink minimum.

NIGHTCLUB 9:30, 930 F St. NW. Tel. 638-2008 or 393-0930.

This funky club features live bands—punk, metal, house/industrial, reggae, rockabilly, and rap—including some well-known performers like Ice T, Run DMC, Nine Inch Nails, Helmet, and the Screaming Trees. Occasionally jazz artists—such as Sun Ra and Sonny Sharrock—play here as well. It's all very un-Washington, not just the music and the crowd but the grotty, black-walled interior with exposed pipes overhead. There are themed dance parties to introduce new artists and releases. The club is open five or six nights a week (it depends on bookings), until 1:30am Sunday through Thursday, to 2:30am on Friday and Saturday, and there's no minimum age for admission—a boon to young teens looking for trouble. No drink minimum; drinks average $3.75. Pizza and snack items are available. Metro: Metro Center.

Admission: $3–$25, depending on the performer.

RIVER CLUB, 3223 K St. NW. Tel. 333-8118.

Isn't it romantic? This elegantly art deco Georgetown nightspot evokes the sophisticated dine-and-dance clubs that flourished in an earlier era (the 1920s and 1930s), bringing unprecedented champagne-and-caviar glamour to the Washington nightlife scene. The clientele is glittery and gorgeous (wear your best), many with limos waiting out front. One often sees local and visiting celebrities here. I've spotted Redskins owner Jack Kent Cooke, Ted Kennedy, Ryan O'Neal, Jesse Jackson, Cher, Lynda Carter, Sen. John Warner, and Sylvester Stallone on various visits. You can hang out at the large bar up front or have dinner (the food's superb) at the tables surrounding the circular dance floor. It's a great place to dance. From 6:30 to 9:30pm a pianist plays show tunes and light jazz; after 9:30pm the music might be Sinatra, Cole Porter, big band and swing, Motown, even a bit of European music. If you can't manage sparkling repartee or kindle the spark of romance in this setting, you never will. Open for dinner Monday through Thursday from 5:30 to 11:30pm, for dancing until 2am; on Friday and Saturday for dinner until midnight, for dancing until 3am. See Chapter 6 for a detailed description of the River Club and its culinary offerings. Drinks average $5.

RUMORS, 19th and M Sts. NW. Tel. 466-7378.

For many years *Washingtonian* magazine's choice as D.C.'s no. 1 singles bar, Rumors is sometimes busy even on Monday nights, when other places offer all the excitement of a wake. In the California-style Neo-Victorian bar (overhead fans, hanging plants, and brass railings) and the dance floor area (featuring a DJ spinning contemporary dance tunes nightly), unless you look like Quasimodo, you're likely to meet someone. Take your new love out for a margarita or a meal at the glass-enclosed café under a striped tent top, where conversation is possible. Food (burgers, salads, Mexican specialties) is served until

11pm, with entrées in the $5 to $13 range. Drinks average $4. You must be 21 or over to get in. Open Sunday through Thursday until 2am, on Friday and Saturday to 3am. Metro: Dupont Circle.

Admission: Free Sun–Thurs, $2 cover Fri–Sat.

SPY CLUB, 805 15th St. NW, between H and I Sts., in an alley. Tel. 289-1779.

The Spy Club's dance floor is punctuated by columns designed to evoke skyscrapers, complete with lighted windows. There are cozy nooks off the dance floor, including the Den (with overstuffed sofas, shaded table lamps, and a working fireplace), the Cubana Room (with palm trees and a roulette wheel), and the Billiards Room (set up with a pool table and backgammon boards). Every Wednesday the club hosts an upscale Latin night, when men in jackets and ties twirl ladies in high heels to sounds of salsa. On Thursday the dance tunes are progressive, Friday features cutting-edge mixes and European music, and on Saturday it's oldies and Top-40 tunes. The dress code prohibits sneakers or T-shirts. The crowd is 25 to 35. If you'd like to dine sometime during the evening, Notte Luna, a fine northern Italian restaurant, is right upstairs. Hours vary, but the club is generally open Wednesday through Saturday from 10pm to 2:30am. Drinks average $4. Metro: McPherson Square. Valet parking is $5.

Admission: $5–$8.

COMEDY CLUBS & CABARET

Though big-name comedians perform around town at places like **Constitution Hall,** and lesser-known comedians and groups at places like **D.C. Space,** there are two clubs in town totally devoted to comedy:

COMEDY CAFE, 1520 K St. NW. Tel. 638-JOKE.

The Comedy Cafe features both local talent and nationally known comics you might have seen in movies or on TV (for example, Larry Miller, Carol Liefer, Danny Bonaduce, Judy Tenuta, David Alan Grier, Jeff Foxworthy, or Soupy Sales). Reservations are recommended, and it's a good idea to arrive early to get a good seat. There are two shows every Friday night (at 8:30 and 10:30pm) and three every Saturday night (at 7, 9, and 11pm). There's no minimum, but you can order food; a reasonably priced menu offers full entrées (such as chicken teriyaki and charcoal-broiled strip steak), as well as sandwiches, burgers, hors d'oeuvres, desserts, and, of course, drinks. Wednesday (from 8:30pm) is open-mike night; that means people are auditioning or, occasionally, pros are working out new material ($4.95 cover, no minimum). And on Thursday (same hours) comics again take the stage ($4.95 cover, no minimum).

The Comedy Cafe is on the second floor. Below, under the same ownership, is **Fanatics,** a sports-themed dance club where a DJ plays oldies and Top-40 tunes and there's karaoke. Plan to go down and dance after the show. Fanatics is open until 2am Sunday through Thursday, until 3am on Friday and Saturday. Metro: McPherson Square or Farragut North.

Admission: Comedy Cafe, $10–$25; Fanatics, no cover or minimum.

THE IMPROV, 1440 Connecticut Ave. NW, between L and M Sts. Tel. 296-7008.

Offering a similar format to the above, the Improv features top performers on the national comedy club circuit. "Saturday Night Live" regulars Ellen Cleghorne (Queen Shenequa), David Spade, and Adam Sandler have all played here. Shows are about 1½ hours long and include three comics (an emcee, feature act, and headliner). Show times are at 8:30pm Sunday through Thursday, at 8:30 and 10:30pm on Friday and Saturday. Best way to snag a good seat is to have dinner here (make reservations), which allows you to enter the club as early as 7pm. Dinner entrées ($8.95 to $11.95) include prime rib, chicken Cordon Bleu, and pasta and seafood selections. Drinks average $3.25. You must be 18 to get in. Metro: Farragut North.

Admission: $8 Sun–Thurs, $10 Fri–Sat, plus a two-item minimum (waived if you dine).

MARQUEE CABARET, in the Omni Shoreham Hotel, 2500 Calvert St. NW, at Connecticut Ave. Tel. 234-0700.

A hotel with a long history of providing great entertainment, the Shoreham today features mostly talented ensembles in its plush art deco nightclub. In the 1930s, people like Sinatra, Chevalier, Bob Hope, and Judy Garland performed at the hotel. And political satirist Mark Russell played the room for 20 years. For the last five years, a politically oriented and very funny musical comedy revue called *Mrs. Foggybottom & Friends* has been playing Thursday through Saturday nights at 9pm. On Monday at 8pm an improvisational comedy group called Now This takes the stage. And singers and comics fill in other nights. There's almost always something on. Reservations suggested. Metro: Woodley Park–Zoo.

Admission: $7–$21, depending on the entertainment.

MUSIC, DANCING & MORE IN THE PARK

From late March through early November, you can attend Friday-night contra and square dances, Saturday-night big-band concerts, and Sunday-night square or folk dances (anything from English country to Bavarian) at the **Spanish Ballroom** at Glen Echo Park, MacArthur Boulevard and Goldsboro Road (tel. 301/492-6282/6229 or 492-6226). Admission costs $5 to $7. Call for hours. There's usually also entertainment on other nights.

4. CINEMA

With the advent of VCRs, classic film theaters are nearly extinct. In addition to the **Mary Pickford Theater,** in the John Adams Building of the Library of Congress (see Chapter 7), there are only two choices in this category, but they're good ones:

AMERICAN FILM INSTITUTE, at the Kennedy Center, New Hampshire Ave. NW and Rock Creek Pkwy. Tel. 828-4000.

This marvelous facility features classic films, cult movies, themed film festivals, and the like in a 224-seat theater designed to offer the highest standard of projection, picture, and sound quality. There's something on almost every night and weekend afternoon. The AFI also sponsors audience-participation discussions with major directors, film stars, and screenwriters—people such as Linda Yellin, Sigourney Weaver, Gore Vidal, Nora Ephron, Jonathan Demme, and Ivan Reitman.

Underground parking at the Kennedy Center is $5 for the entire evening after 5pm. Metro: Foggy Bottom.

Admission: $6; $5 for members (AFI memberships are $15 a year), senior citizens, and students under 18 with ID.

BIOGRAPH, 2819 M St. NW. Tel. 333-2696.

The Biograph, in Georgetown, specializes in small, independent first-run and foreign films, documentaries, and other cinematographic efforts of interest to serious filmgoers. It shows many notable (often award-winning) foreign films and independent-filmmaker productions. Recent offerings have included a Robert Altman retrospective and a Japanese animation festival. Stop by and pick up a calendar if you're going to be in town for a while.

Admission: $6. A discount ticket book good for 10 admissions Monday through Thursday evenings and at all matinee shows is $25.

5. FREE SHOWS

In D.C. some of the best things at night are free—or so cheap they're as good as free in today's inflationary clime.

MILITARY BAND CONCERTS

The **U.S. Army Band, "Pershing's Own"** (tel. 703/696-3718), presents a mix of country, blues, Bach, choral music, jazz, pop, and show tunes every summer, all of it outdoors. There are performances at 8pm every Friday on the east steps of the Capitol and every Tuesday at the Sylvan Theatre on the grounds of the Washington Monument. Every June there's a major American history–themed pageant at the Capital Centre called *Spirit of America* (call 202/475-0685 to obtain free tickets). And beginning early in July (through mid- to late August) the band joins with the Third U.S. Infantry, "The Old Guard," on Wednesday at 7pm to present *Twilight Tattoo*, a military pageant, on the Ellipse; it features the Old Guard Fife and Drum Corps, rifle drills, flag presentations, and a musical salute to America's heritage. Arrive early to get a good seat at any of the above, and bring a picnic dinner and blanket to outdoor concerts. The season's highlight is a performance in August of Tchaikovsky's *1812* Overture with real roaring cannons. There are additional performances in winter at Brucker Hall in Arlington, Virginia. Call for details.

The **U.S. Navy Band, "The World's Finest"** (tel. 433-2525 for a 24-hour recording, or 433-2394), performs a similar variety of music, alternately at 8pm Monday on the east steps of the Capitol and at 8pm Thursday at the Sylvan Theatre, June through August. There are also summer U.S. Navy Band concerts on Tuesday nights at 8pm at the U.S. Navy Memorial, 701 Pennsylvania Ave. NW. The navy band highlight: the *Children's Lollipop Concert* of child-oriented music, in August, with elaborate sets, costumes, balloons, clowns, and free lollipops for the audience. And the band also features the *Navy Summer Pageant,* a multimedia presentation tracing the history of the U.S. Navy, on Wednesday at 9pm at the Washington

Navy Yard Waterfront, 901 M St. SE. Advance reservations are required; call 433-2218.

The **U.S. Marine Band, "The President's Own"** (tel. 433-4011 for a 24-hour recording, or 433-5809), alternates performances June to August on the east steps of the Capitol on Wednesday at 8pm and at the Sylvan Theatre on Sunday at 8pm. It offers additional free concerts January to May at the Marine Barracks, 8th and I Streets SE, including a chamber music series at 2pm every Sunday in January and February (no tickets required). Call for details.

Finally, there's the **U.S. Air Force Band, "America's International Musical Ambassadors"** (tel. 767-5658 for a 24-hour recording, or 767-4310). June through August they (or their jazz ensemble, **The Airmen of Note**) can be seen on the east steps of the Capitol on Tuesday at 8pm and at the Sylvan Theatre on Friday at the same time. And the Friday closest to August 25 is set aside for Christmas in August (carols and other Christmas music).

HEADLINERS — MOSTLY JAZZ

Anheuser-Busch, along with local radio stations, sponsors two fabulous outdoor summer concert series in conjunction with the National Park Service.

Big names in jazz, pop, rock, Latin, and avant-garde music perform in the 4,200-seat **Carter Barron Amphitheatre,** Colorado Avenue and 16th Street NW, in Rock Creek Park (tel. 426-6837 or 619-7222) from mid-June through the end of August on Friday and Saturday nights at 8:30pm. Tickets are very low priced—about $15. They go on sale at Ticketmaster outlets (tel. 432-SEAT) at the beginning of the season and sell out fast. Seating is on a first-come, first-served basis, so arrive early and get on line. Who might you see here? Nancy Wilson, Phoebe Snow, Roberta Flack, Gladys Knight, Phyllis Hyman, or B. B. King, among other stars. In addition, the National Symphony Orchestra presents three or more free summer concerts here, and the *Washington Post* also sponsors free Carter Barron concerts. Call for details.

Under the same sponsorship is a series of jazz concerts on the lawn in the **Fort Dupont Summer Theatre,** Randle Circle and Minnesota Avenue SE, in Fort Dupont Park (tel. 426-7723 or 619-7222), every Friday or Saturday at 8:30pm from sometime in June to the end of August. Bring a blanket and a picnic dinner; arrive early (by 6pm) to get a good spot on the lawn. Past performers here have included Stanley Turrentine, Roy Ayres, Herbie Mann, McCoy Tyner, Betty Carter, the Motown Revue, Flora Purim, and Ahmad Jamal. Admission is free.

MORE OUTDOOR CONCERTS

Concerts at the Capitol, an American Festival, is sponsored jointly by the National Park Service and Congress. It's a series of free summer concerts with the National Symphony Orchestra that take place at 8pm on the west side of the Capitol on Memorial Day, July 4, and Labor Day. Seating is on the lawn, so bring a picnic. Major guest stars in past years have included E. G. Marshall (a narrator and host), Leontyne Price, Johnny Cash, Rita Moreno, Mary Chapin Carpenter, and Mstislav Rostropovich. The music ranges from light classical to country to show tunes of the Gershwin/Rogers and Hammerstein genre. For further information, call 619-7222.

The Corporate Community Family (which is made up of organizations such as Exxon and the *Washington Post*) sponsors free **Music Under the Stars Concerts** on Wednesday nights in summer at the Sylvan Theatre on the lawn south of the Washington Monument (tel. 619-7222). The series offers a mix of big band, jazz, and international music; in the latter category, one night I attended a fabulous Polynesian show, complete with fire dancers. Once again, arrive early to snag a good spot, and bring a picnic dinner. Concerts begin at 7pm.

Concerts on the Canal, sponsored by the Mobil Corporation, are free afternoon concerts right on the C&O Canal between 30th and Thomas Jefferson Streets NW, just below M Street (tel. 653-5844). Featuring jazz, folk, Dixieland, bluegrass, country, and classical artists, they take place every other Sunday afternoon (1:30 to 4pm) from early June to late August or early September.

CHAPTER 10

EASY EXCURSIONS FROM WASHINGTON

1. ARLINGTON NATIONAL CEMETERY
2. MOUNT VERNON
3. ALEXANDRIA

I f possible, consider planning a few days away from Washington, visiting pre-Revolutionary America and other close-to-the-capital attractions. All the destinations below can be visited on day trips, keeping your Washington, D.C., hotel base.

1. ARLINGTON NATIONAL CEMETERY

Originally the land now comprising Arlington County was carved out of Virginia as part of the territory ceded to form the nation's new capital district. In 1847 the land was returned to the state of Virginia, although it was known as Alexandria County until 1920, when the name was changed to avoid confusion with the city of Alexandria.

The county was named to honor Arlington House, built by George Washington Parke Custis (see below), whose daughter, Mary Ann Randolph Custis, married a young army officer named Robert E. Lee. The Lees lived in Arlington House until the onset of the Civil War in 1861. After the first Battle of Bull Run, at Manassas, some Union soldiers were buried here, and the beginnings of the national cemetery date from that time. The Arlington Memorial Bridge at the base of the Lincoln Memorial symbolizes the reunion of North and South after the Civil War.

Note: Keep in mind that this is still an active cemetery and observe the proper decorum.

GETTING THERE Arlington National Cemetery is just across the Potomac River from Washington D.C. **By car,** from the Lincoln Memorial, drive across the Arlington Memorial Bridge. You can park in the huge lots (you're not allowed to drive around the cemetery). Or you can take the **Metro** to the Arlington National Cemetery stop on the Blue Line. If you're sightseeing on the **Tourmobile,** see "Getting Around," in Chapter 4.

GETTING AROUND Upon arrival, head over to the **Visitor Center,** where you can purchase a Tourmobile ticket that allows you to stop at all major sights and reboard when you like. Service is continuous, and the narrated commentary is informative. (See "Getting Around," Chapter 4, for details.) However, if you've ample stamina, consider doing the tour on foot (a free map is available at the Visitor Center). Riding the Tourmobile with crowds of tourists (usually in a holiday mood) makes me feel like I'm at Universal Studios. Walking makes for a more contemplative experience. A good compromise is to walk some and ride some. On hot and humid summer days, walking requires an almost spartan determination.

Arlington National Cemetery is open to visitors daily April through September from 8am to 7pm, until 5pm the rest of the year. Call 703/692-0931 for further information.

WHAT TO SEE

This famous cemetery occupies 612 acres on the high hills overlooking the capital from the west side of the Memorial Bridge. One of America's most famous national shrines, it honors many national heroes and more than 230,000 war dead, veterans, and dependents. Many graves of the famous bear nothing more than simple markers in Arlington. Five-star Gen. John J. Pershing's is one of those. Secretary of State John Foster Dulles is buried here. So are President William Howard Taft and Supreme Court Justice Thurgood Marshall.

The **Tomb of the Unknowns,** containing the unidentified remains of soldiers from both World Wars through the Vietnam War, is located here. It's an unembellished 79-ton white-marble block, moving in its simplicity. Inscribed are the words: "Here rests in honored glory an American Soldier known but to God." Soldiers stationed at Fort Myer guard the tomb day and night. Changing of the guard is performed every half hour from April through September and every hour on the hour from October through March—a ceremony that requires the most meticulous presentation of arms.

Arlington House (tel. 703/557-0613) was for 30 years (1831–61) the residence of Gen. Robert E. Lee. Lee married the great-granddaughter of Martha Washington, Mary Ann Randolph Custis, who inherited the estate upon the death of her father. It was at Arlington House that Lee received the news of Virginia's secession from the Union and decided to resign his commission in the U.S. Army. During the Civil War the estate was taken over by Union forces, and troops were buried there. Soon after the defeat of the Confederate forces at Gettysburg, the estate was bought by the government. A fine example of Greek Revival architecture combined with many features of the grand plantation houses of the early 1800s, it has been under the National Park Service since 1933.

You can take a self-guided tour of the house; hosts in pre–Civil War dress give an orientation talk, hand out brochures, and answer questions. About 30% of the furnishings are original. Servants' quarters and a small museum adjoin. Admission is free. It's open daily: from 9:30am to 4:30pm October to March, until 6pm April through September; closed January 1 and December 25.

Pierre Charles L'Enfant's Grave was placed in Arlington near Arlington House at the point that is believed to offer the best view of Washington, the city he designed.

Below Arlington House is the **Gravesite of John Fitzgerald**

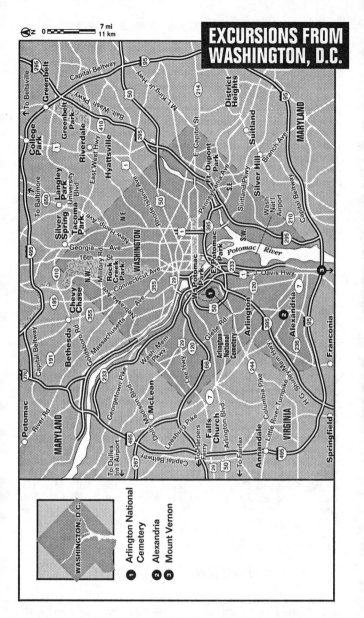

EXCURSIONS FROM WASHINGTON, D.C.

7 mi
11 km

1 Arlington National Cemetery
2 Alexandria
3 Mount Vernon

Kennedy. Simplicity is the key to grandeur here, too. John Carl Warnecke designed a low crescent wall embracing a marble terrace, inscribed with memorable words of the 35th U.S. president, including his famous utterance, "And so my fellow Americans, ask not what your country can do for you, ask what you can do for your country. . . ." Sen. Robert Kennedy is buried nearby, his grave marked by a simple white cross. The Kennedy graves attract streams of visitors. Arrive as close to 8am as possible to experience the mood of quiet contemplation the site evokes when it's not mobbed with tourists. Looking north, there's a spectacular view of Washington.

Close by, the famous statue of the marines raising the flag on Iwo Jima, the **Marine Corps Memorial,** stands near the north (or Orde-Weitzel Gate) entrance to the cemetery as a tribute to marines who died in all wars. In summer there are military parades on the grounds on Tuesday evenings at 7pm.

Close to the Iwo Jima statue is the **Netherlands Carillon,** a gift from the people of the Netherlands, with 49 bells. Every spring over 15,000 tulip bulbs are planted on the surrounding grounds. Carillon concerts take place from 2 to 4pm on Saturday during April, May, and September; from 6:30 to 8:30pm on Saturday from June through August. (Sometimes hours change; call 703/285-2598 before you go.) There's also an annual carillon concert on Easter Sunday. Visitors are permitted into the tower to watch the carillonneur perform and enjoy panoramic views of Washington.

2. MOUNT VERNON

No visit to Washington is complete without a trip to Mount Vernon, the estate of George Washington. Only 16 miles south of the hubbub of the capital, this southern plantation dates to a 1674 land grant to Washington's great-grandfather.

GETTING THERE   If you're going **by car,** take any of the bridges over the Potomac into Virginia to the George Washington Memorial Parkway (Va. 400) going south; the parkway ends at Mount Vernon. **Tourmobile** buses (tel. 554-7950) depart daily, April to October, from Arlington National Cemetery, the White House, and the Washington Monument. The round-trip fare is $16.50 for adults, $8 for children 3 to 11 (free for children under 3), and includes the admission fee to Mount Vernon (for details on the Tourmobile, see "Getting Around," in Chapter 4). You can also get there on a **Spirit of Washington Cruises** riverboat, which from early March to December travels down the Potomac from Pier 4, at 6th and Water Streets SW (tel. 554-8000 for departure times). Round-trip fares— including the admission fee to Mount Vernon—are $20.25 for adults, $18 for seniors, $11.75 for children 6 to 11, and free for children under 6. Book in advance.

TOURING THE ESTATE

Mount Vernon (tel. 703/780-2000) was purchased for $200,000 in 1858 by the Mount Vernon Ladies' Association from John Augustine Washington, great-grandnephew of the first president. Without them, the estate might have crumbled and disappeared, for the federal government and the Commonwealth of Virginia both refused to buy the property when it was offered for sale earlier. The restoration is an unmarred beauty; many of the furnishings are original pieces acquired by Washington, and the rooms have been repainted in the original colors favored by George and Martha.

Mount Vernon's mansion and grounds are stunning. Some 500 of

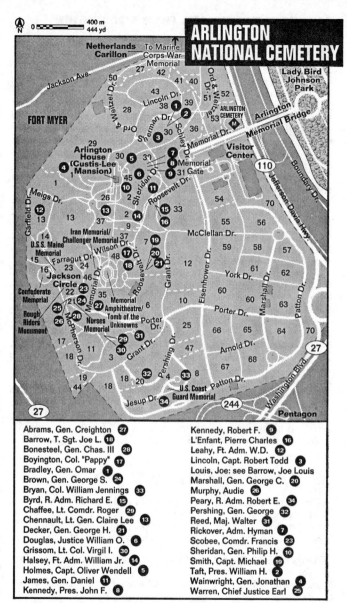

ARLINGTON NATIONAL CEMETERY

the original 8,000 acres (divided into five farms) over which Washington presided are still there. Washington delighted in riding horseback around his property, directing planting and other activities; the Bowling Green entrance still contains some of the trees he planted. The American Revolution and his years as president took Washington away from his beloved estate most of the time. He finally retired to Mount Vernon in 1797, just two years before his death, to "view the solitary walk and tread the paths of private life with heartfelt satisfaction." He is buried on the estate. Martha was buried next to him in May 1802. Public memorial services are held at the estate every year on the third Monday in February, the date commemorating Washington's birthday; admission is free that day.

Mount Vernon has been one of the nation's most visited shrines since the mid-19th century. Today over a million people tour the property annually. There's no formal tour, but attendants stationed throughout the house and grounds provide brief orientations and answer questions. Best time to visit is off-season; in heavy tourist months, avoid weekends and holidays if possible, and year-round, arrive early to beat the crowds. Late afternoon is also usually a good time to visit.

The house itself is interesting as an outstanding example of colonial architecture, as an example of the aristocratic lifestyle in the 18th century, and of course, as the home of our first president. There are a number of family portraits, and the rooms are appointed as if actually in day-to-day use.

After leaving the house, you can tour the outbuildings—the kitchen, slave quarters, storeroom, smokehouse, overseer's quarters, coachhouse, and stables. A four-acre exhibit area called "George Washington, Pioneer Farmer" includes a replica of Washington's 16-sided barn and fields of crops which he grew (corn, wheat, oats, etc.). Docents in period costume demonstrate 18th-century farming methods. A museum on the property contains Washington memorabilia, and details of the restoration are explained in the adjoining annex; there's also a gift shop on the premises. You'll want to walk around the grounds (most pleasant in good weather), see the wharf, the slave burial ground, the greenhouse, the tomb containing George and Martha Washington's sarcophagi (24 other family members are also interred here), the lawns, and gardens.

The house and grounds are open to the public daily from 8am to 5pm from April to August; 9am to 5pm in March, September, and October; and 9am to 4pm from November to February. Allow at least two hours to see everything. Adults pay $7; senior citizens, $6; children 6 to 11 are charged $3; under 6, free. A map is provided at the entrance.

WHERE TO DINE

At the entrance to Mount Vernon you'll find a **snack bar** serving light fare, and picnic tables outside. However, if a picnic is what you have in mind, drive a mile north on the parkway to **Riverside Park,** where you can lunch at tables overlooking the Potomac.

MOUNT VERNON INN, at the entrance to Mount Vernon. Tel. 703/780-0011.
    Cuisine: AMERICAN. **Reservations:** Recommended at dinner.
$ Prices: Appetizers $1.75–$2.50 at lunch, $3.50–$5 at dinner; main courses $4.50–$7.50 at lunch, $12–$23 at dinner; fixed-price dinner $14. AE, DISC, MC, V.
    Open: Lunch Mon–Sat 11am–3:30pm, Sun 11am–4pm; dinner Mon–Sat 5–9pm.
Lunch or dinner at the inn is an intrinsic part of the Mount Vernon experience. It's a quaintly charming colonial-style restaurant, complete with period furnishings and three working fireplaces. Waiters and waitresses are in colonial costume. Lunch here is very reasonable.

Be sure to begin your meal with an order of homemade peanut and chestnut soup. Entrées range from colonial pye (a crock of meat or fowl and garden vegetables with a puffed pastry top) to a 20th-century-style burger and fries. There's a full bar, and premium wines are offered by the glass. At dinner, tablecloths and candlelight make this a plusher choice. Happily, a fixed-price dinner also makes it an affordable one. It includes soup (perhaps broccoli Cheddar) or salad, an entrée such as Maryland crabcakes or roast venison with peppercorn sauce, homemade breads, and dessert (like Bavarian parfait or English trifle).

3. ALEXANDRIA

Founded by a group of Scottish tobacco merchants, the seaport town of Alexandria came into being in 1749 when a 60-acre tract of land was auctioned off in half-acre lots. Colonists came from miles around, in ramshackle wagons and stately carriages, in sloops, brigantines, and lesser craft, to bid on land that would be "commodious for trade and navigation and tend greatly to the ease and advantage of the frontier inhabitants. . . ." The auction took place in **Market Square** (still intact today), and the surveyor's assistant was a capable lad of 17 named George Washington.

Today the original 60 acres of lots in George Washington's hometown (also Robert E. Lee's) are the heart of **Old Town,** a multi-million-dollar urban-renewal historic district. As you stroll Old Town's brick sidewalks and cobblestone streets, you'll see over 2,000 18th- and 19th-century buildings. You'll visit **Gadsby's Tavern,** where two centuries ago the men who created this nation discussed politics, freedom, and revolution over tankards of ale. You'll stand in the tavern's doorway where Washington reviewed his troops for the last time (he trained them in Market Square), visit Lee's boyhood home, and sit in the pews of **Christ Church** where both men worshipped.

Many Alexandria streets still bear original colonial names (King, Queen, Prince, Princess, Royal—you get the drift), while others like Jefferson, Franklin, Lee, Patrick, and Henry are obviously post-Revolutionary.

In this "mother lode of Americana" the past is being ever-increasingly restored in an ongoing archeological and historical research program. And though the present is manifested by an abundance of quaint shops, boutiques, art galleries, and restaurants capitalizing on the volume of tourism, it's still easy to imagine yourself in colonial times—to smell the fragrant tobacco; hear the rumbling of horse-drawn vehicles over cobblestone; envision the oxcarts piled with crates of chickens, country-cured ham, and casks of cheese and butter; and picture the bustling waterfront where fishermen brought in the daily catch and foreign vessels unloaded exotic cargo.

GETTING THERE If you're traveling **by car,** take the Arlington Memorial or the 14th Street Bridge to the George Washington Memorial Parkway (Va. 400) south; it leads right to King Street, Alexandria's main thoroughfare. Parking permits are available from the Alexandria Convention & Visitors Bureau (see below). The easiest way to make the trip is on the **Metro,** and the Old Town is so compact that you won't need a car once you arrive. Take the Metro Yellow Line to the King Street station, but be sure that you get a transfer from your departure station. From King Street, take a blue-and-gold DASH bus (75¢) to the Visitors Center. It's a short walk from the station, and while you could walk the distance, it's better to save your feet for sightseeing.

ORIENTATION

INFORMATION Before you do anything else, visit the **Alexandria Convention & Visitors Bureau** at Ramsay House, 221 King St., at Fairfax Street (tel. 703/838-4200, 703/838-5005 for a 24-hour Alexandria events recording), which is open daily from 9am to 5pm and, frequently, on Thursday night to 9pm (closed January 1, Thanksgiving, and December 25). Here you can pick up a map/self-guided walking tour and brochures about the area; find out about special events that might be taking place during your visit and obtain tickets for them; see a 13-minute video about Alexandria history; and get answers to any questions you might have about accommodations, restaurants, sights, shopping, and whatever else. The bureau has materials in 20 languages.

If you came by car, get a free **three-day parking permit** here for gratis parking at any two-hour meter for up to 24 hours.

Also available at Ramsay House: a **block ticket** for admission to four historic Alexandria properties—Gadsby's Tavern, Lee's Boyhood Home, the Carlyle House, and the Lee-Fendall House. The ticket, which can also be purchased at any of the four buildings, costs $8 to see all four sights, $5 for any two—a saving over purchasing the tickets separately. Children 6 to 17 are charged $3 for all four, $2 for two; children under 6 enter free.

You'll find the staff friendly and knowledgeable; they'll even be happy to book your hotel room or make restaurant reservations.

TOURS Though it's easy to see Alexandria on your own by putting yourself in the hands of guides at the various attractions, you may find your experience enhanced by a comprehensive walking tour. **Doorways to Old Virginia** (tel. 703/548-0100) has tours leaving from the Visitors Bureau at Ramsay House at 11am Monday through Saturday, and at 2pm Sunday (all weather permitting); tours cost $3 for adults and $1.50 for students 7 to 17.

CITY LAYOUT Old Town is contained within several blocks. Park your car for the day, don comfortable shoes, and start walking—it's the easiest way. It's helpful to know, when looking for addresses, that Alexandria is laid out in a simple grid system. Union to Lee Street is the 100 block, Lee to Fairfax the 200 block, and so on up. The cross streets (more or less going north and south) are divided north and south by King Street. King to Cameron is the 100 block north, Cameron to Queen the 200 block north, and so on. King to Prince is the 100 block south and so forth.

SPECIAL EVENTS The below-listed are only the *major* events. If you're planning to participate in any of them, book your accommodations far ahead and contact the Visitors Center for details and necessary advance tickets. Whenever you come, you're sure to run

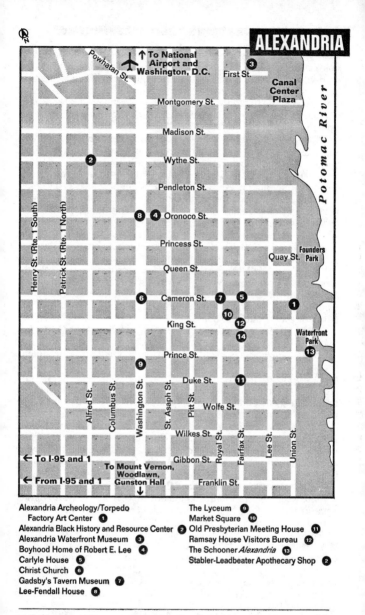

ALEXANDRIA

↑ To National Airport and Washington, D.C.

Powhatan St.

First St.

Montgomery St.

Madison St.

Wythe St.

Pendleton St.

Oronoco St.

Princess St.

Queen St.

Cameron St.

King St.

Prince St.

Duke St.

Wolfe St.

Wilkes St.

Gibbon St.

Franklin St.

Henry St. (Rte. 1 South)

Patrick St. (Rte. 1 North)

Alfred St.

Columbus St.

Washington St.

St. Asaph St.

Pitt St.

Royal St.

Fairfax St.

Lee St.

Union St.

Quay St.

Founders Park

Canal Center Plaza

Potomac River

Waterfront Park

← To I-95 and 1

← From I-95 and 1

To Mount Vernon, Woodlawn, Gunston Hall ↓

Alexandria Archeology/Torpedo Factory Art Center ❶
Alexandria Black History and Resource Center ❷
Alexandria Waterfront Museum ❸
Boyhood Home of Robert E. Lee ❹
Carlyle House ❺
Christ Church ❻
Gadsby's Tavern Museum ❼
Lee-Fendall House ❽

The Lyceum ❾
Market Square ❿
Old Presbyterian Meeting House ⓫
Ramsay House Visitors Bureau ⓬
The Schooner *Alexandria* ⓭
Stabler-Leadbeater Apothecary Shop ❷

into some activity or other—a jazz festival, tea garden or tavern gambol, quilt exhibit, wine tasting, or organ recital. It's all part of Alexandria's *ceād mile failte* (100,000 welcomes) to visitors.

January The **birthdays of Robert E. Lee** and his father, Revolutionary War Col. **"Light Horse Harry" Lee,** are celebrated together at the Lee-Fendall House and Lee's Boyhood Home the fourth Sunday of the month. The party features period music, refreshments, and house tours.

February Throughout the month Alexandria celebrates

George Washington's Birthday. Festivities typically include a colonial costume or black-tie banquet followed by a ball at Gadsby's, a 10-kilometer race, special tours, a Revolutionary War encampment at Fort Ward Park (complete with uniformed troops engaging in skirmishes), the nation's largest George Washington Day Parade (75,000 to 100,000 people attend each year), and 18th-century comic opera performances.

April Alexandria celebrates **Historic Garden Week in Virginia** with tours of privately owned local (usually historic) homes and gardens the fourth Saturday of the month.

June The **Red Cross Waterfront Festival,** the second week in June, honors Alexandria's historic importance as a seaport and the vitality of its Potomac shoreline today with a display of historic tall ships, ship tours, boat rides and races, nautical art exhibits, waterfront walking tours, fireworks, children's games, an arts and crafts show, food booths, and entertainment. This is the nation's largest Red Cross outdoor fund-raiser, attended by over 100,000 people each year. Admission is charged.

There's a **Civil War Living History** program on a selected weekend at Fort Ward, with authentically equipped and costumed military units demonstrating camp life with drills, music, a review of troops, and a torchlight tour. Admission is charged. For details on either of these, call 703/838-4848.

July Gather with the clans for **Virginia Scottish Games,** a two-day Celtic festival the fourth weekend of the month that celebrates Alexandria's Highland heritage. Activities include athletic events (such as the caber toss in which competitors heave a 140-pound pole in the air), musicians (playing reels, strathspeys, and laments), fiddling and harp competitions, a parade of clan societies in tartans, a Celtic crafts fair, storytelling, Highland dance performances and competitions, booths selling Scottish foods and wares, dog trials featuring Scottish breeds, and a Scottish Country Dance Party. Tickets at the gate are about $9 for one day, $15 for the entire weekend; children 15 and under are admitted free with a paying adult. You can get tickets for a little less in advance at the Visitors Center.

September During the **18th-Century Fair** (usually the second week of the month) colonial life is re-created on Market Square and at Gadsby's (an authentic 18th-century tavern) with period food, music, and entertainment.

October Chili enthusiasts can sample "bowls of red" at the **War Between the States Chili Cookoff** in Waterfront Park. Contestants from almost every U.S. state and territory compete, and for a few dollars admission, you can taste all their culinary creations. Proceeds go to charity. Fiddling contests, jalapeño-eating contests, and country music are part of the fun. For details and exact dates, call 703/683-5340.

Explore the ghosts and graveyards of Alexandria on a **Halloween Walking Tour** with a lantern-carrying guide in 18th-century costume. The tour focuses on eerie Alexandria legend, myth, and folklore. Admission is $4 for adults, $2 for students 7 to 17. For details, call 703/548-0100.

November The **Historic Alexandria Antiques Show,** the third weekend of the month, features several dozen dealers from many states displaying an array of high-quality antiques—jewelry, silver, rare books, rugs, paintings, folk art, furniture, pottery, and decorative objects—in room settings. Admission is about $6 per day, including free parking and a catalog. Proceeds go to restoration funds for historic sites. Pricier activities include a gala opening party (about $75 admission) and a champagne brunch with a featured speaker (about $40). Call 703/838-4554 for details.

December There's a **Christmas Tree Lighting** in Market Square the Friday after Thanksgiving; the ceremony—which includes choir singing, puppet shows, dance performances, and an appearance by Santa and his elves—begins at 7pm. The night the tree is lit, thousands of tiny lights adorning King Street trees also go on.

Holiday festivities continue with the **Annual Scottish Christmas Walk,** the first Saturday in December. Activities include kilted bagpipers, Highland dancers, a parade of Scottish clans (with horses and dogs), caroling, fashion shows, storytelling, booths (selling crafts, antiques, food, hot mulled punch, heather, fresh wreaths, and holly), and children's games. Admission is charged to some events.

The **Old Town Christmas Candlelight Tour,** the second week in December, visits seasonally decorated historic Alexandria homes and an 18th-century tavern. There are colonial dancing, string quartets, madrigal and opera singers, and refreshments, too. Tickets—$12 for adults, $5 for students 6 to 17—are available at the Visitors Center.

There are so many holiday season activities, the Visitors Center puts out a special brochure about them each year. Pick one up to find out about decorations workshops, walking tours, tree lightings, concerts, bazaars, bake sales, crafts fairs, and much more.

WHAT TO SEE & DO

In addition to the annual events mentioned above, there's much to see and do. The attractions on the block ticket are in the not-to-be-missed category.

About Admissions: Chances are you'll have purchased the money-saving block ticket described above. If you purchase tickets separately to these first four attractions, adult admission is $3 and children pay $1.

Note: Many Alexandria attractions are closed on Monday.

GADSBY'S TAVERN MUSEUM, 134 N. Royal St., at Cameron St. Tel. 703/838-4242.

Alexandria was at the crossroads of 18th-century America, and its center was Gadsby's Tavern. It consisted of two buildings (one Georgian, one Federal) dating from 1770 and 1792, respectively. Innkeeper John Gadsby combined them to create "a gentleman's tavern," which he operated from 1796 to 1808; it was considered one of the finest in the country. George Washington was a frequent dinner guest (he and Martha danced in the second floor-ballroom), and the tavern was also visited by Thomas Jefferson, James Madison, and Lafayette. It was the scene of lavish parties, theatrical performances, small circuses, government meetings, and concerts. Itinerant merchants used the tavern to display their wares, and traveling doctors and dentists treated an unfortunate clientele (these were rudimentary professions in the 18th century) on the premises.

The rooms have been restored to their 18th-century appearance with the help of modern excavations and colonial inventories that included such minutiae as lemon squeezers. On the 30-minute tour, you'll get a good look at the Tap Room, a small dining room, the

Assembly Room, the ballroom, typical bedrooms, and the underground ice house, which was filled each winter from the icy river. Tours depart 15 minutes before and after the hour, with the final tour at 4:15pm. Inquire about a special "living history" tour called Gadsby's Time Travels (on selected Sundays; call for details). And cap off the experience with a meal at the restored colonial-style restaurant that occupies three tavern rooms (see "Where to Dine," below).

Admission: $3 adults, $1 children 11–17, free for children under 11; or buy the block ticket.

Open: Tours given Apr–Sept, Tues–Sat 10:15am–4:15pm, Sun 1:15–4:15pm; Oct–Mar, Tues–Sat 11:15am–3:15pm, Sun 1:15–4:15pm. **Closed:** All Federal holidays except Veterans Day.

BOYHOOD HOME OF ROBERT E. LEE, 607 Oronoco St., between St. Asaph and Washington Sts. Tel. 703/548-8454.

Revolutionary War cavalry hero Henry "Light Horse Harry" Lee brought his wife, Ann Hill Carter, and five children to this early Federal-style mansion in 1812, when Robert, destined to become a Confederate military leader, was just 5 years old. A tour of the house, built in 1795, provides a glimpse into the gracious lifestyle of Alexandria's gentry. George Washington was an occasional guest of two earlier occupants, John Potts and Col. William Fitzhugh. In 1804 the Fitzhughs' daughter, Mary Lee, married Martha Washington's grandson, George Washington Parke Custis, in the drawing room. And the Curtises' daughter, Mary Anna Randolph, married Robert E. Lee.

General Lafayette honored Ann Hill Carter Lee with a visit to the house in October of 1824 in tribute to her husband, "Light Horse Harry" Lee, who had died in 1818. Lafayette had been a comrade-in-arms with Lee during the American Revolution. The drawing room today is called the Lafayette Room to commemorate that visit.

On a fascinating tour, you'll see the nursery with its little canopied bed and toy box; Mrs. Lee's room; the Lafayette Room, furnished in period antiques with the tea table set up for use; the morning room, where *The Iliad* translated into Latin reposes on a gaming table (both Light Horse Harry and Robert E. Lee were classical scholars), and the winter kitchen. The furnishings are of the Lee period but did not belong to the family. The house was occupied by 17 different owners after the Lees left. It was made into a museum in 1967.

Admission: $3 adults, $1 children 11–17, free for children under 11; or buy the block ticket.

Open: Tours given Mon–Sat 10am–3:30pm, Sun 1–3:30pm. **Closed:** Easter, Thanksgiving, and Dec 15–Jan 31 (except for the Sun closest to Jan 19, Robert E. Lee's birthday).

LEE-FENDALL HOUSE, 614 Oronoco St., at Washington St. Tel. 703/548-1789.

This handsome Greek Revival–style house is a veritable Lee family museum of furniture, heirlooms, and documents. "Light Horse Harry" Lee never actually lived here, though he was a frequent visitor, as was his good friend, George Washington. He did own the original lot, but sold it to Philip Richard Fendall (himself a Lee on his mother's side), who built the house in 1785. Fendall married three Lee wives, including Harry's first mother-in-law and, later, Harry's sister.

Thirty-seven Lees occupied the house over a period of 118 years

(1785–1903), and it was from this house that Harry wrote Alexandria's farewell address to Washington, delivered when he passed through the town on his way to assume the presidency. (Harry also wrote and delivered, but not at this house, the famous funeral oration to Washington that contained the immortal words: "First in war, first in peace, and first in the hearts of his countrymen.") During the Civil War, the house was seized and used as a Union hospital.

Thirty-minute guided tours interpret the 1850s era of the home and provide insight into Victorian family life. You'll also see the colonial garden with its magnolia and chestnut trees, roses, and boxwood-lined paths. Much of the interior woodwork and glass is original.

Admission: $3 adults, $1 children 11–17, free for children under 11; or buy the block ticket.

Open: Tues–Sat 10am–3:45pm, Sun noon–3:45pm. Tours depart continually throughout the day. **Closed:** Jan 1, Thanksgiving, and Dec 24–25.

CARLYLE HOUSE, 121 N. Fairfax St., at Cameron St. Tel. 703/549-2997.

Not only is Carlyle House regarded as one of Virginia's most architecturally impressive 18th-century houses, it also figured prominently in American history. In 1753, Scottish merchant John Carlyle completed the mansion for his bride, Sara Fairfax of Belvoir, who hailed from one of Virginia's most prominent families. It was patterned after Scottish/English manor houses, and furnished lavishly. Carlyle, a successful merchant, was able to import the best furnishings and appointments available abroad to his new Alexandria home.

When it was built, Carlyle House was a waterfront property with its own wharf. A social and political center, the house was visited by numerous great men of the time, George Washington among them. But its most important moment in history occurred in April 1755 when Maj. Gen. Edward Braddock, commander-in-chief of His Majesty's forces in North America, met with five colonial governors here and asked them to tax colonists to finance a campaign against the French and Indians. Colonial legislatures refused to comply, one of the first instances of serious friction between America and Britain. Nevertheless, Braddock made Carlyle House his headquarters during the campaign, and Carlyle was less than impressed with him. He called the general "a man of weak understanding . . . very indolent . . . a slave to his passions, women and wine . . . as great an Epicure as could be in his eating, tho a brave man." Possibly these were the reasons his unfinanced campaign met with disaster. Braddock received, as Carlyle described it, "a most remarkable drubbing."

A **tour** of Carlyle House takes about 40 minutes. Two of the original rooms—the large parlor and the adjacent study—have survived intact; the former, where Braddock met the governors, has its original fine woodwork, paneling, and pediments. The house is furnished in period pieces; only a few of Carlyle's possessions remain. An upstairs room houses an architecture exhibit that explains 18th-century construction methods with hand-hewn beams and hand-wrought nails. Tours are given every half hour on the hour and half hour.

Admission: $3 adults, $1 children 11–17, free for children under 11; or buy a block ticket.

Open: Tues–Sat 10am–4:30pm, Sun noon–4:30pm.

CHRIST CHURCH, 118 N. Washington St., at Cameron St. Tel. 703/549-1450.

This sturdy red-brick Georgian-style church would be an important national landmark even if its two most distinguished members were not Washington and Lee. It has been in continuous use since 1773.

There have, of course, been many changes since Washington's day. The bell tower, church bell, galleries, and organ were added by the early 1800s, the "wineglass" pulpit in 1891. But much of what was changed later has since been unchanged. The pristine white interior with wood moldings and gold trim is colonially correct, though modern heating has obviated the need for charcoal braziers and hot bricks. And for the most part, the original structure remains, including the hand-blown glass in the windows that the first worshippers gazed through when their minds wandered from the service. The town has grown up around the building that was first called the "Church in the Woods" because of its rural setting.

Christ Church has had its historic moments. Washington and other early church members discussed revolution in the churchyard, and Robert E. Lee met here with Richmond representatives to discuss assuming command of Virginia's military forces at the beginning of the Civil War. You can sit in the pew where George and Martha sat with her two Custis grandchildren, or in the Robert E. Lee family pew.

It's a tradition for U.S. presidents to attend a service here on a Sunday close to Washington's birthday and sit in his pew. One of the most memorable of these visits took place shortly after Pearl Harbor when Franklin Delano Roosevelt attended services with Winston Churchill on the World Day of Prayer, January 1, 1942.

Of course you're invited to attend a service. There's no admission, but donations are appreciated. A docent gives brief lectures to visitors. The old Parish Hall today houses a gift shop and an exhibit on the history of the church. Walk out in the weathered graveyard after you see the church. Alexandria's first and only burial ground until 1805, its oldest marked grave is that of Issac Pearce who died in 1771. The remains of 34 Confederate soldiers are also interred here.

Admission: Free.
Open: Mon–Fri 9am–4pm, Sat 9am–noon, Sun 2–4:30pm.

STABLER-LEADBEATER APOTHECARY, 105-107 S. Fairfax St., near King St. Tel. 703/836-3713.

When it closed its doors in 1933, this landmark drugstore was the second oldest in continuous operation in America. Run for five generations by the same family (beginning in 1792), its famous early patrons of course included Robert E. Lee (he purchased the paint for Arlington House here) and George Washington. Gothic Revival decorative elements and Victorian-style doors were added in the 1860s.

Today the apothecary looks much as it did in colonial times, its shelves lined with original hand-blown gold-leaf-labeled bottles (the most valuable collection of antique medicinal bottles in the country, actually), old scales stamped with the royal crown, patent medicines, and equipment for blood-letting. The clock on the rear wall and the porcelain-handled mahogany drawers are from about 1790, as are two mortars and pestles. Among the shop's documentary records is this 1802 order from Mount Vernon: "Mrs. Washington desires Mr. Stabler to send by the bearer a quart bottle of his best Castor Oil and the bill for it."

There's no tour, but a 10-minute recording guides you around the displays. The adjoining antiques shop uses its proceeds to maintain the apothecary.

Admission: $1; free for children under 13.

Open: Mon–Sat 10am–4pm (sometimes closed for lunch).
Closed: Jan 1, Thanksgiving, Dec 25, and occasional days in winter.

OLD PRESBYTERIAN MEETING HOUSE, 321 S. Fairfax St., between Duke and Wolfe Sts. Tel. 703/549-6670.

Presbyterian congregations have worshipped in Virginia since Jamestown days when the Rev. Alexander Whittaker converted Pocahontas. This brick church was built by Scottish pioneers in 1775. Though it wasn't George Washington's church, the Meeting House bell tolled continuously for four days after his death in December 1799, and memorial services were preached from the pulpit here by Presbyterian, Episcopal, and Methodist ministers. According to the Alexandria paper of the day, "The walking being bad to the Episcopal church the funeral sermon of George Washington will be preached at the Presbyterian Meeting House. . . ." Two months later, on Washington's birthday, Alexandria citizens marched from Market Square to the church to pay respects to his memory.

Many famous Alexandrians are buried in the church graveyard, including John and Sara Carlyle, Dr. James Craik (the surgeon who treated—some say killed—Washington, dressed Lafayette's wounds at Brandywine, and ministered to the dying Braddock at Mononga-hela), and William Hunter, Jr., founder of the St. Andrew's Society of Scottish descendants (bagpipers pay homage to his grave the first Saturday of each December). It is also the site of a Tomb of an Unknown Revolutionary War Soldier, and Dr. James Muir, whose distinguished ministry spanned the years 1789–1820, is buried beneath the sanctuary in his gown and bands.

The original Meeting House was gutted by a lightning fire in 1835 but restored around the old walls in the style of the day a few years later. The present bell, said to be recast from the metal of the old one, was hung in a newly constructed belfry in 1843, and a new organ was installed in 1849. The Meeting House closed its doors in 1889, and for 60 years it was virtually abandoned. But in 1949 it was reborn as a living Presbyterian U.S.A. church, and today the old Meeting House looks much as it did following the restoration after the fire. The original parsonage, or manse, is still intact. There's no guided tour, but there is a recorded narrative in the graveyard.

Admission: Free.

Open: Tues–Fri 9am–3pm; Sun services at 8:30 and 11am.

LYCEUM, 201 S. Washington St., off Prince St. Tel. 703/838-4994.

This Greek Revival building houses a museum focusing on Alexandria's history from colonial times through the 20th century. It features changing exhibits (many of them focusing on the decorative arts and architecture) and an ongoing series of lectures, concerts, and films. An adjoining nonprofit shop carries 18th-century reproductions, candles, needlepoint patterns, and such.

In addition, information is available here about Virginia state attractions, highlighting Alexandria attractions in particular. You can pick up maps and brochures, and a knowledgeable staff will be happy to answer your questions.

But even without its manifold offerings, the brick and stucco Lyceum (restored in 1993) merits a visit. Built in 1839, it was designed in the Doric temple style to serve as a lecture, meeting, and concert hall. It was an important center of Alexandria's cultural life until the Civil War when Union forces took it over for use as a hospital. After the war it became a private residence, and still later it was subdivided for office space. In 1969, however, it was only the City Council's use of eminent domain that prevented the Lyceum's demolition for the proverbial parking lot.

Admission: Free.

Open: Daily 10am–5pm. **Closed:** Jan 1, Thanksgiving, and Dec 25.

FORT WARD MUSEUM AND PARK, 4301 W. Braddock Rd. Tel. 703/838-4848.

A short drive from Old Town is a 45-acre museum, park, and historic site that takes you on a leap forward in Alexandria history to the Civil War. The action here centers, as it did in the early 1860s, on an actual Union fort that Lincoln ordered erected to defend Washington, D.C. It was part of a system of Civil War forts surrounding Washington. The Northwest Bastion has been restored, and six mounted guns (there were originally 36) face south waiting for trouble that in fact never came; the fort was not attacked. Self-guided tours begin at the Fort Ward ceremonial gate.

Visitors can explore the fort and replicas of the Ceremonial Entrance Gate and an officer's hut. There's a museum on the premises where you can view Civil War weaponry, armor, correspondence, and other artifacts. Here, too, changing exhibits focus on subjects such as Union arms and equipment, medical care of the wounded, and local war history.

There are picnic areas with barbecue grills in the woods surrounding the fort. Concerts are presented on selected evenings June through mid-September in the outdoor amphitheater. And throughout the summer there are living-history programs on selected weekends (call for details).

Admission: Free.

Open: Park, daily 9am–sunset; museum, Tues–Sat 9am–5pm, Sun noon–5pm. **Closed:** Jan 1, Thanksgiving, and Dec 25. **Directions:** From Old Town, follow King Street west, go right on Kenwood Avenue, then left on West Braddock Road; continue for three-quarters of a mile to the entrance on the right.

TORPEDO FACTORY, 105 N. Union St., near Cameron St. Tel. 703/838-4565.

Studio space for some 175 professional artists and craftspeople who create and sell their own works on the premises is contained in this block-long, three-story building, once a torpedo shell-case factory. Here you can see artists at work—potters, painters, printmakers, photographers, sculptors, and jewelers, as well as those engaged in making stained-glass windows and fiber art.

In addition, on permanent display are exhibits on Alexandria history provided by **Alexandria Archaeology** (tel. 703/838-4399), also headquartered here and engaged in extensive city research. Their special exhibit area and lab are open to the public during the hours listed below, with a docent or staff member on hand to answer questions. An ongoing exhibit here, "Archaeologists at Work," highlights current excavation finds and methodology.

Admission: Free.

Open: Daily 10am–5pm; archaeology exhibit area, Tues–Fri 10am–3pm, Sat 10am–5pm, Sun 1–5pm.

SCHOONER *ALEXANDRIA,* Waterfront Park. Tel. 703/549-7078.

The **Alexandria Seaport Foundation,** a nonprofit organization devoted to maritime heritage, acquired the Swedish three-masted, gaff-rigged, topsail schooner *Alexandria* in 1983, and when it's in port (sometimes it's elsewhere participating in tall-ship festivals) it's docked at Waterfront Park and open to the public. A Baltic trader vessel built in 1929, the ship was remodeled for passenger use in the 1970s. You can tour above and below deck, see one stateroom (the others are used by the crew), and visit the rather elegant Main Salon downstairs.

Admission (and tour): Free. Donations requested.

Open: When in port (usually fall through spring), Sat–Sun noon–5pm.

FRIENDSHIP FIREHOUSE, 107 S. Alfred St., at King St. Tel. 703/838-3891 or 838-4994.

In 1774, Alexandria's first firefighting organization, the Friendship Fire Company, was established. As the city grew, the company attracted increasing recognition, not only for its firefighting efforts but as a ceremonial and social presence at parades and other public occasions. In 1855, Friendship's original building was destroyed by fire and a new brick building, in the fashionable Italianate style (today the restored museum), was erected on the same spot. A strong local tradition centers on George Washington's involvement with the firehouse as a founding member, active firefighter, and purchaser of its first fire engine, although extensive research does not bear out these stories. This interesting museum not only houses exhibits of firefighting paraphernalia, it also documents the Friendship Company's efforts to claim Washington as one of their own.

Admission: Free.

Open: Thurs–Sat 10am–4pm, Sun 1–4pm.

BLACK HISTORY RESOURCE CENTER, 638 N. Alfred St., at Wythe St. Tel. 703/838-4356.

In a 1940s building that originally housed the black community's first public library, the center exhibits historical objects, photographs, documents, and memorabilia relating to African-American Alexandrians from the 18th century forward. Besides the permanent collection, the museum presents twice-yearly rotating exhibits, walking tours, and other activities.

Admission: Free.

Open: Tues–Sat 10am–4pm.

SHOPPING

Old Town has hundreds of charming boutiques, antiques stores, and gift shops selling everything from souvenir T-shirts to 18th-century reproductions. Some of the most interesting are at the sights (like the Museum Shop at the Lyceum), but most are clustered on King and

Cameron Streets and their connecting cross streets. Plan to spend a fair amount of time browsing in between visits to historic sites. A guide to antiques stores is available at the Visitors Center.

WHERE TO DINE

There are so many fine restaurants in Alexandria that Washingtonians often drive over just to dine here and stroll the cobblestone streets.

EXPENSIVE

LANDINI BROTHERS, 115 King St., between Lee and Union Sts. Tel. 703/836-8404.
  Cuisine: ITALIAN. **Reservations:** Recommended.
$ Prices: Appetizers $5.95–$8.95; main courses $11.50–$20.95. AE, CB, DC, MC, V.
  Open: Mon–Sat 11:30am–11pm, Sun 4–10pm.

The classic, delicate cuisine of Tuscany is featured at this rustic, almost grottolike restaurant with stone walls, a flagstone floor, and rough-hewn beams overhead. Diners sit in wicker-seated chairs at white-linened tables. It's especially charming at night by candlelight. There's additional seating in a lovely dining room upstairs. Everything is homemade—the pasta, the desserts, and the crusty Italian bread. At lunch you might choose a cold seafood salad or spinach and ricotta-stuffed agnolotti in buttery parmesan cheese sauce, followed by a dessert of zuccotto (creamy frozen zabaglione). At dinner, get things under way with prosciutto and melon or shrimp sautéed in garlic with tangy lemon sauce. Then you might proceed to an order of prime aged beef tenderloin medallions sautéed with garlic, mushrooms, and rosemary in a Barolo wine sauce. Or perhaps linguine with scallops, shrimp, clams, mussels, and squid in a garlic/parsley/red-pepper and white-wine sauce. Dessert choices include cannoli, cheesecake, and chocolate-mousse cake.

MODERATE

EAST WIND, 809 King St., between Columbus and Alfred Sts. Tel. 703/836-1515.
  Cuisine: VIETNAMESE. **Reservations:** Recommended.
$ Prices: Appetizers $3.50–$4.95 at lunch, $3.95–$6.95 at dinner; main courses $5.95–$8.95 at lunch, $7.95–$13.95 at dinner; fixed-price lunch $6.95. AE, CB, DC, MC, V.
  Open: Lunch Mon–Fri 11:30am–2:30pm; dinner Mon–Thurs 5:30–10pm, Fri–Sat 5:30–10:30pm, Sun 5:30–9:30pm.

The decor of this Vietnamese restaurant is very appealing: Its sienna stucco and knotty-pine-paneled walls are adorned with works of Vietnamese artist Minh Nguyen, and there are planters of greenery, flowers on each pink-clothed table, and a large floral display up front. The owner personally visits the market each morning to select the freshest fish.

An East Wind meal might begin with an appetizer of cha gio (delicate Vietnamese eggrolls) or a salad of shredded chicken and vegetables mixed with fish sauce. One of my favorite entrées is bo dun—beef tenderloin strips marinated in wine, honey, and spices, rolled in fresh onions, and broiled on bamboo skewers. Also excellent is grilled lemon chicken or charcoal-broiled shrimp and scallops served on rice vermicelli. There's refreshing ginger ice cream for dessert. A good deal is the fixed-price lunch which includes soup, an entrée, and coffee or tea.

GADSBY'S TAVERN, 138 N. Royal St., at Cameron St. Tel. 703/548-1288.
   Cuisine: COLONIAL AMERICAN. **Reservations:** Recommended.
$ **Prices:** Appetizers $4.50–$5.25 at lunch, $4.50–$6.25 at dinner; main courses $6.50–$9.95 at lunch/brunch, $12.50–$21.50 at dinner; $25 Publick Table. Half-price portions available for children 12 and under. DC, DISC, MC, V.
   Open: Lunch Mon–Sat 11:30am–3pm; dinner daily 5:30–10pm; brunch Sun 11am–3pm; Publick Table Sun–Mon at 8pm, also at 5:30pm on selected Suns.

In the spirit of history, pass through the portals where Washington reviewed his troops for the last time and dine at the famous Gadsby's Tavern. The setting authentically evokes the 18th century, with period music, wood-plank floors, hurricane-lamp wall sconces, and a rendition of a Hogarth painting over the fireplace (one of several). Servers are dressed in authentic colonial attire. George Washington dined and danced here often. At night, appropriate entertainment—a strolling minstrel or balladeer—adds to the ambience. A flagstone courtyard edged with flower beds serves as an outdoor dining area in good weather.

   All the fare is homemade, including the sweet Sally Lunn bread baked on the premises daily. You might start off with soup from the stockpot served with homemade sourdough crackers, continue with an entrée of baked ham and cheese pye (a sort of Early American quiche), hot roast turkey with bread/sage stuffing and giblet gravy on Sally Lunn bread, or George Washington's favorite—slow-roasted crisp duckling served with fruit dressing and madeira sauce. For dessert, try the English trifle or creamy buttermilk-custard pie with a hint of lemon. Colonial "coolers" are also available—scuppernong, Wench's Punch, and such. The Sunday brunch menu adds items like thick slices of toast dipped in a batter of rum and spices, with sausage, hash browns, and hot cinnamon syrup. And a "desserts and libations" menu highlights items like Scottish apple gingerbread and bourbon apple pie, along with a wide selection of beverages. A strolling violinist entertains Tuesday nights and at Sunday brunch. Wednesday through Saturday night an "18th-century gentleman" regales guests with song and tells the news of the day (200 years ago).

   A special offering at Gadsby's is the "Publick Table," a bountiful 18th-century feast of "the season's best meats, fishes, fowl, vegetables, Sally Lunn bread, relishes, and a fine dessert." Two entrées, an appetizer, coffee, and a glass of port or madeira are included in the price. This is more than just a meal; it's a feast with period entertainment. A server entertains with toasts, songs, news, and humor.

RADIO FREE ITALY, 5 Cameron St., right behind the Torpedo Factory. Tel. 703/683-0361.
   Cuisine: CALIFORNIA-STYLE ITALIAN. **Reservations:** Accepted for large parties only.
$ **Prices:** Appetizers $2.95–$6.95; main courses $5.50–$10.95. AE, CB, DC, DISC, MC, V.
   Open: Sun–Thurs 11am–10pm, Fri–Sat 11am–midnight.
Anchor of the Food Pavilion, a pleasant waterfront dining complex,

Radio Free Italy consists of a downstairs carry-out operation and a fancier upstairs dining room with wraparound windows providing great views of the boat-filled harbor. The latter, with 62 theatrical halogen lights dramatically spotlighting tables at dinner, has a modernistic Italian black-and-white interior with exposed pipes overhead. Both levels offer outdoor waterfront seating in good weather.

There are marvelous salads such as mixed chilled seafood—mussels, clams, calamari, scallops, and shrimp—marinated in lemon and olive oil. The antipasta sampler is also very noteworthy. Oak-fired pizzas have California-style toppings like grilled chicken, goat cheese, spinach, marinara, and quattro formmagio (romano, fontina, parmesan, and provolone). A bowl of mixed seafood is served on a bed of saffron linguine with three sauces—marinara, cream, and pesto. Yet another good entrée choice is fresh fettuccine tossed with pesto, sun-dried tomatoes, garlic-roasted mushrooms, and paper-thin slices of oak-roasted, peppercorn-studded sirloin. There's a full bar, with Italian wines available by the glass. Desserts include a decadently delicious tira misu.

SOUTH AUSTIN GRILL, 801 King St., at S. Columbus St. Tel. 703/684-8969.
  Cuisine: TEX-MEX. **Reservations:** Not accepted.
$ **Prices:** Appetizers $3.25–$7.95; main courses mostly $5.25–$10; lunch specials $4.95–$5.75. AE, DC, DISC, MC, V.
  Open: Sun–Thurs 11:30am–11pm, Fri–Sat 11:30am–midnight.

The South Austin Grill opened in 1991 and immediately became my favorite Alexandria restaurant. This is great Tex-Mex food, totally authentic and brought to its highest culinary level. The two dining floors are cheerfully decorated with roomy booths painted in bright primary hues. Pastel walls are hung with Austin music club posters and other Texiana, and campy copper sculptures of lizards and snakes are suspended overhead. A corner location lets lots of sunlight stream in.

Start with some delicious chili con queso, flavored with finely minced jalapeño, tomato, and onion and spiked with Dos Equis beer. Also not to be missed are crabmeat quesadillas, stuffed with a spicy mix of chorizo sausage, cheeses, and poblano peppers and served with fresh guacamole. For an entrée, South Austin's lime-marinated, mesquite-grilled fajitas (beef or chicken) are out of this world; they come with rice, beans, guacamole, cheese, sour cream, and pico de gallo. Tacos al carbon—pork rubbed with red chilies, garlic, and spices, mesquite grilled, and served up in a tortilla with melted cheese—are also fabulous. Fresh-made iced tea comes with unlimited refills, Texas style, and margaritas are made from scratch. Leave a bit of room for sweet-potato flan—a scrumptious finale. Arrive off-hours to avoid a wait for seating.

BUDGET

CHESAPEAKE BAGEL BAKERY, 601 King St., at N. St. Asaph St. Tel. 703/684-3777.
  Cuisine: SANDWICHES, SALADS.
$ **Prices:** Salads $1.50–$4.50; bagel and croissant sandwiches $1.35–$5. No credit cards.
  Open: Daily 6am–5:30pm.

Happy to say, there's a Chesapeake Bagel Bakery in Old Town. Like its D.C. counterparts (see Chapter 6), it offers fresh-baked New York–quality bagels (11 varieties) with fillings like chopped liver; cream cheese, walnuts, raisins, and carrots; and hummus and sprouts. Of course, you can opt for a traditional cream cheese and Nova as well. There's also homemade soup, and desserts like brownies, blondies, and carrot cake are offered. The white-walled setting is pleasant and unpretentious, and its corner location makes for lots of sunlight.

THE DELI ON THE STRAND, 211 The Strand, entrance on S. Union St. between Duke and Prince Sts. Tel. 703/ 548-7222.
   Cuisine: DELI.
$ Prices: Sandwiches $1.95–$5.25. No credit cards.
   Open: Daily 8am–5pm, with extended hours spring–fall.
Why not a picnic, either combined with a visit to Fort Ward Park (described above), or right in Old Town at Founders Park, bordering the Potomac at the foot of Queen Street? It doesn't have picnic tables, but there are benches and there's plenty of grass to sit on. Market Square is another possibility. Buy the fixings at the Deli on the Strand. They bake breads on the premises, so the aroma is divine, and you can get reasonably priced cold-cut sandwiches on fresh-baked rye and wheat bread, as well as muffins, and on weekends, bagels. Also available are homemade salads like seafood/pasta, cheeses, yummy desserts, beer, wine, and champagne. There are a few picnic tables outside under an awning.

HARD TIMES CAFE, 1404 King St., near S. West St. Tel. 703/683-5340.
   Cuisine: AMERICAN. **Reservations:** Not accepted.
$ Prices: Main courses $3.25–$6.25. MC, V.
   Open: Mon–Thurs 11am–10pm, Fri–Sat 11am–11pm, Sun noon–10pm.
Will Rogers once said he "always judged a town by the quality of its chili." He would have loved Alexandria, where the fabulous Hard Times Cafe serves up top-secret recipe home-made chilis and fresh-from-the-oven cornbread. It's a laid-back hangout where waiters and waitresses wear jeans and T-shirts, country music is always playing on the jukebox, and the Texas decor features Lone Star flags, a longhorn steer hide overhead, and historic photos of the Old West on the walls. The chili comes in three varieties—Texas, Cincinnati (cooked with sweeter spices, including cinnamon), and vegetarian. I favor the Texas style—coarse-ground chuck simmered for six hours with special spices in beef sauce. If chili isn't your thing, order grilled chicken breast, a burger, or salad. Side orders of steak fries cooked with the skins, spicy chicken wings, cheddar-filled jalapeños, and deep-fried onion rings are ample for two. Wash it all down with a bottle of Coors or Lone Star. The menu lists about 30 beers, including many selections from western "micro-breweries." The Hard Times has garnered many a chili cookoff award, and CHILI-U.S.A.—a resolution before Congress "to make chili the official food of this great nation"—was conceived by Oklahoma lobbyists over a "bowl of red" here. There's additional seating upstairs; the Colorado flag overhead was brought in by a senator from that state.

MURPHY'S, 713 King St., between N. Washington and Columbus Sts. Tel. 703/548-1717.

Cuisine: IRISH/AMERICAN. **Reservations:** Not accepted.

$ Prices: Main courses $5.95–$10.95; brunch $6.95. AE, CB, DC, MC, V.

Open: Daily 11am–2am; brunch Sun 10am–3pm.

Murphy's is a self-described "grand Irish restaurant and pub," and it couldn't be more cozy and fun-loving. The bar serves up Irish liqueurs and whiskeys and Irish coffee, and has Guinness stout, Murphy's (from County Cork), Mooney's (a local micro-brewery stout made especially for this restaurant), and 15 draft beers on tap. Fireplaces are ablaze on both floors during the winter, and Irish bands entertain nightly. This is the kind of bar where you can take the whole family; the kids will love it.

The food is fresh and tasty. Order up a meat-and-potato pie (filled with sage-spiced sausage, ground beef, pork, and mashed potatoes), a platter of fried oysters served with cottage fries (they're great), or hearty Irish stew. There's a low-priced children's menu, and desserts include brown-sugary homemade apple crisp topped with ice cream. At Sunday brunch, Murphy's offers champagne with a choice of entrées—perhaps bacon, eggs, sausage, home fries, homemade biscuit, and jelly.

THE TEA COSY, 119 S. Royal St., between King and Prince Sts. Tel. 703/836-8181.

Cuisine: BRITISH TEAROOM. **Reservations:** Not accepted.

$ Prices: Tea cakes and sandwiches $1.95–$4.55; full afternoon tea $7.95; main courses $3.15–$7.50. DISC, MC, V.

Open: Sat–Thurs 10am–6pm, Fri 10am–9pm.

This pristine British tearoom is 100% authentic. It's a charming little place, with posters advertising Bovril and Colman's Mustard on whitewashed walls, a beamed ceiling, and a magazine rack stocked with British periodicals and newspapers. Tables are set with pretty floral-patterned place mats. A shop in the back sells archetypically British foodstuffs—digestive biscuits, ginger wine, Irish oatmeal, chutney, etc.

Come in for a full afternoon tea, including assorted tea sandwiches and oven-fresh scones (date/pecan, lemon, raisin, apricot, or cheese) served with jams and Devonshire cream. Assorted tea sandwiches, crumpets, shortbread, and trifle are also à la carte options. For heartier meals, your choices include steak-and-kidney pie, shepherd's pie, Cornish pastie, Scottish sausage rolls, and bangers and mash. Everything, including vegetables, is fresh and homemade. There are daily dessert specials like apple-blackberry pie with custard. Possible libations: British ales and beers, hard cider, and a soft drink called orange quosh.

INDEX

ACCOMMODATIONS

Key to abbreviations *B* = Budget; *B&B* = Bed & Breakfast; *E* = Expensive; *I* = Inexpensive; *M* = Moderately priced; *VE* = Very expensive.

RESTAURANTS

Now Save Money on All Your Travels by Joining
FROMMER'S ™ TRAVEL BOOK CLUB
The World's Best Travel Guides at Membership Prices

FROMMER'S TRAVEL BOOK CLUB is your ticket to successful travel! Open up a world of travel information and simplify your travel planning when you join ranks with thousands of value-conscious travelers who are members of the FROMMER'S TRAVEL BOOK CLUB. Join today and you'll be entitled to all the privileges that come from belonging to the club that offers you travel guides for less to more than 100 destinations worldwide. Annual membership is only $25 (U.S.) or $35 (Canada and foreign).

The Advantages of Membership

1. Your choice of *three* free FROMMER'S TRAVEL GUIDES (any *two* FROMMER'S COMPREHENSIVE GUIDES, FROMMER'S $-A-DAY GUIDES, FROMMER'S WALKING TOURS *or* FROMMER'S FAMILY GUIDES—plus *one* FROMMER'S CITY GUIDE, FROMMER'S CITY $-A-DAY GUIDE *or* FROMMER'S TOURING GUIDE).
2. Your own subscription to **TRIPS AND TRAVEL** quarterly newsletter.
3. You're entitled to a **30% discount** on your order of any additional books offered by FROMMER'S TRAVEL BOOK CLUB.
4. You're offered (at a small additional fee) our **Domestic Trip-Routing Kits.**

Our quarterly newsletter **TRIPS AND TRAVEL** offers practical information on the best buys in travel, the "hottest" vacation spots, the latest travel trends, world-class events and much, much more.

Our **Domestic Trip-Routing Kits** are available for any North American destination. We'll send you a detailed map highlighting the best route to take to your destination—you can request direct or scenic routes.

Here's all you have to do to join:
Send in your membership fee of $25 ($35 Canada and foreign) with your name and address on the form below along with your selections as part of your membership package to **FROMMER'S TRAVEL BOOK CLUB, P.O. Box 473, Mt. Morris, IL 61054-0473.** Remember to check off your *three* free books.

If you would like to order additional books, please select the books you would like and send a check for the total amount (please add sales tax in the states noted below), plus $2 per book for shipping and handling ($3 per book for foreign orders) to:

FROMMER'S TRAVEL BOOK CLUB
P.O. Box 473
Mt. Morris, IL 61054-0473
(815) 734-1104

[ ] **YES.** I want to take advantage of this opportunity to join FROMMER'S TRAVEL BOOK CLUB.
[ ] **My check is enclosed.** Dollar amount enclosed_____*
(all payments in U.S. funds only)

Name_____
Address_____
City_____ State_____ Zip
All orders must be prepaid.

To ensure that all orders are processed efficiently, please apply sales tax in the following areas: CA, CT, FL, IL, NJ, NY, TN, WA and CANADA.

*With membership, shipping and handling will be paid by FROMMER'S TRAVEL BOOK CLUB for the three free books you select as part of your membership. Please add $2 per book for shipping and handling for any additional books purchased ($3 per book for foreign orders).

Allow 4–6 weeks for delivery. Prices of books, membership fee, and publication dates are subject to change without notice. Prices are subject to acceptance and availability.

AC1

Please Send Me the Books Checked Below:

FROMMER'S COMPREHENSIVE GUIDES
(Guides listing facilities from budget to deluxe,
with emphasis on the medium-priced)

	Retail Price	Code		Retail Price	Code
☐ Acapulco/Ixtapa/Taxco 1993–94	$15.00	C120	☐ Morocco 1992–93	$18.00	C021
☐ Alaska 1994–95	$17.00	C131	☐ Nepal 1994–95	$18.00	C126
☐ Arizona 1993–94	$18.00	C101	☐ New England 1994 (Avail. 1/94)	$16.00	C137
☐ Australia 1992–93	$18.00	C002	☐ New Mexico 1993–94	$15.00	C117
☐ Austria 1993–94	$19.00	C119	☐ New York State 1994–95	$19.00	C133
☐ Bahamas 1994–95	$17.00	C121	☐ Northwest 1994–95 (Avail. 2/94)	$17.00	C140
☐ Belgium/Holland/ Luxembourg 1993–94	$18.00	C106	☐ Portugal 1994–95 (Avail. 2/94)	$17.00	C141
☐ Bermuda 1994–95	$15.00	C122	☐ Puerto Rico 1993–94	$15.00	C103
☐ Brazil 1993–94	$20.00	C111	☐ Puerto Vallarta/ Manzanillo/Guadalajara 1994–95 (Avail. 1/94)	$14.00	C028
☐ California 1994	$15.00	C134	☐ Scandinavia 1993–94	$19.00	C135
☐ Canada 1994–95 (Avail. 4/94)	$19.00	C145	☐ Scotland 1994–95 (Avail. 4/94)	$17.00	C146
☐ Caribbean 1994	$18.00	C123	☐ South Pacific 1994–95 (Avail. 1/94)	$20.00	C138
☐ Carolinas/Georgia 1994–95	$17.00	C128	☐ Spain 1993–94	$19.00	C115
☐ Colorado 1994–95 (Avail. 3/94)	$16.00	C143	☐ Switzerland/ Liechtenstein 1994–95 (Avail. 1/94)	$19.00	C139
☐ Cruises 1993–94	$19.00	C107	☐ Thailand 1992–93	$20.00	C033
☐ Delaware/Maryland 1994–95 (Avail. 1/94)	$15.00	C136	☐ U.S.A. 1993–94	$19.00	C116
☐ England 1994	$18.00	C129	☐ Virgin Islands 1994–95	$13.00	C127
☐ Florida 1994	$18.00	C124	☐ Virginia 1994–95 (Avail. 2/94)	$14.00	C142
☐ France 1994–95	$20.00	C132	☐ Yucatán 1993–94	$18.00	C110
☐ Germany 1994	$19.00	C125			
☐ Italy 1994	$19.00	C130			
☐ Jamaica/Barbados 1993–94	$15.00	C105			
☐ Japan 1994–95 (Avail. 3/94)	$19.00	C144			

FROMMER'S $-A-DAY GUIDES
(Guides to low-cost tourist accommodations and facilities)

	Retail Price	Code		Retail Price	Code
☐ Australia on $45 1993–94	$18.00	D102	☐ Israel on $45 1993–94	$18.00	D101
☐ Costa Rica/Guatemala/ Belize on $35 1993–94	$17.00	D108	☐ Mexico on $45 1994	$19.00	D116
☐ Eastern Europe on $30 1993–94	$18.00	D110	☐ New York on $70 1994–95	$16.00	D120
☐ England on $60 1994	$18.00	D112	☐ New Zealand on $45 1993–94	$18.00	D103
☐ Europe on $50 1994	$19.00	D115	☐ Scotland/Wales on $50 1992–93	$18.00	D019
☐ Greece on $45 1993–94	$19.00	D100	☐ South America on $40 1993–94	$19.00	D109
☐ Hawaii on $75 1994	$19.00	D113	☐ Turkey on $40 1992–93	$22.00	D023
☐ India on $40 1992–93	$20.00	D010	☐ Washington, D.C. on $40 1994–95 (Avail. 2/94)	$17.00	D119
☐ Ireland on $45 1994–95 (Avail. 1/94)	$17.00	D117			

FROMMER'S CITY $-A-DAY GUIDES
(Pocket-size guides to low-cost tourist accommodations and facilities)

	Retail Price	Code		Retail Price	Code
☐ Berlin on $40 1994–95	$12.00	D111	☐ Madrid on $50 1994–95 (Avail. 1/94)	$13.00	D118
☐ Copenhagen on $50 1992–93	$12.00	D003	☐ Paris on $50 1994–95	$12.00	D117
☐ London on $45 1994–95	$12.00	D114	☐ Stockholm on $50 1992–93	$13.00	D022

FROMMER'S WALKING TOURS
(With routes and detailed maps, these companion guides point out the places and pleasures that make a city unique)

	Retail Price	Code		Retail Price	Code
☐ Berlin	$12.00	W100	☐ Paris	$12.00	W103
☐ London	$12.00	W101	☐ San Francisco	$12.00	W104
☐ New York	$12.00	W102	☐ Washington, D.C.	$12.00	W105

FROMMER'S TOURING GUIDES
(Color-illustrated guides that include walking tours, cultural and historic sights, and practical information)

	Retail Price	Code		Retail Price	Code
☐ Amsterdam	$11.00	T001	☐ New York	$11.00	T008
☐ Barcelona	$14.00	T015	☐ Rome	$11.00	T010
☐ Brazil	$11.00	T003	☐ Scotland	$10.00	T011
☐ Florence	$ 9.00	T005	☐ Sicily	$15.00	T017
☐ Hong Kong/Singapore/			☐ Tokyo	$15.00	T016
Macau	$11.00	T006	☐ Turkey	$11.00	T013
☐ Kenya	$14.00	T018	☐ Venice	$ 9.00	T014
☐ London	$13.00	T007			

FROMMER'S FAMILY GUIDES

	Retail Price	Code		Retail Price	Code
☐ California with Kids	$18.00	F100	☐ San Francisco with Kids		
☐ Los Angeles with Kids			(Avail. 4/94)	$17.00	F104
(Avail. 4/94)	$17.00	F103	☐ Washington, D.C. with		
☐ New York City with Kids			Kids (Avail. 2/94)	$17.00	F102
(Avail. 2/94)	$18.00	F101			

FROMMER'S CITY GUIDES
(Pocket-size guides to sightseeing and tourist accommodations and facilities in all price ranges)

	Retail Price	Code		Retail Price	Code
☐ Amsterdam 1993–94	$13.00	S110	☐ Montréal/Québec		
☐ Athens 1993–94	$13.00	S114	City 1993–94	$13.00	S125
☐ Atlanta 1993–94	$13.00	S112	☐ Nashville/Memphis		
☐ Atlantic City/Cape			1994–95 (Avail. 4/94)	$13.00	S141
May 1993–94	$13.00	S130	☐ New Orleans 1993–		
☐ Bangkok 1992–93	$13.00	S005	94	$13.00	S103
☐ Barcelona/Majorca/			☐ New York 1994 (Avail.		
Minorca/Ibiza 1993–			1/94)	$13.00	S138
94	$13.00	S115	☐ Orlando 1994	$13.00	S135
☐ Berlin 1993–94	$13.00	S116	☐ Paris 1993–94	$13.00	S109
☐ Boston 1993–94	$13.00	S117	☐ Philadelphia 1993–94	$13.00	S113
☐ Budapest 1994–95			☐ San Diego 1993–94	$13.00	S107
(Avail. 2/94)	$13.00	S139	☐ San Francisco 1994	$13.00	S133
☐ Chicago 1993–94	$13.00	S122	☐ Santa Fe/Taos/		
☐ Denver/Boulder/			Albuquerque 1993–94	$13.00	S108
Colorado Springs			☐ Seattle/Portland 1994–		
1993–94	$13.00	S131	95	$13.00	S137
☐ Dublin 1993–94	$13.00	S128	☐ St. Louis/Kansas		
☐ Hong Kong 1994–95			City 1993–94	$13.00	S127
(Avail. 4/94)	$13.00	S140	☐ Sydney 1993–94	$13.00	S129
☐ Honolulu/Oahu 1994	$13.00	S134	☐ Tampa/St.		
☐ Las Vegas 1993–94	$13.00	S121	Petersburg 1993–94	$13.00	S105
☐ London 1994	$13.00	S132	☐ Tokyo 1992–93	$13.00	S039
☐ Los Angeles 1993–94	$13.00	S123	☐ Toronto 1993–94	$13.00	S126
☐ Madrid/Costa del			☐ Vancouver/Victoria		
Sol 1993–94	$13.00	S124	1994–95 (Avail. 1/94)	$13.00	S142
☐ Miami 1993–94	$13.00	S118	☐ Washington,		
☐ Minneapolis/St.			D.C. 1994 (Avail.		
Paul 1993–94	$13.00	S119	1/94)	$13.00	S136

SPECIAL EDITIONS

	Retail Price	Code		Retail Price	Code
☐ Bed & Breakfast Southwest	$16.00	P100	☐ Caribbean Hideaways	$16.00	P103
☐ Bed & Breakfast Great American Cities (Avail. 1/94)	$16.00	P104	☐ National Park Guide 1994 (Avail. 3/94)	$16.00	P105
			☐ Where to Stay U.S.A.	$15.00	P102

Please note: if the availability of a book is several months away, we may have back issues of guides to that particular destination. Call customer service at (815) 734-1104.